FLAUBERT

Enid Mary Starkie, who died in 1970, was Reader
Emeritus in French Literature at the University of
Oxford and Honorary Fellow of Somerville College,
Oxford. She was educated and held scholarships at
Alexandra College, Dublin, the Royal Irish Academy
of Music, and Somerville College, Oxford, and also
attended the Sorbonne in Paris. A leading English
authority on French literature, she held many university appointments at Oxford and in America. A
Doctor of the University of Paris, she was also an
officer of the *Légion d'Honneur*, and in 1967 she
received the C.B.E. Among her many publications,
the best known are her studies of the lives and works
of writers such as Baudelaire (also a Pelican Biography), Rimbaud, Gide, Gautier, Eliot and Flaubert.

D0582307

ENID STARKIE

Flaubert

The Making of the Master

PENGUIN BOOKS

Penguin Books Ltd, Harmondsworth, Middlesex, England
Penguin Books Australia Ltd, Ringwood, Victoria, Australia

First published by Weidenfeld & Nicolson 1967
Published in Penguin Books 1971
—
Copyright © Enid Starkie, 1967
—
Made and printed in Great Britain by
Cox & Wyman Ltd.
London, Reading & Fakenham
Set in Linotype Georgian

Contents

Part Two: The Masterpiece

Introduction

FLAUBERT, after going through a long period of comparative neglect, of severe criticism, and even of contempt from the intellectuals, is beginning to come into his own again and to attract sophisticated attention. During the period of committed literature, after the 1930s, he was criticized for not being involved in contemporary problems, for not studying them and for seeming indifferent to them. But during the past twenty years, since the end of the War, readers have begun to grow weary of 'littérature engagée' and are longing to return once more to more disinterested ideals of art. Serious academic study has begun again and there have been, in the past few years, two immense doctorate theses, devoted entirely to his early and posthumously published works, in which the sources of his genius are to be sought.[1]

There has never been, even in France, an entirely satisfactory 'étude d'ensemble' – as the French call it – of Flaubert which produces, as well as an analysis of the writer, a portrait of the human being, with all his complexities and contradictions – he has been more satisfactorily dealt with as an artist – who was a man who cared desperately about things, who was deeply hurt by the ugliness and gross stupidity of the world, and who had a longing for innocence and purity; a man of deep affections and loyalties.

One of the great difficulties in the study of Flaubert is the scattered location of the documents; the unsatisfactory nature, in many ways, of most of the editions of his works – especially of the correspondence – and the impossibility of discovering the whereabouts of the manuscripts of many important early works – as, for instance, *Mémoires d'un Fou*, *Novembre* and also the first *Éducation Sentimentale*.

There is also the difficulty connected with the mass of papers bequeathed by his niece to various scattered libraries, all of which have not yet been sorted and published. 'I've never thrown away a single scrap of paper', Flaubert said in one of his letters.[2] He kept even his school compositions, some of which, but not all, have been published amongst his *Juvenilia*.

In the Municipal Library at Rouen is preserved an immense quantity of notes. For *Madame Bovary* alone, there are almost 4,000 foolscap pages, written on both sides in a minute hand. There is also the completed manuscript of the novel in the author's writing, and the copy transcribed professionally for publication. The Spoehlberch de Lovenjoul Collection at the Institut Library at Chantilly has much of his correspondence and letters addressed to him. The Bibliothèque de la Ville de Paris has various notebooks – the *Carnets* – particularly his travel notes. Finally, the Bibliothèque Nationale in Paris possesses the manuscripts of many of his early works – amongst them the interesting *Passion et Vertu* – but, as has already been mentioned, it is not known where the manuscripts are of the important *Mémoires d'un Fou*, *Novembre* and the first *Éducation Sentimentale*. It also possesses all the notes which René Descharmes took when he was preparing his masterly thesis, *Flaubert, sa Vie, son Caractère, et ses Idées avant 1857*, which are invaluable for a study of Flaubert.

There is also the immense bulk of work, of a very varied nature, which Flaubert composed as a child and as a youth, before he left school, which is contained in the three volumes of *Juvenilia*, posthumously published. He never considered printing them himself, though he never destroyed them, and they show diversity of inspiration and great range of reading.

The reputation which has come down to us of his performance at school is of a poor scholar – even his niece repeated this opinion in her *Souvenirs* of her uncle, published after his death – but this seems strange to us today, now that we have access to what he was writing then. This opinion was, however, only possible because French literature was not taught or studied in the lower forms at school, but only in the higher classes of Rhetoric and Philosophy, and then merely in the form of 'Dissertation', and no one knew, at that time, what his talents were. On the contrary, what is astounding is the range of his reading, and the number of compositions he found the time and the inspiration to produce. From his earliest days he had had the vocation of a writer, and there never was anything else that he wanted to be. Yet, even after fame came his way, he remained modest and unsure of himself and, as late as 1876, only four years before he died, he talked of his wasted life.[3]

The publication of his *Correspondance* by Conard, in nine volumes, with the four supplementary volumes since the War, has made a fuller study of the novelist an easier task. Nevertheless this publication is not, even yet, thorough or complete, and too many of the letters have been cut – probably for reasons of decency – and whole letters have been omitted altogether, for reasons not easily explicable. The letters of Flaubert to Louise Colet are no longer available in manuscript to the scholar, but it does not seem to be generally known that they must have been accessible to Descharmes, when he was working on his thesis, and that he had typewritten copies made of them, which are preserved amongst his notes in the Bibliothèque Nationale in Paris. It is possible to read there the passages and letters omitted in the Conard edition of the *Correspondance*. To my knowledge only one edition has used these documents, a Swiss edition by Maurice Nadeau for the Éditions Rencontre published in Lausanne in 1964 – though not all of them.

There are, as well as the omissions in the Conard edition of the *Correspondance* – the one most frequently used and in all libraries – other serious errors, as, for instance, the same letter to Louise Colet being published in one volume under the date 17 January 1852 and, in the following volume, as 15 January 1853. In the second case it is only an extract pub-

lished as a letter but, in the first, it is part of a longer letter.
It can however be dated accurately, by internal evidence, as
it mentions the award of the decoration of Officer de la
Légion d'Honneur to Du Camp, which occurred in 1852.[4]
Many of the letters are obviously wrongly dated; and the
Index is virtually useless as most of its entries are incorrect.
It is to be hoped – and it is expected – that the edition being
prepared by Jean Bruneau for the Éditions de la Pléiade,
will be more satisfactory. He has certainly seen the Des-
charmes documents, for he has used them for his thesis, *Les
Débuts Littéraires de Gustave Flaubert*, published in 1962.

Before the publication of his *Correspondance*, it used to be
believed that Flaubert wrote with difficulty, that he was a
'constipated' author. But we now realize that, on the contrary, he wrote with amazing fluency but that, in his published works, he curbed his natural fluency, put obstacles in
the way of its flow, and was then obliged to surmount them.
After he had developed his method and technique, he never
again wrote easily, whether it was on a romantic or a modern
subject.

When readers have suddenly come upon the correspondence they have felt inclined to think that they would willingly sacrifice the novels if they could only keep the letters
– but, of course, the letters are interesting chiefly in view of
what the author says about his art. The correspondence is
certainly amongst the most fascinating and absorbing in
French literature, and here we find the author in all his variety, in complete naturalness. André Gide once wrote:[5] 'For
a long time I loved Flaubert as a master, as a friend, as a
brother. His *Correspondance* was my bedside book, and, for
five years, it replaced the Bible on my bedside table. It was a
reservoir of strength. It offered to my ardour a new kind of
sainthood.'

Through most of his life Flaubert's closest and most
affectionate friendships were with men, to whom, at
different times, and in different ways, he gave a great deal of
devotion and to whom he owed very much. The closest of

these were Ernest Chevalier, Alfred Le Poittevin, Maxime
Du Camp and Louis Bouilhet. It is possible to believe that
there was some homosexual basis in these attachments,
though nothing positive can be proved in this respect, except
perhaps in the case of Louis Bouilhet, in unpublished passages in Flaubert's letters to him, preserved in the Spoehlberch de Lovenjoul Collection in the Bibliothèque de
l'Institut at Chantilly.[6] It is difficult to believe that these
passages, which do not figure in any published *Correspondance*, do not indicate the existence of some homosexual practices. He said of himself once:[7] 'Am I not a
feminine nature, and Lesbos is my mother-country.' And, in
his *Souvenirs, Notes et Pensées Intimes*, he wrote, when he
was nineteen: 'There are days . . . when one would like to be
a woman.'[8] He once told Louise Colet that, when he was a
student of nineteen in Paris, he had often wanted to castrate
himself.[9] It is true that he had many women friends and
correspondents, especially in middle age, after the publication of *Madame Bovary*, when this brought him into
touch with those who had found themselves in his heroine –
like many homosexuals he liked the company of women, especially as correspondents. There is however no proof that
these attachments were other than platonic.

He is only known to have had one passionate relationship
with a woman, with Louise Colet, who was his mistress over
two periods of almost three years each – from 1846 to 1848
and from 1851 to 1854 – but this ended in disaster. The other
feminine relationships seem to have been tender friendships
and not real love affairs – one of the women correspondents,
Mademoiselle Leroyer de Chantepie, he never even met. It is
sometimes suggested that he may have had a closer attachment with the second English governess of his niece, Juliet
Herbert – he certainly visited her on several occasions, after
she returned to England, and his niece stayed with her
during the Franco-Prussian War – but nothing definite is
known about this, as no letters from him to her have come
down to us, nor any of hers to him.

He never seems to have had any truly satisfactory relationship with a woman. This may have been due to his homosexual tendencies; and probably also to his emotional fixation on Élisa Schlésinger, with whom he fell romantically and innocently in love when he was fourteen and she twenty-six – all the women whom he is known to have loved, or for whom he cherished a romantic feeling, were older than himself. After his emotional feelings were set in the channel of Élisa Schlésinger, he was never again able to love truly another woman. Perhaps also his feelings for his mother inhibited him. Even as a grown man, he went in awe of her, and always had his eyes on her, fearing that she might disapprove of him, or discover something in his private life, and he took great pains to conceal it from her. He always had Louise Colet's letters to him addressed to a friend's house, who sent them on to him in another envelope. He lived with his mother until the day of her death in 1872, only eight years before his own death and, after she died, he wrote that he then realized that she had been the human being who had meant most to him in his whole life.[10] It was as if it was a mother figure whom he sought in all the women whom he loved, especially in the great love of his life, Élisa Schlésinger, for, when he first met her, she was nursing a baby at her breast.

There was always in him, also, the fear that, if he became too intimate with a woman she would encroach on his private life and hinder his artistic work. Du Camp relates[11] that Gautier once asked Flaubert about a woman who had fallen in love with him: 'Why are you always so hard on that unfortunate woman?' Flaubert is alleged to have answered: 'She might try to force her way into my study.'

This book was originally planned to be the first of two volumes dealing with Flaubert; and it was intended to show how the great novelist was formed, taking his life, reading, and works up to the publication of his first printed book, *Madame Bovary*, in 1857, when he was thirty-five; to show, in fact, how Flaubert became Flaubert. When he had completed that novel, he had found his technique, which altered very little thereafter. In the period of its composition, between 1851 and 1856, he crystallized his method; everything which had happened before it, came into its own; everything converged to make the great work, and to enrich it. After that he utilized this mastery and art for other works, drawing on them for the rest of his life – in *Salammbô, L'Éducation Sentimentale, La Tentation de Saint Antoine, Trois Contes*, and the unfinished and posthumously published *Bouvard et Pécuchet*.

This first volume studies the development of the artist, from the early tentative efforts to the finished masterpiece, when its author reaches maturity.

The second volume was originally intended to study the rest of the writings, and to show what Flaubert had achieved in general. Bad luck, however, has pursued the first volume from the very beginning, and, as there seemed to be the danger of its being the only volume – if, in fact, it was ever written at all – more has been included in the Conclusion of the present book than would, otherwise, have been the case, so that it could stand on its own, as a complete book in its own right. There is in it, therefore, some anticipation of future events, of the possible second volume.

In the multiplicity of critics who have studied Flaubert, it is difficult to know whom to select for special attention – in any case, only those useful for this particular volume are mentioned. René Descharmes' *Flaubert, sa Vie, son Caractère, et ses Idées avant 1857* still remains, after more than half a century, one of the best books available on the subject, and indispensable; though I personally have found more help for this particular book in Jean Bruneau's thesis, *Les Débuts Littéraires de Gustave Flaubert*, which is a mine of information. Démorest's *L'Expression Figurée et Symbolique dans l'Oeuvre de Gustave Flaubert* is a model of its kind, but it refers to the whole of the novelist's work, and not only to the early writings. Claudine Gothot-Mersch's valuable thesis, *La Genèse de 'Madame Bovary'*, published only in 1966, came too late to be of service to me. I have, however, seen all the papers on which she has worked, in the Bibliothèque Municipale at Rouen.

Unless otherwise stated, the edition always referred to in this book is that of the *Oeuvres Complètes*, in twenty-eight volumes, published by Conard.

I would like particularly to express my gratitude to Dr Constance West for having most kindly and generously permitted me to consult her notes on the Tennant papers which I was unable to see on my own. I would like to thank Mademoiselle Gabrielle Leleu, the former Librarian at the Bibliothèque Municipale at Rouen, for her helpful advice; also the present Librarian, Mademoiselle Jeanne Dupic, for giving me access so easily to the library and all the papers; Monsieur Jean Pommier, for his invaluable help and advice when I was working at the Spoehlberch de Lovenjoul Collection in the Institut Library at Chantilly; Monsieur de Saint Rémi, the Librarian at the Bibliothèque de la Ville de Paris, for permission to consult Flaubert's *Carnets*; Monsieur Julien Cain, formerly Administrateur of the Bibliothèque Nationale in Paris, who has done so much in collecting the Flaubert manuscripts and documents in the library, for his invaluable advice and help; Monsieur Jacques Suffel, for many useful suggestions. And finally my former students, Miss Joanna Richardson and Miss Sonia Spurdle; the former for much valuable material; and the latter for devoted help in checking references in Paris, which I was prevented from investigating myself.

Oxford, September 1966   ENID STARKIE

BOOK ONE

SPRING SOWING

PART ONE

The Child Father to the Man

[1]

The Family Background
(1821–31)

ROUEN is one of the oldest cities in France and it dates back to pre-Roman days, but its real character arose later. The Normans came there from Scandinavia in 841 and again in 876 under Rollo, who made it the capital of his Duchy, establishing himself there finally in 911. There were fourteen Norman dukes who died there, amongst them William the Conqueror of Britain. The town suffered greatly during the Hundred Years War, especially during the siege which ended in 1419, when the town surrendered to Henry V. Joan of Arc was burnt at the stake there in May 1431, but the town was finally reconquered in 1449 by Charles VII, who entered it in triumph. It suffered again during the Religious Wars, but the Edict of Nantes brought in an era of great prosperity which continued even after the Revocation of the Edict, when 20,000 Protestants emigrated.

In Flaubert's day it was the third largest and most notable city in France, a very important industrial town with its two hundred factories employing thousands of operatives. It possessed some of the wealthiest families in France, the bourgeoisie which Flaubert was to satirize later in his works. But it had, as well, a large number of very hard-worked and poorly-paid working people. It was a typical medieval town, often called the Florence of the north, with its churches, palaces and fortresses. Hugo has described it in a poem of *Les Feuilles d'Automne*:[1]

> La Ville aux cent clochers carillonnant dans l'air,
> Le Rouen des châteaux, des hôtels, des bastilles,
> Dont le front, hérissé de fleches et d'aiguilles,
> Déchire incessamment les brumes de la mer.

There are the medieval buildings – the Hôtel de Ville, the Cathedral which plays such an important part in *Madame Bovary*, and the other churches – but there are, as well, some lovely eighteenth-century buildings – the boulevards built on the fortifications, the Hôtel Dieu where Flaubert was born and where he spent his youth until the age of twenty-two, and the Église Sainte Madeleine where he was christened.

The countryside is very varied with its rich meadows and dairy herds, but Rouen is also an important port and one never feels far from the sea. The town is at easy distance from many popular seaside resorts, which we find as background in some of Flaubert's works. He knew this country well, and loved it in spite of his diatribes against its people; all his early works – also some of the later ones – take place there, and he has described it with great emotion in *Mémoires d'un Fou, Novembre* and *L'Éducation Sentimentale* as well as in *Un Coeur Simple*.

Flaubert's father was not a Norman, but came from lower middle-class stock from Champagne where, since the seventeenth century, his forebears had been veterinary surgeons – his father and uncle were of that profession, as well as his father's cousin, who had served in the army in Napoleon's Russian campaign.

Flaubert's father, Achille Cléophas, seems to have been of higher intelligence and education than the rest of the family. He received university training and studied medicine, becoming Dupuytren's favourite and most distinguished student in Paris. He obtained his doctorate in 1810, at the age of twenty-six, then became Laumonier's assistant at the Hôtel Dieu in Rouen in 1815, eventually succeeding his teacher, on his death, as Master of the hospital in 1818. He was very hard-working, devoted to learning and to his students, and he started the medical school at Rouen. At 5.30 every morning, even in winter, with his candle. he left his residence at the Hôtel Dieu and made his way into the adjoining hospital. All the morning he carried out oper-

ations, and, in the afternoons, he attended to his private
patients.

In 1815 he was elected a member of l'Académie des Sciences, Belles Lettres & Arts in Rouen, and in 1824 he was
elected an Associate Member of l'Académie Royale de
Médecine. At that time an inquiry was set on foot about
him, on account of his liberal and free-thinking opinions
which shocked the Catholic authorities under Charles X,
and there was a secret dossier concerning him, but the report
was entirely favourable.[2] It was stated that his opinions
were in fact liberal, but that he never tried to propagate
them, and that he had earned the confidence of even those
who did not share his views: 'His lofty moral qualities, and
particularly his gentle character, have earned for him public
consideration and esteem.'

He was made Chevalier de la Légion d'Honneur in 1839.

Flaubert greatly admired his father and one of the kindest
portraits in *Madame Bovary* is the one he drew of him in the
person of Dr Larivière.

All his patients were devoted to him on account of his
qualities of integrity and devoted service. He was a careful
and economical man and, in his thirty-five years of work, he
saved a great deal of money, investing it in land, especially
along the coast, which eventually left his family in very
comfortable financial circumstances, so that his second son
was never obliged to take up a profession. Flaubert could
have lived thus to the end of his life, without anxiety, if he
had not, finally, felt obliged to sell his lands to use the
money to save his niece's husband from bankruptcy.

In the meantime, in 1812, Dr Flaubert had married Caroline Fleuriot, the daughter of a physician, when she was
living with her godfather, Laumonier, at the Hôtel Dieu.
Her mother had died at her birth, and her father soon afterwards; she was fated also to lose her only daughter in childbirth. She was born in a higher social class than her
husband, though she was not as aristocratic as her grand-
daughter would like us to believe.[3] Her mother was a cer-

tain Charlotte Cambremer de Croixmare, who married
François Prosper Fleuriot, a physician, and her grand-
daughter considered this a misalliance. One of Caroline
Fleuriot's uncles died on the scaffold during the Terror, and
another was the engineer who planned the Orleans Canal. A
Cambremer had been a 'Conseiller à la Cour des Comptes,
Aides & Finances' and he was raised to the minor nobility in
1763 for his services to the State.

She was also connected with the family of Dunycan of
Saint Malo, who were sailors. In 1692 one of them seized a
piece of the coast of Newfoundland; and another, in 1703,
became an explorer and discovered a small group of islands
beyond the Falklands to which he gave his name. Another
was with Duguay-Trouin at the attack on Rio de Janeiro in
1711.

Thus Flaubert came, on her side, from adventurous
stock.

From his father he inherited, as well as many bourgeois
qualities, his love of learning and his attention to detail,
qualities which might have made him a great scholar if he
had not become a great novelist. From his mother he inherited aristocratic pride and contempt for worldly
success.

Achille Cléophas Flaubert's marriage to Caroline Fleuriot
was a love match, and Flaubert told Louise Colet later that
she had loved her husband, after thirty-five years of married
life, as passionately as on the first day.[4]

They lived at first in the rue du Petit Salut, but moved
later to the Hôtel Dieu when Achille Cléophas became its
Master in 1818. Madame Flaubert later told her grand-
daughter that her years in the rue du Petit Salut were the
happiest in her life.

Most of the critics and biographers describe the Master's
Lodgings at the Hôtel Dieu as gloomy and depressing. Yet
it has always seemed to the present writer a beautiful house,
built in a good period when domestic architecture was at its
height. The 'pavillon', as the Master's house was called, was

built in 1755 for the Master at that time, Lecat, after whom
the street in which the hospital stands is called. There is a
fine nobly proportioned room on the ground floor, with long
windows on to the rue Lecat, which are now blocked, but two
further long windows open on to the garden. According to
Georges Duboso,[5] this room was used by Dr Flaubert as a
laboratory and dissecting room. Flaubert and his little sister
used to climb up to the windows and look in at their father
working on the naked bodies laid out for dissection, until he
chased them away.[6]

Above, on the first floor, were the 'salon', the billiards
room where Flaubert and his friends used to perform their
plays, and the large bedroom where he was born. The passage leading to that looked on to the courtyard of the hospital, and it was from there that he used to gaze down at the
patients sunning themselves in the garden, and saw stret-
chers passing. On the floor above were the rooms of the
children and their guests.

In that house Flaubert lived the first twenty-two years of
his life. He was born there on 12 December 1821, and
christened in the nearby Église Sainte Madeleine on 13
January 1822.

At school Madame Flaubert had been a close friend of a
certain Mademoiselle Turin who, in 1815, married Paul Le
Poittevin, a rich industrialist in Rouen. Their son Alfred,
born in 1816, had Dr Flaubert as godfather, and in 1821 Gustave Flaubert was to have Paul Le Poittevin as his godfather.
Alfred's sister, Laure Le Poittevin, three months older than
Flaubert, was to become the mother of Guy de Maupassant.
Alfred Le Poittevin, although five years older than Flaubert,
was to become one of his closest friends, the one whose
influence on him was most deep-rooted.

The atmosphere at home was gloomy, for there had been
many deaths in the family, and only three of the six children
born out-lived infancy. Three – a girl and two boys – between Gustave and his elder brother, Achille, had died at
about the age of eighteen months; and each had died a few

months before the next child was born. The brother just ahead of Gustave, Jules Alfred, died at the age of nineteen months, six months before Gustave was born. It was small wonder that Madame Flaubert was of a gloomy disposition. Gertrude Tennant, née Collier, describes her in *Recueil de Souvenirs*.[7] She had known her first in 1842, but she wrote only at the end of the century, when she knew of all the tragedy in her life: the serious illness of her second son, the death of her husband and of her young daughter at the age of twenty-one. 'She was as dusky as a gypsy,' wrote Gertrude Tennant, 'with dark melancholy eyes, and black glossy hair. Her face was pale, imposing and solemn as if she never smiled. She looked as if she had suffered a great deal, in the presentiment of other suffering to come.'

Gustave Flaubert himself spent a delicate childhood and his life was often despaired of. Louis Bertrand tells us that when Dr Flaubert bought a plot in the cemetery for a family grave, he had only a small grave dug for his younger son, as he thought he would not survive childhood.[8] Later, when he was finally buried there, his coffin had to be forced in as the space was so short. His shorter head-stone and grave, beside those of his father and mother, look like a child's cot beside the bed of his parents.

After Gustave there was a further child, a girl, two and a half years his junior. She too spent a delicate childhood, suffering probably from tuberculosis, and finally died in childbirth, of puerperal fever, at the age of twenty-one.

She was one of the great affections of his childhood and youth and he used to supervise her reading. The majority of his letters as a student in Paris are addressed to her. As long as she lived she was the chief feminine influence in his life.

His brother Achille was much older than he – nearly nine years – and there was no possibility of close friendship between them. When Gustave was a schoolboy, Achille was already a medical student in Paris. He was eventually to join his father at the Hôtel Dieu, and to succeed him as Master on his death in 1846. Gustave often refers to him in his correspondence without much warmth, and there was obviously no deep sympathy between them; but, from this lack of enthusiasm, to deduce – as some critics do – that Gustave hated him, is an exaggeration; and also to conclude that it was to depict him unfavourably that he composed *La Peste à Florence*, in 1836, concerning two warring brothers.

One of the most vivid memories of Flaubert's childhood was of the old servant, Julie, who entered his parents' service when he was three and remained with the family until her death, which occurred in 1883, three years after Flaubert's, having outlived all the children whom she had reared, for the last of them, Achille, died in 1882. She used to tell Gustave stories and folklore of the region and she was for him 'la servante au grand coeur' of Baudelaire's poem. She appears often in his work and she seems to have been someone who gave him some confidence in human nature. She was, particularly, the model for Félicité in *Un Coeur Simple* from *Trois Contes*.

Flaubert always remembered with excitement the Revolution of July 1830, when he saw the white flag of the Bourbons being hauled down and the tricolour being hoisted in its stead, for he was a democrat already at the age of eight.

Even before he went to school he was seeing himself as a writer and, in a letter to his friend Ernest Chevalier, on 31 December 1830, when he had only just reached his ninth birthday, he talked of the plays he was writing. However, on the following 4 February, he had changed his mind about being a playwright, and was going to write novels inspired by *Don Quixote*, which was then, and always, one of his favourite books. He told Louise Colet later[9] that he had known the whole of it by heart before he was able to read.

All the same, the stage was, on the whole, his main interest as a child, and, between 1830 and 1840, most of the famous actors from Paris appeared in Rouen and he attended their performances. He and his friends produced plays of their own. These were acted in the billiards room, rarely used for its original purpose. The table was pushed back against one wall and served as a stage, while the audience sat on chairs below. All sorts of plays were acted there – classical and modern plays – and it was Flaubert who planned and directed everything, though helped later by his older friend Alfred Le Poittevin. Little Caroline looked after the scenery and the costumes, and Ernest Chevalier was handy-man for moving accessories, but both were also roped in for acting at times.

The stage remained Flaubert's chief interest, even when he went to school, and indeed for many years after that; witness the number of scenarios of plays which are amongst the notes preserved in the Bibliothèque Municipale at Rouen; and the play *Le Château des Coeurs*, which he wrote in collaboration with Bouilhet, in 1863, and *Le Candidat* which he produced in 1874, but which was withdrawn after a few days.

There was one play which he never forgot and which, even as a child, so marked his imagination that he could never free himself from its influence, and that was the puppet show produced every year at La Foire Saint-Romain in Rouen by an old man called Legrain, which enacted the temptations of Saint Anthony who was assailed by the Devil but eventually was able to withstand his blandishments. La Foire Saint-Romain occurred each year in the third week of October and continued until the beginning of November. Flaubert attended it every time but, out of all the excitement, it was the puppet show which most impressed him. He kept some lines of it for the first version of his *Tentation de Saint Antoine:*

> Messieurs les démons,
> Laissez-moi donc!
> Messieurs les démons,
> Laissez-moi donc!

What might be called Flaubert's *Opus One* is an essay on Corneille, written when he was nine and which he mentions to Ernest Chevalier in a letter of 4 February 1831. It is a rather ordinary piece of writing – though very good for his age – vastly inferior to the composition written by Arthur Rimbaud at the same age, for it contains many clichés and commonplace ideas – probably suggested by his teacher. It is preserved amongst his manuscripts at the Bibliothèque Nationale in Paris.[10]

However, so good did the old family friend, Mignot, think it – he who used to read him *Don Quixote* – that he had it transcribed in copper-plate writing, to look as if it had been printed. Indeed Flaubert thought that it had, in fact, been published, for he told Ernest Chevalier in a letter: 'They've printed my piece in praise of Corneille.'[11]

The *Éloge de Corneille* is accompanied by a study on constipation, which is very much more original and had obviously not been suggested by anyone else. It takes the form of a medical treatise and one can perceive in it the influence of the scientific home tradition. It is unpublished – probably for reasons of decency. It is entitled *La Belle Explication de la fameuse Constipation*:[12]

La constipation est un resserrement du trou merdarana, et quand le passage est stérile, c'est à dire quand le débouché est rétréci, on appelle cela constipation. Il ressemble alors à la mer qui ne produit plus d'écume, et à la femme qui n'a pas d'enfants. On appelle ce qui sort du trou merdana, gros et menu. Voilà la production du trou fameux.

Gustav F* * *
C'est digne de lui!

He was very proud of his production and even permitted himself a vulgar joke about it to Ernest Chevalier – he liked Rabelaisian jokes and always favoured puns, as we see from many of his letters.[13] 'J'avais raison de dire que la belle explication de la fameuse constipation ... tournerait à la postérité, c'est à dire au postérieur!'

This is not bad for a boy of nine.

[2]

Ernest Chevalier
(1831–6)

FLAUBERT had his first lessons from his mother but, judging from the spelling in his earliest letters, written before he went to school, she did not succeed in training him in the rudiments of grammar. It is true that his epistolary style is more ambitious and mature than is usual at that age.

He entered the Collège Royal de Rouen in the eighth class in the autumn of 1831 when he was nine. He was, at first, a day boy but, in March 1832, he became a boarder.

The Collège de Rouen was founded by Charles de Bourbon, Archbishop of Rouen. He had invited the Jesuits to establish a school for the education of the sons of the nobility and the rich bourgeoisie. It was begun in 1569 but the Archbishop died a prisoner at Fontenay-le-Vicomte in 1590 before the work was completed. It was finally opened in 1595 under the name Collège Archépiscopal de Bourbon. It was closed when the Jesuits were obliged to flee from France but was reopened in 1604. A Jesuit church, which was built between 1614 and 1704, became the chapel of the school. Thereafter the college flourished, and the great Corneille was educated there; later, Bernardin de Saint Pierre, Delacroix, Corot and Flaubert. None of the seventeenth-century construction remains and most of the buildings date from the eighteenth century, when it was rebuilt with government funds. When Catholicism was prescribed during the Revolution, the college was temporarily ruined, but, in 1796, the Directory established a school in the old buildings. In 1802 Napoleon, with his vast plans for education in France, founded the Lycées Impériaux and the college was then called Le Lycée de Rouen. In 1819, under the Restoration, it became once more Le Collège Royal, and remained so until the Revolution of 1848, when, under the Second Republic, it became Le Lycée National. Under the Second Empire, it became Le Lycée Impérial, but, after the fall of Napoleon III, it was just a lycée and, finally, in 1873, it became Le Lycée Corneille, after one of its most famous old boys, and so it remains to this day.

The school still occupies the place in the square where it stood in Flaubert's day and it has not changed much in appearance. La Place de l'Hôtel de Ville, as it is now called, was, in those days, La Place Saint Ouen. It was there, at the Café National, that Flaubert, in his last year, used to sit and smoke while waiting for the bell for school to ring.[1]

What we know about the school in Flaubert's day, we learn from F. Bouquet, who was a boarder there from 1829 to 1835, so that he overlapped, for some of his time, with him.[2] The school was run on military lines – a relic of the age of Napoleon. The teachers all wore cap and gown, and white bands. The boys carried horn inkstands, divided into two sections, one for black and one for red ink; also quill pens and a knife with which to cut them. There were no desks in the classrooms and the boys wrote on their knees, holding their books and papers there. To and from school they carried them in a strap fastened with a large brass buckle.[2]

The schoolrooms were enormous, like university amphitheatres, but they had no kind of heating, and, during the severe cold in the early part of 1830 – the coldest winter in living memory – the ink froze in its containers.

As Bouquet tells us,[2] French was sacrificed to Latin, and all they studied in their mother tongue was rules of grammar – that was in the lower classes. Only in the Class of Rhetoric did they begin to study French, in the form of 'Discours Français' and only in the top class, the Class of Philosophy, did they practise 'Dissertation Française'.

The Censeur did his rounds at 5 o'clock in the morning. At the first sound of the drum, the thirty or forty boys in the dormitory used to jump out of bed and hurriedly dress.

They washed at the fountain in the courtyard, then went
back to their dormitories where they stood by their beds,
ready to form ranks for roll call. They were allowed only
twenty minutes in which to get ready. The Inspector, who
used to carry out his inspections at 4 o'clock in the morning,
reported that matters were improving as, on his earlier visits,
the boys had taken half an hour.[3]

Flaubert has given a vivid picture of the life at school, and
its rigours, in his *Mémoires d'un Fou*.

To set off against the severity of the living conditions, the
discipline was, on the whole, relaxed – not to say lax – and
the boys had a high degree of personal independence. This
sometimes led to incidents. A few months before Flaubert
entered the school, in March 1831, there occurred what was
in truth a real rebellion.[3] Several boys refused to go to confession, and the Proviseur declared that, if they did not
comply with the regulations, they would be expelled from
the school. The boys shouted 'à bas l'aumonier!' and there
were cat-calls and boos when the ring-leaders were expelled.
The revolt spread to all the classes, and the whole school
demanded that the order be rescinded. When this request
was turned down, the boys barricaded themselves in their
dormitories and refused to go to class. Then the Recteur, accompanied by the Governing Body of the school – 'Le Con-
seil Académique' – went to parley with the pupils who
would not listen.[2] The Governing Body was hissed and
bombarded with missiles, but fire hoses were turned on the
boys, who were forced to surrender. Then the Recteur declared: 'Gentlemen, all classes are suspended for the time
being. Subsequently a notice will be posted advising when
they will be resumed.'

Next the whole school was expelled. An inspector was sent
down from Paris to investigate the matter, who seems to
have behaved with wisdom and diplomacy, and who forth-
with resolved the dispute. However the subversive activities
of the boys and the lack of discipline seem to have continued
all through Flaubert's schooldays.

Flaubert's first close friend was Ernest Chevalier, and it was to him that most of his earliest letters were written. Chevalier was little more than a year his senior, but it was the younger boy who always took the lead in their association. Flaubert's first letter, which for some reason has remained unpublished in the standard collection of the correspondence, is addressed to him.[4] It was written when he was eight years old but its spelling is erratic.

Cher ami.

Je pense que tu est hors de danger. Nous nous verrons tous à Radeport Dieu merci. J'ai reçu ta lettre, elle ma fait beaucoup de plaisir. J'ai reçu des nouvelles de ta bonne famille, je commençait à avoir peur de ta maladie, si ton bon père n'était venu me donner des nouvelles de toi, je serait dans l'inquiétude du meilleur de mes amis. Je suis dévoré d'impatience de voir le meilleur de mes amis, celui avec lequel je serait toujours amis, nous nous aimerons ami qui sera toujours dans mon coeur. Oui ami depuis la naissance jusqu'à la mort. Ton ami Gustave Flaubert.

Flaubert was certainly devoted to him, and kept on assuring him that he was the life of his life, his dearest friend, and that nothing would ever part them. 'Yours to death' he wrote to him[5], and again, 'Come back, come back! life of my life, soul of my soul, you will give me back life, if you return to me'.[6] Ernest Chevalier was the great love of his life at this time; he had a ring made, with both their names entwined on it, and Flaubert adds, in the letter where he mentions it, 'persons who will never be parted'.[7] They did in fact remain close friends until life eventually separated them and they went their different ways.

Ernest Chevalier studied Jurisprudence and took up a law career. He became a magistrate in Corsica, and subsequently occupied various legal posts in Lyons, Metz, Lille and Grenoble. In 1870 he finally retired from public office at the age of fifty, and went to live at Chalonnes-sur-Loire, becoming eventually a member of parliament. His career was one of devoted public service, but there was nothing in it to appeal to Flaubert as a man, when he was the passionate servant of literature. As a small boy he discussed his literary plans with him – or perhaps found in him a receptive audience, one who also aroused his emotions.

Even in his earliest days at school, Flaubert began to show traces of the love of documentation which was to be a characteristic trait of his maturity, and which made him then a scholar as well as a novelist. When he was barely ten, he described to Chevalier, in a letter, all the notes he was taking of his reading.[8] He was certainly not being as idle a boy as most of his biographers maintain. In fact, in 1833, when he was eleven, he won a second 'Prix d'Excellence' for having been five times first in composition.

One perceives already in the boy of eleven the furious and biting irony of the mature man, when he described to Ernest Chevalier Louis-Philippe's official visit to Rouen in September 1833.[9]

Louis-Philippe is now, with his family, in the town which gave birth to Corneille. How stupid men are! How limited the populace! To run after a king, to vote thirty thousand francs for the celebrations, to send to Paris for two thousand five hundred francs worth of musicians, to take so much trouble, for whom? For a king! To queue up at the doors of a theatre from three o'clock until half past eight, for whom? For a king! Ah!!! How stupid the world is!

And the following year, when he was twelve, he wrote again to his friend:[10]

If you thought I was bored on account of your absence, you wouldn't be far wrong; and if I hadn't in my head, and at the point of my pen, a queen of France of the fifteenth century, I'd be so disgusted with existence, that a bullet would long ago have freed me from this poor joke called life.

One need not, however, take too seriously the pessimism and cynicism of a boy of twelve who sees himself as a romantic hero.

During his first years at school, Flaubert's chief interest was in history, and it is astonishing all that he read and digested. He had here, as guide and mentor, a most remarkable teacher, who helped him rather in the same way that des Essarts helped Mallarmé, or Izambard helped Rimbaud, and later, Alain so many modern writers. This man, Pierre-Adolphe Chéruel, had been a student of Michelet and brought his teaching to Rouen. He was born in 1809 and was himself a former pupil of the Collège Royal de Rouen, as a scholar. From there he went to the École Normale Supérieure in Paris, but returned to the school, in 1831, at the age of twenty-two, the youngest teacher, having already obtained his Licence and his Agrégation. He taught history and geography, and lectured to the boys in the beautiful romantic periods of Michelet, trying to introduce the same method into the school. He taught there until 1849, when he went as a lecturer to the École Normale Supérieure in Paris, and eventually became a professor at the Sorbonne. He took a great interest in his pupils and led them on archaeological expeditions round the town and the country, insisting that they should know their own neighbourhood well, not only in the present but in its historical past as well. He had the greatest influence on Flaubert, who, although he was to develop other interests as well, never lost his passion for history, and never forgot the historical method he had learnt from Chéruel, witness his work in *Salammbô* and *Hérodias*. He kept up his friendship for his teacher until the end of his life and used to visit him on frequent occasions when he was a professor at the Sorbonne. He persuaded Flaubert, when he taught him, to read a great many early texts, such as Froissart, Commines and Brantôme, as well as the historical works of Hugo and Dumas. Encouraged by him, Flaubert composed a great many historical works between the age of eleven and fourteen. Many of these are obviously elaborations of school exercises, such as *La Lutte du Sacerdoce et de l'Empire Chronique Normande, Dernière Scène de la Mort de Marguerite de Bour-*

gogne, La Mort du Duc de Guise, Le Moine des Chartreux, and very many others. They all show a remarkable range of knowledge and intelligent use of texts. They also reveal great natural fluency of style, and promise for his age, though they are not intrinsically significant. Many of them are derivative from other historical works of the day, but what is noticeable is how much his descriptive talent develops as he writes, and that is probably the most valuable quality that he gained from his historical writings at this time. This is seen particularly in *La Peste à Florence,* written towards the end of his fourteenth year, at the close of 1836, the last of his historical compositions of youth, in which his talent for description is seen at its best, and shows a hand which does not falter.

Encouraged by Chéruel, Flaubert won, for several years, prizes in history and it was considered his best subject.

His historical writings at this time were, according to his correspondence, of two kinds, plays and stories, but the plays have not come down to us. One of these, *Frédégonde et Brunehaut* he mentions several times, and discusses the possibility of having it published. His best play, *Loys XI,* which has reached us, belongs to a later stage in his development, and it is more purely romantic than historical, with a strong influence of Hugo and Dumas – it was written the year of the production of Hugo's *Ruy Blas,* in 1838 – and it also reveals Flaubert's philosophical preoccupations at the time of writing, which did not yet exist in 1836.

It was not only in history that Flaubert was being encouraged at this time. There was another remarkable master at the school besides Chéruel, the teacher of literature called Gourgaud-Dugazon, who arrived there in 1834, just when Flaubert was beginning to take himself seriously as a writer. He interested him in questions of method and led him to read more widely in literature than hitherto, as, for instance, such writers as Byron. It was in the school year, from 1834 to 1835, that Flaubert edited a paper entitled *Art et Progrès* – indeed he was its sole contributor. But the only interesting article is the 'Voyage en Enfer', part of which he used three years later in *Agonies*.

Here Satan appears to him and shows him the beauties of the world, all that it can offer him of joy and pleasure, but nothing satisfies him for he sees evil everywhere. In the end he asks Satan to show him his own kingdom which may provide more satisfaction than the rest:[11]

> Montre-moi ton royaume, dis-je à Satan.
> – Le Voilà!
> – Comment donc?
> Et Satan me répondit:
> – C'est que le monde c'est l'enfer.

This is the beginning of Flaubert's philosophic reflection.

It might have been in November 1834 – or, as we shall see, it could have been in 1835 – that Flaubert enjoyed the idyllic episode with the little English girl, which is related in *Mémoires d'un Fou*. He says that he believes that he was 'en cinquième' at the time, which would make it 1834; on the other hand, he declares that the events occurred two years before he was writing that particular part of the story, which was in December 1837, before he had thought of the whole work, which was composed between the autumn and Christmas of 1838. There is no doubt about this, for he gave the manuscript to Alfred Le Poittevin on 1 January 1839 as a New Year's gift. This would suggest that it was in 1835 that he met the English girl, and he would then have been 'en quatrième' and not 'en cinquième'. He relates that one single glance from Maria completely effaced from his memory the thought of the English girl. Maria, as we shall see, is Élisa Schlésinger, whom he met in the summer of 1836 – this is incontrovertible. It does not greatly signify whether the events occurred in 1834 or 1835, whether he was twelve or thirteen, and time would not be spent on discussing the problem if other critics had not brought forward so many conflicting theories about it. An objection to the second date would be that it would not have been easy for all the events related to take place in less than a year. It is a delightful episode, all spring and innocence:

C'était quelque chose de doux, d'enfantin, qu'aucune idée de possession ne ternissait, mais par cela même, manquait d'énergie; c'était trop niais cependant pour être du platonisme.[12]

There were no more than occasional kisses exchanged – fraternal and innocent on his side, though more passionate and enterprising on hers, for she was nearly two years older, and mature for her age – but it all petered out eventually when he encountered Maria, and when the English girl fell in love with her drawing master:

Voilà comment finit cette liaison, qui promettait peut-être une passion avec l'âge, mais qui se dénoua d'elle-même.

Est-il besoin de dire que cela avait été à l'amour ce que le crépuscule est au grand jour, et que le regard de Maria fit évanouir le souvenir de cette pâle enfant?

C'est un petit feu qui n'est plus que de la cendre froide.[13]

Since Flaubert is known to have been closely acquainted with an English family, children of Admiral Collier, it has usually been assumed by all critics and biographers, even the most recent – witness Philip Spencer's biography, published in 1952, and Jacques Suffel's in 1958 – that the English girls in *Mémoires d'un Fou* are, in fact, the Collier girls; and, in the Pléiade edition of Flaubert's works, published in 1951, the date of their meeting with Flaubert is given, in the chronology, as 1835; also in Jean Bruneau's Edition du Seuil, published in 1964. Yet it is perfectly clear from Caroline Flaubert's letters to her brother that they met for the first time in the summer of 1842. These letters should have been known to the biographers and critics, as they were published as long ago as December 1936, by Lucie Chevalley-Sabatier, in *La Revue Hebdomadaire*. C. West, who had knowledge of Caroline Flaubert's letters, still believed that the English girls in *Mémoires d'un Fou* were the Collier girls, and her solution of the problem was to suggest that the section in question had been composed later, after 1842.[14] There are many objections to this theory, the chief being that, after 1 January 1839, the manuscript, signed and dated by Flaubert himself, was in the hands of Alfred Le Poittevin, where it remained until his death in 1848, when it passed to his son, and it is from this manuscript, which showed no signs of later additions, that the work was first published in *La Revue Blanche*, from 15 December 1900 to 1 February 1901; and in subsequent editions. It is the only version known.

Until recently it had not occurred to critics that there might be other English girls in the cosmopolitan town of Rouen whom Flaubert might have known – friends, for instance, of his sister's English governess, since Flaubert tells us that they were schoolmates of Caroline.[15] Jean Bruneau is the first person, in print, to have expressed doubts about these girls being the Collier girls.[16] Now Lucien Andrieu, the librarian at the Flaubert library at Canteleu, near Croisset, where the novelist's personal books are preserved, comes forward with a suggestion concerning the identity of the girls, a suggestion which has verisimilitude, although nothing can be proved definitely.[17] The problem was to discover an English girl, living with her mother in Rouen who was separated from her husband; who, one January, married a drawing master; and who, one November was about fifteen. He unearthed, from the local papers at the time, a certain Caroline Anne Heuland, who was born in London in 1820, and was living in Rouen with her mother at the time of her marriage to an artist in January 1838 – Flaubert calls his English girl Caroline in the story. She would have been fifteen in November 1835. Andrieu states that the events occurred in the autumn of 1836, two years before the composition of *Mémoires d'un Fou*. He forgets, however, that this particular section was written a year before the rest of the work and that the episode occurred before his meeting with Maria in the summer of 1836. Writing in December 1837, Flaubert declares that it is eighteen months since he

has seen the English girl, which would mean that it was in
the spring of 1836, and this would fit in well with his meeting
with Maria in the summer of 1836; and it would fit in
whether he met the English girls in November 1834 or in
1835.

It was early in 1836, when he was fourteen, that Flaubert
began to write his philosophical tales, on the model of those
of Balzac, which are in striking contrast with his historical
stories. *Un Parfum à sentir* was composed in April 1836. It
tells, very lengthily, with many digressions, of the life of
acrobats, of a woman who is hated on account of her ugliness
and eventually drowns herself in despair. Her corpse is
fished out of the river, and there is a vivid and accurate
description of its appearance, which may be a remembrance
of what he had seen in his father's dissecting room, when he
had climbed up to look in as a small child. It may also be a
remembrance of the terrible cholera epidemic a few years
earlier, in 1832. Many years later, in a letter to Mademoiselle
Leroyer de Chantepie in 1861, he described how there
was only a thin partition between their dining-room and
the hospital ward, where the patients were dying like flies.[18]
Flaubert's description is surprising from a boy of fourteen:[19]

On venait de retirer un cadavre de l'eau, et il était exposé à
la morgue; c'était une femme, un bonnet de dentelle avec des
fleurs sales lui couvraient la tête, ses habits étaient déchirés et
laissaient voir des membres amaigris; quelques mouches venaient
bourdonner à l'entour et lécher le sang figé sur sa bouche
entr'ouverte, ses bras gonflés étaient bleuâtres et couverts de
petites taches noires.

Le soleil était à son déclin et un de ses derniers rayons,
perçant à travers les barreaux de la morgue, vint frapper sur
ses yeux fermés et leur donner un éclat singulier.

Ce corps couvert de balafres, de marques de griffes, gonflé,
verdâtre, déposé ainsi sur la dalle humide, était hideux et faisait
mal à voir. L'odeur nauséabonde qui s'exhalait de ce cadavre en
lambeaux, et qui faisait éloigner tous les passants oisifs, attira
deux élèves en médecine.

At this period in his development, Flaubert wrote easily and with great fluency – this is very different from the diatribes against composition of his maturity. At the end of *Un Parfum à sentir,* he writes:[20]

Vous ne savez peut-être pas quel plaisir c'est: composer!

Ecrire, oh! écrire, c'est s'emparer du monde, de ses préjugés, de ses vertus et le résumer dans un livre; c'est sentir sa pensée naître, grandir, vivre, se dresser debout sur son piédestal, et y rester toujours.

Je viens donc d'achever ce livre étrange, bizarre, incompréhensible. Le premier chapitre je l'ai fait en un jour; j'ai été ensuite pendant un mois sans y travailler; en une semaine, j'en ai fait cinq autres, et en deux jours je l'ai achevé.

He wrote to Ernest Chevalier in the same period: 'Let us always be occupied with art, which, greater than all peoples, crowns and kings, is always there, soaring above us in enthusiasm, with its godly crown.'[20]

What is most striking in Flaubert at this early age is how much he has read and assimilated, amazing for a boy as yet only fourteen.

His general philosophy of life was radical and against all authority and accepted values – one would say today that he was opposed to the establishment. In *La Peste à Florence,* written when he was fourteen, one can see already his later revolt against the injustice of man, and his sympathy for those in a lowly position in life, his hatred of those who are privileged.

Most noticeable is his tremendous eagerness for learning, his interest in everything; and the immense amount of his time that was spent in writing. There must be few – if any – examples like his of so much work being produced by a boy between the ages of ten and fourteen.

During the summer of 1836, when he was fourteen and a half, there occurred the episode with the 'fantôme de Trouville' which marked him for the rest of his life.

[3]

Élisa Schlésinger
(1836–7)

THE summer holidays were always very important for the Flaubert family. They possessed properties in various parts of Normandy within easy reach of Rouen, places which have since become popular seaside resorts – such places as Trouville and Deauville. These properties were later to appreciate considerably and to ensure the financial independence of the family after the death of the Doctor. It was in Trouville that they spent frequent holidays, as they had a small house there, and it was very different in the 1830s from what it was later to become. It was then a simple fishing village, with only one small and unpretentious hotel on the quayside, and life was carried on very quietly, as the families went there mostly for the bathing. There were no bathing-boxes and everyone undressed in their houses or on the sea-shore. It was then beginning to be discovered by painters and musicians.

It was in the summer of 1836 that Flaubert experienced the illumination which permanently fixed the pattern of his emotional life, when he met Élisa Schlésinger. Various dates have been suggested for the episode, but a careful study of the autobiographical work, *Mémoires d'un Fou*, as well as the correspondence,[1] where he states that her daughter was three months old when he first encountered her – she was born in April 1836 – proves that it must have been in the summer of 1836 that they met, when he was fourteen.

One morning, as he was wandering along the sea-shore, he saw a red cloak in danger of being overwhelmed by the incoming tide. He moved it out of the path of the waves and the cloak felt soft and light to his touch, so that it moved him deeply. Later, in the hotel, at the moment of lunch, he was thanked by its owner. She looked at him and he lowered his eyes, blushing. She repeated her thanks and the words sank into his mind never to be forgotten; nor was the vision of her face ever to be effaced from his memory:[2]

Elle me regarda: Je baissai les yeux et rougis. Quel regard en effet! comme elle était belle cette femme! je vois encore cette prunelle ardente sous un sourcil noir se fixer sur moi comme un soleil. Elle était grande, brune avec de magnifiques cheveux noirs qui lui tombaient en tresses sur les épaules; son nez était grec, ses yeux brûlants, ses sourcils hauts et admirablement arqués, sa peau était ardente et comme veloutée avec de l'or; elle était mince et fine, on voyait des veines d'azur serpenter sur cette gorge brune et pourprée. Joignez à cela un ton mâle et énergique à faire pâlir les beautés blondes. . . . Elle parlait lentement; c'était une voix modelée, musicale et douce.

Élisa Schlésinger was at this time twenty-six to Flaubert's fourteen and a half, and she was at the height of her beauty. His attitude to her was very like that of Baudelaire for *La Vénus Blanche*, a mixture of admiration and respect. His love was here permanently fixed in a maternal channel, and his most vivid memory of her was suckling her child at her breast. His only attempt at evasion was later, with Louise Colet, but this ended in disaster.

Flaubert wrote of the episode twice: first, as a youth, in *Mémoires d'un Fou*, and finally, in middle age, in the second *Éducation Sentimentale*.

Who was Élisa Schlésinger who was to play such an important part in Flaubert's life? The fullest and most accurate account of her is to be found in a book by her great-grandson, Helmuth Steinhardt Leins, entitled *Flauberts Grosse Liebe*. From this we learn that she was born Élisa Foucault, in 1810, in Vernon in France; that in 1829 she married a man called Judée. Through a sister and brother-in-law, she made the acquaintance of Maurice Schlésinger who was then the editor of *La Revue Musicale* in Paris, and a prominent figure in musical circles. Maurice Schlésinger and Élisa Judée fell in love and became lovers. In 1835 Judée returned to Germany and it is not known whether he and his wife ever met again. There was no divorce in France in those days and the lovers could not marry, but she was always known as Madame Schlésinger. Judée eventually died in November 1839 and Élisa married Maurice Schlésinger in September 1840. A legitimate son was born in 1842, but the daughter, born in 1836, recognized by Schlésinger, was registered as his by an unknown mother. Schlésinger was said to have been good to Judée and to have paid his debts. This might explain the loyalty Élisa felt for her second husband, in spite of all his infidelities, and why, later, she was never to become Flaubert's mistress – though he was not to know the true cause of her resistance. She had property in Trouville – what was later to become the Hôtel Bellevue was hers – and she and her husband often went there for holidays.[4]

That is all that we need, for the moment, to know about the Schlésingers. Flaubert spent a great deal of the time during the holidays when he was fourteen with them, and he did not separate husband and wife in his enjoyment. He went boating with them, and for picnics. Schlésinger seems to have been a gay and generous companion who was kind to the young boy. He called him his son and Flaubert called him 'my venerable father, Maurice'. Arnoux, in the final *Éducation Sentimentale*, seems to be a faithful portrait of him.

Flaubert was happy though, at the same time, sad, but he did not yet understand what had happened to him, and he imagined that he felt equal friendship for both husband and wife. The adventure was, however, written in his mind in invisible ink, but it needed further experience to develop it.

The following summer Flaubert just missed Schlésinger at Trouville, but he heard that he had been there with another woman. The next year, in 1838, when he returned there the Schlésingers did not come; but now, matured and changed by his reading of personal literature, and visiting the same scenes again, he finally realized what use he could make of his own emotional adventure. It was then that he composed *Mémoires d'un Fou*, in the autumn of 1838, the seed of which had lain buried in his heart for two years and was now ready to bear fruit. This work will be discussed in a later chapter.

In the summer of 1836 Flaubert probably had a further experience which greatly affected him, when, for the first time, he attended a grown-up ball. He relates that it was during the holidays between the fourth and the third class, and that would have been in the late summer of 1836.[5] He mentions it particularly in a letter to Louis Bouilhet from Egypt, describing how, in the early morning, after he had just left the house of the courtesan Kuschiuk Hanem, he was shooting with his guide and it was not of what he was doing that he thought but of an earlier morning:[6]

In the morning, at seven o'clock, we departed and I went shooting with a sailor in a cotton field. ... The wind was blowing in the branches of the trees. It was whistling as if through reeds; the mountains were pink; the sun was rising; my sailor was walking in front of me, bending down to get under the hedges; and pointing out to me the turtle-doves which he saw in the branches. I didn't kill a single one. I didn't even see them. I walked, pushing my feet before me, thinking of similar mornings, of one in particular, at the Héron, the house of the Marquis de Pomereu, after a ball. I hadn't gone to bed at all, and, in the early morning, I went for a row in a boat on the pond, alone, in my school uniform. The swans stared at me as I passed, and the leaves from the branches dropped into the water. It was a few days before school opened. I was fifteen.

If it was at the end of the holidays in 1836, he would not have been fifteen until the following December, but he was, at all events, in his fifteenth year. Jean Bruneau seems somewhat perverse in trying to insist that it must have been in 1837, because he used the episode of the ball in a story, *Quidquis Volueris*, which was written, according to his own dating, between September and October that year.[7] There is no reason why it should not have happened the previous year, and been stored in his mind to be used a year later.

This ball, given by the Marquis de Pomereu, one of the richest land-owners in the neighbourhood, impressed Flaubert greatly, so that he thought of it on several occasions, many years later, and used it as a very important episode in *Madame Bovary*, the ball at the castle of La Vaubyessard, as well as in *Quidquis Volueris*. From this ball he carried away an impression of luxury and, as he walked in the garden in the early morning, he thought about his past life just as Emma Bovary was to do after her ball, and her reflections are like his as a schoolboy.

It was in this year, in the third class, when he was fifteen, that Flaubert began to show real originality as a writer. He had started his writing with plays and then, under the influence of his teacher Chéruel, he had written historical tales. The last of these, *La Peste à Florence*, was composed in September 1836. Now he was turning away from the historical and picturesque side of Romanticism, to the melodramatic. He now was influenced by the frenetic side of the movement,[8] the Romanticism of the Bouzingos who flourished in the 1830s, which we find in the works of Petrus Borel, Philothée O'Neddy, and in the writings of Aphonse Rabbe, which Flaubert must have known. Rabbe, in his *Oeuvres Posthumes*, published in 1835, has a section entitled *L'Enfer du Maudit*, with sub-titles, *Deuils, Souffrances, Gémissements, Cris de Douleur*. All Flaubert's writing at this time abounds in presentiments, weird portents, and he chose the most horrifying subjects. There is no proof that he had actually read the Marquis de Sade, though he has much in common with him at this time, but he could have obtained the influence from Jules Janin or other horrific writers of the 1830s. In a letter to Louise Colet,[9] he tells her that he used to have a human skull on his writing table – this was typical of the Bouzingo school. In one of his tales, *Rage et Impuissance*, he describes the feelings of a man buried alive who, in desperation, eats his own arm. This may also have been a memory of the cholera epidemic of 1832 mentioned earlier, when several people were known to have been buried alive. There is also *Quidquis Volueris*, the story of a creature, the product of an ape and a Negro girl, who falls in love with a white woman, goes berserk and rapes and mutilates her most horribly, then kills himself by dashing his brains out against a wall. Flaubert tries to give weight to his account by claiming that he had undertaken it for scientific purposes; that he was studying the ape-man, and there had recently been various articles in a local literary paper called *Le Colibri*, directed by his friend Alfred Le Poittevin, dealing with the problem. One tale, in particular, published there on 24 November 1836, entitled *Jack en bonne fortune*, was concerned with an orang-outang from the Jardin des Plantes in Paris, which was found unconscious near a woman, 'à moitié ivre de cidre et d'amour'.

In Flaubert's story the scientific aspect is swamped, and only the horror comes through. It is very much in the tradition of the 1830s, but, nevertheless, one feels already the compassion of the young author for the suffering of others, which will be one of the outstanding characteristics of his work in maturity.

Remarkable, and very typical of his writing at this time, is *Rêve d'Enfer*, written in March 1837, in which the philosophic content is more marked, though this sometimes takes the form of somewhat trite cynical sayings such as 'ce prodigieux bourbier qu'on nomme la vie'.[10]

It relates the story of a Satanic character, Duc Arthur d'Almaroës, an alchemist whom the local people consider the devil incarnate. The old man lives in a decaying tower, where he carries on his experiments, very typical of the literature of the time, abounding in owls and bats, and he lives with nothing but ghosts. He himself is pure spirit, a man without heart and soul who can never die. He is bored with existence, which has nothing for him but emptiness, and he cannot commit suicide since he is immortal. Satan

comes to visit him and offers to help him to make gold. He
comes in horrible guise and is instrumental in causing many
horrific events, such as when the milk in the pails turns to
blood. He promises the Duke to cure him of his ennui by
love and asks, in return, for his soul. The Duke answers that
he possesses none, but Satan replies that he will grow one
when he falls in love and becomes a man. He causes Juliette,
a simple country girl, to fall in love with the Duke, but she
does not know that he is not human. She destroys herself
with love of him but nothing moves him and Juliette, whose
love is inspired by hell in its violence, eventually commits
suicide and is taken away by the Devil. The Duke then begs
Satan to kill him, but the Devil has no power over him since
he is not a man. They fight in what looks like mortal
combat, but it is Satan who is vanquished. The tale ends
with a plea from mankind to God, begging him never to
create any other worlds:[11]

Et plusieurs siècles se passèrent.
La terre dormait d'un sommeil léthargique, point de bruit à
sa surface, et l'on n'entendait que les eaux de l'océan qui se
brisaient en écumant; elles étaient furieuses, montaient dans l'air
en tourbillonnant, et le rivage remuait à leurs secousses comme
entre les mains d'un géant. Une pluie fine et abondante obscur-
cissait la lumière douteuse de la lune, le vent cassait la forêt, et
les cieux pliaient sous leur souffle comme le roseau à la brise du
lac.
Il y avait dans l'air comme un bruit étrange de larmes et de
sanglots, on eût dit le râle d'un monde.
Et une voix s'éleva de la terre et dit:
– Assez! assez! j'ai trop longtemps souffert et ployé les reins,
assez! Oh! grâce! ne crée point d'autre monde!
Et une voix douce, pure, mélodieuse comme la voix des anges,
s'abattit sur la terre et dit:
– Non! non! c'est pour l'éternité, il n'y aura plus d'autre
monde!

In 1837 Flaubert became very much interested in natural
history, and this had a profound influence on his writing. It

was then that he composed, on the model of the popular 'Physiologies' of Balzac, the physiology of the clerk, entitled *Une Leçon d'Histoire Naturelle. Genre Commis.* Le Poittevin published it in *Le Colibri* on 30 March 1837.[12] It is a very good example of Flaubert's ironic and satiric vein which will later produce Homais in *Madame Bovary* and the grotesque characters in *Bouvard & Pécuchet.* It is a clever and amusing piece of work for a boy of fifteen:[13]

Pour moi, que ma longue expérience a mis à même d'instruire le genre humain, je puis parler avec la confiance modeste d'un savant zoologue. Mes fréquents voyages dans les bureaux m'ont laissé assez de souvenirs pour décrire les animaux qui les peuplent, leur anatomie, leurs moeurs. J'ai vu toutes les espèces de Commis, depuis le Commis de barrière jusqu'au Commis d'enregistrement. Ces voyages m'ont entièrement ruiné et je prie mes lecteurs de faire une souscription pour un homme qui s'est dévoué à la science et a usé pour elle deux parapluies, douze chapeaux (avec leurs coiffes en toile cirée) et six ressemelages de bottes.

Le Commis a depuis 36 ans jusqu'à 60; il est petit, replet, gras et frais; il a une tabatière dite *queue de rat,* une perruque rousse, des lunettes en argent pour le bureau et un mouchoir de rouennerie.

Il crache souvent et lorsque vous éternuez il vous dit: 'Dieu vous bénisse.' Il subit des variations de pelage suivant les saisons.

En été, il porte un chapeau de paille, un pantalon de nankin, qu'il a soin de préserver des taches d'encre en étalant dessus son mouchoir. Ses souliers sont en castor et son gilet en coutil. Il a invariablement un faux col de velours. Pour l'hiver c'est un pantalon bleu avec une énorme redingote qui le préserve du froid. La redingote est l'élément du Commis comme l'eau est celui des poissons.

Originaire de l'ancient continent, il est malheureusement très répandu dans nos pays. Ses moeurs sont douces: il se défend quand on l'attaque. Il reste le plus souvent célibataire et mène alors la vie de garçon. La vie de garçon! C'est à dire qu'au café il dit 'Mademoiselle' à la dame du comptoir, prend le sucre qui lui reste sur son plateau et se permet parfois le fin cigare de trois sous. Oh! mais alors le Commis est infernal! Le jour qu'il a

fumé il se sent belliqueux, taille quatre plumes avant d'en trouver une bonne, rudoie le garçon de bureau, laisse tomber ses
lunettes et fait des pâtés sur ses registres, ce qui le désole
considérablement.

It is in the same vein as the creation of 'Le garçon', whom
he and his friends invented and to whom they attributed
every grotesque and ludicrous characteristic they could imagine.

At the examinations in the summer of 1837, Flaubert won
first prizes in natural history and literature. It is after that,
at the end of the year, that we have, from his pen, his most
interesting work to date, *Passion et Vertu*, which is a great
advance, in style and psychology, on all that he had written
hitherto. This is really a first sketch for *Madame Bovary*, for
it is the account of an adulterous woman who ends by com-
mitting suicide.

Flaubert obtained the subject from an article entitled 'La
Moderne Brinvilliers', published in *La Gazette des Tri-
bunaux* on 4 October 1837.[14] There can be no doubt that
here is the source of his tale, for the details are the same.

The heroine of the true story fell passionately in love with
a young man and they became lovers. Eventually, to escape
from a relationship which seemed bound to end in disaster,
he fled from France and took up a position in Brazil. From
there he wrote to her to explain the reason for his departure
and begged her to forget him, since their happiness could
not be obtained without sin and remorse. From this moment
she became obsessed with the idea of becoming free so that
she could marry him. She poisoned her husband without
arousing any curiosity, but when her two children later also
died, then the authorities became suspicious and a warrant
for her arrest was issued. When the police broke into the
house, they found her lying dead with a bottle of prussic
acid in her hand.

Flaubert's tale is very much fuller than the press account;
there are more descriptions, more analysis, and he has taken
more pains to portray the main characters, who are well

differentiated. He was now beginning to be fascinated by his most typical character, the frustrated woman, dreaming beyond her powers of attainment, who possessed the quality which always appealed to him, of loving greatly. Mazza, the heroine, has the same romantic exaltation as Emma Bovary, the same habit of seeing her emotions through literature:[15]

Souvent, dans les transports du délire, elle s'écriait que la vie n'était que la passion, que l'amour était tout pour elle; et puis, les cheveux épars, l'oeil en feu, la poitrine haletante de sanglots, elle demandait à son amant s'il n'aurait pas souhaité, comme elle, de vivre de siècles ensemble, seuls sur une haute montagne, sur un roc aigu, au bas duquel viendraient se briser les vagues, de se confondre tous deux avec la nature et le ciel, et de mêler leurs soupirs aux bruits de la tempête; et puis elle le regardait long-temps, lui demandait encore de nouveaux baisers, de nouvelles étreintes, elle tombait entre ses bras, muette et évanouie.

She too, like Emma Bovary, had an unsatisfactory, materialistic husband, who thought of nothing but making money, and did not understand her dreams or need of love:[16]

Et quand, le soir, son époux, l'âme tranquille, le front calme, rentrait chez lui, lui disant qu'il avait gagné aujourd'hui, qu'il avait fait le matin une bonne spéculation, acheté une ferme, vendu une rente, et qu'il pouvait ajouter un laquais de plus à ses équipages, acheter deux chevaux de plus pour ses écuries, et qu'avec ces mots et ces pensées il venait à l'embrasser, à l'appeler son amour et sa vie, oh! la rage lui prenait à l'âme, elle le maudissait, repoussant avec horreur ses caresses, ses baisers, qui étaient froids et horribles comme ceux d'un singe.

Il y avait donc dans son amour une douleur et une amertume, comme la lie du vin, qui le rend plus âcre et plus brûlant.

Ernest, her lover, however, began to tire of her ardour, and also to be afraid, for he understood that her passion was a terrible thing which would end by destroying him, and he resolved to break the relationship, by leaving for Mexico where he hoped to obtain a post. He wrote her a letter of farewell, telling her to forget him for the sake of her future happiness; that she must love duty and virtue. In a state of deep distress, which is admirably drawn, she follows him to Le Havre – a nightmare journey – but arrives only to see the white sails of his ship disappearing on the horizon. The despair of her return is described with great insight and sensitiveness. Like her model, she decides that the only obstacle to her happiness is the presence of her husband and children, and she poisons them. She writes to Ernest to tell him that she is now free and can go to him without guilt. But she receives a letter from him asking her not to importune him further, that he is about to wed a girl of seventeen and that he has an assured position in Mexico. She decides then to kill herself, and her feelings as she returns home with the poison are very similar to those of Emma as she leaves Rodolphe. She writes first to the police to tell them what she is about to do; then, having wept and thought of bygone days, she drinks the poison and lies down on the couch, where she had so often lain with Ernest, to wait for death. When the police break in they find her dying.

The main difference between Flaubert's tale and the newspaper account is that he is sympathetic towards the predicament of the woman. The reporter had thought that the man had behaved reasonably, and that all the blame was on the side of the wife, but Flaubert had been struck by the baseness and the meanness of Ernest. He has the same caddishness which we shall find in Rodolphe, in *Madame Bovary*, especially in the matter of the farewell letter. Flaubert remembered all this later when writing his great novel.

In style there is marked development in comparison with his earlier works, many more metaphors, and there are many fine descriptions as, for instance, the passage where Mazza stands on the jetty watching Ernest's ship sailing away on the horizon. There is here the same close sympathy of feeling between the character and nature which will be a characteristic of his maturity:[17]

Il était parti! parti pour toujours, et quand elle releva sa figure toute couverte de larmes, elle ne vit plus rein . . . que l'immensité de l'océan.

C'était une de ces brûlantes journées d'été, où la terre exhale de chaudes vapeurs comme l'air embrasé d'une fournaise. Quand Mazza fut arrivée sur la jetée, la fraîcheur salée de l'eau la ranima quelque peu, car une brise du sud enflait les vagues, qui venaient mollement mourir sur la grève et râlaient sur le galet. Les nuages noirs et épais s'amoncelaient à sa gauche, vers le soleil couchant, qui était rouge et lumineux sur la mer; on eût dit qu'ils allaient éclater en sanglots. La mer sans être furieuse, roulait sur elle-même en chantant lugubrement, et quand elle venait à se briser sur les pierres de la jetée, les vagues sautaient en l'air et retombaient en poudre d'argent.

Il y avait dans cela une sauvage harmonie, Mazza l'écouta longtemps fascinée par sa puissance; le bruit de ces flots avait pour elle un langage, une voix; comme elle, la mer était triste et pleine d'angoisse; comme elle, ces vagues venaient mourir en se brisant sur les pierres et ne laisser sur le sable mouillé que la trace de leur passage. Une herbe qui avait pris naissance entre deux fentes de la pierre, penchait sa tête toute pleine de la rosée, chaque coup de la vague venait la tirer de sa racine, et chaque fois elle se détachait de plus en plus; enfin elle disparut sous la lame, on ne la revit plus; et pourtant elle était jeune et portait des fleurs. Mazza sourit amèrement, la fleur était, comme elle, enleveé par la vague dans la fraîcheur du printemps.

Il y avait des marins qui rentraient, couchés dans leur barque; en tirant derrière eux la corde de leurs filets, leur voix vibrait au loin, avec le cri des oiseaux de nuit, qui planaient en volant de leurs ailes noires sur la tête de Mazza et qui allaient tous s'abattre vers la grève, sur les débris qu'apportait la marée. Elle entendit alors une voix qui l'appelait au fond du gouffre, et, la tête penchée vers l'abîme, elle calculait combien il lui faudrait de minutes et de secondes pour râler et mourir. Tout était triste comme elle dans la nature, et il lui sembla que les vagues avaient des soupirs et que la mer pleurait.

This is very similar to Emma Bovary's sensations when she leans out of the attic window after she has received Rodolphe's farewell letter, when she is tempted by suicide and feels the village square beneath her beckoning to her and drawing her down towards it.[18]

Flaubert finished *Passion et Vertu* a few days before his sixteenth birthday, and it is a most remarkable, mature and polished piece of work for so young an author.

The manuscript is preserved in the Bibliothèque Nationale in Paris. It is very neatly written but does not give the impression of a fair copy, for there are certain corrections and alterations in it, and it seems as if it had been fluently written. For some reason which has never been explained, the third page of the manuscript has been omitted in the Conard edition of Flaubert's works.[19]

Flaubert seems to have been troubled and saddened by his new discovery in the human heart and, writing to Ernest Chevalier, he said:[20]

It's a sad thing, in criticism and study, to reach the limits of knowledge only to discover vanity; to analyse the human heart only to find egoism; to understand the world only to see misery. How much more do I prefer poetry, cries from the heart, sudden aspirations, deep sighs, the voice of the soul, meditations of the heart. There are days when I'd give the whole of knowledge, the whole of vain erudition . . . for two lines of Lamartine, of Victor Hugo. Here am I turning against reason, against truth, for what is beauty except the impossible . . .

[4]

Alfred Le Poittevin
(1837–8)

THE closest friend of Flaubert's youth – probably of his whole life – was Alfred Le Poittevin. We have seen that he had known him from a child and that Alfred used to contribute to the theatrical performances in the billiards room at the Hôtel Dieu. Alfred Le Poittevin was five years the elder and he left school in 1834 when Flaubert was still in the junior classes. He then started studying law in Rouen, but there is no evidence that there was any close friendship between the two youths before 1837; then, until 1838, when Le Poittevin left to complete his studies in Paris, they spent together as much time as circumstances permitted. The first mentions of Le Poittevin in Flaubert's correspondence are found in two letters to Ernest Chevalier, of 24 March and 24 June 1837.

Flaubert was to say after Le Poittevin's death:[1] 'I see that I've never loved anyone (man or woman) as I loved him.' And he wrote on the copy of *Madame Bovary* which he presented to Alfred's sister, Laure de Maupassant:[2] 'Please accept this book, dear Madame, in memory of the affection which you had always shown me; and also (and especially), in the name of remembrance. If *He* were still alive, it is to him that this work would have been dedicated. His place has remained empty in my heart and our burning friendship has not been quenched.' And Le Poittevin himself said to his friend: 'We are something like one single man, and we live of the same life.'

Most of the critics concentrate on the friendship between the two young men during the forties, when Flaubert was living in Croisset and Le Poittevin was in Rouen, when Flaubert's closest friend at that time, Maxime Du Camp, was away on a trip abroad. However, it is in the period between 1837 and 1838 that Le Poittevin's influence on him is most marked, sets its seal most deeply on him, at a time when he was beginning to be interested in philosophy and occult thought.

It was a romantic friendship that the two young men shared, and Flaubert felt for Alfred Le Poittevin hero worship for a man five years his senior, who had therefore for him more glamour than Ernest Chevalier could ever possess, who was his equal in age, and who does not seem to have had any marked gifts for literature or thought. With Ernest Chevalier Flaubert took the lead, but his feminine nature, on the whole, preferred to be dominated by his friends.

There is no definite proof that there was anything actively homosexual between the friends, but there was undoubtedly a very warm, not to say emotional friendship between them. Once, when they were parted, Flaubert wrote to him:[4] 'On the bridge, I watched the water flowing by, thinking of you, without knowing that you desired it also, as you tell me in the letter which I received this morning . . . I thought of you again in the Arènes at Nimes, and under the arches of the Pont du Gard; that is to say that, in these places, I desired you with a strange appetite; for, far from each other, there is something lost in us, something incomplete.'

Flaubert wrote to him, while telling him of his love:[5] 'If you were to fail me, what would there be left to me? What would I have in my inner life, that is to say my true life?' This was in 1845, and the following year Le Poittevin married. When this happened Flaubert was outraged and, writing much later to Laure de Maupassant, he said:[6] 'I experienced, when he married, a very deep stab of jealousy, it was a rupture, a tearing away. For me he died twice.'

Le Poittevin also had for Flaubert the glamour of someone who was connected with a paper, and we have seen that, when he was attached to *Le Colibri*, he published in it two of Flaubert's contributions in 1837.

Le Poittevin, without being a great writer – he had, in fact, little time to become one, for he died at the age of thirty-two – was a very typical figure of the Romanticism of the 1830s; a period of great pessimism, when the influence of Byron was at its height in France. But he also expressed the philosophic ideas of the time, the theories of those authors who, like Edgar Quinet, in his *Ahasvérus*, endeavoured to solve the problem of man's destiny. He became very critical of the Christian explanation of the universe, and, with growing awareness of human suffering, he reached complete scepticism. Like many of his contemporaries, he was much attracted by the occult philosophy of the East and believed that it was there that all wisdom lay.

At this time, when he had just reached manhood, the time of his close friendship with Flaubert, he seems to have been going through a crisis in his life, and he emerged from it abandoning the faith of his youth. He revolted against God and particularly attacked the Christian explanation of human destiny. He was much obsessed by the problem of evil and how, if God exists, he can tolerate evil, if he is good. He then delighted in giving expression to the vanity of life and the futility of all effort.

At this time Le Poittevin was writing mostly poetry, which he published in *Le Colibri,* in Rouen, so that it was not known outside the narrow confines of the province. The poems are all very pessimistic and cynical, and their atmosphere is that of the *Cain* by Byron. The titles, *Satan, Heure d'Angoisse, La Foi, Allégorie, Ahasvérus,* express their nature. They all investigate the problem of evil. They are not of a very high quality – one must, however, remember that their author was only twenty – and do not deserve the immortality which they failed to gain. His most important work, *Une Promenade de Bélial,* was planned ten years later, in 1845, but was abandoned and then taken up again in 1847, in the last year of his life. But even this is not of lasting interest, and is a rather ordinary nineteenth-century philosophic tale.

We shall see the impact of Le Poittevin's ideas on

Flaubert's writings at this time, when he was becoming engrossed in philosophical problems, especially in the problem of human destiny. Here he follows the regular current of mid-nineteenth-century mystical inspiration, the current which gave rise to the tremendous prose epics dealing with Man's fate, such works as the *Ahasvérus* by Quinet, published in 1833. His ideas are coloured by the cynicism and pessimism of Le Poittevin, and these are seen in the works which he composed during 1838 and the first half of 1839. This was one of the most richly productive years of his youth – probably of the whole of his life. In March 1838 he composed the last play of his youth – the only one which has come down to us – *Loys XI*, which is also his last historical work until *Salammbô*. It has, however, more than historical interest, for it is also inspired by his new philosophic conceptions. Louis XI represents for him the close of the Middle Ages and the opening of the modern period; he is for him the defender of the people, the enemy of aristocracy and privilege. The play also clearly demonstrates that, in spite of his passion for the stage, Flaubert was not gifted dramatically – this will also be amply evident in the plays of his maturity – for he needed more space in which to build up his characters.

The following month, in April, he composed *Agonies, Pensées Sceptiques*, the first work dedicated to Alfred Le Poittevin, and truly influenced by him. In May he wrote *Danse des Morts*, his first attempt in the manner which was to reach fruition in *La Tentation de Saint Antoine*; and in June, *Ivre et Mort*. Then there was a slowing down in his literary production on account of the examination season, except that he won the history prize at school in July, with a long composition entitled *Histoire Moderne*, which is, in fact, an original essay on the Renaissance, dealing especially with Rabelais, who was beginning to interest him at this time, and whom he read under the guidance of Le Poittevin.

Between October and Christmas he composed his only deliberately autobiographical work, *Mémoires d'un Fou*, and, immediately after that, he began *Smarh*, which was completed in April 1839; and, in August, he wrote *Les Funérailles du Docteur Mathurin*, the last of his tales until *Trois Contes*, although it was the form which he most favoured in his youth.

The first of Flaubert's philosophic works is *Agonies, Pensées Sceptiques*, the second section of which is entitled *Angoisses* and it recalls Le Poittevin's poem *Heure d'Angoisse*. This expresses weariness and ennui with life, and the narrator wonders why he is alive, since everything on earth bores him so inexpressibly; why he is alive, since there is nothing round him but emptiness, 'le néant'. The work shows its author more firmly set than ever in his early conviction that there is nothing but cruelty and injustice in man. He declares that his only weapon against despair is his delight in cynical aphorisms. Yet everything is vain, since death is the end of all and awaits each of us:

En moins d'un an les vers déchirent un cadavre, puis c'est la poussière, puis le néant; après le néant . . . le néant, et c'est tout ce qui reste.[7]

Then follows the description of an exhumation, with full realistic detail, which shows that Flaubert has not lost his early obsession with death and decay, but which is also in the style of the 'charogne' literature of the day; it must be remembered that Théophile Gautier published his *Comédie de la Mort* in 1838.

Then he asks himself what becomes of the soul, but his answer is only cynical:[8]

Mais l'âme? Ah! oui, l'âme! Si tu avais vu l'autre jour le fossoyeur avec un chapeau de cuir ciré sur le coin de l'oreille, avec un brûle-gueule bien culotté; si tu avais vu comment il a ramassé cette cuisse en pourriture, et comme tout cela ne l'empêchait pas de siffler en ricanant: jeunes filles, voulez-vous danser? tu aurais ri de pitié, et tu aurais dit: L'âme, c'est peut-être cette exhalaison fétide qui sort d'un cadavre.

Il ne faut pas être philosophe pour deviner cela.

The narrator seeks out a cleric for spiritual help but he only finds a priest more interested in his potatoes cooking in the

kitchen next door than in his charge of souls. He is the first
sketch for Father Bournisien in *Madame Bovary*.[9]

The tale ends – if indeed it can be called a tale – with
Satan showing the narrator all the evil and misery of the
world, and the passage is almost word for word a page from
the very early work, *Voyage en Enfer*, mentioned previously. The manuscript is unfinished, but the implication is
that we need not look further for Hell since we have it with
us here below.

La Danse des Morts, composed a month later, is Flaubert's
most ambitious work to date – certainly his longest, more
than fifty pages – but it is too diffuse and not well planned,
as the author does not seem very clear about his central idea,
or where he is going. Its main theory is that the world is
composed of suffering and that everything aspires to
nothingness, 'le néant'.

It is written in the romantic style of nineteenth-century
mystical thought, but it possesses what is not usually found
in other texts: Flaubert's typical grotesque sense of irony
and comic humour, as when he declares that the Holy Ghost
has died many years ago from congestion of the lungs.[10]

The work ends with Satan telling God that he will outlive
him, and be finally left in control of the universe. Then
Death departs on his horse, Christ returns to the bosom of
his father, but Satan, uttering a hideous laugh, more
hideous than that of Death, spreads his wings over the whole
earth:[11]

La Mort siffla son cheval, on le vit accourir, d'un bond elle
s'élança dessus.

Et puis le Christ pleura, s'entourant d'un nuage blanc, alla
retrouver son père qui l'endormit dans son coeur.

Et Satan, poussant un plus horrible rire que celui de la Mort,
un rire de joie et d'orgueil, s'abattit sur la terre, étendant sur elle
ses deux ailes de chauve-souris qui l'entourèrent comme un linceul noir.

Le Poittevin did more than inspire Flaubert in literature,
and he is said also to have encouraged him in all kinds of

self-indulgence and debauch. This is seen in the correspondence between the two young men, which is very different from that with Ernest Chevalier, which is much more light-hearted and innocent. A large batch of Le Poittevin's letters is preserved in the Bibliothèque Nationale in Paris.[12] When René Descharmes was publishing his memoir of the poet,[13] he felt that he could not publish many of his letters as he considered them too pornographic. Public opinion is less squeamish now than in 1924, and the letters would be valuable for the light they throw on Flaubert. They are certainly very coarse but most of them belong to a later period, when Flaubert was more mature than he was in 1838 at sixteen. Not all the letters of Le Poittevin to Flaubert have been preserved, for the latter wrote on the envelope containing Eulalie Foucaud's letters to him, 'Opened and reread the day when I burned Alfred's letters, a Sunday morning at the end of January.' This may have been after Le Poittevin married, when Flaubert had felt such a violent pang of jealousy; he then may have reread the letters from the first woman who had ever loved him.

It is said that Le Poittevin encouraged Flaubert to drink; indeed it is sometimes claimed that it was addiction to alcohol which caused Alfred's early death, or was partly responsible for it.

Under his influence Flaubert composed two bacchic tales in glorification of drink and drunkenness, *Ivre et Mort* in June 1838 and *Les Funérailles du Docteur Mathurin* in August 1839.

Ivre et Mort relates the adventures of two men who undertake a drinking contest, in which one of them dies. It expresses the same disillusionment with life as do Flaubert's other works at this time. What is noticeable here is the author's talent for realistic description and his attention to external detail.

Les Funérailles du Docteur Mathurin is similar in inspiration, the story of a man who wants to enjoy one final drinking bout before he dies. It is coloured by the pessimism which had become habitual to Flaubert, but the tale contains some very good writing and brilliant dialogue. Jean Bruneau considers that it is the masterpiece amongst Flaubert's stories,[14] but not all would agree with this verdict and many would prefer *Passion et Vertu*, written eighteen months earlier.

As has been mentioned earlier, *Les Funérailles du Docteur Mathurin* is Flaubert's last story until *Trois Contes*, published thirty-six years later.

It was under the influence of Le Poittevin that Flaubert began to read the works of Rabelais with passionate interest, as can be seen from his correspondence. Writing to Ernest Chevalier, he said that there were only two men whom he really admired, Rabelais and Byron.[15] We have seen that his prize composition in July 1838 on the Renaissance dealt largely with Rabelais; but he wrote, as well, an essay on him after the examination. We know that he took Rabelais's works away with him for the holidays of 1838;[16] and, in September, he told Ernest Chevalier that he proposed to write a literary and philosophic study of Rabelais and Montaigne.[17] The essay on Rabelais was composed probably towards the end of 1838, or the beginning of 1839 – the critics have argued endlessly about the matter, which is not of great significance – it was certainly not before the end of October 1838, when he finished reading Rabelais.[18] Jean Bruneau expresses admiration for this composition,[19] yet it does not reveal much more than competence and does not express his true originality; it shows wide reading, and a good use of the material, but it was probably produced as a school 'dissertation' – perhaps even on a suggested plan.

Flaubert's most ambitious work of his schooldays is *Smarh*, and it is also the most important of those influenced by Alfred Le Poittevin. Even though it was written after *Mémoires d'un Fou*, which was composed in the autumn of 1838, it is studied first since it is part of the same inspiration as the work of this period. *Mémoires d'un Fou* belongs to another spiritual and literary climate, and it will be studied in the following chapter.

Smarh was begun in December 1838, as soon as Flaubert
had completed *Mémoires d'un Fou*; he abandoned it
shortly afterwards, but took it up again in March and
finished it on 14 April 1839. The sub-title *Vieux Mystère*
seems to indicate that he intended to suggest that it derives
from the mysteries of the Middle Ages so popular with
Romantic writers – though more in theory than in practice –
but he is more likely to have been thinking of the two mysteries of Byron, *Cain* and *Heaven and Earth,* especially the
former. We have seen that he was enthusiastic about Byron
at this time, and he could have read him in French, for there
were many current translations – some of them in popular
editions in one volume.

He drew some inspiration also from the *Faust* of Goethe,
the first part of which was translated by Gérard de Nerval in
1829. He had certainly read the German poet before he composed *Smarh*, for he mentions *Werther* in *Mémoires d'un
Fou*.[20] But, as Bruneau points out,[21] he did not borrow
more from *Faust* than two scenes, notably the one where
Satan appears as a doctor and discusses philosophy with
Smarh.[22] The most fruitful source of inspiration was undoubtedly Quinet's prose epic *Ahasvérus*, which was also
one of the favourite works of Alfred Le Poittevin. It is divided into four days, with a prologue and an epilogue. Like-
wise *Smarh* is in four parts with a prologue and an epilogue.
Flaubert intended, like Quinet before him, to express sym-
bolically the history of the miserable state of humanity, the
restlessness of mankind never satisfied with what it achieves
and always longing for something beyond its grasp. In his
pride man believes that he can dominate everything, but he
is always fated, in the end, to stumble and fall to destruction.
Flaubert's metaphysical style has many resemblances to that
of Quinet.

From Byron Flaubert borrowed the main philosophy of
the work, which is revolt against everything – the world and
God; revolt especially against human destiny. It is one of the
most pessimistic works he ever wrote, and he was only seventeen at the time. He favoured such cynical and pessimistic

statements as:[23] 'La vie, c'est un linceul taché de vin, c'est
une orgie où chacun se soûle, chante et a des nausées;
c'est un verre brisé, c'est un tonneau de vin âcre, et celui qui
le remue trop avant y trouve souvent bien de la lie et de la
boue.' And again Smarh says:[24] 'Où suis-je? où suis-je?
J'ai monté dans l'infini, et j'ai eu vite un dégoût de l'infini;
je suis redescendu sur la terre, et j'ai assez de la terre. Aussi
que faire? La nature et les hommes me sont odieux. Oh!
quelle pitoyable création!'

Smarh is a very long work – one hundred and ten pages –
but it is very much better planned than *La Danse des Morts*.
Flaubert gives what he claims is a synopsis of the work in
a letter to Ernest Chevalier,[25] but it was somewhat altered
later in the writing.

In the introduction Satan addresses the Archangel
Michael and tells him that he is about to tempt a man, a
saint amongst saints, Smarh, who has been a contented hermit until a thirst for knowledge destroyed serenity in him.

Then follow the temptations of Smarh by Satan; and his
experiences under the direction of both Satan and Yuk – in
nature, the world and eternity; then all the passions – of the
senses, of knowledge and glory.

The mystery closes with an account of the end of the
world and the victory of Yuk.

Yuk is a unique character in Flaubert, and does not occur
in other nineteenth-century epics. He is the personification
of the grotesque, and represents laughter in the midst of
anguish and despair. His attitude before ambition, delight
or suffering is laughter, bitter laughter and irony. His irony
does not spare the finest actions, which he shows up as
interested; nor the noblest thoughts, which he reveals as
commonplace and vain; his greatest joy is in making clear to
man the baseness of his condition. He is a recurrent figure in
Flaubert's mature work, the symbol of the grotesque
conquering everything. He sums up the young author's philosophy of life, stating that the only attitude that man can
oppose to the injustice and absurdity of the world is the cyni-

cal laughter of someone who believes in nothing. It is the bitter laugh, the 'humour noir' to be found in the work of Petrus Borel, in *Champavert* and *Madame Putiphar*, published in the 1830s.

Smarh was first planned as a play, and Flaubert discussed the various scenes with Ernest Chevalier.[26] This is more noticeable in the first two parts than in the others, for they are written in dialogue with stage directions. In part three there is a mixture of dialogue and narrative. Part four is largely narrative, and there is also a difference which does not exist in the other three parts: the author intervenes in his own person – this is the influence of the confessional literature which Flaubert had been reading when composing *Mémoires d'un Fou*. He speaks particularly in the person of the poetic young man who renders most expressively the vague longings of boyhood, which are those of the young author himself:[27]

Pourquoi donc s'ennuyait-il déjà, le pauvre enfant?

Il avait voulu un horizon plus vaste que celui qui s'étendait sous ses yeux, quelque chose de plus resplendissant que le soleil. Lorsqu'il voyait, dans les belles nuits d'été, les bouquets de roses et les jasmins secouer aux souffles des vents leurs têtes fleuries, que la brise agitait les feuilles vertes et qu'elle remuait, dans ses plis invisibles, des échos lointains d'amour et des parfums de fleur, que la lune brillait toute pure et toute sereine, avec ses lumières qui montent et brillent et coulent silencieusement là-haut, avec les nuages qui s'étendaient comme des montagnes mouvantes ou les vagues géantes d'un autre Océan, il avait senti qu'il y avait encore dans son âme quelque chose de plus doux que tous ces parfums, de plus suave que toutes ces clartés, comme s'il y avait en lui des sources intarissables de volupté et des mondes de lumières qui rayonnaient au dedans.

Ce n'était plus assez de rester dans le fond de la vieille barque grêle, de se laisser bercer par la marée montante, couché sur les filets aux mailles rompues, alors que le soleil brillait sur les flots et que la quille venait battre le sable et les cailloux qui erraient sous elle, ni de voir au crépuscule les flots s'avancer et les sauterelles de mer rebondir comme la pluie sur le rivage, ni de sentir dans ses cheveux le vent de l'automne qui roule les feuilles

jaunies et les plumes de la colombe, et qui semble murmurer des
pleurs dans les rameaux morts; rien de tout cela.

The only thing which could ease his infinite distress would
be to become a poet and to express the emotion artistically,
and, by poet, he understood any creative artist:[28]

> Oh! poète! se sentir plus grand que les autres, avoir une âme
> si vaste qu'on y fait toujours entrer, tout tourner, tout parler,
> comme la créature dans la main de Dieu; exprimer toute l'échelle
> immense et continue qui va depuis le brin d'herbe jusqu'à
> l'éternité, depuis le grain de sable jusqu'au cœur de l'homme;
> avoir tout ce qu'il y a de plus beau, de plus doux, de plus suave,
> les plus larges amours, les plus longs baisers, les longues rêveries
> la nuit, les triomphes, les bravos, l'or, le monde, l'immortalité!
> N'est-ce pas pour lui, la mousse des bois fleuris, le battement
> d'ailes de la colombe, le sable embaumant de la rive, la brise
> toute parfumée des mers du Sud, tous les concerts de l'âme,
> toutes les voix de la nature, les paroles de Dieu, à lui, le poète.

Flaubert came out of his metaphysical experience bewildered and shattered, as he said to Ernest Chevalier:[29]
'Recently, in the composition of my mystery, when I found
myself face to face with infinity, I did not know how to
express what was shattering my soul.' He was left, after finishing the work, with the same feeling of despair as
Smarh:[30]

> Il pleura amèrement pendant longtemps, et chacune de ses
> larmes était une malédiction pour la terre, c'était quelque chose
> du cœur qui tombait et s'en allait dans le néant; c'était l'agonie
> de l'espérance, de la foi, de l'amour, du beau, tout cela mourait,
> fuyait, s'envolait pour l'éternité; toute la sève, toute la vie, toutes
> les fraîcheurs, tous les parfums, toutes les lumières, tout ce qui
> navre, ce qui enchante, tout ce qui est volupté, croyances,
> ardeurs, avait été arraché par le vent d'éternité qui venait de la
> terre, rasait le sol, emportait les fleurs.

Smarh is a work with many faults of prolixity and
diffuseness, with too much exuberance of imagery; but it has
many passages of fine writing, and shows a power of metaphysical reflection unusual in a young man barely seventeen
years of age.

[5]

Mémoires d'un Fou
(1838-40)

AFTER the end of the school year in 1838 Flaubert went, with his family, for their usual summer holiday to Trouville, but, as we have seen, the Schlésingers were not there. He wandered round the places where he had seen Élisa, longing for her presence; he looked everywhere for her image, and only then became conscious of what had happened to him two years before:[1]

Quoi! rien du tout cela ne reviendra? Je sens comme mon coeur est vide, car tous ces hommes qui m'entourent me font un désert où je meurs. Je me rappelai mes longues et chaudes après-midi d'été où je lui parlais sans qu'elle se doutât que je l'aimais, et où son regard indifférent m'entrait comme un rayon d'amour jusqu'au fond du coeur. Comment aurait-elle pu en effet voir que je l'aimais, car je ne l'aimais pas alors, et en tout ce que je vous ai dit, j'ai menti, c'était maintenant que je l'aimais, que je la désirais; que, seul sur le rivage, dans les bois et dans les champs, je me la créais là, marchant à côté de moi, me parlant; me regardant.

He was now reading confessional literature and turning towards the introspective aspect of Romanticism. He was enthralled by Rousseau's *Confessions*, much interested in Goethe's *Werther*, which is really a personal confession; and also by *La Confession d'un Enfant du Siècle* by Musset, published in 1836.[2] Now, ripened by this reading, it came to him what personal and artistic use he could make of his own emotional experience. It was then that he formed the plan of producing his own autobiography, *Mémoires d'un Fou*, the only truly autobiographical work he was ever to compose, although there are many personal details and emotions in

his other works, it is the only one in which he set out deliberately to tell the story of his life.

He was perhaps also encouraged by Le Poittevin's description of a girl whom he had met in 1838, whom he called
Flora, and for whom he seems to have felt the same emotion
that Flaubert had experienced for Élisa Schlésinger:[3]

> When I arrived at Havre, it was almost nightfall. There were,
> sitting at a window of the Hôtel de l'Amirauté, two women, one
> young and the other older. I thought they were Flora and her
> mother and I returned in the evening to linger under the light
> that fell from the windows. . . . It was not she, she had left Havre
> a fortnight before, and I had wasted my emotion.
>
> Why did this young girl, whom I don't know, remain thus in
> my memory? I don't know, and doubtless a few hours more
> would have disenchanted me with her as with all the others. But
> I like to think of her from time to time. Is it because I addressed a
> couple of poems to her? and is the memory of her only a form of
> vanity?

In October 1838, when the school reopened, Flaubert
ceased being a boarder and became a day boy again, and he
tells Ernest Chevalier that he will now be able to smoke his
cigar at the Café National, waiting for the school bell to
ring.[4] He talks about how happy and calm he is now that he
is no longer living in the college.[5] Nevertheless, he is count-
ing the days until he can say goodbye to school for ever:[6] 'Il
est vrai que je suis maintenant externe libre, ce qui est on ne
peut mieux, en attendant que je sois tout à fait parti de
cette sacrée nom de Dieu de pétaudière de merde de collège.'

In spite of his delight in his freedom, sadness settled on
him and he was lonely and depressed. His two closest friends,
Alfred Le Poittevin and Ernest Chevalier, were in Paris and
he does not seem to have had any other close associates. In
particular, he missed Ernest, whom he had seen every day of
his life at school, when they were both boarders together.
His letters at this time to Chevalier are valuable as an indi-
cation of his state of mind – probably those to Le Poittevin
have been destroyed; at least none are known to exist.

In his solitude he was analysing himself and dissecting himself more,[7] but this only led to further depression and boredom. 'Je m'emmerde à la perfection', he said to Ernest Chevalier.[8] And again:[9] 'I dissect everything and that amuses me. Then, when I've discovered corruption in what is considered pure, and gangrene in what is fine, then I lift up my head and roar with laughter.'

Mémoires d'un Fou was begun in the autumn of 1838 and finished by Christmas. It was dedicated to Alfred Le Poittevin and given to him as a New Year's gift on 1 January 1839:[10]

A toi mon cher Alfred
                         ces pages sont dédiées et données.
Elles renferment une âme tout entière. Est-ce la mienne? est-ce celle d'un autre? J'avais d'abord voulu faire un roman intime, où le scepticisme serait poussé jusqu'aux dernières bornes du désespoir; mais peu à peu, en écrivant, l'impression personnelle perça à travers la fable, l'âme remua la plume et l'écrasa.

J'aime donc mieux laisser cela dans le mystère des conjectures; pour toi, tu n'en feras pas.

Seulement tu croiras peut-être, en bien des endroits, que l'expression est forcée et le tableau assombri à plaisir; rappelle-toi que c'est un fou qui a écrit ces pages, et si le mot paraît souvent surpasser le sentiment qu'il exprime, c'est que, ailleurs, il a fléchi sous le poids du coeur.

Adieu, pense à moi, et pour moi.

It is in the typical 'roman personnel' style of the early years of the nineteenth century, and, in form, pretends to be a personal record of the author's life. It is the same form as Chateaubriand's *René*, or Goethe's *Werther* – especially the latter. *Werther* is also in the form of a day-to-day diary, Goethe also saw himself as a madman, and Flaubert's attitude to Élisa Schlésinger is very similar to that of Werther for Charlotte. It is, in the opinion of this author at all events, Flaubert's most interesting work to date, though it is not without its faults of planning and construction, as well as of balance.

It is difficult to study the work critically, as the manuscript has not been available for more than half a century. It is not one of those which belonged to Flaubert's niece and were sold after her death; or were bequeathed to various libraries. But, as we have seen, it belonged to Alfred Le Poittevin, and after his death in 1848, it passed to his son, who, at the end of the century, sold it to Pierre Dauze, the editor of *La Revue Blanche*, who published it serially in the magazine, between 15 December 1900 and 1 February 1901. The same text, with slight typographical errors, was published by Flourey in 1901, and this is the one which has been reprinted ever since.

René Descharmes, when preparing his thesis, *Flaubert avant 1857*, published in 1907, studied the manuscript – he is the last person to have seen it – and described it in his notes, which are preserved at the Bibliothèque Nationale in Paris.[11] He has described it very fully, page by page.

There can be little doubt that the only extant version of *Mémoires d'un Fou* is the one in the manuscript given to Alfred Le Poittevin in January 1839, and that there is no possibility of later additions to it. Descharmes describes the episode of the little English girls as being written on different paper from the rest, of a different colour and format than the bulk of the manuscript, but this is easily explainable, since it was composed a year before the rest.[12]

Mémoires d'un Fou is written in a variety of styles, with many episodes, and often one does not see the reason why some of them are strung together. The work lacks unity.

The first nine sections are a somewhat conventional Romantic confession showing an influence, in spirit, of Byron. Flaubert says that he is going to put down all his thoughts as they occur to him, and that he is going to write the story of his life:[13]

Seulement je vais mettre sur le papier tout ce qui me viendra à la tête, mes idées avec mes souvenirs, mes impressions, mes rêves, mes caprices, tout ce qui passe dans la pensée et dans l'âme; du rire et des pleurs, du blanc et du noir, des sanglots partis d'abord du coeur et étalés comme de la pâte dans des périodes sonores, et des larmes délayées dans des métaphores romantiques. Il me pèse cependant à penser que je vais écraser le bec à un paquet de plumes, que je vais user une bouteille d'encre, que je vais ennuyer le lecteur, et moi-même; j'ai tellement pris l'habitude du rire et du scepticisme, qu'on y trouvera, depuis le commencement jusqu'à la fin, une plaisanterie perpétuelle, et les gens qui aiment à rire pourront à la fin rire de l'auteur et d'eux-mêmes.

All these first sections express somewhat conventional Romantic pessimism and cynicism, but his diatribes against life and love must not be taken too seriously, nor must everything that he says about himself at school be believed as truth. It is not true, as he states, that he was disliked and mocked at by his schoolmates, but it was fashionable for the hero to have everyone's hand against him. On the contrary he had many friends, amongst whom he took the lead. It was not true either to say that all the teachers were despicable. On the contrary there were many talented and distinguished masters at the college: Chéruel in history, Gourgaud-Dugazon and Mallet in literature. It was clever then, as now, to hate school and to have been misunderstood there. Nor should one attribute too much importance to the youthful cynicism of the boy of sixteen, derived from Byron: 'Malheur aux hommes qui m'ont rendu corrompu et méchant, de bon et pur que j'étais.'[14] This is very like the French version of a passage from *Childe Harold*, translated, in 1838, by Laroche, Canto III:

> Le seul soulagement à mon âme plaintive
> C'est d'avoir épuisé la coupe du malheur.
>
> Ce qu'on rencontre au fond de cette coupe amère,
> Ne le demande pas. Ne cherche pas à voir
> Ce qu'un coeur d'homme peut contenir de misère,
> Et l'enfer qui bouillonne en cet abîme noir.

This conventional Romantic confession ends with typical disgust of life and longing for nothingness:[15]

A peine ai-je vu la vie qu'il y a eu un immense dégoût dans
mon âme; j'ai porté à ma bouche tous les fruits, ils m'ont semblé
amers, je les ai repoussés et voilà que je meurs de faim. Mourir si
jeune, sans espoir dans la tombe, sans être sûr d'y dormir, sans
sçavoir si sa paix est inviolable! Se jeter dans les bras du néant et
douter s'il vous recevra!

Oui, je meurs, car est-ce vivre de voir son passé comme l'eau
écoulée dans la mer, le présent comme une cage, l'avenir comme
un linceul.

Then follows a pause, as if the author were reluctant to
begin, as if he could not bear to embark on the serious part of
his narrative, on the burning memories. After a three weeks'
break, as he says, he starts again:[16]

Ici commencent vraiment les mémoires . . .

Ici sont mes souvenirs les plus tendres et les plus pénibles à la
fois, et je les aborde avec une émotion toute religieuse. Ils sont
vivants à ma mémoire et presque chauds encore pour mon
âme, tant cette passion l'a fait saigner. C'est une large cicatrice
au coeur qui durera toujours, mais, au moment de retracer cette
page de ma vie, mon coeur bat comme si j'allais remuer des
ruines chéries . . .

Pour moi tout semble vivre encore. J'entends et je vois le
frémissement des feuilles, je vois jusqu'au moindre pli de sa robe;
j'entends le timbre de sa voix, comme si un ange chantait près de
moi, voix douce et pure, qui vous enivre et qui vous fait mourir
d'amour, voix qui a un corps, tant elle est belle et qui séduit,
comme s'il y avait un charme à ses mots.

This portion – sections X to XIV – is something quite
different from the first nine sections, as it is written with
sincere emotion, and with great simplicity. It is the account
of his meeting with Maria – Élisa Schlésinger – and the
summer that they spent together. There is no attitudinizing
here, and the author is no longer looking at himself, play-
acting. He manages to be direct and moving when describing the places where they met, in Trouville, in the days
before it had been spoilt by too many summer visitors:[17]

Alors, tout était simple et sauvage, il n'y avait guère que des artistes et des gens du pays. Le rivage était désert et, à marée basse, on voyait une plage immense avec un sable gris et argenté qui scintillait au soleil, tout humide encore de la vague. A gauche, des rochers où la mer battait paresseusement dans ses jours de sommeil les parois noircies de varechs; puis, au loin, l'océan bleu sous un soleil ardent, et mugissant sourdement comme un géant qui pleure.

Et quand on rentrait dans le village, c'était le plus pittoresque et le plus chaud spectacle. Des filets noirs et rongés par l'eau étendus aux portes, partout les enfants à moitié nus marchaient sur un galet gris, seul pavage du lieu, des marins avec leurs vêtements rouges et bleus; et tout cela simple dans sa grâce, naïf et robuste, tout cela empreint d'un caractère de vigueur et d'énergie.

This portion ends with the close of the summer holidays when the visitors left, and he returned to school:[18]

Il fallut partir; nous nous séparâmes sans pouvoir lui dire adieu. Elle quitta les bains le même jour que nous. C'était un dimanche.

Elle partit le matin, nous le soir; elle partit et je ne la revis plus. Adieu pour toujours! Elle partit comme la poussière de la route qui s'envole derrière ses pas. Comme j'y ai pensé depuis! combien d'heures confondu devant le souvenir de son regard, ou l'intonation de ses paroles! ... Adieu pour toujours à ces belles fleurs de la jeunesse si vite fanées et vers lesquelles plus tard on se reporte de temps en temps avec amertume et plaisir à la fois! Enfin je vis les maisons de ma ville, je rentrai chez moi, tout m'y parut désert et lugubre, vide et creux; je me mis à vivre, à boire, à manger, à dormir.

L'hiver vint et je rentrai au collège.

Next follows section XV, dealing with the episode of the English girls, written in a completely different style, and not intended, at first, as we have seen, to be part of the work, which, as we have also seen, is a charming idyll. He says, however that its memory was completely wiped out by the experience with Maria.

Then, as if he needed a sensual contrast to the innocent adventure, he gives an episode with a bought woman, which

does not ring true, but which he says left him with nothing
but remorse, as if Maria had been a religion which he had
desecrated. This is section XVII. Sections XVIII to XX
discuss philosophic and aesthetic problems, and are written
in the style of the first nine sections; they also contain meditations on death and decay which we now recognize as the
climate of Flaubert's thought in adolescence. Sections XXI
and XXII are in the nature of an epilogue. The young
author returned to the scene of his platonic adventure two
years later, but he did not find Maria there, and he realized
then for the first time that he had loved her, and that she
had set the pattern for his emotional life. He felt now
capable of writing of her, and of recounting the story of his
episode with her, *Mémoires d'un Fou*, since he is a madman
to have remembered a vain love for so long. Then he says
farewell to her for ever:[19]

O Maria! Maria! cher ange de ma jeunesse, toi que j'ai vue
dans la fraîcheur de mes sentiments, toi que j'ai aimée d'un
amour si doux, si plein de parfum, de tendres rêveries, adieu!

Adieu! d'autres passions reviendront, je t'oublierai peut-être,
mais tu resteras toujours au fond de mon coeur, car le coeur est
une terre sur laquelle chaque passion bouleverse, remue et
laboure sur les ruines des autres. Adieu!

Adieu! et cependant comme je t'aurais aimée, comme je
t'aurais embrassée, serrée dans mes bras! Ah! mon âme se fond
en délices à toutes les folies que mon amour invente. Adieu!

Adieu! et cependant je penserai toujours à toi; je vais être
jeté dans le tourbillon du monde, j'y mourrai peut-être, écrasé
sous les pieds de la foule, déchiré en lambeaux. Où vais-je? que
serai-je? je voudrais être vieux, avoir les cheveux blancs; non, je
voudrais être beau comme les anges, avoir de la gloire, du génie,
et tout déposer à tes pieds pour que tu marches sur tout cela; et
je n'ai rien de tout cela et tu m'as regardé aussi froidement qu'un
laquais ou qu'un mendiant.

Et moi, sais-tu que n'ai pas passé une nuit, pas une heure,
sans penser à toi, sans te revoir sortant de dessous la vague, avec
tes cheveux noirs sur tes épaules, ta peau brune avec ses perles
d'eau salée, tes vêtements ruisselants et ton pied blanc aux

ongles roses qui s'enfonçaient dans le sable, et que cette vision
est toujours présente, et que cela murmure toujours à mon
coeur? Oh! non, tout est vide.

Adieu! et pourtant quand je te vis, si j'avais été plus âgé de
quatre ou cinq ans, plus hardi ... peut-être. ... Oh! non, je
rougissais à chacun de tes regards. Adieu!

He was, in fact, never to forget her, but this was not their
last meeting, for he met her again when he was a student
in Paris.

With all the different topics and episodes, the general conclusion of *Mémoires d'un Fou*, like that of *Smarh*, is that it
is from man's pride that all his errors derive, and most of his
sorrows.

It is at this time that we perceive, in Flaubert, the beginning of a preoccupation, of an interest, in perfection of
form. This is seen in a school essay, produced in January
1839, 'Les Arts et le Commerce', in which his theories are
similar to those of the Art for Art's Sake Movement, as expressed in the famous Preface to *Mademoiselle de Maupin*
by Théophile Gautier, published in 1836. Flaubert had declared in *Mémoires d'un Fou* that the only consolation for
the misery of life was to be found in art.[20] 'Si j'ai éprouvé
des moments d'enthousiasme, c'est à l'art que je les dois.'
The essay is a discussion of the relative merits of the arts and
material progress, and he comes down on the side of art, declaring that it will outlive all materialistic considerations. It
is not particularly brilliant or original as a composition, but
it is intelligent and well reasoned.

We know that Flaubert began composing *Smarh* in December 1838, as soon as he had completed *Mémoires d'un
Fou*, and that he finished it in April 1839. It is, as we have
seen, his longest and most ambitious work, but it left him
drained of all literary effort for many months – for nearly
three years – except for some school essays and *Les
Funérailles du Docteur Mathurin*, composed during the
summer holidays, in August 1839. Writing to Ernest Chevalier, in July, he said:[21] 'As for writing, I have given it up

completely, and I'm sure that no one will ever see my name in print, I've no longer the strength for it, and I don't feel capable of it any more, that is, fortunately, or unfortunately, true. I'd have distressed all those around me.'

He was also beginning to be concerned about his future and the choice of profession. 'The future is the worst thing in the present,' he said to Chevalier,[22] 'that question flung at a man *what are you going to be,* is a yawning chasm in front of him, and which approaches nearer and nearer as he advances. . . . Don't imagine that I'm undecided about the choice of profession, I've decided never to take up any, as I've too great a contempt for men to wish to do them either good or harm.' Later he became resigned and accepted his family's plan that he should embark on the study of law.[23] 'Well! I'll be like everyone else, respectable; like everybody, a lawyer, a prefect, a notary, a barrister, any judge, a stupidity like all stupidities, a man of the world or of an office, which is even more stupid, for one must be something of all that there is no middle way. Well! I've chosen, I've decided, I'll go and study law, which, instead of leading to everything leads to nothing. I'll spend three years in Paris, and catch pox, and what then? And I long for one thing only, to spend my days in an old ruined castle beside the sea.'

Flaubert was looking forward to his final year at school, his year in Philosophy, but he was in a state of pessimism, of lack of enthusiasm and lack of any conviction. He was doing well in class, being now thoroughly appreciated, and he liked the master of the Class of Philosophy, a certain Mallet, who realized his true worth and placed him first in the form.[24] Mallet was, however, a very poor disciplinarian, though an excellent and inspiring teacher. He could not keep order and he was replaced by a man called Bezout.[25] The boys, who liked and admired Mallet, took exception to this and organized a rebellion against the newcomer. Bezout sent in an unfavourable report to the Censeur about the boys. This report, dated 11 December 1839, said:

I have the honour to address this report to you concerning the disturbance which occurred during the class of philosophy when I was replacing Monsieur Mallet. The boys came in very noisily, talking at the tops of their voices, and it was only with the greatest difficulty that, having finally obtained silence, I was able to start the lesson, which was interrupted three times by the pupils Flaubert, Scentreuil and Poittevin, whom I was obliged to punish separately from the rest. The disturbance continued and the boys went as far as to shuffle their feet and to murmur. As I was expounding a complicated commentary, I was obliged, regretfully, to inflict a communal punishment on the whole class. I am well aware of the drawback of not differentiating between the guilty and the innocent; I hesitated for a long time, and it is only at the third warning that I gave a thousand lines to the whole class, promising however to raise the punishment if the guilty would own up. My intention had also been to take advantage of the first moment of silence to exempt them from this punishment, but the disturbance having continued, I was obliged to retain the punishment.

The boys, egged on and encouraged by Flaubert, refused to carry out the punishment, and they got up a protest against Bezout. Flaubert, and thirty other boys, drew up a petition against the master and the imposition. Amongst its signatories were Louis Bouilhet who, some years later, was to become one of Flaubert's closest friends and his literary mentor; and Émile Hamard, who was to marry his sister. The protest was headed: 'The boys, whose names follow, have refused to carry out the imposition inflicted on them by Monsieur Bezout.'

The new Censeur chose three 'unruly' boys as he called them, and threatened them with expulsion if they did not comply; these were Flaubert, Piedelièvre and Dumont. Flaubert drew up a further protest, in the name of the class, and this was signed by twelve members, again including Bouilhet and Hamard; and it was sent to the Proviseur. The letter is in Flaubert's hand and signed with the twelve names:[26]

Monsieur le Proviseur.
They told us that we were children and behaving like children;

we shall try, by our moderation, and our loyalty, to convince you of the contrary.

We handed to the 'Censeur' a letter from all the boys who refused to do the imposition. Without taking any notice of that list, the 'Censeur' contented himself with selecting three boys whom he threatens with nothing less than total expulsion from the school, that is to say to wreck their future, that is to say to debar them for evermore from the career they might have chosen. It would have been wise, before resorting to such a serious and decisive measure, to weigh in an impartial balance the justice or injustice of the imposition which was demanded today so imperiously. We are not afraid to state that such an investigation would have alleviated the harshness which the 'Censeur' showed towards us. Nevertheless, since the imposition is a general one, and, as such, must be borne by the whole class, by all the boys, by all those who signed the list which is in the possession of the 'Censeur', and which we do not repudiate, we sign here once more and we declare to you, Monsieur le Proviseur, first that we are prepared to put before you the reasons which make us act as we do today, and then if, notwithstanding these arguments, and then, if the class is still to continue to be 'decimated', we demand, for the undersigned, the imposition, if there is to be an imposition, and expulsion, if there is to be expulsion, which, if it were to be inflicted on a few separately, would no longer be a general imposition. If they inflict a thousand lines on the whole Class of Philosophy, they could just as easily expel the whole Class of Philosophy.

Finally we rely, Monsieur le Proviseur, on your justice and impartiality, which we know you like to exert in favour of boys who deserve it, boys of the Philosophy Class, boys who do not behave inconsiderately like lower form boys, but who have reflected deeply and meditated before taking a step which they think just, and which they are resolved to pursue to the bitter end.

Here follow the names of the boys who signed the list which is in the possession of the Censeur, and who assure you, Monsieur le Proviseur, of their respect and consideration.

It was signed 'Gustave Flaubert' followed by the eleven other names.

The Proviseur however did not allow himself to be moved;

he remained adamant and upheld the Censeur, declaring that the boys Flaubert, Piedelièvre and Dumont, having refused to do their imposition, had, by this very act, barred the doors of the school against themselves and were expelled. Nevertheless they refused to capitulate.

Flaubert, at the time of the rebellion, had shown courage and determination, but he must have been ordered, or advised, by his parents, to keep quiet about the matter for he does not seem to have discussed it with anyone – his father was a governor of the school and may have advised him to remain silent. He merely informed Ernest Chevalier that he had left school, in December 1839.[27]

He had then to prepare for his 'baccalauréat' alone, and with the help of Ernest Chevalier's notes of the previous year – we have seen that Chevalier was, at this time, in Paris, studying law, being a year older than Flaubert.

While working for his examination Flaubert was also studying Greek, and he declared that for his 'baccalauréat', he was learning Demosthenes and Homer *by heart*.[28]

Flaubert was in a very depressed state of mind after his expulsion from school. There is an interesting record of this time, a unique document, *Souvenirs, Notes et Pensées Intimes*, which he began to keep in February 1840, the first time he ever kept a private diary. The text is sixty-five pages long, and it was sold, after the death of his niece, in November 1931. It is not known whether the title is his, as it was in his niece's handwriting on the folder which contained the notes. Short extracts were printed in the catalogue of the sale, but fuller passages were published in *Le Figaro* on 7 November 1931; only in 1965 was it published *in extenso* by Lucia Chevalley-Sabatier.

The first dated entry is 20 February 1840, while he was working at home for his examination; and the last 'night of 2 January 1841', that is on his return from his trip to Corsica, when he was thinking about his future.

Flaubert was lonely at this time, working alone at home; not only were his close friends, Chevalier and Le Poittevin,

away but he had no longer even the companionship of his
other schoolmates. Once, when he had spent three days in
the country with Chevalier, he wrote to him afterwards to
express his loneliness on leaving:[29]

> Oh! my dear Ernest, I left you with a smile on my lips, but
> with rage in my heart, and I'm now terrifyingly sad. I've now
> sunk back into my everyday life, into that sterile, banal and
> laborious life. What boredom! It seems to me three years since I
> left you! What wonderful days you gave me! What a difference
> between my life three days ago and now! When I think of it I am
> overwhelmed and my soul is desolate with melancholy, is con-
> fused and useless! How yesterday seemed long to me!

He goes on to say how he went back to Rouen, after seeing
his friend off, feeling as if his happiness were evaporating.
Seated on top of the bus he felt as if the whole of his youth
was vanishing, disappearing beneath him, like the road, and
every step brought him nearer to Rouen and the daily grind.
He thanks his friend for the treat he has given him and says
that he will never forget it. 'Good-bye! Answer me soon and
forgive me!'

Flaubert was, at this time, showing symptoms of overwork,
without sufficient companionship and relaxation. His life
seems to have been a very unhealthy one and unnatural for
a young man of eighteen.

He was particularly longing for someone to love him:
'And nevertheless I've been in love, like anyone else, but no
woman has ever known anything about it.'[30] And again:

> Who would ever want me? It should already have happened,
> for I need a lover, an angel, I am complacent they say, why then
> this doubt that I have for each of my actions, this void which
> terrifies me, all these vanished illusions.

> Oh! a woman, what a beautiful thing! ... I like dreaming of
> her form, I like dreaming of all the graces of her smile, of the
> softness of her white arms, of the shape of her thigh, of the pose
> of her bent head.

These are not the sentiments of a young man who has
enjoyed sexual experience.

At that time he doubted his capacity, and this was the greatest suffering of all:[31]

And now, although I still have the conviction of my vocation, or rather the fulness of immense pride, I doubt more and more! If you only knew what anguish that is! If you only knew my vanity – what a savage vulture it is, how it eats into the heart – how lonely I am, isolated, suspicious and jealous, selfish and fierce – Oh! the future that I dreamed, how fine it was! Oh! the life I built for myself, like a novel, what a beautiful life! and how hard it is to give it up!

And again:[32]

What is wrong with me today? My head is sick and my heart empty! Habitually I have what is called a gay heart, but now there is nothing but emptiness there, a hideous void, into which I fall, broken and overwhelmed. I don't write any more. Formerly I used to write and was passionately interested in my own ideas; I knew what it was to be a poet, and I was a poet, inside, at least, in my soul.

He talks of his agony of not being able to write as he felt:[33]

When one writes one feels what should be; one understands that, at such and such a place, one needs this, at another that; one builds up pictures that one sees; one has, to a certain extent, the feeling that one is going to cause them to appear; one senses it in one's heart, like the distant echo of all the passions that one is going to bring to light; but one's impotence to render all that is the eternal despair of all those who write.

His longing for love and understanding turned him temporarily towards religion and the search for God. But when, at the end of the year, he found physical experience and love in Marseilles, on his trip to Corsica, he abandoned the search for mysticism for the time being:

How does it happen that I long for Jesus Christ to have existed, and that I am certain of it? It is that I find the mystery of the passion the most beautiful thing in the world . . .[34]

He was to remember these sentiments later, when describing Emma Bovary's dreams of religion:[35]

I would like to be a mystic. There must be some wonderful joys in believing in Heaven, in drowning in floods of incense, in being overwhelmed at the foot of the cross, in taking flight on the wings of a dove – First Communion is something innocent, and do not let us make fun of those who weep at it – the altar is a beautiful thing, covered with sweet-smelling flowers. The life of the saints is a beautiful thing; I would like to have died as a martyr, and if there is a God, a good God, the father of Jesus, let him send me his grace, and I shall receive it and bow down before Him.

Flaubert passed his 'baccalauréat' in August 1840, when he was eighteen, and his father, to recompense him for his diligence and success, gave him a trip to the south of France and to Corsica. He started off in a state of gloom – or even despair – but he returned transformed and full of courage for the future. He had seen many of the southern landscapes of which he had dreamt all his life; and he had experienced a romantic sexual adventure, being loved at last by a woman, for the first time in his life.

[6]

Eulalie Foucaud
(1840–41)

As it was not considered that, at the age of eighteen, it was suitable for him to travel alone, Flaubert was accompanied on his trip to the South by a friend of his father's age, Dr Cloquet, his spinster sister and an Italian priest called Father Stephani. It was strange company for a young man and he cannot be blamed for feeling some misgivings as he set out. He tells Chevalier that all his instincts tell him to accept the trip, if it were not for his travelling companions. In the end, however, it turned out better than he had anticipated, for he found the companionship of Cloquet in particular very sympathetic, and he formed a close attachment for him.

Before he left his father gave him much wise advice, telling him to keep a diary of what he saw and of what was happening to him.[1] 'Take advantage of your trip, and remember your friend Montaigne, who wants one to travel principally in order to bring back the humours of the different nations, and to rub and sharpen one's mind against that of others. Look around you, take notice of everything, take notes and do not travel like a grocer or a commercial traveller.'

Flaubert took his advice and bought ten notebooks to fill with his observations; they were intended to serve him on the various journeys he planned to make in the future. 'I am keeping the ten notebooks of good paper which I had intended to be blackened during the journey, I shall seal and put them away carefully, after having written on the cover: "White paper for other journeys".'[2] He used them for the present trip, and, in 1849, for his journey to the East but, for some reason, he did not use them for his journey to Italy in 1845, nor for his trip to Brittany in 1847.

This trip to the south of France and to Corsica – largely written up on his return to Rouen – was eventually published in the volume of his collected works entitled *Par les Champs et par les Grèves*.

At no moment since he was a very small boy did Flaubert ever forget that he was a man of letters, and he embarked on the narrative of his travels in the classical manner. There was a tradition of travel writing in the nineteenth century in France and he, as usual, had read a great deal. There were works such as Chateaubriand's *Itinéraire de Paris à Jérusalem* and Dumas's *Impressions de Voyage* as examples to copy. He obviously wanted to compete with them as he carefully composed and, afterwards, transcribed his daily journal. A great deal of it is somewhat pedantically and academically written, and he gives far too much information, but certain scenes and episodes struck him with force, so that some passages are written with vividness and humour. Then he forgets to pontificate but tells about the commonplace events he notices, or the dramatic effort he made at life-saving in Biarritz, when he vainly attempted to save two swimmers from drowning.[3] One realizes that even he is, at times, weary of the duty of writing and once, when he was obliged to stay indoors, he asks himself what else there is to do but write. 'But write what?' he complains. 'There is nothing as tiring as to make endless descriptions of a journey, and to annotate the slightest impression that one feels; by dint of expressing everything, of rendering everything, there is nothing left in one.'[4] He wonders then what is the point of telling everything. 'Isn't it delightful, on the contrary, to keep in one corner of your heart, unknown things that no one else but you could imagine, and that you suddenly recall on dark days like today, the remembrance of which illuminates you with joy, and charms you as in a dream.'

One evening he ventured to read what he had written to

his travelling companions, but they do not seem to have appreciated it, and he felt lonely and isolated. He wrote in *Souvenirs, Notes et Pensées Intimes*:[5] 'I read my notes to M. Cloquet and Mlle Lise, little approbation and little intelligence on their part; I'm offended; in the evening I write to mother; I'm very sad and, at dinner, I've the greatest difficulty in restraining my tears.'

They drove first down the west coast, to Bayonne and Biarritz and other places in the Pyrenees; then crossed over to the east coast, to Toulon, Marseilles and the Riviera, and eventually sailed for Corsica. It is interesting to note that Flaubert was more moved by the classical towns and oriental influences on the east coast than by the medieval on the west. 'You can't imagine', he wrote to his sister,[6] 'what the Roman monuments are like, my dear Caroline, nor the immense pleasure that the view of the "Arènes" gave me.' The trip for him was really an oriental and classical journey and left him with a burning longing to see more of the East. He adds, however, that he will probably end by only going on Sunday to Déville and, if it is fine, in the summer to Pont l'Évêque.[7]

The Corsican part of the travel notes is less learned and pedantic than that describing the Pyrenees – probably because there were many fewer printed documents to consult. He was able to view the country directly and not through history or what he had read. He took a boy's interest in all the stories of bandits, was fascinated by their personalities. The strongest and most memorable of all was the great pantheistic experience which he underwent at Sagone in Corsica, his account of which is quite different in the quality of its writing from the bulk of the diary:[8]

C'était alors en plein midi, et nous longions le bord de la mer que le chemin suit jusqu'à l'ancienne ville de Sagone. Elle était calme, le soleil, donnant dessus, éclairait son azur qui paraissait plus limpide encore; ses rayons faisaient tout autour des rochers à fleur comme des couronnes de diamant qui les auraient entourés; elles brillaient plus vives et plus scintillantes que les

étoiles. La mer a un parfum plus suave que les roses, nous le
humions avec délices; nous aspirions en nous le soleil, la brise
marine, la vue de l'horizon, l'odeur des myrtes, car il est des jours
heureux où l'âme aussi est ouverte au soleil comme la campagne et, comme elle, embaume de fleurs cachées que la
suprême beauté y fait éclore. On se pénètre de rayons, d'air pur,
de pensées suaves et intraduisibles; tout en vous palpite de joie et
bat des ailes avec les éléments, on s'y attache, on respire avec eux,
l'essence de la nature animée semble passée en vous dans un
hymen exquis, vous souriez au bruit du vent qui fait remuer la
cime des arbres, au murmure du flot sur la grève; vous courez
sur les mers avec la brise, quelque chose d'éthéré, de grand, de
tendre plane dans la lumière même du soleil et se perd dans une
immensité radieuse comme les vapeurs rosées de matin qui
remontent vers le ciel.

What is strange is that, neither in the travel notes, nor in
his letters, does Flaubert give any hint of the great
emotional experience which he underwent at Marseilles, when he found sexual experience, for the first time in
his life. He was twice at Marseilles during the trip – before
he went to Corsica and after his return. Bruneau is of the
opinion that it occurred on the return journey.[9] This seems
more likely than before the trip to Corsica, for Flaubert shed
two of his travelling companions after that, and only kept
Dr Cloquet. It would have been easier to evade his vigilance
than that of all three – especially that of the spinster sister.
Also Flaubert wrote, on his return to Rouen, in *Souvenirs,
Notes et Pensées Intimes*:[10] 'How much I've changed and
lived since then.' He then asks: 'Is it the same man who
stood at the edge of the Gulf of Sagone?' This would indicate
that the episode had occurred after the trip to Corsica, and it
suggests how much it had altered him.

The adventure occurred with a creole woman, who, with
her mother, kept the Hôtel Richelieu, in the rue de la Darse
in Marseilles, where Flaubert and Cloquet stayed for a few
days. It seems that Cloquet had already known the two
women and that this was why they had chosen this particular hotel.[11] It appears that she enticed Flaubert into her

room one day and that they became lovers. He was to say later to Louise Colet that he had never loved her, but this may only have been to allay the retrospective jealousy of his mistress. He certainly never forgot her and, on all his later visits to Marseilles, he went to search for traces of her, but in vain. In 1845, on his trip to Italy, he found that the hotel had changed hands and was deserted. He scarcely recognized it.[12] The last time he went to Marseilles was on his way to North Africa in 1858, to collect material for *Salammbô*, and he found everything still more altered. The hotel was gone and, instead, on the ground floor, there was a bazaar, and a barber's saloon on the first floor, where he went to be shaved.[13]

There can be no doubt that Eulalie Foucaud loved Flaubert passionately, and we have, as witness to this, four love letters which she wrote him, after his return to France, between January and August 1841. Only fragments of these letters have been published, by Maurice Monda, in *Le Figaro* on 14 November 1931, but Flaubert's letters to her have, unfortunately, not come down to us and we have therefore no direct record of what his feelings for her really were.

The relationship lasted only a few days, and the correspondence is spaced over a period of eight months. He was obviously not a very fluent correspondent – and this is very different from his later relationship with Louise Colet – for she frequently complains of his long silences. With the caution he was also later to show with Louise Colet, he did not have Eulalie Foucaud's letters addressed to his home, but had them sent care of his old school friend Émile Hamard, in Paris, who would forward them to him in another envelope.

Eulalie Foucaud was a woman of thirty-five, and Flaubert was eighteen at the time. It is possible to believe that, in appearance, she was the type of his fixation, the woman who appears so often in his writings – dark-haired, amber-skinned and maternal, with something strong and almost masculine in her personality. Flaubert, at the time, was a

remarkably good-looking young man, with his slim, tall
stature, wide shoulders and narrow hips; with his golden
curling hair and beard. Gertrude Collier describes him as he
was when she met him first two years later:[14] 'No young
Greek was ever more beautiful than Gustave, then still in his
teens. He was tall, slight, elastic in his movements, with the
most faultless limbs and the great charm of utter unselfconsciousness of his own physical and mental beauty, and
perfectly indifferent to all forms of ceremonies. His dress
consisted of a red woollen shirt, dark blue woollen trousers
such as French fishermen wear, a dark blue scarf tied tightly
round his waist and a slouching hat, often bare-headed.'
Maxime Du Camp, who also knew him at the same time,
describes him as follows:[15] 'He was of heroic beauty, with
his white skin, slightly pink on the cheeks, his soft long hair,
his tall stature, wide shoulders, his full beard of a golden
brown; his enormous eyes, colour of the sea, overshadowed
by dark brows, with his reverberating voice, like the sound of
a trumpet; his wild gestures and his loud laughter; he was
like one of those Gaulish chiefs who fought against the
Romans.'

Eulalie Foucaud talks, in her letters, of the pleasure she
had from his 'corps jeune et vigoureux', and how much good
her kisses had done him.

A reflection of the relationship is to be found in Flaubert's
novel *Novembre*, composed two years later, and from that
can be seen how sweet was the affair, how rich for him in
emotional and physical enlightenment, and how little harm
it brought him. He was lucky that his first experience happened in this way, for, in spite of what he had written in
Mémoires d'un Fou – which, after all, is fiction – it can be
believed that, when he encountered Eulalie Foucaud, at the
age of eighteen, he was still a virgin in body, if not in
mind.

Eulalie Foucaud's letters to him were intimate and
passionate from the first, and she addressed him as 'tu'. She
tells him that she is dying far from his arms, and she

wonders whether another woman has replaced her in his affections, for he does not reply to her letters. She assures him that it is the first time in her life that she has ever truly loved. 'Receive my whole soul,' she says to him, 'all my love, all my thoughts and all my desire.'

In her letter of 16 February 1841, she writes:

Dear soul, everything which is you, which is connected with you, cannot be foreign to me or indifferent to me, and henceforth my soul is so utterly identified with yours, that they form only one single entity, for joy or suffering. To have possessed you and to be deprived of you, is a terrible torture, a torture of hell. . . . I'm discouraged, overwhelmed, Gustave, oh! my beloved Gustave, I pity you if you suffer as I do, poor woman, exiled on this earth, and indifferent to everything.

She accused him of forgetting her and making her suffer:

Why was it granted to us to love one another, to know, through each other, heavenly happiness, since we were to part so soon, and especially if you were to forget me so quickly. . . . Since you've left me this house is for your lover an immense desert. This room, these walls . . . how many times have I gone to kiss them, to interrogate them, and to seek for the signs of a happiness so soon vanished, and which will have served only to poison the rest of my life.

At one moment there was the possibility that she might come to Paris and that they might meet. She expresses delight at the prospect and declares that if it could ever happen then she would die happy.

He must eventually have written to her, for she tells him, in her third letter, of 6 May 1841, that his long-awaited letter has at last arrived, and that her pain and her anguish have thereby diminished. She mentions a trip to America which she may be obliged to make, but she does not know when it will be, and she talks of her grief at leaving France, her mother and daughter, and himself, but her departure is necessary. Her only consolation is the hope that she may see

him before she leaves, or after she gets back, and that he will
be the first person she will press to her heart on her return.

Later, on 6 August 1841, she writes the last letter which we
have from her pen, and mentions her immediate departure
for America, but she assures him that it will not be for long
and that her hair will not yet be white by her return. 'I'll be
able, with the same ardour, the same happiness, to take you
in my arms and cover you with mad and voluptuous kisses,
and to show you still a gaze full of fire and desire.' She prays
that Heaven may still have, in reserve for her, a few happy
days, which are all the more precious at her age for it is only
then that one really knows what love is. He will realize the
truth of that, she says, in ten years' time. She goes on to tell
him that a woman sums up for a man all the joys and
pleasure he can ever hope for. Love means to devote oneself
to a woman, to give her all one's thoughts and desires, to
have no other will but hers, and to feel that, through her, he
will be able to attain the highest achievements. To abandon
everything to devote himself to her, to breathe the same air,
and to die on her heart and in her arms, that is love. 'But,
dear friend,' she adds, 'you will never be able to love as the
woman who is writing to you loves.' She ends by begging
him not to forget her and to write to her.

Knowing the attitude that Flaubert was later to adopt
when a passionate woman was to try to encroach upon his
private life, one may surmise that it was eventually the excessive ardour of Eulalie which brought the correspondence
to a close. He certainly lost sight of her and never discovered
what had become of her or of her family. He cannot therefore have answered her exhortations of writing to her frequently. As we know, the hotel in Marseilles was eventually
given up and he was never able to find out what had become
of its inmates. But he kept her letters, sealed them in an
envelope, after re-reading them, and wrote on the envelope:
'Is it really possible that she may have loved me?' He read
the letters again as he watched beside the death-bed of his
beloved sister. It may have been that the only woman in his

life at that time having died, he thought of what might have been if he had responded better to the love of another woman.

He seems to have said nothing about Eulalie to any of his friends – certainly not to his family – and, writing to Chevalier at the very moment when he was receiving her letters, he said:[16] 'Woman is a vulgar animal, of whom man has always cherished too fine an ideal.'

Flaubert returned to Rouen in November 1840, disgusted at being back in a country where there was no sun, and he declares that he will go one day to Constantinople and buy himself a slave.[17]

He had left for his trip to the South in a very unhappy frame of mind, but he returned home somebody different. With the successful experience of love, his personality seemed to have been released and to blossom, and he had regained confidence in himself. He told Chevalier that he was now resigned to taking up the study of law, that he was tired of dreams and determined to go the whole hog right up to the doctorate.[18] Perhaps the prospect of having to go to Paris to complete his studies had some weight with him. He had by now abandoned mysticism and idealism and said that he had become a materialist.[19]

We do not know what Flaubert was doing during the year which followed his return from his trip to the South, for he does not mention anything in particular in his letters to Chevalier, his chief correspondent. He does not discuss any works of literature that he is writing or projecting. He was going to study law, but he could not do that in Rouen, as there was no law school there. He took out his first 'inscription' at the École de Droit in Paris on 10 November 1841, and he intended to go to Paris in January 1842, to follow lectures and to prepare his first year of law, proposing to sit for the examination in the summer.

On New Year's Eve he was alone, and he had just reached his twentieth birthday. He wrote to Chevalier reflecting on all they used to say that they would do when they had

reached the age of twenty. They had so often spent that
night together, as children and as youths, staying awake
until after midnight and, as they waited for the New Year to
appear, they used to smoke their pipes in their respective
beds, talking endlessly, and were up the following morning
at five o'clock. But this year Flaubert was alone, he would get
up at four in the morning, read Homer, looking out at the
moon shining on the roofs opposite; he would not go out all
day and he would not pay a single call.[20]

Although, in his letters, he does not mention any writing,
he must, during the year which followed his return from his
Mediterranean trip, have been composing something, or
have corrected previous works, for in January 1842 he wrote
to his former literature master, Gourgaud-Dugazon, who
was now teaching at the Collège Royal at Versailles, to ask
for his help and advice on his writings. The letter shows
considerable trust and intimacy, and one regrets that
further letters are not forthcoming, and no answer. From its
tone it is unlikely to have been an isolated example:[21]

First I must begin by declaring that I'm anxious to receive an
answer. I hope to see you in April and, as your letters are so often
delayed for terms, it might happen that I had no news from you
before that. Come! surprise me by being punctual for once! It is a
scholastic virtue of which you should pride yourself since you
possess all the others. I've been to Paris at the beginning of the
month, I was there for two days, and, as I was overwhelmed with
business and messages, I had no time to go and greet you. In the
spring I'll go and see you one Sunday morning, and willy-nilly,
you'll have to devote the whole of your day to me. The hours slip
by so quickly when we are together, and I've so many things to
say to you, and you're such a good listener!

More than ever now I need your conversation, your competence and your friendship. I'm in a critical moral state, you
understood that when we met last time. I hide nothing from you,
and I speak to you, not as if you were my former master, but as if
you were only twenty, and as if you were here, in front of me,
beside my fire.

And so I'm studying law; that is to say I've bought the law books and signed on. I'll begin work presently and I expect to sit for my examination in July. I carry on my study of Greek and Latin, and I'll probably always study them. I love the flavour of these beautiful languages. Tacitus is for me like a bronze bas relief; and Homer is as beautiful as the Mediterranean – the same pure blue waves, the same sun, the same horizon. But what comes over me every moment, what knocks the pen out of my hand, if I'm taking notes, what tears the book away from me if I'm reading, is my old love, the same old fixed idea, the desire to write! That is why I'm not doing much although I rise up very early every morning, and go out less than ever.

I've reached a decisive turning in my life, where one must advance or retreat; that is the main thing for me. It is a matter of life or death. When I've made up my mind, nothing will deter me, even were I to be hissed or mocked at by everyone. You know enough of my obstinacy and my powers of endurance to be convinced by them. I'll qualify as a barrister but I doubt very much whether I'll ever defend the case of a partition wall, or an unfortunate father robbed by a rich ambitious man. When they talk to me of the bar and say: 'That fellow will speak well because he has a strong and sonorous voice,' I must say that I've an inner feeling of revulsion, and I don't feel cut out for that trivial and materialistic life. Each day, on the contrary, I admire poets more and more, and I discover in them thousands of things I hadn't noticed formerly. I perceive connections and antitheses, the accuracy of which astounds me! Here then is what I've resolved, I've in my mind three novels, three tales of different kinds, which require a very special way of writing. It will be sufficient to prove to myself whether I've any talent or not.

I'll put in these everything I can of style, passion and wit, and after that we'll see.

In April I hope to show you something. It is that sentimental, love hotch-potch that I've already mentioned to you. The action is non-existent. I couldn't possibly give you a synopsis of it, since it is entirely composed of analyses and psychological dissections. It's perhaps very beautiful; but I fear very much that it's very false, and fairly pretentious and affected.

Good-bye! I must stop now as you've had, perhaps, enough of my letter, where I've done nothing but speak of myself and of my miserable passions. But I've nothing else to talk to you about, as I never go out dancing and never read any papers.

Good-bye again!

p.s. Answer me soon! I would very much like to correspond with you more frequently, for, as soon as my letter is finished, I find myself only just at the beginning of what I've got to say to you.

It is not known which of his works Flaubert is referring to in this letter. It might be something which has not come down to us, though that is unlikely, since he never destroyed anything. The description does not at all fit *Smarh*, though it might conceivably refer to *Mémoires d'un Fou*, but he gave the only manuscript of that to Alfred Le Poittevin three years before. What it most resembles is *Novembre*, generally believed not to have been begun before September 1842, and certainly only finished in October that year. He might, however, have begun it after he returned to Rouen, in November 1840, and then have finished it two years later. He told Du Camp, years afterwards, that he was nineteen when he had composed it and, writing on 7 April 1846, he said that it was nearly six years earlier. That would mean that it was in 1840 and, in November that year, he would have been almost nineteen.

Flaubert set out for Paris in January 1842, at the age of twenty, feeling that he had left childhood behind him and that adult life was about to begin. He was already formed as a writer; all his different strands of inspiration were there, but he had not yet found a method. He had a large stock of compositions in reserve, of various kinds, and he was to draw deeply from this rich fund for the rest of his life. In philosophy he was theoretically a pessimist, but there were in him, nevertheless, immense resources of animal optimism, and his expressions of youthful despair must not be taken too seriously.

PART TWO

The Apprentice

[7]

Novembre
(1841–2)

FLAUBERT signed on at the École de Droit in Paris on 10 November 1841, and he went there in January 1842 to arrange about his courses and examinations.[1] He returned to Rouen two days afterwards, to prepare for his examination at home, but the plan was that he should go back to Paris in April. He confessed to Chevalier, on 22 January 1842, that he had not yet begun to study but that, in April, he would start serious work, and that he would then do fifteen hours a day – he was accustomed to long hours of concentrated intellectual effort, and he had worked in this way for most of his life – he had thus prepared for his 'baccalauréat'. He did not seem, however, to be applying himself to anything, and, in a letter to Chevalier a month later,[2] he admitted that he was not studying, nor reading, nor writing, that he was being completely idle. He had, nevertheless, made a beginning at his law books, but he does not seem to have understood a word of what he had been reading. In March he began to worry about his examination, for which he had to sit in the summer, and in April he went for a few days to Paris. In June the time for his longer stay in Paris, for lectures and classes, was drawing nearer, and he confessed to Chevalier the difficulties he was encountering in the study of law:[3]

You demand long letters, but I'm absolutely incapable of writing them. Law stupefies me, kills me, wears me to shreds, and it's impossible for me to work at it. When I've spent three hours with my nose glued to the statute books, during which time I've understood nothing, it's impossible for me to go beyond that; I could commit suicide (which would be a pity for I show great promise!). The next day I've to begin all over again what I did the day before, and, in this way, one doesn't make much progress at all. . . . How bored I'll be in Paris preparing for my exam.

He could not, nevertheless, help a feeling of delight at the thought of his visit to the capital:

What always seems to me most beautiful in Paris is the Boulevard, and each time that I cross it when I arrive in the morning, I feel a sort of galvanic contraction in the soles of my feet, which the asphalt pavement produces on me, on which, each evening, the prostitutes shuffle their feet, and trail the hems of their garish garments. At the hour when the gas lamps shine through the panes of glass of windows, when the knives and forks tinkle on the marble-topped tables, I go for a walk, at peace and enveloped in the smoke of my cigar, staring at the women who pass. There prostitution is spread out before you and eyes are bright.

Flaubert, like Baudelaire, at just the same time, was romantically attracted by the prostitution in Paris, and this passage in his letter could be the subject of one of Baudelaire's *Fleurs du Mal.* Later he wrote to Louise Colet:[4]

It is perhaps a perverted taste, but I love prostitution for itself and independently of what it means underneath. I've never been able to see one of these women, in low-cut dresses, pass, beneath the light of the gas lamps, without my heart beating fast.

His work was not progressing very fast and, even before he went to Paris, he was already contemplating the possibility of not sitting for his examination in the summer, for, in the same letter to Chevalier, he says:

I think it would be wise if I gave up all idea of sitting for my examination in August, as I know almost nothing – not to say absolutely nothing. I need at least a fortnight for my Roman Law and, as for French Law, I'm still only at article 100, but I would certainly be failed if I was questioned on any one of the hundred. And when I think I've still got three years of such a glorious prospect! It's enough to make one die of rage.

He went to Paris at the end of June,[5] but was, sur-

prisingly, bored with the capital in the middle of summer,
with everyone away, and he himself was only longing to be
back with the family at Trouville, by the sea. He did, however, do some work, and even went to see others being examined, for candidates seemed to have been examined
individually and only orally. His own examination seems to
have been fixed for 20 August and he worked for it every
night until one o'clock in the morning. Each candidate was
obliged to sign on at the École de Droit in Paris every term.
The first term began on 2 November, the second on 2 January, the third on 1 April and the fourth on 1 July. The registers were available for signature in the secretariat of the
Faculty for a fortnight at the beginning of each term.
During term there was nothing to oblige students to be in
Paris or to attend lectures, but they could get permission to
sit for the examination only after having obtained a
certificate from the professor whose classes they were supposed to be following. It was to attend classes and to obtain
the certificate that Flaubert had gone to Paris in June 1842.
Unfortunately, what he called his 'fool of a professor' would
only deliver such a certificate on the production of the notes
of his lectures. Flaubert had none but he tried to obtain
some from a class-mate, though he wondered whether they
would pass muster with Oudot, the professor in question,
who was alleged to scrutinize all notes very carefully. Flaubert failed to obtain the certificate and so he was not able to
sit for his examination.

He decided to join his family immediately, not waiting for
daylight, and he arrived in the middle of the night, after
experiencing an 'illumination', a mystical illumination, similar to the one he had undergone at Sagone in Corsica two
years before. Writing to Louise Colet many years later, he
said, of his pleasure at his various visits to Trouville:[6]

But the arrival at Trouville which surpasses all others is the
one I made in 1843 [he means 1842]. It was at the end of my first
year of law. I arrived alone from Paris, and had left the coach at
Pont l'Évêque, nine miles from here. I arrived home on a

moonlit night, towards three o'clock in the morning. I can still remember the linen jacket I was wearing, the white stick I was carrying, and what ecstasy I felt as I breathed, from afar, the salt tang of the sea.

A reflection of this experience is found in a passage from *Novembre* composed soon after he arrived at Trouville:[7]

Je suis descendu en courant au bord de la mer, à travers les terrains éboulés que je sautais d'un pied sûr, je levais la tête avec orgueil, je respirais fièrement la brise fraîche, qui séchait mes cheveux en sueur; l'esprit de Dieu me remplissait, je me sentais le coeur grand, j'adorais quelque chose d'un étrange mouvement, j'aurais voulu m'absorber dans la lumière du soleil et me perdre dans cette immensité d'azur, avec l'odeur qui s'élevait de la surface des flots; et je fus pris alors d'une joie insensée, et je me mis à marcher comme si tout le bonheur des cieux m'était entré dans l'âme. Comme la falaise s'avançait en cet endroit là, toute la côte disparut et je ne vis plus rien que la mer; les lames montaient sur le galet jusqu'à mes pieds, elles écumaient sur les rochers à fleur d'eau, les battaient en cadence, les enlaçaient comme des bras liquides et des nappes limpides, en retombant illuminées d'une couleur bleue; le vent en soulevait les mousses autour de moi et ridait les flaques d'eau restée dans le creux des pierres, les varechs pleuraient et se berçaient, encore agités du mouvement de la vague qui les avait quittés; de temps à autre une mouette passait avec de grands battements d'ailes, et montait jusqu'au haut de la falaise. A mesure que la mer se retirait, et que son bruit s'éloignait ainsi qu'un refrain qui expire, le rivage s'avançait vers moi, laissant à découvert sur le sable les sillons que la vague avait tracés. Et je compris alors tout le bonheur de la création et toute la joie que Dieu y a placée pour l'homme; la nature m'apparut belle comme une harmonie complète, que l'extase seule doit entendre; quelque chose de tendre comme un amour et de pur comme la prière s'éleva pour moi du fond de l'horizon, s'abattit de la cime des rocs déchirés, du haut des cieux; il se forma, du bruit de l'Océan, de la lumière du jour, quelque chose d'exquis que je m'appropriai comme d'un domaine céleste, je m'y sentis vivre heureux et grand, comme l'aigle qui regarde le soleil et monte dans ses rayons . . .

Puis ce fut tout; bien vite je me rappelai que je vivais, je revins à moi, je me mis en marche, sentant que la malédiction me reprenait, que je rentrais dans l'humanité; la vie m'était revenue, comme aux membres gelés, par le sentiment de la souffrance, et de même que j'avais un inconcevable bonheur, je tombai dans un découragement sans nom.

It was on this summer holiday at Trouville, in 1842, that Flaubert met the English family called Collier who were to play a part in his life, intermittently, until the end, though not as important as some of the earlier biographers – indeed also the latest – have claimed. Much has always been made of the relationship with the Colliers because, as has been previously discussed, it was believed that they were the English family described in *Mémoires d'un Fou*, but it has been shown that this is impossible. Caroline Flaubert had written to her brother in Paris, on 14 July 1842:[8]

We've just made the acquaintance of an English family who live in the house with the shutters. There are four girls one of whom is ill, I think of some spinal complaint. She comes every day to sit in our garden and she stays there for hours on end. We offered her an armchair and cushions, and it is thus that we've got to know them. The second daughter is very pretty, talks perfect French, adores Mademoiselle Rachel and knows all Shakespeare by heart. The other two are nice enough, but they speak very little and walk along the edge of the sea from five until ten o'clock at night. Their father is an old captain from the English Royal Navy, and could be quite amusing if he didn't stutter so.

An intimacy soon sprang up between the two families, who were much of an age. The eldest girl, Gertrude, was two years older than Flaubert, and the second, Henrietta, two years younger – the two youngest girls do not seem to have counted much, as they are never mentioned, but there was also a boy of eight who became a great favourite of Flaubert's at the time, and also later when he was a student in Paris.

Flaubert does not seem, according to his own accounts, to have taken much interest in the girls – unless his seeming indifference was a youthful pose. Le Poittevin, in an unpublished letter, tells him that he admires his coldness towards the woman with whom he bathes, but speculates on the real cause of his indifference.[9] Flaubert seems only to have mentioned the Collier father and the little boy, Herbert. Le Poittevin expresses surprise that he should be pleased to spend all his time with a 'stupid sailor and a child of eight'.[10]

The summer of 1842 is the only one which the Colliers and the Flauberts spent together at Trouville and, because of the Tennant papers, we know a good deal about the period, as we have in them one of the most vivid pictures of the atmosphere in the Flaubert family.[11]

The papers by Gertrude are of three categories. The first, entitled *Recollections of Bygone Times*, written for her grandchildren between 1880 and 1911, contains much that does not concern Flaubert, but tells the life of her father in his youth, and how he came to settle in France for nearly twenty-five years. It had been thought that he was a naval attaché at the British Embassy in Paris, but the truth is that he left England to escape from his creditors and to live more cheaply in France. The banker to whom he had entrusted all his fortune had gone bankrupt. This was in 1823, and the family went to Paris to live on what they could salvage. They had an apartment near the Champs Elysées, and it was there that Flaubert used to visit them as a student, after he had settled in Paris, in the autumn of 1842.

Collier seems to have been almost a caricature of an Englishman and, although he lived in France for close on a quarter of a century, he never learned to speak the language and prided himself on his ignorance. He despised the inhabitants of the country, saying that one Englishman was worth half a dozen Frenchmen. The Colliers were in Paris when the Obelisk was erected in 1836, in the Place de la Révolution, now Place de la Concorde, and the father was delighted because English sailors had helped to put it up. With an air of supreme contempt he declared, 'Ho! they could never have done anything without Englishmen.'

Gertrude tells us that the Flauberts were the first French family they had known, which is strange considering that, at the time, they had lived in France for twenty years.

Gertrude's second text, entitled *Written by Request*, is pure fiction, and the names of the characters are disguised. It should be treated with caution and not used, as it generally is, as irrefutable evidence of fact. She talks of being nearly seventeen during the summer which they spent at Trouville, when, in fact, she was twenty-three – but girls are always seventeen in Victorian fiction. Accepting this as fact has upset Philip Spencer's chronology. She talks about being in love with César, intended for Flaubert, and says that he was the first person she had ever loved. She also makes it appear as if he had returned her affection. 'I knew that I loved him passionately, adoringly,' she wrote, 'years have passed over my head but I have never felt the worship, the love and yet the fear that then took possession of my soul. Something told me I should never be his. I knew as certainly that he would be in one world and I in another, as far as the stars in heaven. I knew that we had nothing in common. His people were not my people; his ways were not my ways. ... But I knew, in the deepest recesses of my heart, how truly I could love him, honour him and obey him. But – I suppose it was not to be.'

She mentions an evening at the opera, when they went to hear *Faust* by Spohr, and of a kiss she and César exchanged; we have, however, no way of knowing whether this is true or not as it is only in the fictional work. She says that her father would never have consented to her marrying a Frenchman, and he assured her that Flaubert did not think of her in this way – in which he was probably right. In 1847 she married Charles Tennant and died at the age of ninety-nine, at the end of the First World War, in 1918. Delicate Henrietta died in 1909 at the age of eighty-six.

Gertrude wrote this piece of fiction very much later, when Flaubert was famous and dead, when it would have re-dounded to her credit if he had returned her love. In it she does not mention Henrietta at all, towards whom he had, obviously, had a deeper feeling.

More interesting and more true in atmosphere is the *Memoir* which she wrote for Flaubert's niece, after his death, in 1884, part of which was translated and published in the Introduction to the *Correspondance*. She was then recalling events which had happened forty years before, and it is astonishing how clear and vivid is her memory of them.

What appears clearly from all these documents is the extraordinary beauty and charm of Flaubert at twenty, and the originality and naturalness of his bearing. As we have already seen, he was tall, slight and graceful in all his movements, he had the most faultless limbs and the great charm of utter unselfconsciousness in his own physical and mental beauty. She describes his sadness – or pose of sadness – and how he used to say the kind of things to which we have grown accustomed in his correspondence: 'Misfortune saddens me but never surprises me!'

Gertrude may have loved him but it seems as if it was delicate Henrietta towards whom he was attracted at first. He had carried her in his arms to safety from death by burning and that intimacy was more than he had enjoyed with Gertrude:[12]

During our stay at Trouville, one hot summer evening, the windows were left open in my sister's bedroom. The summer breeze blew the muslin curtains on to the lighted candle. My sister was supposed to have something wrong with her spine, and was kept continually in a recumbent position. She found herself alone and helpless, the danger was great for the house was built of wood entirely. The Flauberts saw the flames from their windows and father and son ran to our assistance. Gustave went direct to the upper room from which the flames were issuing and carried down my sister. By that time help had arrived, the fire was extinguished, and all had gathered round my sister fearing that the shock might have seriously affected her. The Flauberts begged that she might be carried to their house. From that day we saw the Flauberts hourly – Caroline became my constant companion, and after much consultation, my sister was placed under Doctor Flaubert's medical care.

Admiral Collier was glad of this friendship, for he greatly approved of Caroline's fair beauty, and he declared that she might be English – which was the highest compliment he could pay her. Although he did not generally like Frenchmen, he admired Flaubert and said: 'What a superb young fellow that is, what a pity he's a Frenchman.'

Caroline, for her part, did not greatly like Gertrude, whom she considered superficial and hard – indeed she may have been right in her disapproval, for a not very pleasant personality emerges from the pages of her personal documents. There is a letter to Henrietta from one of her sisters, concerning a book alleged to be by her cousin Hamilton Aidé, which she considers to have been really written by Gertrude and she says:

You must by some means get a book called *Rita* (an Autobiography, it is Hamilton's, given out as such) but every incident in the story and every character almost you can trace it all comes from Gertrude, beginning in the rue Ponthieu. There is no mistaking. . . . Pray read it. It does not *reflect any credit on her;* and it is a most heartless and silly thing. . . . None but the family of course would understand. She herself stands out as the heroine, and *the wonder of the house.* As a novel, I was made the remark by a lady, 'Oh! it's a very bad book but very amusing'; when you have read it you feel a disagreeable sensation, and what good to either of them, it's difficult to say, and when one reflects how wilful, spoilt she was and everything sacrificed for her; it leaves a bitter feeling of *disgust,* at least that was my feeling when I read it, though one would never acknowledge to anyone that she was the person, in my own mind there is little doubt about it.

In a letter, in February 1843, Caroline warns her brother against Gertrude, who, she says, is frivolous and worldly.[18] In a letter, Gertrude had boasted to her of having placed Gustave in an unfavourable light at a party at her house, putting him in the position of a 'chevalier servant'. Caroline was indignant that her beloved and admired brother should be treated in such a manner.

But she loved Henrietta and did her best to foster her brother's affection for 'la douce Henriette'. She would have liked him to have married her. On 30 March 1843, she tells him that she has received a letter from Henrietta, who hopes that he will come and read Hugo's recent play, *Les Burgraves*, to her.[14] Caroline hopes that he will do this, as how could one refuse her anything when she says: 'you're so good!' He seems, indeed, on various occasions to have gone to her house to read to her when he was a student in Paris. It is clear that she cherished a tender feeling for him and that, at one moment, he realized her affection. Writing to Louise Colet, in September 1846, he said:[15]

I used to be a frequent visitor at a house where there was a charming young girl, wonderfully beautiful, with a Christian and almost Gothic beauty, if I may put it in that way. She had an ingenuous mind and was easily moved to emotion; she used to weep and laugh alternately, as rain and shine follow one another. I could move, at the will of my words, this beautiful heart, where there was nothing save what was pure. I can see her still, lying against her pink pillow, and gazing at me when I was reading, with her large blue eyes. One day we were alone, seated on a sofa; she took my hand in hers and twined her fingers through mine; I let it happen, without thinking anything because I'm innocent most of the time, and she gazed at me with a look ... which brings a chill to my heart even now. At that moment her mother came in, she understood what was happening, and was dreaming already of fulfilment in a son-in-law ...

I'm sure that the poor girl had yielded to a moment of invincible tenderness, to one of these commonplaces of the soul, when it seems as if everything in you liquefies and melts, a voluptuous death, which would be full of delight, if one were not ready to burst into sobs and to melt into tears. You can't imagine the sensation of terror that I felt. I came home deeply upset, and I reproached myself with still being alive. I don't know whether I exaggerated matters to myself, but I, who did not love her, I would have given my life with pleasure, to redeem that sad and loving gaze to which mine had not responded.

This means that, towards the month of March 1845, there

was a relationship of some closeness between Henrietta Collier and Flaubert, and that her mother had hoped for their union. This, with a young man of his temperament – he was twenty-three at the time – was sufficient to frighten him away. Three years had passed since their first meeting, and she was now twenty-one but, by this time, he had met Élisa Schlésinger again; he had his warm friendship with Maxime Du Camp; had had his various sexual adventures in Paris; and he no longer thought of marriage. It was also a year after his illness, when his vitality was low with the tranquillizing drugs he was taking. But all this is a later story. In the meantime they were all at Trouville together, in the summer of 1842, with no cloud on the horizon, and Flaubert treated the girls with comparative indifference. Before them he posed as being an agnostic and a cynic, against all accepted values and impervious to all emotion. He mocked at Collier's French and his conventional views; at the concessions which the whole family felt obliged to make to society; at their strict Sunday observances. Gertrude describes Flaubert as trying hard to avoid them but, as there was no one else at Trouville, this was not easy, and he could not help but see them frequently.

Gertrude describes Madame Flaubert several times in the documents as being a sad-looking woman, always dressed in black, who looked like a character from a Rembrandt picture, and she noticed that Flaubert seemed more attached to her than to anyone else – his father did not seem to understand him. She, on her side, seemed to have eyes for her daughter alone, anxious that she should not overtire herself, for she seems to have been very delicate and often stayed in bed. Gertrude describes Dr Flaubert as a very forcible character, thoroughly the French man of science, always exquisitely courteous. He was a noble nature, she said, who commanded universal respect. Though his massive forehead was without a line, and his light brown hair without a thread of silver, he looked older than his fifty-eight years.

Madame Flaubert looked Spanish and was as brown as a

gypsy, with melancholy dark eyes and glossy black hair. Her face was perfectly colourless and she rarely smiled.

When the holidays were over Dr Flaubert was obliged to return to his hospital duties, but it was decided that the Colliers should follow them to Rouen, and take up their abode at the Grand Hotel, for the Doctor had taken on Henrietta as one of his patients. Gertrude, who was bored at being at the hotel with nothing to do, spent a great deal of time at the Hôtel Dieu, especially with Caroline. She describes Madame Flaubert as spending most of the day in her bedroom, a gloomy and solemn room, with its dark green furniture. But frequently she stayed to lunch and always sat next 'the dear old doctor'. What struck her most forcibly about the family was the noise and loudness with which they carried on their conversation, particularly Gustave whose voice usually drowned all the rest. A strong bond of love seemed to unite the whole family, they were happy with one another, and they treated her as one of themselves.

Flaubert may have pretended indifference to Gertrude and he did not say good-bye to her when she left, but he sent her, through his sister, his annotated copy of Montaigne, with the inscription, 'Souvenir d'une inaltérable affection'. These are the very words which he was to use fifteen years later, when sending her a copy of *Madame Bovary*, but we shall see that she did not appreciate the gift, and wondered how he could ever have brought himself to write such a work.[16]

Though Gertrude may have imagined that she loved Flaubert – especially writing forty years later, after his death – there was much in him of which she did not approve. Later in the year, when he came to Paris to study law, she says that they saw much less of him. 'I was growing to womanhood,' she said, though she was, in fact, twenty-three, 'and his eccentricities were more noticeable in a drawing-room in Paris than on the plage at Trouville. He ridiculed all the conventionalities of fashionable society, which he called "these pleasures without happiness, so full of infinite emptiness", in which he never attempted to take part and pitied me for so doing.'[17]

This reads very much like pique or disappointment, and may have been due to his attentions to Henrietta. In the *Memoir*, she says nothing of the episode at the opera, which may, therefore, be fictitious; nor of any intimacy between herself and Flaubert.

In the meantime, in October 1842, Flaubert had not yet returned to Paris, as the term did not start until November. He was occupied with finishing *Novembre*, which he had been meditating at Trouville, and probably had even begun to write.[18] He dates the manuscript as having been finished on 25 October 1842, and he was normally accurate about such matters.

Flaubert wrote *Novembre* to say farewell to his dead past, and it ends with the death of the hero, who owes much to him. He saw himself also as dying, as dying spiritually to all that he had formerly believed in, for he had given up his literary ambitions, and had consented to study law.

Critics have spent a great deal of time in discussing the problem of where he obtained the title for his book, whether it came from a poem by Hugo, or from Quinet. It has not occurred to any of them that the title might merely have come from himself, because it corresponded with his mood and with his own view of the work. Coleman believes that the title comes from a poem by Victor Hugo, entitled 'Novembre' in *Les Orientales*.[19] While Shanks thinks that it comes from a passage in *Ahasvérus* by Quinet.[20] Why should he not have been thinking of All Souls Day, 'Le Jour des Morts', on 2 November, for his hero eventually dies, and it is on All Souls Day that we remember the departed? It might also be because he had begun writing the book in November 1840 – it is true that this cannot be proved – and it might also have been for a hundred equally good reasons.

Although *Novembre* was finished before he was twenty-one, Flaubert never lost interest in it, though he did not think of ever publishing it. Writing about it to Louise Colet in 1853, he said: 'Ah! what a good nose I had, in my youth, not to publish it. How I would blush about it today if I had.'[21]

He used, however, on frequent occasions, to show it to his friends, and to read it to them. He showed it to Baudelaire as late as 1860, after the publication of *Madame Bovary*;[22] to the Goncourts in 1863;[23] and to Louise Colet in 1846.[24]

The novel is very much better composed than any of his previous works, better also than the first *Éducation Sentimentale,* begun a year later and finished only in 1845.

The book divides logically into three parts. The first, before the sexual experience with Marie; when the hero is young and his romanticism is vague and sentimental. The second is his affair with Marie, when he grows up and becomes mature. The third describes the disillusionment after possession. This part is divided in two, the second section of which is narrated in the third person, and this narrator winds up the action and recounts the death of the hero. This was a device frequently adopted by Romantic writers of the 'roman personnel'.

It must not be forgotten that *Novembre* is a work of fiction, and the amount of autobiographical detail must not blind one to this fact. It certainly belongs to Flaubert's autobiographical cycle, showing an influence of Goethe's *Werther*, Chateaubriand's *René*, and Musset's *Confession d'un Enfant du Siècle*, and there are many echoes of these works in the novel. But the book arranges the events so as to form a fictional pattern, and care is shown in the planning – more than in his earlier works. There is a logical development of the hero right through, from birth to death. The book ends with his death, for he had in fact to die after his failure, since there was no other outcome for him.

It is interesting to note here that analysis is beginning to replace dialogue, and that there is more effort at generalization in order to draw an eternal and universal lesson.

Flaubert handles the different styles very competently, as a practised writer. After showing the heights of lyrical and romantic dreams of the hero, a more dispassionate style was required for the logical, observant narrator; and a looser, more illiterate prose was needed for Marie's account of her youth, for she was an uneducated prostitute.

The mood of the first part is the same as in the early pages of *Mémoires d'un Fou*, and is more derivative than the latter parts. It is inspired by the same aimless melancholy and *Weltschmerz*, but it is a very sensitive evocation of the distress of youth trying to find itself. This was probably the first section to be written – perhaps in November 1840, just after his return from Marseilles.

The first part expresses the vague longing of youth, an aimless yearning for something – anything – the young man feels that he could love anyone, that the object would not matter, and he reflects sadly that he may die without ever having loved, and without having found anyone worthy of his love. He is eighteen and still a virgin, and all he has seen of passion is in the poets he has read:[25]

Oh! comme j'aurais aimé si j'avais aimé, si j'avais pu con-centrer sur un point toutes ces forces divergentes qui retombaient sur moi! Que quefois, à tout prix, je voulais trouver une femme, je voulais l'aimer, elle contenait tout pour moi, j'attendais tout d'elle, c'était mon soleil de poésie, qui devait faire éclore toute fleur et resplendir toute beauté. Je me promettais un amour divin, je lui donnais d'avance une auréole à m'éblouir, et la première qui venait à ma rencontre, au hasard, dans la foule, je lui vouais mon âme, et je la regardais de manière à ce qu'elle me comprît bien, à ce qu'elle pût lire dans ce seul regard tout ce que j'étais, et m'aimer. Je plaçais ma destinée dans ce hasard, mais elle passait comme les autres, comme les précédentes, comme les suivantes, et ensuite je retombais, plus délabrée qu'une voile déchireé trempée par l'orage.

He has many treasures in his heart to squander, but there is no one worthy of them. In revenge for his frustration, he is seized with violent and impotent rage against life, and he would willingly have destroyed the whole of creation. Then he longs for death with youthful and poetic yearning, making sad reflections on it:[26]

Alors la mort m'apparut belle. Je l'ai toujours aimée. . . . Il est
si doux de se figurer qu'on n'est plus! il fait si calme dans tous les
cimetières! là, tout étendu et roulé dans le linceul et les bras en
croix sur la poitrine, les siècles passent sans plus vous éveiller que
le vent qui passe sur l'herbe. Que de fois j'ai contemplé, dans les
chapelles des cathédrales, ces longues statues de pierre couchées
sur les tombeaux! leur calme est si profond que la vie ici-bas
n'offre rien de pareil; ils ont, sur leur lèvre froide, comme un
sourire monté du fond du tombeau, on dirait qu'ils dorment,
qu'ils savourent la mort. N'avoir plus besoin de pleurer, ne plus
sentir de ces défaillances où il semble que tout se rompt, comme
les échafaudages pourris, c'est là le bonheur au-dessus de tous les
bonheurs, la joie sans lendemain, le rêve sans réveil.

Nature might be a consolation and there are, in the novel,
many beautiful descriptions of the landscape, the Norman
countryside which Flaubert knew so well, and which has
nothing to do with Marseilles or the Mediterranean. It is a
western landscape, with the sun setting over the sea. We
have already seen the ecstasy of his description after his solitary walk to Trouville in the dead of night, on his arrival
there in September 1842.

However, the ecstasy and contemplation of nature cannot
last and the hero has to return to reality. He remembers that
he is alive and the curse of living seizes hold of him again;
life comes back to him as it returns to frozen limbs. As he
has experienced great happiness, he now feels immense and
nameless unhappiness.

The first part could, with advantage, have been shorter,
for it is largely the over-fluent expression which is found so
often in Flaubert's early works.

The hero is longing to love someone and he makes a
sudden decision to call on a prostitute whose house he has
often noticed as he passed, and his heart had always beaten
more quickly as he went by. This part, the second, is the
most autobiographical of the novel and is a reflection of the
episode with Eulalie Foucaud in Marseilles in 1840. She, in
fact, was not a prostitute but only a woman of somewhat

easy virtue, prepared to seduce the handsome youth who crossed her path. Marie is, however, the noble courtesan of the Romantic tradition, and she is legion in the literature of the time – Marion Delorme, the young woman in *Rolla* by Musset, and later Marguerite Gautier in *La Dame aux Camélias*. She is also, in appearance, the type of woman who is a fixation with Flaubert, with a strong resemblance to Élisa Schlésinger:[27]

> Je me sentis d'abord frappé du regard brillant de ses deux grands yeux; quand je pus relever mon front, affaissé sous le poids de ce regard, je vis une figure d'une adorable beauté; une même ligne droite partait du sommet de sa tête dans la raie de ses cheveux, passait entre ses grands sourcils arqués, sur son nez aquilin, aux narines palpitantes et relevées comme celles des camées antiques, fendait par le milieu sa lèvre chaude, ombragée d'un duvet bleu, et puis là, le cou, le cou gras, blanc, rond; à travers son vêtement mince, je voyais la forme de ses seins aller et venir au mouvement de sa respiration.

There is no doubt that the episode is inspired by a real adventure, but it is also a wonderful description of the first experience of sexual love, and it has verisimilitude as well as truth.

One sees, in this part, the novelist's talent for accurate description and his eye for detail which will be one of the outstanding features of *Madame Bovary*:[28]

> Et puis je ne sais plus, tout cela est parti, c'est déjà si vieux! Cependant il y a certaines choses que je revois comme si c'était hier; sa chambre par exemple; je revois le tapis du lit, usé au milieu, la couche d'acajou avec des ornements en cuivre et des rideaux de soie rouge moirée; ils craquaient sous les doigts, les franges en étaient usées. Sur la cheminée, deux vases de fleurs artificielles; au milieu, la pendule, dont le cadran était suspendu entre quatre colonnes d'albâtre. Çà et là, accrochée à la muraille, une vieille gravure entourée d'un cadre de bois noir et représentant des femmes au bain, des vendangeurs, des pêcheurs.

With possession comes disillusionment and the hero asks himself whether this is all that love is:[29]

Ce n'était donc que cela, aimer! ce n'était donc que cela, une femme! Pourquoi, ô mon Dieu, avons-nous encore faim alors que nous sommes repus? pourquoi tant d'aspirations et tant de déceptions? pourquoi le coeur de l'homme est-il si grand, et la vie si petite! il y a des jours où l'amour des anges même ne lui suffirait pas, et il se fatigue en une heure de toutes les caresses de la terre.

He does not, however, want to accept this disillusionment, and he returns to see Marie. She then gives him a long account of her life, for she has formed a deep attachment for the handsome young man.

This long account is very typical of Romantic literature and does not ring true. Also it mars the unity of the tale and holds up the action. There is in her dreams and aspirations something of what will be found in Emma Bovary. She makes the interesting reflection that none of the men in her life had ever truly known her, they had only seen in her their own dream, she was for them what Maya was for her lovers, in Simon de Gantillon's play of the same name; she was, for each of them, his own illusion.

Flaubert has succeeded in rendering in a poignant manner the sadness of the woman who is no longer young and knows that her days of satisfaction are numbered. This shows compassion and understanding on the part of a young novelist of twenty. He cleverly uses the fading violets to symbolize the ageing woman:[30],

Il y avait sur la table de nuit un bouquet de violettes dans un verre d'eau, j'étendis la main, je le pris, je cassai le fil avec les dents et je les respirais. La chaleur de la veille, sans doute, ou bien le long temps depuis qu'elles étaient cueillies les avait fanées, je leur trouvai une odeur exquise et toute particulière, je humai une à une leur parfum; comme elles étaient humides, je me les appliquai sur les yeux pour me refroidir, car mon sang bouillait, et mes membres fatigués ressentaient comme une brûlure au contact des draps. Alors, ne sachant que faire et ne voulant pas l'éveiller, car j'éprouvais un étrange plaisir à la voir dormir, je mis doucement toutes les violettes sur la gorge de

Marie, bientôt elle en fut toute couverte et ces belles fleurs
fanées, sous lesquelles elle dormait, la symbolisèrent à mon
esprit. Comme elles, en effet, malgré leur fraîcheur enlevée, à
cause de cela peut-être, elle m'envoyait un parfum plus âcre et
plus irritant; le malheur, qui avait dû passer dessus, la rendait
belle de l'amertume que sa bouche conservait, même en dor-
mant, belle des deux rides qu'elle avait derrière le cou et que le
jour, sans doute, elle cachait sous ses cheveux. A voir cette
femme si triste dans la volupté et dont les étreintes mêmes avaient une joie lugubre, je devinais mille passions terribles qui
l'avaient dû sillonner comme la foudre à en juger par les traces
restées.

After possession the hero feels much older and experienced, but there is also a sensation of failure, for he has
placed love on too high a pedestal. Before his encounter with
Marie, his ennui had been beautiful and poetic, but now it is
only stupid. He tries to find refuge in nature, in dreams of
exotic countries, and he longs to escape from boredom in
some wonderful place in the world.

Here the personal manuscript ends and the third-person
narrator takes over. He has known the hero and he recounts
the end of his life. However, some of the material which he
relates could have been utilized in the person of the hero. He
enlarges on his pessimism and depression, and on the ways
by means of which he tries to escape from them. He tries to
see his friends, but is surprised that they have nothing to say
to one another. Then he is tempted by suicide, as he sits
alone and weeping at the edge of the sea:[31]

Il pleurait, était-ce de froid ou de tristesse son coeur crevait, il
avait besoin de parler à quelqu'un . . .

Le soir il voulut encore sortir, il alla se coucher dans un trou
qui sert aux chasseurs pour tirer les canards sauvages, il vit un
instant l'image de la lune rouler sur les flots et remuer dans la
mer, comme un grand serpent, puis de tous les côtés du ciel des
nuages s'amoncelèrent de nouveau, et tout fut noir. Dans les
ténèbres, des flots ténébreux se balançaient, montaient les uns
sur les autres et détonnaient comme cent canons, une sorte de
rythme faisait de ce bruit une mélodie terrible, le rivage, vibrant

sous le coup des vagues, répondait à la haute mer re-
tentissante.

Il songea un instant s'il ne devait pas en finir, personne ne le
verrait, pas de secours à espérer, en trois minutes il serait
mort.

Eventually he dies out of a lack of will to live, out of mere
weariness and sadness. But, before he dies, he casts aside all
personal expression and subjective literature. In the same
way, at this time, Flaubert was laying aside his past, his romanticism and the lyric writers whom he had previously
admired, and he was turning towards the future. He felt that
Novembre closed a period of his life. Writing to Louis Colet,
in December 1846, he declared that the novel marked the
end of his youth, that it had 'clôturé' his youth.[32]

The book is vastly superior, in every way, to the others
which preceded it, and already it fulfils many of his later
ideas on life and literature. It is the first of his books in
which one really feels the creative artist at work, and it is no
wonder that it should have been the one of his early works
which he preferred. It is a remarkable achievement for a
young man not yet twenty-one, and it makes a good end to
his youth.

[8]

Maxime Du Camp
(1842–4)

FLAUBERT went to Paris in November 1842, to become a regular university student – his first settlement away from home – and he found a little apartment, in the rue de l'Est, looking out over the Luxembourg Gardens, a street which later disappeared when the Boulevard Saint Michel was constructed. It was very cheap, he tells his sister, only £12 a year and, as it was unfurnished, he bought furniture for it, also very cheaply, as he only expended £8.[1] It was in the centre of the Latin Quarter, very handy for lectures and other student activities. He lived, at first at all events, a very diligent and frugal life, going to bed at three in the morning and rising again at eight. He went to lectures and studied at home, and worked to such good purpose that he passed his examination in December, the one for which he had failed to sit in August; it was, in fact, the only examination he was ever to pass.

At that time he seemed to his fellow-students awkward and provincial. Du Camp says that he always went to lectures, even at eight in the morning, dressed in black, with white tie and white gloves, looking like a bridegroom.[2]

He talks, in his letter, of the dissolute life he was leading, but most of his details read like the boastfulness of youth and do not ring true. He could not afford a mistress but was obliged to go to brothels, and he describes his escapades with cynicism – the idea of prostitution still excited him – and he mentions how he always spent the last day of the year in a brothel, selecting the ugliest girl he could find, then made love to her with a cigar in his mouth to show his contempt.[3] This is probably only bravado. During his whole period as a

student in Paris – barely fifteen months – there were only
two Decembers. On New Year's Eve 1843 he was with the
Schlésingers at Vernon, and it seems certain that in 1842 he
was in Rouen. In his letters to his sister, in December that
year, he talks of his longing for home, of his imminent
examination and how, when he had finished it, they must
spoil him to make up to him for the rigours of its preparation. He passed the examination on 28 December 1842,
and it is very likely that he went home immediately after
that, for there was nothing further to keep him in Paris.

Nevertheless it is possible that it was at this time, in Paris,
that he caught the venereal disease which he mentions,
much later, to Ernest Chevalier, in a letter dated 6 May 1849,
and to which he himself was inclined to attribute the
nervous ailment which started in January 1844:[4]

You must know that your friend is, apparently, undermined
by some kind of pox, the origins of which are lost in the mists of
time. Although the symptoms get cured, it reappears again from
time to time. My nervous complaint, from which I still suffer
intermittently, and which cannot be cured in the circumstances
in which I live, may well have no other cause.

It is now known, of course, that he contracted syphilis in
1850, on his journey to the East,[5] but he may well have
caught another form of venereal disease much earlier.

Flaubert renewed his summer friendship with the Colliers,
and it was an easy almost family relationship, in which he
still seemed to take most notice of little Herbert. He often
went to dine with them in their apartment at the Rond Point
des Champs Élysées. If he cared more for one of the girls
than for the others, at this time, it could only have been for
Henrietta. He went several times to read to her – she was still
an invalid on a couch and could not go out much. He spent
Christmas of 1843 with them and read her Victor Hugo's
play *Hernani*. He mentions her several times in his letters to
Caroline, saying once how pretty she looked in a pink frock;
but he is very critical of Gertrude, who, he says, 'has always

something to teach you'. Also he thought her admiration for the Royal Family misplaced, and her distress over the death of the Duke of Orleans.[6] Le Poittevin certainly believed that, in November 1842, Flaubert was toying with plans for marriage, though no name was mentioned.[7] If indeed he cherished ideas of matrimony at that time, it can only have been with Henrietta Collier. We have seen that, later, Mrs Collier would have favoured their union. Nevertheless, if feeling there was, it cannot have been very deep, for, when the Colliers moved to Chaillot, beyond the Bois de Boulogne, he considered it too far to go to visit them.[8] They must, two years later, have moved back to the Champs Élysées, for, in a letter to Alfred Le Poittevin, he mentions calling on them there, where everything looked exactly as it had done when he had first visited them.[9]

A house he very much liked to visit, because its free and easy bohemian atmosphere was greatly to his liking, was the studio of the sculptor Pradier who, at this time, was at the height of his powers and was one of the most admired sculptors of the day. He was generally called Phidias by his friends. At one time, some years earlier, he had been the lover of Juliette Drouet who, in 1833, became Victor Hugo's life-long mistress. Claire P., for whom poems in *Les Contemplations* were composed, was her daughter by Pradier.

Flaubert became acquainted with the sculptor through a schoolmate, Charles Darcet, whose sister Louise – called Ludovica by her intimates – was Pradier's wife, and her father was a close friend of Dr Flaubert. She was eventually to become one of the models for Emma Bovary. She was a gay, extravagant and unfaithful wife. In 1845 Pradier was to feel that he must separate from her, as she was ruining him by her extravagances and her infidelities. Victor Hugo said of her once: 'Monsieur Pradier, the excellent sculptor, has a marvellous talent and a coquettish wife. His talent enriches him but his wife impoverishes him.'

Flaubert kept an attachment for Louise Pradier most of his life and he used to go to visit her after her divorce. There was possibly some element of psychological study in this, for he wrote to Alfred Le Poittevin: 'Ah! la belle étude que j'ai faite là.'[10] At Pradier's studio Flaubert met many of the eminent men of letters of the day, amongst others, Victor Hugo in January 1843. He described him in a letter to his sister:[11]

You want details about Victor Hugo. What can I tell you about him? He's a man like any other. His face is ugly enough and his appearance fairly common. He has fine teeth, a superb forehead, neither eye-lashes nor eye-brows. He doesn't talk much and he seems all the time to be keeping a watch over himself, and to be reluctant to give himself away. He's very polite and somewhat stiff. I like very much the sound of his voice. I took great pleasure in observing him from close quarters.

But the people with whom he was most anxious to renew his acquaintance were the Schlésingers. He must have met them on one of his short visits to Paris, before he settled there as a student, for he mentions it, in a letter to his sister, in April 1842.[12] But, when he was living there, they became his closest friends and he dined with them every Wednesday. Many years later, he recalled to Élisa Schlésinger the pleasure he had derived from these parties, and how he had never forgotten their dining-room in the rue de Grammont.[13]

At this time Maurice Schlésinger was a well-known character in the musical world, for he was then editing *La Gazette Musicale* and was acquainted with most of the musicians of the day, including Wagner, who described him in his *Histoire de ma Vie*.[14]

Wagner contributed to the paper, but he did not long keep his esteem for the editor. When he wrote for the magazine, in 1848, he described the extraordinary manner in which Schlésinger calculated what was due to his authors. The text was put in an iron frame and measured. The title and the author's name were subtracted, and also all the blank spaces. Wagner, having imagined that he had contributed a whole page, was, in fact, only paid for half a page. He complained that his collaboration with *La Gazette Musicale* had brought him nothing, and yet he had contributed some very successful articles.[15]

There is considerable difference of opinion concerning the problem of whether Flaubert and Élisa Schlésinger ever became lovers. Both Bruneau and Pommier believe that his love for her was over by the time he was eighteen or twenty, and they produce as evidence the letters which he wrote to Louise Colet where he denies having loved her for more than a few years.[16] But what he said to jealous Louise Colet is not reliable evidence, and, moreover, if his correspondence is taken into account, he spoke very little of his deepest feelings. During his years in Paris, he spent a great deal of time with the Schlésingers, and it is difficult to imagine that Maurice, the tricky Philistine bourgeois, whom Flaubert normally despised, and whom he portrayed in the final *Éducation Sentimentale,* could have been the main attraction.

Those who support the thesis that Flaubert and Madame Schlésinger did, in fact, become lovers, use as evidence the first *Éducation Sentimentale*, where Émilie Renaud becomes the mistress of the hero, Henry. It is, however, fiction and although some of the events may have happened to Flaubert in real life, in his youth, there is no resemblance whatsoever between the heroine of the novel and Élisa Schlésinger as she is portrayed in Maria in the *Mémoires d'un Fou* and in Madame Arnoux in the second *Éducation Sentimentale*. She is far more like Eulalie Foucaud, who did, in fact, become the mistress of Flaubert.

Marie-Jeanne Durry, in *Flaubert et ses Projets Inédits,* published the plans and notes which served for the final *Éducation Sentimentale*, in which Flaubert discusses whether or not to make Frédéric become the lover of Madame Arnoux.[17] He decides that it would make a stronger situation if they were not to be lovers. She concludes from this that, in real life, they had been lovers, but this does not necessarily follow.

It seems more true psychologically to Flaubert's character that he should never have made her his mistress. He resembled Baudelaire in wishing to keep his madonna in her shrine. In his case possession was invariably followed by disillusionment – both in life and in his writings – and it is hard to believe that there had been possession, since he kept his idealistic view of her until the end. It does not seem possible that he could have retained this romantic conception of her if he had gone through the disillusionment which inevitably followed possession.

It seems likely that Élisa Schlésinger loved Flaubert, and he may have tried to make love to her, but it is probable that she repulsed him. As we have seen, he was always bewildered by her faithfulness to Maurice Schlésinger in spite of all his infidelities. In his letters to her, during the lifetime of her husband, he wrote to her with distant and respectful affection, letters which any husband might read. It was only during his last years, when she was a widow, that he wrote to her with deep emotion and heartfelt affection. It is hard to believe that this could have happened if there had been possession and consequent disillusionment. But, throughout his life, he kept her image unsullied in the walled-up chamber of his heart.[18]

All through the spring of 1843 Flaubert was working for his second law examination, which he was to take in the summer. He had been studying now for eighteen months and he had only passed one examination. He was now growing to dislike Paris because his life there was being poisoned by his work. He had spent a month in Rouen at Easter but he had returned to Paris with nostalgia for home, and loathing for the kind of life he was obliged to lead, with the prospect of the examination at the end, which he was very unlikely to pass. In all his letters to his sister, he describes his loneliness and his disgust with his predicament. One sees how vulnerable he was, although he was an adult of twenty-one. Just after he got back to Paris, he wrote to her, at the end of April:[19]

How lonely I am for you, my poor little rat! It seems to me at least a fortnight since I left you. The weather too is of a most awful sadness; it has snowed all day, and I'm alone thinking of you, and imagining what you're doing. You're all sitting round the fire, and I alone am missing. You're playing dominoes; everyone is laughing and shouting; you're all together, while I'm here like an idiot, leaning with my elbows on the table, not knowing what to do. The month which has just gone by was so wonderful and sweet, that I think of it still and long for others like it to come quickly. I'd recovered at home; I'd got so well accustomed to embracing you again, that I wanted to be with you at all minutes, my poor little rat; that, being deprived of that seems harder than ever. Today I saw again the eternal streets of my quarter, and the look of these pavements on which I pass two or three times a day. I found on my table my cursed law books, where I'd left them. I much prefer my old room in Rouen, where I spent so many sweet and peaceful hours, when I could hear round me the movement of the house, when you used to come at four o'clock, to do some history or English, and then instead of doing history, you gossiped with me until dinner time. To be happy in a place one must have lived there for a long time. It's not in one day that one can warm one's nest and be comfortable in it. In the day-time it's all right, but it is in the evening, when I've come in, and find myself in this empty room, that I think most of Rouen. Answer me immediately my poor little rat. Tell me how you are, if you've not been ill again, etc. Draw, paint, play the piano, try to spend your time the way you like best, and, although you say you don't like writing, write me long letters.

Nevertheless, he continued to work, but to very little purpose, for he could not remember what he read. Sometimes he would hit his table with his two fists, in impotent rage, and then, when the fit of anger had passed, he noticed that half an hour had gone by when he had done nothing, and he turned over the pages more desperately than ever. Then, when evening fell, he used to go out alone to a dingy restaurant, to eat his solitary meal and to dream of the family seated round the dinner table, with their happy laughing faces. It is only where one is at home that one can eat with a good appetite, and where one can laugh aloud.

He even gave up going to dine with the Colliers, as he only came out of his lair once a week.[20]

He still attended his lectures, but he was no longer able to listen to the professor droning on, and his hatred of law went on increasing.

He was also in financial difficulties – either through extravagance or because he was kept short of money. His father, who heard of his straits through his friend Dr Cloquet, sent him something to help him, with a letter which shows the warm-hearted generosity of the great man:[21]

You're twice foolish, firstly to allow yourself to be fleeced like a real provincial; an idiot who allows himself to be caught by the lords of industry or venal women, who can only get hold of feeble minds and foolish old men; and, thank God, you're neither stupid nor old; your second mistake is not to have had confidence in me. ... I imagined that I was sufficiently your friend to deserve to know what was happening to you, either good or bad. Farewell my Gustave, spare my purse a little and especially be well.

His examination was fixed for August and, as the time approached for it, he was becoming more desperate. Writing to his sister shortly before it, he said:[22]

If my examination, instead of taking place in a week, were to take place only in two months time, I think I would throw it up. I'm beginning to be worn out. It is finally too much annoyance for one man. If, unfortunately, I were to fail, I swear, on my honour, that I'd not do any more work for the second attempt, and that I'd sit for the examination, each time, with what I now know, until finally they passed me. I began to work for my examination in too great detail so that I'm overwhelmed by it . . .

If you only knew, my dear old rat, how much I'm thinking of that happy end of the month of August, and how I'll dash out of the Law School, when I've passed, and all the foolish things I'll say and do in the carriage with you.

However, this was not to be and, in spite of all his hard work, he failed in his examination; it was the last for which he was ever to sit.

The family had gone to Paris to take him home, and had stayed at the Hôtel Bristol, but there was a weight over the holiday on account of Gustave's failure.

For some time past he had been considering the plan of giving up the study of law as soon as he had got his diploma and not waiting, as he originally intended, to work for the doctorate. Le Poittevin wrote to him on 28 July 1843:[23] 'I'm longing to hear how your father will take the resolution which you've just announced to me, of ending your active studies with the diploma!'

It was in 1843, in Paris, that Flaubert made the third close friendship of his life, comparable to his friendships with Ernest Chevalier and Alfred Le Poittevin. It had, for some years at all events, the emotional intensity of his association with Le Poittevin. This was his friendship for Maxime Du Camp, who became, during his student days, his dearest and closest friend. Maxime Du Camp was very near to him in age, only two months younger, and, in his youth, was a man of great attraction and charm, and good looks, with his tall stature, his shining eyes and his thick curling hair, closely cropped. He was an orphan, and his only near relation was an old grandmother. There is no doubt that he and Flaubert loved one another very dearly. Very many years later, in 1877, when they decided to destroy their correspondence, Flaubert reread some of the letters he had written to his friend and he said:[24] 'Weren't you nice in those days, and didn't we love one another.' This was long after life had separated them and had blunted their affection.

Du Camp tells us in his *Souvenirs Littéraires* how he first met Flaubert, in March 1843, in the room of Ernest Le Marié, who had been a schoolmate of Flaubert in Rouen, near the Hôtel de Ville. Le Marié was thumping out on the piano Beethoven's *Funeral March* when they heard the bell ring, and he saw a tall youth with a fair beard appear, with his hat set jauntily on the side of his head. Le Marié introduced the young man to him as an old school friend from Rouen, Gustave Flaubert.[25]

Maxime Du Camp and Gustave Flaubert soon became close friends, and Du Camp seemed to Flaubert a highly polished young man, very much more experienced and sophisticated than himself, less provincial; very much the Parisian man about town. There was something energetic about him – bossy even – which made others have belief in themselves, and Flaubert allowed him to gain ascendancy over him. He was always prone to hero-worship, until he saw the feet of clay, and none were visible in Du Camp at this time. He also liked to be led by others. Even at the age of twenty-one, Du Camp knew where he was going, and that was to the top of the ladder, but he was prepared to carry his new friend up with him. At this time his energy and ambitions had charm, he was very persuasive and his susceptibilities had not yet been blunted by the pursuit of fame and success.

Critics have been universally hard on Du Camp and have suggested that his attitude towards Flaubert was inspired by jealousy. This opinion seems unjustified, and it will be seen later that, on the contrary, there was some jealousy – perhaps only envy – in Flaubert towards him when Flaubert was struggling to make concrete his difficult theory of art, and was misunderstood. Du Camp had no reason to be jealous of Flaubert for he was, in every way, more successful, and there were no honours which he did not gain – the rank of Officier de la Légion d'Honneur before he was thirty and election to the French Academy, whereas Flaubert was only to be made Chevalier in the last years of his life, through the kind offices of Princesse Mathilde. He genuinely admired Flaubert's early talent, his great natural fluency, and he considered that he had narrowed it by placing obstacles in its way. But most of the critics of the day also shared this opinion. He was inclined to attribute the discipline and restriction of his inspiration to his nervous disorder. It is true that his illness came just at the time when he was beginning to develop his austere talent.

Du Camp has also been blamed, as a friend, for having

said, in his *Souvenirs Littéraires*, after Flaubert's death,
that he had suffered from epilepsy. That was certainly believed at the time – and still is – and there is nothing shameful in it. But the authority with which he stated this disease
may have been in order to hide the fact of another which
would have been considered more shameful. We have seen
that Flaubert admitted to Chevalier that he had caught a
venereal disease, to which he attributed his nervous disorder.
Maxime Du Camp, who was his closest friend at the time,
would have been aware of this, and he certainly knew that
he had contracted syphilis on the journey to the East in 1850.
Du Camp may well have thought that the reputation of epilepsy was preferable to that of venereal disease as an explanation of his undoubted physical disorders.

There was certainly on Du Camp's part a desire to help
Flaubert to reach success and fame – perhaps later with a
certain condescension, but, by then, it would have been
difficult for him to consider his friend's activities as important as his own, which were certainly far more generally appreciated. Most critics have been hard on his worldly
ambitions, but idealism cannot be expected from everyone,
nor noble self-sacrifice to a cause. Du Camp's ambitions were
those of most of his contemporaries, and he succeeded in
attaining them.

On his side Flaubert certainly looked up to him as a
leader, and indeed cherished for him an almost schoolgirl
'crush'. But the attraction was mutual, and, when he published his first book, Du Camp dedicated it to Flaubert 'Solus
ad Solum'. They also gave each other rings, and Du Camp
said: 'When we exchanged rings, it was a kind of be-
trothal.'[26]

Du Camp's letters to Flaubert, when he was on his first
trip abroad,[27] have an intensity which is not normally
found in the letters from one man to another. Otherwise
their correspondence has been largely destroyed. Du Camp
said: 'It was not without regret that we decided to do away
with these pages where the best of our souls had been poured

out.'[28] The letters in the Institut library at Chantilly were
preserved probably because they made a travel diary for Du
Camp. He numbered them and was always anxious to find
out whether they had arrived in their correct order, and he
was always eager that they should be carefully preserved.

Du Camp is often inaccurate in his *Souvenirs Littéraires*,
which was written forty years after the events described; but
the letters were written at the time, and the material is first-
hand. The writing is very difficult to decipher; the letters are
immensely long and often very uninteresting with their
mass of detail. But what shines through all of them is the
deep affection of the writer for his friend and his concern on
his behalf. This was after Flaubert had fallen ill. The letters
abound in passionate terms of endearment. 'I love you, I love
you,' he wrote, in the first letter, on 15 May 1844, 'I embrace
you, strongly enough to smother you.' And he adds, in a
postscript: 'Fare well, fare well! I kiss you on your large
beautiful eyes.' In the second letter he wrote: 'Fare well, dear
sick child. I embrace you and I love you.' In most of the
letters, he says: 'I embrace you tightly enough to stifle you. I
embrace you and I love you.' On 31 October 1844, Du Camp
wrote to him: 'You'll never be forsaken by your old Du
Camp, who would sacrifice immediately all his future hopes
of bourgeois happiness, and even happiness itself, to wipe
one single tear from your eyes. I forbid you ever to doubt
me, and, unless you send me away, you'll always find me at
your side, and, as long as I live, you'll never be alone.'

Du Camp seems to have been, as well, a full-blooded
heterosexual, and many women are known in his life. There
was especially Suzanne, who was the Portia of his *Chants
Modernes* and *Chants d'Amour*. There were also Viviane,
Valentine and particularly Madame Delessert, Mérimée's
friend, who was to be the model for Madame Dambreuse in
Flaubert's final *Éducation Sentimentale*. He would have
liked also to have made Louise Pradier his mistress but, at
that time, she was attracted by Flaubert and did not think of
anyone else. But Flaubert did not want Louise Pradier as

a lover. Du Camp wrote to Flaubert on 25 December 1848:[29]

> She took my hands in hers, and said to me that she loved me dearly, but that it could not happen because, *in her heart she was certain that it would grieve you. You know that that has been my secret opinion this long time.* ... I realized that she was only yielding to my caresses, so I was stupid enough – or loyal enough – to stop short. ... She then spoke of her children whom she had seen that day, and she wept a lot on my shoulder. ... She then admitted to me 'Please don't let us do anything, *before that I must see Gustave and discuss it seriously* with him; perhaps it was harder for me to resist than for you.' That is *literally* my evening, what do you think of it? What do you wish me to do?

It was in 1843 that Flaubert began writing his first *Éducation Sentimentale*, which was only to be published posthumously, and which bears no relation to the final version of the same title.

It has been universally believed by the critics that this is an account of Flaubert's attachment for Élisa Schlésinger, the second version – the first being *Mémoires d'un Fou* – but it is difficult to see any resemblance to the heroine of *Mémoires d'un Fou* or to that of the final *Éducation Sentimentale* in the Émilie Renaud of the present novel. The author uses, it is true, elements of himself in both heroes, Henry and Jules, but the woman is far more like Eulalie Foucaud than Élisa Schlésinger. Émilie Renaud is far more vulgar and obvious and she does not inspire the same feeling of worship and adoration.

Flaubert intended, in the book, to give a picture of his generation as he saw it, to show the emotional education of the young men of his day.

He began writing the book in February 1843, shortly after his successful passing of his examination. He abandoned it for a time when working for his next test, which he failed at the end of August, but he took it up again in September and October and worked at it intermittently until he fell ill on 1 January 1844. He was then forced to drop it, taking it up

again in May, and finally finished it in January 1845. This
would mean that the longest time of composition was after
he had fallen ill.

Flaubert was very much changed by his illness, in his life
and character, and critics have tried hard to decide what
point he had arrived at before he fell ill, but it is impossible
to reach any certain conclusion. It is likely that the character
of Jules had grown in importance and depth with further
reflection, but it existed in the original plan, as the author
said later to Louise Colet, when she tried to persuade him to
remove Jules from the novel as unnecessary and as dividing
the interest.[30] Flaubert needed him as a contrast, a 're-
poussoir' he calls him. Gérard-Gailly believes that the break
occurs when Henry and Émilie elope to the United
States.[31] There is, however, proof, in a letter from Flaubert
to Louise Colet,[32] that the passage which he mentions was
written in August 1844, and it comes from Chapter 17, *before*
the elopement, so that the change after the illness must have
occurred before he wrote the journey to America.

There is no possibility of discovering the truth, but what
can be believed with confidence is that the major part of the
book was composed after he fell ill, between May 1844 and
January 1845, when it was completed. The work is thus
largely the first work of his altered self, of his changed life
and outlook, the first of his maturity. The novel will be more
fully discussed in the following chapter.

What seems clear is that when he started writing Flaubert
considered Henry as the main character, in whom he saw
himself, who represented the outward events of his life – not
necessarily his deepest self. However, as he progressed, he
came to see Jules as representing what he would like to be,
and he became, eventually, the most important character in
the novel.

Flaubert was twenty-one when he began composing
L'Éducation Sentimentale, and twenty-three when he completed it. Although it is still a subjective work, and the
influence of Rousseau, Chateaubriand and Goethe still per-

sists, it is more of a novel than anything else that he had
written so far. It also crystallizes many of his later views on
art.

Flaubert spent Christmas 1843 with the Colliers, and New
Year's Eve with the Schlésingers at their property at
Vernon; then he went home to Rouen on 1 January 1844.
This was the last time that he was in full health, for it was
then that he suffered the first attack of the illness which
completely altered his life.

L'Éducation Sentimentale
(1844–5)

FLAUBERT returned home from Vernon to Rouen on New Year's Day 1844, but left for Deauville immediately, where the family had been thinking of building a villa, and it was on the road been Pont l'Évêque and Rouen, when driving with his brother Achille, while he himself was holding the reins, that he had his first seizure – whatever it may have been, epilepsy or some other nervous ailment. He fell to the ground; his brother carried him to the nearest house and bled him, fearing that he was dead. After repeated bleedings he seemed to recover and he was brought home to Rouen, where he came under his father's treatment. So terrible was this treatment that it seems to us marvellous today that he did not, in fact, succumb to it. A seton was put on his neck to draw off the blood, fastened permanently in position, and he was kept on a very low diet, with little meat and no wine or tobacco, although he had always enjoyed these pleasures. Writing to Chevalier he said:[1]

My dear old Ernest, without knowing it you've almost had to mourn the death of the honest man who is writing you these lines. Yes, old fellow; yes young man; I almost departed to see Pluto, Rhadamanthus and Minos. I'm still in bed, with a seton on my neck, which is a stiff collar less yielding than that of an officer of the national guard; with masses of pills, tisanes, and especially with that spectre, a thousand times more terrible than all the illnesses in the world, a diet. You must know, my dear friend, that I've had a congestion of the brain, which is something like a miniature attack of apoplexy, accompanied by aching nerves, which I still have because it is fashionable. I almost croaked in the hands of my family. . . . They bled me three times all at once, and, at last, I opened my eyes. My father wants to keep me here

for a long time, and to look after me carefully, although my
moral condition is good, as I don't know how to worry. . . . I'm in
a cursedly low state and, at the slightest feeling, all my nerves,
vibrate, like fiddle strings; my knees, my shoulders, and my belly
tremble like an aspen leaf. However, that is life, *sic est vita, c'est
la vie*. It is likely that I'm not near going back to Paris, except
perhaps for two or three days towards April, to give notice to my
landlord, and to settle some little pieces of business.

His letter crossed one from Chevalier, and he wrote again a
few days later:[2]

I've a seton which oozes and itches, which holds my neck stiff,
and irritates me so much that it makes me sweat. I'm purged and
bled; leeches are stuck on me; good food is prohibited to me,
wine is forbidden to me; I'm a dead man.

But the worst deprivation was the absence of his pipe, for he
had always liked smoking better than anything else.

He went to Paris to sign on again at the law school, but he
suffered another attack – indeed several, and these seizures
became a daily occurrence, as he told Chevalier:[3] 'Not a
day goes by that I do not see skeins of threads or fireworks.'
At one of these attacks, Dr Flaubert was so much alarmed
because the blood did not come immediately when he was
bled that he withdrew the lancet and poured boiling water
on his son's arm, burning him so badly that there was a scar
there for the rest of his life.

As a result of these various attacks, Dr Flaubert decided
that his son was to abandon his study of law and to give up
all idea of having a professional career. Flaubert did not
regret this decision, which now permitted him to devote
himself to the work for which he felt suited. Psychologists
might think that his illness was a subconscious attempt to
escape from the life which he thought was destroying him,
taking away all his joy in living, and which was bound, in
the long run, to kill him artistically. It was an unconscious
bid for escape from a man whose nervous system had never
been strong. His illness caused a complete change, a total

break in his life. Writing to Alfred Le Poittevin in May 1845, he said:[4] 'My nervous disease has been the transition between two states.' And to Louise Colet, in August the following year, he wrote:[5] 'I've had two completely distinct existences; outward events were the symbol of the end of the first, and the birth of the second; all that is mathematical. My active and passionate life, full of emotion and contradictory movements, and of multiple sensations, ended when I was twenty-two. At that time I made great strides forward and something else came.'

Whatever may have been the disease from which he suffered, it certainly altered his life radically. Dr Flaubert sold the land at Deauville and bought the property at Croisset, a few miles downstream from Rouen, which, in those days, was an outlying village. He bought the house especially to be a home and a refuge for his invalid son. So the family gave up living in the Master's Lodgings at the Hôtel Dieu, and moved to the pleasant eighteenth-century château, with its garden running along the length of the river, and the beautiful avenue of lime trees, where he used to wander under the sweet-smelling blossoms. In those days there were none of the factories which now disfigure the landscape and impede the view. In this house at Croisset Flaubert was to live for the remaining years of his life, except for odd journeys abroad and intermittent trips to Paris. After his death the house was sold immediately by his niece, pulled down to make way for a factory, and the only part now left of the original place is the little summer house at the edge of the river, which has been turned into a Flaubert museum though it has very little connection with him.

At Croisset Flaubert tried to lead a normal life – indeed that was what his father prescribed for him. He went sailing, but his mother was always anxious lest a seizure might come on him while he was out alone. He had always been powerfully built and was used to taking a great deal of physical exercise in swimming and boating.

He was living very quietly and, writing to Chevalier, he said:[6]

I'm now almost set in my mould, and I live in a calm and regular way, occupying myself almost exclusively with literature and history. I've taken up Greek again, and I continue to persevere with it, and my master Shakespeare, whom I read with ever-increasing love.

I've never spent better years than the two which have just gone by, because they've been the freest, the least hindered in their development. I've sacrificed a lot to that liberty, and I'm prepared to sacrifice much more. My health is neither better nor worse; it is long, long, very long, my poor old fellow; not for me, but for my family, for my mother whom this illness is slowly wearing out and is making even iller than I am myself.

One may say, perhaps, that Flaubert might never have become the great artist he was to become without this disorder which took him away from regular life, and which permitted him to reflect in solitude. In his days and nights of illness he had thought of many things which he had never before considered, and he began to see the falseness of much of what he had earlier admired. He was now withdrawn from that ambitious life of the world, from the place-seeking and scramble for honours. He who, in his early youth, had dreamt of publication and approbation was now indifferent to all these things. With his portfolios crammed with works which he might have published, he did not seek to do so; and he was waiting to be satisfied with himself. Writing to Maxime Du Camp, he said:[7]

Do you know what would be a beautiful idea, that would be that a strong fellow who, until the age of fifty, had published nothing would then, at one fell swoop, publish, one fine day, his complete works, and then would stop at that.

He was helped, it is true, by being a man of independent means, but he never used his affluence for luxurious living, or pleasure, or for any extravagance, but only to avoid the soul-killing job which would have left him little leisure for his own work.

It was Flaubert's changed view of art and life which, eventually, led to the diminution of his friendship with Du Camp. Du Camp had been the close friend of his time as a student in Paris, when he was full of joy in living, and belief in his own worldly success. Just before he went to Paris, at the age of nineteen, he had written:[8]

Quand j'avais dix ans, je rêvais déjà de gloire – et j'ai composé dès que j'ai su écrire, je me suis peint tout exprès pour moi de ravissants tableaux – je songeais à une salle pleine de lumière et d'or, à des mains qui battent, à des cris, à des couronnes. On appelle l'auteur – l'auteur c'est bien moi, c'est mon nom, moi, moi, moi, moi, on me cherche dans les corridors, dans les loges, on se penche pour me voir – la toile se lève, je m'avance – quel enivrement! on te regarde, on t'admire, on t'envie, on est près de t'aimer.

Du Camp had fostered Flaubert's ambitions and his self-confidence, which indeed were also his own. He wanted wordly success for himself as soon as possible, but he wanted, as well, to carry Flaubert along with him. He did not understand, and he was never to understand, his friend's holding back, and his ideal of meticulous art.

Du Camp's departure for his journey to the East, in May 1844, loosened the close bonds of friendship which had united them during the previous year. While he was away abroad Flaubert renewed his earlier friendship with Le Poittevin, whose influence worked on him once more, and whose ideals now seemed to him more in harmony with his own than those of Du Camp. Their friendship grew deeper and Flaubert recognized that they were always mistaken when they parted:[9]

We would be really very wrong to part, to deviate from our vocation and our sympathy. Each time that we've tried to do so, we've found out our mistake. I've felt it recently, at our last parting, a painful impression which, although it may have roused less astonishment than formerly, is always full of sorrow. For the past three months we were happy together, alone, alone in ourselves, and alone both together. There is nothing in the world like these strange conversations beside that dirty fireplace where you come and sit, isn't that the case my dear poet? Delve down into your life and you'll admit, as I do, that we've no better memories, that is to say, intimate and tender things, by dint of being elevated. I've revisited Paris with pleasure; I saw the Boulevard, the rue de Rivoli, the pavements, as if I'd come to revisit all that after an absence of a hundred years, and I don't know why I breathed more freely, feeling myself in the midst of all that noise and all that human bustle. But I've no one with me alas! As soon as we part, we land in a foreign land where no one speaks our language, and where we speak that of no one else.

Le Poittevin admitted that he had been somewhat hurt, and had felt neglected, during the period of the height of Flaubert's friendship with Du Camp:[10]

If I've seemed to you, dear child, to draw away from you somewhat for some time now, it is because it seemed to me, on recent occasions, I'd found, on your part, less frankness than I'd expected. That led me to hide from you various things which, without that, I'd have been prepared to tell you. It was sad for me to act in this way but I'd be most happy to have been wrong.

And later he wrote to him:[11]

Come back, I'm thirsty for you! We're like two trappists who speak only when we're together, and then a language understood by ourselves alone. . . . I've a great longing to see you again; there is, in spite of everything, something in us which bleeds when we are too long parted. The distance prevents us, at first, from feeling it, but our attention is not distracted for long, and the habit awakens again.

While Flaubert wrote to him:[12]

No! I don't consider that I'm to be pitied, when I reflect that I've got your friendship, and that we've whole free hours to spend together. If you were ever to fail me, what would there be left for me?

Their friendship grew in depth and intensity, and Flaubert took up again his metaphysical interests, which he had lately somewhat neglected. In his letters he mentions an oriental tale which is preoccupying him; it is unknown whether this is the old *Smarh* or some new work. The interest in metaphysics, which he now resumed, made it possible for him, during his trip to Italy in 1845, to be influenced by the picture of Saint Anthony by Breughel, which he was to see in Genoa, and which eventually led to his *Tentation de Saint Antoine*. His interest in this kind of work had almost disappeared during the time when he was preoccupied with modern life, and was composing *L'Éducation Sentimentale*.

Maxime Du Camp did not approve of this renewal of friendship between Flaubert and Le Poittevin. There was probably a large element of jealousy in his feelings, but he did not think that Alfred had a good influence on Gustave. He described him as 'devious like a woman, and saying the most outrageous things in a calm voice'.[13] This was probably true, and the obscene nature of Le Poittevin's conversation and correspondence has been observed in an earlier chapter.

In one of his interminable letters, while he was on his journey to the East, Du Camp said:[14]

You saw happiness where it does not exist, you became enthusiastic for insignificant things, the artistic side of which ought not to have blinded you to their horrible and ridiculous aspect. You've denied your own heart. You've mercilessly mocked at sacred things; you who have a noble intelligence, you've made yourself the monkey of a corrupt being, a Greek of the decadence, as he calls himself; and now, I give you my sacred word of honour, he's pulling your leg and doesn't believe one single word of what he said to you. Show him this letter and you'll see that he'll not dare deny it. Forgive me, my very dear child, it's very reluctantly that I've felt obliged to talk to you in this way, but friendship is inexorable and I had to speak to you as I did. Don't be angry with me. I'd be so happy to see you at peace, calm, and enjoying all the happiness which you've got within your grasp, and which, nevertheless, you seek so far away. It's a good thing to love art, but one must not sacrifice everything to it. One may be a strong man but there's always something lacking when the joys of the heart aren't complete. . . . Farewell! In two or three days time, I'll write to you at greater length. I'll never speak about all this to you again. You must be tired of these four pages! Forgive me for them, but you may be sure that they've burnt me more to write than they will cost you to read. Nevertheless rest assured that it is my extreme love for you that has dictated them. Farewell, dear old chap. . . . I love you and embrace you with all my heart. Don't be angry with me and write to me that you still love me a little.

Earlier, in the same letter, he had said:

If you only knew how much I love you and how much I suffer to see you finding happiness where it doesn't exist. I'd give everything in the world to have you live my life for six months and then you'd appreciate it, and I'm certain that you'd go back calm and collected to enjoy that life which now seems to you intolerable.

All through this correspondence from Du Camp to Flaubert, during his absence abroad, one sees that he thought of his friend constantly, and always with deep affection bordering on passion. He begs him again and again for letters, lamenting the fact that he is so far away, and he thinks that he would have been wiser if he had never left him at all:

Talk to me of a thousand things, it is only in this way that your absence can be made bearable to me, and to which I grow accustomed only with the greatest difficulty.[15]

The longing for his friend was poisoning his trip, and he never got sufficient news from him: 'Either you're ill . . . or you've cruelly forgotten me. If you're well then your carelessness is unpardonable.'[16]

In another letter he says:[17] 'I'd like to follow everything that you're doing, to know what you're doing, minute by minute.'

And he seems to have spent writing to him every minute that he could spare:[18]

I've still four letters to write and yet I talk only to you. You get the finest and biggest share. Write to me lengthily and often. Tell me of your life and about your thoughts. You know that, in me, you'll always find an echo – in spite of myself.

He seems as if unable to tear himself away from his letter:

Nevertheless, my dear child, if you wish me to be able to endure my trip, you must write to me often and at great length.

If you only knew with what impatience I await the posts from France.[19]

Du Camp was away from France from May 1844 until March 1845, and it was during that time that Flaubert finished his first *Éducation Sentimentale*.

The first *Éducation Sentimentale*, as has already been noted, has no more connection with the second than its title. It is true that there are certain similarities in physical characteristics between Madame Renaud, the heroine of the first, and Madame Arnoux, the heroine of the second, but this may be due only to the fact that each is the kind of woman who appealed to Flaubert, and her type is found in many of his works. We have seen that Eulalie Foucaud resembled Élisa Schlésinger – indeed that may be why Flaubert was attracted by her. Louise Colet seems to have been the only woman in his life who was not dark, but a rich Flemish blonde.

L'Éducation Sentimentale was not planned to be, as were some of his earlier works, a cosmic vision of the universe; nor was it meant to serve as self-revelation or an expression of himself. It was intended to be a picture of life as it is lived every day in a modern world; and also to be a criticism of that life. It was particularly intended to show the 'sentimental education' of the young men of his age, and by 'sentimental' we have seen that he did not merely mean passionate. In a letter to Le Poittevin shortly after he had finished the book he said:[20] 'My own "sentimental education" is not yet completed, but perhaps I'm nearing its end.' It is clear from the context that he is not referring to his love life. Naturally, since he was still very young, he used elements from his own character and events from his own experience.

From the outset, he conceived the two characters, Henry and Jules, as a contrast to one another; but, after his illness, Jules began to take on for him a new importance, becoming the spokesman for his recent ideas and expressing his new philosophy of art.

We find, in the novel, the sentimental education of the two young men. At first the author was, obviously, more interested in Henry, who was then really a hero, than in Jules. Henry's sentimental education is an effort at adaptation to the world as it is. He accepts it in the end, making his peace with it and becoming blunted by it. He finally makes a great success of life in a worldly way, but he thereby loses his soul and becomes a bourgeois.

That is why some critics see in him a deliberate portrait of Maxime Du Camp, but Flaubert himself shared these ambitions in his youth, before the great change in his life. Then he feared that he might have gone the same way as Henry if he had remained in Paris and had kept his ambitions.

Henry fails in love but so, too, does Jules. This at first turns the latter in on himself, making him hate the world and see himself as a Byronic hero. He even contemplates suicide, but eventually becomes inured to his misery. He seeks consolation everywhere and thinks that he would find it in literature, but he finds there only himself. Eventually he reaches serenity in his conception of art, believing that the artist must be able to understand everything, the present and the past, the living and the inanimate; only then would he be able to reach the forgetfulness of self which is peace.

The plot of the novel is based on the contrast between the destinies of the two friends. Jules remains in the provinces, and falls passionately in love with an actress who treats him badly.

Henry goes to Paris as a student and is seduced by – or seduces – the wife of the head of the pension where he boards. After much passionate love-making, he persuades her to elope with him to America. But, as is usually the case with Flaubert, with possession comes disillusionment. The two lovers are crushed by the hardships which they have to endure in the New World. He is unable to obtain work, and she hankers after the pleasures of Paris. He finally brings her back to France, and she returns to her husband.

Then the interest shifts from Henry to Jules, who now

usurps the main attention. This is undoubtedly due to Flaubert's meditations during and after his illness, when he had withdrawn from the gay life of Paris, and had had leisure to reflect on its vanity. His conclusions, and his views on life and art, are probably the most important part of the novel.

Henry returns to the life of futile pleasure and ambition, and eventually makes a success in a worldly way. It is obvious that, by then, Flaubert was less interested in that life than in the life of the mind of Jules, who is shown as superior to Henry, as he is an artist.

The construction of the novel is not perfect. The two separate stories of Henry and Jules are linked together by letters, but the device is not very successfully worked out and the two portions remain divided and distinct. Flaubert was himself conscious that the construction was faulty and he considered that the novel required replanning, that a further chapter was needed to link the two parts and to show how the characters became what they did become.[21] In this chapter he would show 'how such and such an action brought such and such a result, in this character rather than in another. The causes are shown and the results also, but the connecting links between the cause and the effect are less well demonstrated. That is the vice of the book and how it belies its title.'

A very important part in the novel is the formulation of a philosophic conception of life and art.[22]

Jules, after his disappointment in love, at first seeks self-expression in Romantic literature, but, eventually, he comes to see the weaknesses of this ideal. This was the period in France when Romantic ideals were being seriously criticized, the beginning of the Art for Art's Sake Movement. The failure of *Les Burgraves* by Victor Hugo, in 1843, is generally accepted as the closing date of the Romantic Movement.

Jules abandoned Romanticism, as Flaubert was also to do:[23]

La tempête aussi perdit considerablement dans son estime; le lac avec son éternelle barque et son perpétuel clair de lune, lui parurent tellement inhérents aux keepsakes qu'il s'interdit d'en parler, même dans la conversation familière.

This is a criticism of Lamartine and we shall later see, in *Madame Bovary*, his ironic treatment of this poet:

Il dit un adieu sans retour à la jeune fille chargée de son innocence et au vieillard accablé de son air vénérable, l'expérience lui ayant vite appris qu'il ne faut pas toujours reconnaître quelque chose d'angélique dans les premières ou de patriarcal dans les seconds.

This leads Jules, like Flaubert, to study antiquity, to develop a passion for the past and to see the greatest poets amongst those who studied humanity and not themselves. He was to say the same thing to Louise Colet the following year, using Byron and Shakespeare to contrast the two ideals of literature.[24]

Jules has an intuition of the unity in the world, and his aim is to try to explain it. In this unity even ugliness has its place, and the duty of the artist is to find the harmony between the two elements of beauty and ugliness, and to express it:[25]

Alors il songea que tout ce qui lui paraissait si misérable autrefois pouvait bien avoir sa beauté et son harmonie; en les synthétisant et en les romenant à des principes absolus, il aperçut une symétrie miraculeuse rien que dans le retour périodique des mêmes idées devant les mêmes choses, des mêmes sensations devant les mêmes faits; la nature se prêtait à ce concert et le monde entier lui apparut reproduisant l'infini et reflétant la face de Dieu; l'art dessinait toutes ces lignes, chantait tous ces sons, sculptait toutes ces formes, en saisissait leurs proportions respectives, et par des voies inconnues les amenait à cette beauté plus belle que la beauté même, puisqu'elle remonte à l'idéal d'où celle-ci était dérivée, et qui produit en nous l'admiration, qui est la prière de l'intelligence devant la manifestation éclatante de l'intelligence infinie, l'hymne qu'elle lui chante dans sa joie en se reconnaissant de sa nature, et comme l'encens qu'elle lui envoie en gage de son amour.

Everything blends into this harmony and unity:[26]

Alors la suprême poésie, l'intelligence sans limites, la nature

sur toutes ses faces, la passion dans tous ses cris, le coeur humain
avec tous ses abîmes, s'allièrent en une synthèse immense dont
il respectait chaque partie par amour de l'ensemble, sans vouloir
ôter une seule larme des yeux humains ni une seule feuille aux
forêts.

Flaubert's view of beauty is very similar to that of Baudelaire, namely that beauty does not exist in the object itself
but only in what the artist brings to it.

Jules reaches the same point which Flaubert attained
when he finished composing his novel, that is to write for his
own pleasure alone, without any thought of worldly success
or appreciation. Writing to Louise Colet, the following year,
he said:[27]

No, I don't despise fame; one can't despise what one can't
attain. More than anyone else my heart used to beat at the sound
of that word. Formerly I spent long hours dreaming up for
myself startling triumphs, the acclaims of which used to make
me shiver as if I already heard them. But, I don't know why, one
fine day, I awoke completely freed from this desire, and more
completely than if it had been satisfied. If one has any value at
all then to run after success is to ruin oneself deliberately, and to
seek glory is perhaps to lose oneself entirely.

Jules's views of art were to be developed by Flaubert more
fully later in his correspondence with Louise Colet, and especially during the years when he was composing *Madame
Bovary*.

Jules's main ideas on art are that it must be impersonal
and not express the author; that Beauty and Truth are one
and the same thing; as are also form and substance. That
there is a unity in Beauty – as Flaubert was to say to Louise
Colet, many years later – that 'there is only one Beauty; it is
the same everywhere, but it has different aspects'.[28]

L'Éducation Sentimentale is Flaubert's first book with a
coherent philosophy of art, based on the unity in the world;
it is the duty of the artist to discover this unity. That con-
stitutes the great joy and ecstasy of the artist and his only
remedy against despair.

A philosophy of art and life does not necessarily make a good novel, but *L'Éducation Sentimentale* is very much more of a true novel than any of Flaubert's previous works. It has the texture of real life and takes into account the circumstances of the characters and their everyday life.

As fiction, the chief interest in *L'Éducation Sentimentale* is psychological, in the characters, and there is much more variety in their portrayal than in Flaubert's previous works; many more different types – especially amongst the minor people. Here is seen his later gift for outward portrayal, for significant detail, and his sense of irony and comedy. There is, for example, the portrait of Renaud, the head of the pension:[29]

Il paraissait malin à la première entrevue et bête à la seconde, il souriait souvent d'une manière ironique aux choses les plus insignifiantes, et, quand on lui parlait sérieusement, il vous regardait sous ses lunettes d'or avec une intensité si profonde qu'elle pouvait passer pour de la finesse; sa tête, dégarnie sur le devant et couverte seulement sur la nuque de cheveux blonds, grisonnants et frisés, qu'il laissait pousser assez longs et qu'il ramenait soigneusement sur les tempes, ne manquait pas d'intelligence ni de candeur; toutes les lignes saillantes de sa stature, qui était petite et ramassée sur elle-même, se perdaient dans une chair flasque et blanchâtre; il avait le ventre gros, les mains faibles et potelées comme celles de vieilles femmes de cinquante ans, ses genoux étaient cagneux et il se crottait horriblement dans la rue. ... Madame Renaud lui avait brodé une calotte grecque, fond de velours brun avec des fleurs bleues, dont il se couvrait le chef dans son cabinet.

There is also the spinster music teacher, Mademoiselle Aglaé:[30]

Mademoiselle Aglaé était une vieille fille de vingt-cinq ans, professeur de piano dans les *boarding schools for young ladies*, une femme très gracieuse et très maigre, ayant de superbes papillotes à l'anglaise qui lui caressaient les clavicules et les omoplates, qu'elle découvrait volontiers, en toute saison sans jamais attraper de rhume ni de fluxion de poitrine, quoiqu'elle semblât d'abord d'une délicate et tendre constitution. Ses pieds n'étaient

guère beaux, quoique le lacet de ses bottines de peau verdâtre
fût si serré que les oeillets manquaient de s'en rompre. Chose
déplorable, surtout pour une femme sentimentale, ses mains
étaient rouges et, l'hiver, abîmées d'engelures.

There are many more: Bernardi the actor manager; the
Lenoir family, with their little boy dressed as an artillery
officer, with his spurs and sword.

There are many dramatic and comic scenes, which show
great sense of humour and irony: the reception and ball at
the house of Madame Renaud; Henry's call on the fashionable man of letters; and many others.

In this novel Flaubert shows emotional maturity and
understanding in his description of the early ecstatic stage of
passion, followed by the satiety when love has grown sour.
This is very like the rising and waning of Léon's love for
Emma Bovary, when, as Henry realizes, 'leur passion, longtemps fermentée, commençait à s'aigrir comme les vieux
vins'.[31]

One of the strangest episodes in the whole novel is that of
Jules's nightmarish encounter with the dog. One evening
late, as he is wandering in the countryside, meditating on his
future and his past, he is followed by a mangy dog which
seems lost, and, try as he may, he cannot get rid of it. The
beast reminds him of a spaniel he had once owned, in his
youth, and which later he had given to Lucinde, the actress
with whom he was in love, because she had expressed a wish
to possess it. He is much affected by the dog which he imagines is a supernatural creature sent to warn him of the
death of his beloved. Then, having examined it from closer
quarters, he realizes that it is quite different, a very sick but
also very much alive dog, quite unknown to him. He tries all
sorts of means of getting rid of it, including stoning it so as
to wound it, but he is left only with a feeling of horrified
guilt. He manages at last to evade it and returns home, but,
going down later, he finds it lying on his doorstep. This ends
the chapter, and the dog is never mentioned again.

This episode has been more studied and analysed than

any other in the novel, and critics have tried to expound the
symbolism which they imagine they have found in it. There
have been various interpretations which are often more logical than imaginative. Shanks sees it as a kind of parable
proving that one cannot escape from one's past.[32] Demorest
believes it is an effort to fuse dream and reality.[33] While
Marianne Bonwit sees it as Jules's attempt to crystallize his
philosophy of life.[34] And Bruneau believes that the dog
represents everyday reality in contrast with the ecstasy which
Jules had experienced just before he encountered it. There
are many similar elucidations.[35] But enjoyment and appreciation of the episode do not depend on a logical solution,
and it is one of the most moving and terrifying passages in
the novel.

It is a very skilful and powerful evocation of a nightmarish
experience which many of us have lived through, which
seemed, at the time, to hold particular and sinister
significance, and which would only lose its terrifying and
moving quality if a key could be found for it.

In a masterly fashion Flaubert has succeeded in conveying
the various states of emotion of the hero. Particularly when
they pass near the water-mill, at the river-side, where he had
once contemplated suicide. The dog's barks increase in
volume and he seems to want to drag Jules to the edge of the
water to show him something:[36]

Puis il se rappela qu'un jour – oh! qu'il y avait longtemps! – il
était venu sur ce point et qu'il avait désiré mourir. Était-ce là ce
que voulait dire la bête funèbre qui tournait autour de lui? Qu'y
avait-il donc de caché dans la rivière pour qu'elle en parcourût
sans cesse le bord en se dirigeant toujours, il semblait, de la
source à l'embouchure, comme pour montrer quelque chose qui
aurait coulé dessus, qui serait descendu? N'était-ce pas Lucinde?
grand Dieu! était-ce elle? serait-elle noyée, perdu sous le torrent?
si jeune! si belle! morte! morte! Et plongeant ses regards dans les
ténèbres, au loin, bien avant, il s'attendait à voir ... il la voyait
avec sa robe blanche, sa longue chevelure blonde épandue, et les
mains en croix sur la poitrine, qui s'en allait doucement au courant, portée sur les ondes; elle était peut-être là, à cette place,

ensevelie sous l'eau froide, couchée au fond du fleuve, sur les
cailloux verts! 'Est-ce là ce que tu veux dire, avec ta voix qui
pleure comme si tu hurlais sur un tombeau?' Et il se figurait son
cadavre, la bouche entr'ouverte, les yeux fermées.

  Les nuages s'ouvrirent, et la lune, se dégageant de leurs flocons
grisâtres, apparut sur un fond du ciel bleu sombre bordé de
nuées noires; elles couraient vite et s'amoncelaient les unes sur
les autres au haut du ciel; la lune montait en suivant sa course,
quelquefois un de ses rayons tombait sur la rivière ou bien faisait
luire au loin les flaques d'eau restées dans les ornières de chemins
creux. En ce moment sa lumière éclaira le chien maudit qui hur-
lait toujours, elle dardait sur sa tête; il semblait, dans la nuit,
sortir de chacun de ses yeux deux filets de flamme minces et
flamboyantes, qui venaient droit à la figure de Jules et se rencon-
traient avec son regard; puis les yeux de la bête s'agrandirent
tout à coup et prirent une forme humaine, un sentiment
humain y palpitait, en sortait; il s'en déversait une effusion sym-
pathique qui produisait de plus en plus, s'élargissait toujours et
vous envahissait avec une séduction infinie. 'N'es-tu pas son ami,'
se demanda-t-il, 'que tu me regardes ainsi comme si tu voulais
entrer dans mon amitié? que veux-tu de moi?'

In superstitious terror Jules tries to kill the dog, but it always
returns to him. Finally he manages to make it flee, and he is
able to reach home:[37]

  Il pleuvait, c'était une nuit sombre, toute la ville dormait, les
réverbères suspendus balançaient leur lueur rougeâtre à
travers le brouillard, on n'entendait que la pluie tomber sur le
pavé, les gouttières crachaient du haut des toits, les ruisseaux
grossis coulaient dans les rues. Celle où demeurait Jules était
toute droite et rapide, les eaux du quartier supérieur s'y étaient
déversées et avaient passé par là, les grès brillaient comme si on
les eût lavés, la pluie fouettait dessus et rebondissait, c'était un
bruit grêle, régulier, continu; il détourna la tête ... non! il
s'était trompé.

Finally he reaches his home and locks himself in. He does
not go to bed, but remains for long hours, going over in his
mind the various stages of his experience with the monster,
and he comes to the conclusion that it had not been a dream
or a hallucination, that it had been a reality, though of

another kind than the one he was used to, but as true, never-theless, as common reality, even though it seemed to con-tradict it. He then decides that he would like another encounter with the creature, to see whether he would be, this time, the stronger. He wonders whether the dog has followed him home, and he longs for it, in spite of the terror it had inspired in him. He goes down to the door, saying to himself that this was only madness, and how stupid to contemplate such a thing – but supposing it was there. He opens the door and discovers the dog lying on the threshold.

This is the end of the story; no more is heard of the dog and no explanation is given. It is the most vivid and power-ful episode in the whole novel, leaving the reader with the horrified sensation of awaking from a nightmare, the mys-tery of which cannot be elucidated. This feeling could only be weakened by a logical and allegorical interpretation.

This episode could be extracted from the novel and pub-lished separately as a short story or a prose poem. It is, in the work, really a literary 'hors d'oeuvre', having little con-nection with the main trend of the novel.

Flaubert never thought of publishing *L'Éducation Sen-timentale*. He always lost interest in his books once they were completed, and Jules expresses the same indifference to his own work:[38]

Insoucieux de son nom, indifférent du blâme qu'il soulève ou de l'éloge qu'on lui adresse, pourvu qu'il ait rendu sa pensée telle qu'il l'a conçue, qu'il ait fait son devoir et ciselé son bloc, il ne tient pas à autre chose et s'inquiète médiocrement du reste.

He did once try to read it to his father, in an attempt to interest him in his literary future, but Du Camp tells us that Dr Flaubert fell asleep after a few pages.[39]

In this novel, finished when he was barely twenty-three, Flaubert laid the foundation of his future work. He knew now that nothing would ever again hold him back, as he was no longer wasting his time on the senseless study of law, and he saw what was to be his ideal of art.

But, although there is great technical progress and maturity between this novel and his earlier works, although it is more perfect as fiction than the others, for one reader, at least, it does not possess the lyric charm, nor the youthful moving quality of the best passages in *Novembre*, in spite of its technical imperfections.

Du Camp returned from his trip to the East in March 1845, determined to work hard and to further his literary career, but he intended also to help his friend, and to drag him along with him up the steep and slippery slopes of Parnassus. There is a touching quality in his earnestness and seriousness.

It was inevitable that there should, eventually, be opposition between the two friends. Du Camp imagined that Flaubert was still at the same stage where he had left him, and he did not realize the extent of the change which had taken place in him. He had been very much scarred by his experience; life, in the ordinary sense, no longer interested him, and worldly ambition meant nothing to him. There was bound to be a clash between their temperaments, so that their friendship would eventually wear thin. Nevertheless they took it up again, on Du Camp's return to France, where they had dropped it the previous year, and the following year, so warm was their affection still for one another, that Flaubert was able to say to Louise Colet:[40]

I'm very glad that you like Max. He's a fine, beautiful and great nature whose qualities I guessed from the first day, and to whom I've clung, as to a great discovery. There are, between us, too many points of contact in mind and in nature for us ever to fail one another. We've known one another now for four years; and it seems like a century, so much have we lived together, and through various kinds of fortune, through rain and shine. Love him like a brother of mine in Paris; trust him as you would me, and more in him than in me, for he's better than I am. He possesses more courage and delicacy than I do.

The break in their friendship was not to occur until five or six years had gone by.

[10]

The Tragic Year
(1845–6)

AFTER finishing *L'Éducation Sentimentale* in January 1845, Flaubert spent his time reading and studying; and discussing philosophical and occult subjects with Alfred Le Poittevin. He did not seem in a hurry to start on another book, nor did he consider trying to publish the novel which he had just completed.

It was in November 1844 that Flaubert's beloved sister Caroline had become engaged to Émile Hamard, who had been a school friend of his at the Collège Royal in Rouen. Hamard had lost his brother in April 1843, and his grief had drawn Caroline close to him in sympathy, then sympathy ripened into love.[1] He was an unhappy young man who already showed symptoms of the mental instability which was to develop later into insanity. Flaubert did his best to prevent the marriage, of which he did not approve, but in vain. Maxime Du Camp, on the contrary, was full of praise of him and delight at the thought of their union, but he was not such an acute judge of character as Flaubert.[2]

The young people were married on 3 March 1845, and, at first, lived in the lodgings which Hamard had occupied as a bachelor, postponing their honeymoon for some weeks. The honeymoon was planned in the extraordinary manner of the habitual journeys of the Flaubert family, and it recalls the trip which Flaubert had taken after he had passed his 'baccalauréat' in 1840. The newly-wed couple was accompanied by the bride's parents and her brother, and it was no wonder that it turned out such a disappointment to everyone.

On his way south Flaubert passed through Paris but he felt like an old Rip Van Winkle returning to his past after a century of sleep. He called on the Colliers, who had returned to the Champs Elysées, and found everything exactly the same as three years previously. The invalid was still reclining on her couch; the furniture and rugs were still the same; and the same old barrel-organ was playing, in the streets outside, the same old tunes. Nothing had changed, except himself, since the days when he had read *Hernani* and *René* to Henrietta. It was then that he realized her feelings for him but, although he was only twenty-three, he felt too old and weary for love.[3]

He did not see the Schlésingers on this visit, but he called on Madame Pradier who, by then, was separated from her husband, and added to his store of psychological knowledge for his later novels.

Flaubert spent most of the trip in a state of irritation, for he was feeling himself growing more different each day from others. Writing to Le Poittevin, he said:[4]

The more I advance the more incapable I feel of living the life of everyone, and of participating in family joys, of growing excited about what raises enthusiasm in others, of blushing at what makes others indignant. I try as much as I can to hide the sanctuary of my soul. Vain effort, alas! ... By everything that you hold most sacred, by Truth and Greatness, dear and gentle Alfred, don't travel with anyone! with no one! I wanted to see Aigues-Mortes; la Sainte Baume, and the grotto where Madeleine wept; the battle-field of Marius, etc. I've seen nothing at all because I wasn't alone, I wasn't free. This is the second time that I see the Mediterranean – like a grocer! Will the third time be any better?

On this trip he felt very close to Le Poittevin, so that he thought of him continuously and not of Du Camp.[5] He had planned, on passing through Marseilles, to call on Eulalie Foucaud. 'It will be strangely bitter and comic,' he wrote to Alfred,[6] 'especially if I find her grown ugly, as I fully expect.' But, in Marseilles, he found the hotel deserted. He wrote to Alfred Le Poittevin:[7]

They no longer own the Hôtel Richelieu – I passed in front of it – I saw the steps up to the door – the shutters are barred; the hotel is deserted – I could scarcely recognize it, isn't that a symbol? – how long have the shutters of my heart been barred, its steps neglected, a hotel formerly full of movement, but now empty and echoing like an enormous tomb without a corpse.

He talks to Le Poittevin of having given up all idea of love and he declares that art is a better substitute:[8]

The only way of not being unhappy is to bury oneself in art, and to count all the rest for nothing; pride replaces everything if it is founded on a broad enough base. As for me I'm well enough since I've accepted to be always ill! . . . But I regret neither riches, nor love, nor the joys of the flesh, and people are astonished to see me so wise. I've said a final and irrevocable farewell to life.

Flaubert kept a diary on the journey, but it is mostly in rough notes, though there are occasional well-written passages which show talent and mastery, as the one which describes the Place aux Foins at Toulon, where he draws a comparison between the square and the heart of man.[9] It looked exactly the same as it had looked when he had seen it last, when his heart had been young:

Quelle différence avec le coeur! les arbres ne conservent point la trace des orages qui ont courbé leurs branches, ni les sables légers que le vent fait mouvoir, celle des pas qui s'y sont imprimés; il n'en est pas de même de l'âme et de la figure des hommes: tout y marque. Eternel travail de mosaïque! les petites pierres s'incrustent par-dessus les grandes, le noir sur le blanc, le bleu à côté du rouge, les privations et les excès, les colères, les découragements et les enthousiasmes, bei mihi! bei mihi!

During the trip he was still thinking of what he calls his 'conte oriental' about which we have no information, whether it is *Smarh* or something else.[10]

But he received, at the Balbi Palace in Genoa, an 'illumination' – one of the strongest in his life – when he came upon the picture *The Temptation of Saint Anthony* by Breughel. This moved him greatly when all the other pictures in the gallery left him cold.[11] And he told Le Poittevin that he would give the whole collection of *Le Moniteur* and a hundred thousand francs to be able to purchase it.[12]

His first idea was that he would like to write a play on the subject. This was not to be, but, three years later, he was to compose his first *Tentation de Saint Antoine*, a philosophic work which is a return to his oriental inspiration and resembles his earlier *Smarh*. He had been prepared for his experience at the Balbi Palace by his renewed closer friendship with Alfred Le Poittevin during the previous year.

The trip was not proving a success. Dr Flaubert was suffering a great deal from his eyes, and Caroline seemed so continuously ill that her mother was very anxious on her behalf, for she had always been very delicate. Also Achille, who was taking most of his father's private patients in his absence, was beginning to complain that he was overworked, and he begged them to come back. It was eventually decided to cut short the honeymoon and to return to Rouen.[13] They were back home on 15 June 1845.

Caroline and her husband remained in Paris to look for a suitable apartment, but the rest of the family returned to Rouen, and they settled again in the house at Croisset. Flaubert was still at a loose end but he hoped to spend the summer bathing. His mother, however, would never allow him to go out alone for fear he should have another seizure, and he gave up sailing for he found it distasteful to have a servant always dragging round after him. He spent the summer studying Greek and reading Shakespeare and Voltaire. His passion for Shakespeare grew, but he found Voltaire's theatre boring to analyse; yet he persevered with it as he thought that it might be useful to him later.[14]

The family spent the summer at Tréport and after that there is complete silence in Flaubert's correspondence for some months, as it is then that all the tragedies occurred.

In November Dr Flaubert fell ill, with an abscess, or growth, in his thigh. His son performed an operation on him, which was not successful, and he died on 15 January 1846. He had been greatly beloved in the town and there was general mourning on the day of his funeral, as all work in the city closed down.

Six days after her father's death Caroline gave birth to a daughter. At first her condition gave rise to anxiety but then she seemed to mend and to be well on the road to recovery. Flaubert went to Paris to deal with some business in connection with his father's inheritance but, after some days, he was recalled home as she had contracted puerperal fever and was in a very dangerous state. Du Camp recounts[15] how, two days after Flaubert had left, his old great uncle Parrain arrived at eleven o'clock at night, with a letter from Madame Flaubert to say that her daughter was dying, that the doctors said that nothing further could be done for her, and begging him to bring Raspail immediately to her as he alone might be able to save her.

Then a nightmare adventure ensued. Du Camp did not know where Raspail lived, but he and Parrain went out to seek him. They managed to obtain his address from a chemist who had not yet shut up shop. There were two streets of the same name, in different parts of the city. At the second they discovered that Raspail had only a consulting room there and that he lived at the other end of Paris in the suburbs at Montrouge, but that he never let anyone in after eight o'clock at night.

At Montrouge they found everything in total darkness, but a butcher, who was preparing his load of meat for the following day, indicated Raspail's house to them. They knocked at the door for half an hour, and at last it was opened a crack by the terrified concierge, who did not dare answer their question as to where Raspail lived – at this time the old scientist was suffering from persecution mania and had the delusion that Louis-Philippe wanted to poison him. Du Camp assured him that the old man did not run any danger with them, and he finally explained that Raspail lived in the house at the end of the courtyard, in a garden surrounded by high walls, but he warned them that they would not be able to get in. Du Camp dragged old Parrain after him and, when they reached the wall, he managed, with his help, to climb up on to it. He could see nothing in the gloom but he jumped down into the garden and wandered in the darkness until he at last reached the two-storied house, in front of which a flight of stone steps led to a glass door. He put his finger on the bell and kept it there. A few minutes later a light appeared at one of the upstairs windows; it opened and a woman asked him what he wanted. After he had answered, the glass door downstairs lit up and he heard the bolts being drawn back. With his hat in one hand and his letter in the other, Du Camp ran up the steps, but he was received by a rifle held against his chest by Raspail who shouted: 'Halt!' Du Camp begged him to read Madame Flaubert's letter, which Raspail handed to his housekeeper asking her to read it to him, while he still kept Du Camp under aim. Then he said: 'You are indeed foolhardy, my dear boy. You've had a lucky escape, I took you for an officer of the watch!' However, he agreed to Madame Flaubert's plea and promised to be at the Gare de l'Ouest for the first train to Rouen in the morning. He kept his promise, but he found that he could do nothing for Caroline, as she was beyond human aid. 'The unfortunate young woman is doomed,' he said. 'They've perforated her stomach with their sulphate of quinine. I knew her father, Dr Flaubert, a man of great ability, but too sceptical. He would never believe that Louis-Philippe wanted to have me poisoned.' One is reminded of the scene in *Madame Bovary*, where Dr Larivière is called to the death-bed of Emma and has to explain to the distracted husband that he could do nothing for his wife.

Du Camp had been entrusted with two thousand francs to give Raspail for his trouble – about £80 in the currency of the day – but he refused to take a penny.

Flaubert arrived home to find his sister delirious and unable to recognize anyone. She was no longer aware that her father had died, and she thought that Ernest Chevalier, the friend of the whole of her life, was in the house.[16]

Writing to Maxime Du Camp, Flaubert said:[17]

Hamard has just gone out of my room, where he was sobbing, standing near the fire-place. My mother is a weeping statue. Caroline speaks, smiles, caresses us, says kind and affectionate words to all of us; she is losing her memory: she didn't know if it was I or Achille who had gone to Paris. What grace sick people have, and what strange gestures! The little baby feeds and cries. Achille says nothing, and doesn't know what to say. What a house! what hell! . . . It seems as if misfortune is going to pounce on us again, and that it won't leave until it has taken its fill of us. Once more I'll see the black hangings, and I'll hear the horrible sound of the nailed shoes of the coffin-bearers, coming down the stairs. I prefer to have no hope but, on the contrary, to enter in imagination into the grief to come.

Caroline Hamard died, after great suffering, on 20 March 1846, and she was only twenty-one.

Flaubert, as he watched beside his dead sister, opened the letters which he had received five years before, from Eulalie Foucaud. After he had read them, he wrote on the packet as he resealed it: 'Opened and read during the night of 20 to 21 March 1846, when I reread the letters from Marseilles with a strange sensation of regret. Poor woman, can she really have loved me? All my old affections repeat in my mouth like food which has not been properly digested, but has rotted in the stomach. A quarter to two.'

What made him reread these letters at this tragic time? Perhaps it was that Caroline had been, so far, the only feminine influence in his life, the only woman with whom he had been really intimate. The episode with the Colliers had not penetrated very deeply into his nature, and Élisa Schlésinger had been far above him, like a star. Then he thought of the woman who had written him the burning love letters, and he began to wonder whether she had really loved him and whether he might have loved her.

In a beautiful letter to Maxime Du Camp, Flaubert described his sensations at the funeral of his sister.[18] Some critics have accused him of being hard and insensitive because he could recount in so much detail these tragic personal feelings. The truth is that he minded it so much that he felt the necessity of making it concrete and not allowing it all to evaporate into nothingness. At such moments no palliative or comfort could be of any use to him, nothing could make it less horrible, and he wanted to feel it at its worst, with its full tragedy. The situation could not be made beautiful or fine; our grief and pain must be accepted and made permanent so that they should never fade:

I didn't want you to come here, as I was afraid of your affection, I had enough with the sight of Hamard without you. Perhaps you'd have been even less calm than we were. In a few days I'll call on you, and I count on you. It was yesterday, at 11 o'clock, that we buried the poor child. They dressed her in her wedding gown, with bunches of roses and violets. I spent the whole night at her wake. She was lying straight on her bed, in that room where you heard her playing. She seemed taller and more beautiful than when she was alive, with the long white veil which hung down to her feet. In the morning, when everything was over, I gave her a last kiss in her coffin. I bent over her, put my head in and I felt the lead yielding under my hands. It is I who had the death mask made. I saw the thick paws of these coarse fellows handling her and covering her with plaster. I'll have her hand and her face. I'll ask Pradier to do a bust of her and I'll put it in my room. I've got her big multi-coloured shawl, a lock of her hair, the table and the desk on which she wrote. That is all; that is all that remains of those whom we've loved! Hamard wanted to come with us. When we arrived up there, in the cemetery, behind the walls of which I used to go for a walk with the college, Hamard, at the edge of the grave, was sending her kisses as he wept. The grave was too narrow, the coffin wouldn't fit in. They shook it, turned it, pulled it in all directions; they took levers and, at last, one of the grave-diggers stamped on it – it was the place of her head – to fit it in. I was standing near, my hat in my hand; I threw it away, crying. I'll tell you the rest verbally, for I would write it too badly . . .

We are back at Croisset since Sunday. What a journey! alone with my mother and the child who was crying. The last time I left it, it was with you, do you remember? Of the four people who lived in it then, there are only two left. The trees haven't yet got their leaves, the wind is blowing, the river is full; the rooms are cold and neglected. My mother is better, better than she could be. She looks after the child of her daughter, puts her to bed in her own room, looks after her to the best of her ability. She is trying to become a mother once more; can she succeed in this? The reaction hasn't yet come, and I'm afraid of it.

Madame Flaubert retired permanently to Croisset, a figure of tragedy, and Flaubert feared for her reason and health; he thought that she could not live long, but, in fact, she was to live for another twenty-six years.

Achille Flaubert succeeded his father as Master of the Hôtel Dieu and moved into the Lodgings. Flaubert inherited from his father what was a good income for these days, especially as it was in the nature of pocket money, for he lived at home with his mother and had no living expenses.

He imagined now that he was going to console himself with the closest and dearest of all his friends, Alfred Le Poittevin, and continue his friendship with him. Alfred, however, married in July that year, 1846, a Mademoiselle de Maupassant – the sister-in-law of his sister Laure Le Poittevin – and Flaubert felt that this was his third bereavement of the year, for Alfred would be twice dead for him, first by his marriage and secondly because he was leaving Rouen. He was heartbroken at this break in his long and valued friendship with the man he held nearest to his heart and mind. He wrote to him to express his disappointment and his grief:[19]

As you didn't ask for my advice, it would not be seemly for me to give you any. It won't thus be of that that we'll speak. I've many presentiments. Unfortunately I've very long sight – I believe that you are in a state of illusion, in an enormous one, as moreover one is each time that one takes any Action, of whatever kind it may be. Are you certain, great man, that you won't end up as a bourgeois? I linked you in all my dreams of art. It is that side which makes me suffer most of all.

It is too late! Let what may be happen! You'll always find me there. It remains to be seen whether I'll still find you. Don't contradict me! Time and things are too strong for us. It would need a whole volume to enlarge on a single word in this page. If nobody more than I wishes for your happiness, no one more than I doubts of it. By the very fact that you are seeking it, you are doing an abnormal thing. If you love her, so much the better. If you don't love her try to love her.

Will there still be, between us, these *arcana* of ideas and feelings inaccessible to the rest of the world? Who can answer? No one.

Come to see me, or I'll go to see you when you wish. Only write to me at least a day in advance because now I occasionally go to Rouen to help in the move . . .

If nothing prevents you, try to come on Tuesday, that would suit me very well.

Farewell, *Carissimo*.

[11]

Louise Colet
(1846–8)

In July 1846 Flaubert went to Paris to commission from Pradier a bust of his sister Caroline, and, one day, in the studio, he met a beautiful and brilliant woman. Pradier introduced him to her, saying: 'Here is a young man whom you can help with your literary advice.'

This was Louise Colet, poet and Academy prizewinner, then thirty-six years old and at the height of her beauty and fame.

Flaubert fell in love with her at first sight, and this was the one passionate attachment of his life, the only one to which he gave himself wholeheartedly – in the first stages at all events. He may have posed as having had a wide experience of love but, up to date, it was largely theoretical, and the only relationship he is known to have had before that with Louis Colet was the one with Eulalie Foucaud when he was eighteen, which had lasted little more than a day.

Louise Colet, née Revoil, was born in Aix-en-Provence in 1810.[1] From her earliest years she had possessed great beauty, which caused her to be spoilt by her family and everyone whom she met. Even as a girl she showed talent for poetry and she reached the age of twenty in 1830, at the height of the Romantic Movement, when literature was particularly favourable to women.

Louise Revoil was taken up by Julie Candeille, who, as Madame Périé, held one of the most famous salons in Nîmes at that time.

Unfortunately Monsieur Périé died in 1833, and his wife in 1834, in the same year as Louise's mother, and she was left alone. She went, for a time, to live with a married sister in

Nîmes and there she met Hippolyte Colet once more, whom she had known earlier at the salon of Madame Périé. He was a musician of some talent, though not of the highest, and he had missed the Prix de Rome, but, in 1834, he obtained a post at the Paris Conservatoire. He fell in love with Louise, as most men did, and she saw in him the means of escaping from her restricted circumstances, and of getting to Paris. They were married on 5 December 1834, when they were both twenty-four. They went immediately to Paris, but they lived very poorly as his salary was low, and they could not afford a servant. She felt that she was getting nowhere and that she had made a great mistake in marrying Colet. He was not being a success at the Conservatoire and he managed to antagonize the Director, Cherubini, so that he destroyed his hopes of promotion.

Then Louise thought of making a book of her earlier poems, but she needed someone important to introduce her, and her choice fell on the most eminent writer of the day – she was never one to err through modesty – on Chateaubriand himself. She sent him a selection of her poems and called on him to flatter him. Then she dared to ask him to write a preface to her collection of poems. He refused politely, in a conventionally worded letter, saying that only a poet should introduce a poet, and threw in a few empty compliments to pacify her. She managed to find a publisher for her collection of poems, *Fleurs du Midi,* which appeared in 1836, and she printed, as a preface, Chateaubriand's letter. This was her first act in pushing herself forward into the notice of men in high places. It must be admitted that few withstood the power of her beauty, and most of the great writers of the day wrote flatteringly to her, and of her.

In the meantime *Fleurs du Midi* was not receiving a very favourable press and Louise Colet was beginning to despair. She was, however, very good at becoming acquainted with important people, and somehow she managed to get to know Marie-Louise of Orleans, the daughter of Louis-Philippe, who obtained for her her first government grant. At the

Archives Nationales in Paris, there is a complete dossier of the amounts which she received at various times in her career, and they represent considerable sums of money.[2]

Next she brought herself to the notice of the fashionable poet Béranger, who was flattered by the attentions of the pretty young woman, and he encouraged her to compete for one of the Academy poetry prizes. The subject for the prize that year was *Le Musée de Versailles*. It happened that one of the pieces of sculpture in the museum, in the new historical gallery, was a statue of Joan of Arc by Marie-Louise of Orleans. The young princess had died in January 1839, and Louise Colet, very cleverly, based her poem dealing with the museum of Versailles on the statue and on the tragic death of the princess. She was awarded the prize and had her day of triumph when she received it at a public session of the Academy.[3]

It was probably then that she met Victor Cousin, the eminent philosopher, who was to become Minister of Education the following year, in 1840, and he helped her assiduously to obtain further government grants. They became lovers, and she bore him a daughter. He was to provide for her for the next eighteen years until they finally parted.

Louise Colet received a gold medal from the King in 1843, which was said to be as 'a reward and an encouragement'.[4]

She was merciless in her pursuit of people to publish notices of her books. There was, however, one critic who was able to withstand her wiles, who was not captivated by her beauty, and that was Sainte-Beuve. When she tried to extract an article from him he answered:[5]

I do not understand the letter which you have paid me the honour of writing to me. . . . I do not think that there is any decree which obliges me to speak, in public, of your poetry. What! must I, under pain of seeming to fail you, explain to the public where I admire and where I cease from admiring you.

And again:[5]

Since the first day, a long time ago now, when I had the honour of meeting you at the house of Dr Aliberti, when you asked me for a preface; until the last time when I had the honour of meeting you, when you asked me for an article, this question of an article and literary criticism, has always been the first between us. I ask you for one thing only, and that is to be permitted to admire you in silence, without being obliged to explain to the public where I cease from admiring you. This request seems to me, Madame, a modest one, and I believe that you will not try to insist on my dropping it. It would, in any case, be in vain, for I have no leisure, and I am determined to choose for myself the subjects which I wish to study.

She took her revenge on him later – but only after his death – by publishing a vindictive article against him.

However, some journalists were antagonistic to her and Alphonse Karr attacked her, in his satirical paper, *Les Guêpes – The Wasps* – in June 1840, on the score of her pregnancy:

Madame Revoil, after a union of several years with M. Collet (sic) has, at last, seen Heaven bless her marriage – and she is about to give birth to something other than an Alexandrine – when the venerable Minister of Education heard of the circumstances – he understood his duty to literature – and he did for Madame Collet what he would doubtless have done for every other woman of letters. He surrounded her with care and attention; he does not allow her to go out except in his own carriage. At dinner at M. Pongerville's house – although tired and longing to go home, he waited for the interesting poet, to bring her home in his own brougham. . . . Everyone hopes that he will not refuse to be the godfather of the expected child.

It has been generally said that Karr had declared that the event was due to 'une piqûre de cousin', that is to say the sting of a gnat – the word 'cousin' in French means gnat. But this is a later invention which does not exist in the article – it is the kind of joke which a wit would not be able to resist.

When Louise read the article, incensed by Karr's venom, she went to his house and attacked him with a kitchen knife. He managed to disarm her and he hung the knife on the wall of his study with the inscription 'donné par Madame Colet, née Revoil, dans le dos.'

What Louise never doubted was her beauty and her intellect. One day she informed an assembled company: 'You know they've now found the arms of the Venus of Milo!' Someone asked 'Where?' and she replied: 'In the sleeves of my dress!'[6]

In a poem entitled *À La Gloire*, published in her collection *Ce qu'on rêve en aimant*, she speculates on her future fame with a complete absence of self-consciousness:

> La poésie un jour m'a dit: 'Tu seras reine!'
> Et dans ma frêle main j'ai pris son étendard,
> Et je poursuis la route étoilée et sereine,
> Que l'idéal altier me traçait au départ.
>
> J'entrevois sur ma tombe une foule soumise,
> Un immortel vieillard me dit: 'Tu m'es promise!'
> Et mon front couronné s'appuie au fond du Temps.

Flaubert later, when he had grown tired of her airs, said to her about this poem:[7] 'It is the same as your sonnet *À la Gloire*, that is unreadable, and the reader will always be indignant about the superiority which the author attributes to herself.'

At the time when Flaubert met her, in 1846, Louise Colet was still married to Hippolyte Colet, and kept by Victor Cousin, who was supporting her and her daughter. This did not, however, prevent her from indulging her affections elsewhere as well.

It was on 29 July 1846 that Louise and Flaubert first met, and, on 4 August, they became lovers. Since the death of his sister, six months before, he had been living with his mourning mother and his orphaned infant niece, and he was starved for feminine companionship. It was no wonder that he fell in love with the beautiful woman who flung herself at his head. There is no doubt that he was passionately in love with her, and she also with him. She felt, she declared in a poem, entitled *Le Baiser du Poète*, dated 4 August 1846, and published in *Ce qui est dans le Coeur des Femmes*, inspired by him:

Si du bonheur j'ai le tressaillement,
C'est que je sens une clarté divine
Par ce baiser passer dans ma poitrine,
C'est que je crois, poète créateur,
Que votre esprit que la muse domine,
Répand en moi son souffle inspirateur.
Oui, par un Dieu, mon âme est possédée,
Et dans mon sein il fait germer l'idée,
La fleur, dit-on, est ainsi fécondée
Par le baiser des vents de l'équateur.

Their relationship is divided into two parts, with a break of more than three years separating them. The first part, the more passionate, lasted less than two years and was terminated by Flaubert in the spring of 1848. He took up the relationship again in July 1851, just when he was planning *Madame Bovary*. It may have been a deliberate action on his part, because he needed her material for the creation of his heroine.

It was to Louise Colet that Flaubert wrote the six score letters which are amongst the most interesting in the French language. Those in the two periods of their relationship are very different in quality. In the first they were passionate at the beginning, and then full of recriminations, but literary discussion does not play the most important part in them. Those of the second period contain Flaubert's most interesting reflections on the nature and the function of art. For the whole of that time he was in the throes of the composition of *Madame Bovary*, and he seems to have been trying out his theories on Louise Colet – or else he was merely expressing what was uppermost in his mind.

At first he used to write every day – sometimes even twice a day – immensely long letters which take up seven, eight or nine pages in the printed edition of his correspondence. But, even then, the thought that she might expect a letter every single day, he felt, would inhibit him. Even at the beginning she seems to have been insisting on constant attention from him:[8]

You tell me, for instance, to write to you every day, and if I don't do it, you'll accuse me. Well! the idea that you want a letter each morning, would prevent me from doing it. Allow me to love you in my own way, in the way of my own being, with what you call my originality. Don't force me in anything, and I'll do everything. Understand me and don't accuse me. If I considered you frivolous and foolish, like other women, I'd pay you in words, promises, pledges. What would it cost me? But I prefer to remain rather below than above the truth of my heart.

Nevertheless, he lived in a state of bliss when he thought constantly of her. He carried away her bedroom slippers with him, and he could conjure up her image by gazing at them. There was some fetishism in his emotion and he was to remember this later when depicting Léon in *Madame Bovary*.

At first they were ecstatically happy together. Writing to her, when he got home, after their first night together, he said:[9]

Twelve hours ago we were still together; yesterday, at this time, I was holding you in my arms ... do you remember? ... How far away that all seems! The night is now warm and sweet; I hear the tulip tree, which is under my window, trembling in the wind, and, when I lift my head, I can see the moon which is reflected in the river. Your little slippers are there while I'm writing; I have them under my eyes and I'm looking at them. I have just put away, alone and locked up, the things that you gave me; your two letters are in the embroidered case; I'm going to reread them when I've sealed mine. I didn't want, to write to you, to use my usual notepaper, which is black bordered; so that nothing sad should go from me to you. I would like to cause you nothing but joy and to surround you with calm and continuous happiness, to repay you a little for all that you gave me in handfuls out of the generosity of your love. I'm afraid of being cold, dry and selfish, and yet God knows what, at this moment, is happening in me. What a memory and what desire! Ah! our two drives in the carriage! How beautiful they were, the second especially, with the fireworks! I remember the colour of the trees lit up by the lamps, and the movement of the springs; we were alone and happy. I gazed at your head in the darkness, I saw it in spite of the night; your eyes lit up your whole face. It seems to me that I'm writing all this very badly; you'll read it coldly; I'm not saying anything that I'd like to say. My sentences beat together, like sighs; to understand them one would need to fill in the blanks, which separate one from the other; you'll do it, won't you? Will you pause to dream at each letter, at each sign of the writing? As I do, as I gaze at your little brown slippers, I think of the movement of your foot when it filled them, and that they were warm.

Her letter, however, when it came, expressed doubt of his love, complaints of his coldness, and offers to release him, never to see him again – this was to be her theme song with him, through all the years of their relationship. Or perhaps he feared that she might have misunderstood the cause of his temporary physical failure with her:[10]

And I, tell me how do I strike you? How does my image arise before your eyes? What a poor lover I am, am I not? Do you know that what happened to me with you had never happened to me before (I was worn out from the previous three days, and my nerves were stretched taut like cello strings). If I'd been a man to have a high opinion of my own person, I'd have been bitterly dismayed; I was, but for your sake. I was afraid that you might, on your part, have suppositions insulting to yourself; others might have thought that I was insulting them. They would have thought me cold, indifferent or worn out. I was grateful to you for your spontaneous understanding, which was astonished by nothing; as for me I was astounded by it all as an unheard of monstrosity.

But misunderstandings grew between them. She understood love very differently from the way he did. She thought that he should want to go to Paris constantly to see her, to be with her, whenever she called on him. He said that he was coming soon, but 'soon' meant something different to her than to him. To her it was immediately. It was incomprehensible to her that he should tell her that he needed a pretext to leave home, as he did not want to add to his mother's worries, and she was always anxious when he was long out of her sight.[11] Neither could he invite her to Croisset as he was afraid of what the neighbourhood would say, as they would know of her visit the very next day.[12] 'So you're guarded like a young girl?' she asked contemptuously.[13] He answered her:[14]

Accuse me, abuse me in your heart, as much as you like. God, if there is a God, can read in my conscience, if I've got a conscience. A word of advice while I think of it, if you want at all costs to come and see me; and do you not believe that I don't dream of that, and that I don't imagine lovely pictures of it. Don't ever come here, it would be impossible, topographically speaking, for us to meet ... it would be better if you stopped at Rouen, you'd come in the morning, having given me notice the day before; I'd give the pretext of some business, and I'd be back here at six o'clock.

He never allowed her letters to be addressed directly to himself; they had to be sent care of Du Camp, who knew what they were and redirected them in another envelope.[15]

Like many creators – like Balzac, for instance – he could be quite happy writing to the object of his love, thinking of her, gazing at the things which had belonged to her – as he did with her bedroom slippers, her handkerchief and her lock of hair; all these he kept in a special casket, always at his side:[16]

Then night falls, and I'm alone, safe from being disturbed, and when, around me, everyone is asleep, I open the drawer of the little wall-rack, which I've mentioned to you, and I take out my relics, and spread them on my table; the little slippers first, the handkerchief, the locks of your hair, the case which contains your letters; I reread them, I touch them again. It is the same with letters as with kisses, the latest is always the best. This morning's one is there, between my last sentence and the one which isn't finished yet; I've just reread it, so as to be able to see you better, and to smell more strongly your perfume. I see, in imagination, the pose you must have had as you wrote to me, and the long gaze you must have had as you turned the pages. It was beneath the lamp, which illuminated our first kisses, and on the table where you compose your poems. Light it in the evening, your alabaster lamp; look at its pale white light, as you remember that night when we loved one another. You said to me that you didn't want to use it again. Why? It is something of us. I love it.

Soon she began to make him feel guilty, as he was not able to respond to her as she would have liked. She wanted all his thoughts at all hours of his waking day, and she was always accusing him of not loving her enough:[17]

Do you know that you are cruel? You accuse me of not loving you, and you use the argument of my departures. That is wrong! Can I stay? What would you do in my place?

You talk of your grief; I believe in it, I have the proof of it, and I feel it in me, what is more. But I see another grief, a grief here at my side, which never complains, which even smiles and beside which yours, however deep it may be, will never be more than a sting beside a burn, a convulsion beside a death rattle. Here is the vice in which I'm held. The two women whom I most love have put in my heart a bit with two reins, by which they hold me; they pull me alternately, by love and by grief. Forgive me if this angers you again. I no longer know what to say to you; I hesitate now when I speak to you, I'm afraid to make you cry, and, when I touch you, to wound you . . .

I love in my own way; more or less than you? God only knows. But I love you, and when you tell me that I've perhaps done for common women what I've done for you, I've done it for *no one*, no one – I swear it. You're the only person for whom I've made a journey, and that I've loved enough for that, because you're the first person who has loved me as you love me. No, never before you has anyone else wept the same tears, or looked at me with such a tender and sad look. Yes, the memory of the night of Wednesday is my sweetest memory of love. It is that one, if I were to become old tomorrow, that would make me regret life.

But what terrified him most of all was her insistence, from the very beginning of their relationship, on wanting a child by him. Scarcely three weeks after their first night together, he reproached her with this 'idée fixe' in an unpublished portion of a letter:[18]

You consider complacently, in the sublime egoism of your love, the hypothesis that a child might be born. You want it, admit it, you wish it as a link that would unite us more, like an inevitable contract that would rivet one to the other our two destinies. Oh! it must be because it is you, my dear and too tender friend, that I don't bear you a grudge for a desire so frightful for my happiness.

And he went on to say that, if it was necessary, in order to prevent this child from being born, for himself to die, he would willingly throw himself into the Seine with a weight around his neck.

She kept on begging him to go away with her so that they could be alone together:[19]

What would be royal, and magnificently beautiful, would be if you could go the sixty leagues to spend a few hours in the little summer house over here. . . . But what is the point of dreaming of such madness. It's impossible; for the whole country would know of it the very next day; and there would be never-ending gossip. A long kiss, nevertheless, for having thought of it.

At last he agreed that they should meet at Mantes, a pretty little town, half-way between Paris and Rouen, and on one of the few railway lines, the direct one from the capital to the coast. There they were to meet at the Hôtel du Grand Cerf, which still stands there and has little altered in the intervening years. He stipulated, however, that he must get home the same night, as it would be impossible otherwise, but they would have the whole afternoon together.[20]

It was her turn now to be difficult, and she made him feel petty and mean for having offered only so short a time, and she sent him a letter of abuse.[21] Finally she agreed to his plan, and he was overcome with grateful delight:[22]

Ah! we'll be alone, quite alone, by ourselves, in this village in the country (and around us silence). Why are you so sad? I've the anticipation of a day of happiness. One day is very little isn't it? But a wonderful day illuminates a whole year, and one has so few days to live that, when it happens, a good day is worth the trouble of enjoying. But will you be good? Will you weep again?

They ended by spending also the night at Mantes as they could not tear themselves away from one another, but he had not warned his mother that he might not be home, and she had been anxious all night:[23]

I arranged a little story that my mother believed, but the poor woman was very anxious yesterday. She went at eleven o'clock to the station; she spent an entirely sleepless night worrying. This morning I found her at the arrival platform, in a state of extreme anxiety. She made no reproach, but her face was the greatest reproach anyone could make.

This day at Mantes was the highest point in the happiness of the two lovers, and Flaubert always kept a special affection for the place, so that he could hardly bear to go back to it – it is true that he later also associated Louis Bouilhet with it, who had lived there for a time. When a friend asked him, very much later, in 1873, to visit her there, he had answered:[24]

When you insist that I should go to visit you at Mantes, don't you feel that you're asking me to do something which is not without sorrow for me? Every time I go by the station and catch sight of the spire of that dear little town, where I spent so many delightful hours, my heart turns over in me, and I can scarcely keep back a sob. That's the truth.

After he got back to Croisset, Flaubert wrote immediately to Louise to express his joy:[25]

It was I who stayed last. Did you see how I was looking at you, until the end? You turned your back, you left and I lost sight of you. . . . Do you know that this was our finest day. We loved one another even better than ever. We experienced exquisite pleasure. Oh! I'm not tired this evening. I slept for three hours this afternoon, and if you were here, you would find me, like yesterday, fresh, strong and passionate . . .

How good was our hotel at Mantes, our boatman, and the intelligent assistant in the bookstall, at the railway station. How far away all that seems now. How well filled were these twenty hours! I was proud when you told me that you'd never experienced such happiness. Your joy inflamed me. And I, did I please you? Do tell me, it is sweet to me.

When shall we meet again?

Everything was so happy wasn't it? Nothing constrained us, and I didn't say anything, it seems to me, to wound you, and neither did you to me. What a beautiful memory! . . .

You said one thing, which gave me great pleasure, and that is: 'Even if we were to separate, we would always keep each of the other, a good memory, *un bon souvenir.*'

Louise was to call the poem, which commemorates this afternoon, *Souvenir*.

Enclosed in one of Flaubert's notebooks – *carnets* – which are preserved in the Bibliothèque de la Ville de Paris, there is a text called *Souvenir*, which is certainly by Louise Colet, and which gives a reflection of what they had experienced at Mantes.[26] She begins with a quotation from a letter by Flaubert:[27]

It seems to me as if ten years had gone by since we were at Mantes. It is far, far away. That memory appears to me in a glorious and melancholy distance, shimmering in a vague colour and, at the same time, bitter and burning. It is beautiful in my memory, like a sunset on snow. The snow is my present life; the sun shining on it, is the memory, a burning reflection which illuminates it.

Then follows a poem by Louise Colet, dated September 1846, and after that a reflection, also by herself:

I wrote these lines for you alone, and I would like them to be better, to please you better. In sentiment and rhythm, there is perhaps some beauty in the poem, but its form is not pure enough, not polished enough. I would like perfection. The necessity of finishing another piece of work prevents me. But if, a year hence, you still love me, if this memory of Mantes does not then find you indifferent, I shall work on the piece, line by line, composed especially for you, I shall try to make it more worthy of you.

Although Flaubert could laugh, when he read, in the poem, the description of himself as 'un buffle indompté des déserts d'Amérique', and could gently chide her for describing the shrimps that were fished out of the Seine for their supper, which he called 'a geographical culinary howler',[28] his critical faculty seems to have deserted him when he praised a certain verse in the poem:[29]

> Ton bras enlaçait ma ceinture;
> Ton cou vers mon cou se tendait
> Et ta lèvre embaumée et pure
> A ma lèvre se suspendait.
> Deux langues dans la même bouche
> Mêlaient d'onctueux lèchements,
> Nos corps unis broyaient la couche
> Sous leurs fougueux élancements.

'These are moving lines,' he said, 'which would stir a stone, all the more myself.'

We have seen how often Louise had expressed a longing to have a child by him, although he assured her that such an idea brought cold shivers down his spine. After the visit to Mantes there was terror in his heart for some time. He expressed anxiety at her intermittent bouts of sickness, 'and that cursed blood that doesn't come'.[30] She assured him that she had often missed before without any specific reason, but he urged her to make certain. 'If you don't try, what I advise, some medicine to bring back the English' – that is the redcoats – 'how will you ever be able to be certain about the reason for their absence?' He ends by begging her to destroy his letter as it would be, he says, 'more prudent'. It is surprising to find Flaubert, the apostle of 'le mot juste', using such a comic euphemism as 'the English soldiers' for the menses.

A few days later, however, anxiety was relieved. He wrote to her in an ecstasy of happiness:[31]

So much the better if I've no posterity. My obscure name will die with me, and the world will go on its way, as if I was leaving an illustrious one . . .

Oh! I must embrace you I'm so moved! I'm weeping! Oh! let me kiss you on that poor heart which beats for me. Oh! you're so good and devoted. . . . No! I've never been loved as you love me, you're right to say it. I'll never be so again! It only happens once in a life-time, so that one should remember it for ever, and so that, when one dies, one blesses the memory.

Nevertheless, she continued to tell him of her longing to have a child and, in December, there was a further alert which, like the previous one, was eventually unfounded. He wrote to her in December:[32] 'Thank goodness, if the English have landed! I've not spoken to you about the subject for some time; you told me that it distressed you, but I thought about it none the less.'

He was very often now weary of her and was discovering how different they were in all their ideas about everything. He was clear-sighted and accurate, while she was sentimental and gushing. He thought that passionate love was unimportant, while she believed in all the romantic clichés of eternal love. He tried to discuss matters reasonably and sincerely with her, but that was not what she wanted; she needed constant flattery and protestations of undying love. His letters – in the early days at all events – were passionate, but that was not sufficient; she wanted his physical presence and to be installed in the centre of his life. Yet, scarcely two months after they first met, he said to her:[33]

It isn't everything to be loved! Life can't be spent in expressions of tenderness. That is good, it is exquisite at rare and solemn moments. What makes the days sweet, is the expansion of the mind, a communion of ideas, confidences of one's dreams, of all that one longs for, of all that one thinks.

He went on to say that he was shocked and scandalized with her attitude to art, and how little she cared for it. 'Art the only true and good thing in life. How can you compare a human love with it.'

She once had the audacity to suggest that they should write a book together, in collaboration, and this was a mark of condescension on her part as she was the famous author and he had published nothing. He pretended to be flattered by her suggestion and put her off by saying that he was not yet ready for publication.[34]

For her, art was a means of self-expression – a *déversoir* for personal feelings Flaubert called it. What she prized was the tinsel fame and she wanted the same thing for him. But she wanted, most of all, that he should glorify her as Lamartine had glorified Elvire; as Victor Hugo had sung Juliette Drouet. What was the point otherwise of having an artist as a lover? For her, art was the means of bringing glory – *la gloire* – to the individual. Even the memory of their day at Mantes was poisoned for him by the difference in their ideals, and he realized that they could never be at one on this subject:[35]

You wish me to be frank? Well, I'll be so! One day at Mantes, under the trees, you said that you would not give your happiness for the fame – *la gloire* – of Corneille. Do you remember? Haven't I a good memory? If you only knew what ice you poured into my entrails, and what amazement you caused me! *La gloire! la gloire!* But what is fame? It is nothing! It is the external noise of the pleasure that Art procures us. For the fame of Corneille! but to be Corneille! to feel oneself Corneille!

Besides I've always seen you mix up with Art a host of other things, patriotism, love – what have you? A heap of things which for me, are foreign to it and which, far from ennobling it, in my eyes, diminish it. Here is one of the chasms between us. It is you who dug it and who showed it to me.

Their views on art were very different. He had been horrified, when she had expressed delight at some 'tableaux vivants' which she had seen and which, she said, were preferable to the paintings of the Masters because they were pulsating with life:[36]

Tu me dis: Aime l'art, il vaut mieux que l'amour;
Tout sentiment s'altère et doit périr un jour!

Pour que le coeur devienne une immortelle chose,
Il faut qu'en poésie il se métamorphose.

Et moi je te réponds: La langue du poète
Ne rend du sentiment que l'image incomplète;
Concevoir le désir, goûter la passion,
Nous fait dédaigner l'art et sa création;
Formuler les pensers dont notre esprit s'enivre,
Ce n'est que simuler la vie: aimer, c'est vivre:
C'est incarner le rêve, et sentir les transports
Dont l'art ne peut donner que les emblèmes morts!

Des maîtres les plus grands les oeuvres les plus belles,
Auprès du beau vivant, compare, que sont-elles?
Corrège et le Poussin, Titien et Raphaël,
Rubens, dont la palette est prise à l'arc-en-ciel,
Éblouissant nos yeux, ont groupé sur leurs toiles
Des visages divins et de beaux corps sans voiles!
Mais hier, quand soudain à nos regards charmés
Ces tableaux immortels se trouvaient animés,
Lorsqu'au lieu de la chair que la couleur imite,
Nous avons admiré cette chair qui palpite,
Où le sang à travers l'épiderme soyeux,
Circule en répandant des reflets lumineux.

Lorsque nous avons vu d'exquises créatures,
Dont les beaux torses nus, les bras aux lignes pures,
Le sein ferme et mouvant, le visage inspiré,
Faisaient vivre à nos yeux quelque groupe sacré,
Oh! n'as-tu pas senti combien sont imparfaites
Toutes ces oeuvres d'art que les hommes ont faites,
Et ne t'es-tu pas dit, du réel t'enivrant:
La beauté seule est belle, et l'amour seul est grand.

She took offence at everything he said, and saw insults
where none were intended. When he called her 'chère vieille
amie' she imagined that this was a reflection on her
age.[37]

She accused him of talking literature with her, as with
anyone else, when they might be discussing themselves; of
talking art as to some indifferent person:[38]

And do you discuss Art with indifferent people? You consider the subject as secondary, as something amusing, between politics and the news. Not me, not me!

She was jealous of his past – of his earlier women friends, particularly of Eulalie Foucaud. She was jealous of his present and suspected what he might be doing when he was not with her. One evening she forced her way into a private room at the restaurant, *Les Trois Frères Provinciaux*, expecting to find him with a rival, but she found him alone with Du Camp and Bouilhet, who had taken a private room in order to be able to discuss their literary business away from the noisy restaurant below.[39]

She made a fuss because he did not send her gifts to celebrate anniversaries; when he left her without kissing her:[40]

I felt guilty for having left you, as if I had done wrong; but I couldn't do otherwise, I had to. You say that I didn't want to kiss you; but it is you who refused. Do you remember that I wanted to take your hand in your muff and that you held it closed? But not for a second did I bear you any grudge. You were making me too unhappy; all this turned against me and tore me inwardly. How weak I am! I who thought myself so strong, here am I trembling as I write to you; my heart is beating. Oh! before the week is out, on Friday or Saturday at latest, I'll see you again. I count the hours, I remain beside my fire waiting for the days to pass, thinking of you and of nothing but you.

In letter after letter she wanted assurance that he loved her and she put the question again and again. This obviously got on his nerves and he answered several times harshly, in impatience:[41]

You want to know if I love you, to settle the matter once and for all and to end it frankly. Isn't that what you wrote to me yesterday? It is a question too big to be answered by 'YES' or 'NO'. Nevertheless it is what I'll try to do so that you shan't accuse me any more of being devious . . .

For me, love is not, and cannot be, in the forefront of life; it must remain in the background. There are other things before it, in the soul, which are, it seems to me, nearer to the light, nearer to the sun. So if you consider love as the main meal of existence: NO. As a dressing YES!

If you understand by loving to have an exclusive pre-occupation with the loved one, to live only for him, to see only him in the world, in all that there is in the world, to be full of thought of him ... to feel that your whole life is bound to that life and that that has become a particular organ of your soul: NO!

She called him mean and miserly, and declared that his attitude of mockery – she must have meant his irony – had killed her love. She tried to diminish him in his own eyes:[42]

Formerly I seemed to you sublime; but now I seem to you pitiable. But I'm neither one nor the other, and at bottom I am no more of a scoundrel than anyone else.

In the end she thought – or said – that it would be better that they should part, and he agreed with her:[42]

Well since you are so keen on it, agreed! Since you find nothing further to say to me, frankness compels me to confess that I've no more on my side, having exhausted all possible forms to make you understand what you've refused to understand for the past five months. Nevertheless I've used up in it all the refinements of my heart and all the varieties of my pen. Why did you try to encroach on a life which did not belong to me, and to change that existence at the whim of your love? I suffered very much seeing the vain efforts you were making to shake the rock which makes all hands bleed which touch it.

You accuse me ceaselessly of egoism and hardness; in your heart, this long time, you have decided that I didn't love you. False, false, my poor dear. I love you as much as ever; I love you in my own way, in my fashion, according to my nature. You should have had – I told you so from the first day – a man younger and more naïve than I, whose heart was less mature and was fresher.

But there was much play-acting in the attitude of both of them. The very next day he expressed surprise and regret at

not having heard from her. Their correspondence was resumed, but the recriminations and scoldings went on in her
daily letters. At the end he decided that he could not continue any longer in this way which made it impossible for
him to work or to think of anything else:[44]

It is impossible for me to continue any longer with a correspondence which is becoming epileptic. Please change your tone.
What have I done to you (since it is *vous* now) that you spread
out before me the pride of grief, the spectacle of a despair against
which I know no cure? If I had deceived you, made you the cause
of gossip; if I had sold your letters, etc., you would not write me
more frightful or desolating things.

What have I done, God! what have I done?

You know well that I can't come to Paris. You want to force me
to answer you with cruelty. I am too well bred to do so, but it
seems to me that I've told you often enough so that you can
remember it.

I had formed a very different idea of love. I thought that it was
something independent of everything else, and even from the
person who inspired it. Absence, insults, infamy, all that
wouldn't alter it. If one loves another one can spend ten years
without seeing the other without suffering.

Louise had written against this last reflection: 'What can
one think of such a sentence.'

You declare that I treat you like *a woman of the lowest rank*. I
don't know what a woman of the last rank is, nor of the first or
second ...

As for me, I'm tired of grand passion, of noble sentiments, of
wild loves and howling despair. I like common sense before
everything else, perhaps because I haven't got any myself.

I don't understand your anger and your sulks. You make a
mistake as you are good, excellent, amiable and one cannot help
being grieved as you spoil all that wilfully.

This letter did not end their correspondence, which continued again in the New Year of 1847, but always with bitterness. There seems to have been a quarrel more fierce than
the rest in March 1847, which caused a virtual break between

them. On the letter which Flaubert then addressed to her, Louise Colet had written 'His last letter' though it was not, in fact, to be the last. It is a very long letter, six typed pages, which is not included in the *Correspondance*.[45] Something very terrible must have happened between them when he left very hurriedly, and wrote to her later:

The letter in the third person which I received on Tuesday evening, finally persuaded me to leave. When I read your suspicions concerning the wife of Phidias '– that is to say Louise Pradier –' I said to myself, this is the last straw, it only needed this!

Let's speak of ourselves now. You ask me to send you at least one last word. . . . I know that you would have done anything for me, that you would still do it, that your love would have deserved an angel – I grieve at not having been able to respond to it. But is it my fault? Is it my fault? I'd have liked to have loved you as you loved me. But liking peace before anything else and rest, I only found in you, turmoil, storms, tears and anger.

He went on to tell her of all the rows which she had caused on so many occasions and which had always left him spent; how she had sworn at him in the railway station because he had missed an appointment which, in fact, he had never made:

All the trouble came from the first error. You made a mistake in accepting me, or else I should have changed. Your ideas of morality, patriotism, of devotion; your tastes in literature, all this was antipathetic to my ideas and my tastes.

He repeats again that it was a pity that she ever got to know him, that she had always wanted him to be otherwise than he was, and could never accept him as he really was. He ended by saying:

Farewell! Imagine that I've gone away for a long trip. Goodbye again! Meet someone more worthy of you. To give him to you I'd go to find him at the far end of the world. Be happy.

There was, however, no finality yet in their relationship –

and indeed little real sincerity in their desire to part. Although he did not go to see her when he was passing through Paris, on his way to Brittany with Du Camp, in April 1847, he expected to find letters from her at every port of call, and was bitterly disappointed when there were none. Their friendship and their love staggered on all through 1847 and into 1848, with the same accusations and recriminations. He was in Brittany for the first anniversary of their meeting, 29 July, and she wrote to complain that he had sent her no flowers:[46]

You declare that I *ought* at least to have sent you flowers for 29 July. You know well that I don't admit any duties. You strike badly in trying to strike too hard. I don't laugh about all that as you imagine, for I don't laugh and for a very good reason. For the last fortnight I've experienced such things that I've lost the habit of it, for the present at least. It will come back perhaps. It seems to me, nevertheless, that the letter which I wrote to you from Saint Malo was affectionate and kind. It appears not! I'm mistaken perhaps . . .

You ask for complete oblivion. I might give you the signs of it; so let it be, but in my heart, no. . . . You couldn't resign yourself to accepting me with the infirmities of my position, with the exigencies of my life. I'd given you the depths. You wanted also the surface, the appearances, the cares, the attentions, the visits, everything that I killed myself to explain to you that I couldn't give you.

Let it be as you wish. If you curse me, I'll always bless you and my heart will always be moved at the sound of your name.

You imagine that I didn't celebrate the anniversary last Wednesday, and that I didn't think of it!

Farewell.

Flaubert was home by August 1847, but he does not seem to have met Louise during the latter part of the year, though the letters continued, with recriminations on her part, and excuses on his. Her husband seems to have been living with her then, as there are frequent allusions in Flaubert's letters to 'l'Officiel', and she must have complained of his presence for he mentions 'the unbearable Officiel' and 'the Officiel who poisons your existence'.[47] 'It's the greatest torture one can endure to have to live with those whom one doesn't love.'

There is no letter extant between December 1847 and March 1848, but Flaubert was in Paris during the February Revolution, and they may have met while he was in the capital. Then the break came, and the last real letter from Flaubert to Louise Colet, in this series, is one in March 1848, a reserved and slightly distant letter, though with expressions of friendship. In the meantime she had become pregnant by Hippolyte Colet, and, when he heard the news, Flaubert answered:[48]

What was the good also of all your preambles to announce *the news* to me. You could have told it to me straight out without all these circumlocutions. I'll spare you the reflections which it aroused in me, and the expression of the feelings which it caused me. There would be too much to say. I pity you, I pity you very much indeed. I've suffered for you, and, much more, *I imagined everything*.

Whatever happens you can always count on me. Even if we were not to write to one another any more, even if we weren't to see one another again, there will always be between us a bond which nothing will ever wipe out, a past, the consequences of which will always survive.

My *monstrous personality*, as you so kindly call it, is not such that it obliterates in me all honest sentiment, human if you prefer it. One day, perhaps, you'll recognize it and you'll be sorry for having expended, on my account, so much sorrow and so much bitterness.

Farewell. I embrace you. Yours ever.

A son, born in June 1848, who did not long survive his birth, was the final cause of the break in this period of the relationship between Flaubert and Louise Colet. His last note to her is dated 21 August 1848:[49]

Thank you for the present.
Thank you for the beautiful verses.
Thank you for the memory.

Louis Bouilhet
(1846–8)

WE have seen the shock which Flaubert felt on the marriage of Alfred Le Poittevin in July 1846, and how he considered that here was the third bereavement which he had suffered during the year. It was then that he took up with Louis Bouilhet, a young man barely a year younger than himself, whom he had once known at school, but with whom he had not then been intimate. We have seen that he had been, with him, one of the signatories of the school protests in 1839.

Louis Bouilhet had been a very good scholar at school, especially in Latin, and he had won the 'Prix d'Honneur', in 1839, in the Class of Rhetoric.

After he passed his 'baccalauréat' he decided to take up the study of medicine, because his father had been a doctor, a surgeon, in the army during the Russian campaign. He had died when his son had not yet finished his studies, and had left a widow and two daughters as well as Louis. Louis Bouilhet became one of Dr Flaubert's pupils, and he reached the stage of 'interne' in the hospital at Rouen in 1842, when he was twenty. He hated his medical studies and he finally abandoned them in 1845. He then founded what is called in French a 'boîte à bachot', a cramming establishment to prepare boys for university entrance. He was badly paid and worked eight hours a day at his lessons; he was miserably poor, as he had made over to his mother and sisters the legacy which he had inherited from his godfather.

His chief passion and occupation were the writing of poetry, and he was interested in all the new theories of the Art for Art's Sake Movement, which was beginning at this time, and which concentrated on the form of poetry – a great contrast with the loose writing favoured by the Romantic School. He was then composing the poems which he was to publish in his collection *Festons et Astragales*. Flaubert thought highly of him as a poet and considered that he would earn immortality. Bouilhet, however, knew better and, in a poem entitled *La Dernière Nuit*, from *Dernières Chansons*, he wrote prophetically about his ultimate fate:

> Pareil au flux d'une mer inféconde,
> Sur mon cadavre au sépulcre endormi
> Je sens déjà monter l'oubli du monde
> Qui tout vivant m'a couvert à demi.

It is not known how he and Flaubert renewed their acquaintanceship, but Flaubert's first letter to him was written on 15 August 1846, a month after the marriage of Le Poittevin. Du Camp tells us that, when he visited Flaubert at Croisset in May 1847, he talked to him about his new friendship with his former schoolmate.[1]

Bouilhet was obliged to work all the week to earn his living but on Saturdays he went out to Croisset to visit Flaubert and stayed there until Monday morning. They soon became very close friends, twin spirits, who thought alike and came to look so much alike that it was often rumoured that Bouilhet was Dr Flaubert's illegitimate son, but there is no truth whatsoever in this suggestion.

Bouilhet's intimacy with Flaubert soon rivalled that of Alfred Le Poittevin. Flaubert may not have considered him so romantically as he had done Alfred – he was, after all, of his own age – and he did not hero-worship him to the same extent, but he met him at a later stage in his development, when he was moving away from romantic ideas. He was the last of Flaubert's really close friends, and we have seen that there was probably some homosexuality in their relationship.[2]

He became Flaubert's literary mentor and guide, and the latter never wrote anything without his advice. He might never have become the pure artist he was to become if it had not been for his literary guidance. After his death, in 1869, Flaubert asked himself what was the good of continuing writing since Louis Bouilhet was no longer there to appreciate what he was doing. 'I say to myself what is the point of writing now that he is no longer there.'[3]

Bouilhet aroused once more Flaubert's interest in the theatre, and there are many plays that they planned together. These are preserved in Flaubert's notes in the Bibliothèque Municipale in Rouen, and in the Bibliothèque Nationale in Paris.[4] Flaubert mentions to Louise Colet that he and Bouilhet spent three evenings a week preparing these scenarios.[5] None of them are at all good – in fact, they are mediocre – but they never seem to have considered publishing or producing them.

The first of Flaubert's works on which we can see the influence of Louis Boulhet is the one which he wrote in collaboration with Maxime Du Camp, an account of their journey through Brittany in the spring of 1847, of which his own part was published posthumously under the title *Par les Champs et par les Grèves* in 1886. This is his first real attempt at carrying out the ideals of the Art for Art's Sake Movement; the first in which we see the true attention to style of the mature master. Later he was to say: 'This book gave me a great deal of trouble, it is the first that I wrote with pain and difficulty.'[6] And while he was composing it, he declared:[7]

You ask me for news of our book, Max's and mine. You must know that I'm harassed by writing! Style, which is a thing that I take seriously, disturbs my nerves most terribly, I get infuriated, I fume with rage. There are days when I'm ill from it all, and nights when I'm in a fever. The more I advance the more incapable I become of expressing the *Idea*. What a strange mad occupation, to spend one's life wearing oneself out over words, and sweating all day to round off periods. There are times, it is true, when one experiences great joy; but at the price of how much discouragement and bitterness, does one buy that pleasure! Today, for instance, I spent eight hours correcting five pages, and I think I've worked well! Imagine the rest! It is piti-able! Whatever happens, I'll complete this work, which, by its very object, is a stiff exercise.

One could almost imagine that Flaubert was here talking of the composition of *Madame Bovary*, for these are the same lamentations which he was later to make.

It was Du Camp who planned the journey to Brittany – he was a great planner of trips and was a very efficient organizer. He managed to persuade Madame Flaubert to allow her son to embark on this expedition – he would probably not have ventured on it otherwise as he was always afraid of causing her anxiety. She had not yet recovered from her tragic shocks of the previous year, and was always in a nervous and apprehensive state. She was to accompany them in her carriage part of the way and to meet them in the towns in which they stopped.

They started out in May 1847 and, from their accounts, and their letters, one would not have known that they had anyone else with them, and there must have been long stretches when they were alone, as they travelled very roughly, staying at very low hotels and lodging houses, not suitable for a woman. The conditions in Brittany were very primitive in those days, and even the food was very poor and often insufficient. They usually travelled along very rough paths where it would not have been possible for a carriage to pass.

Although Flaubert was in fairly good health during the trip, he did suffer one seizure and Du Camp had to send for the local doctor to treat him, but this was the only attack.[8] This was the happiest time in Du Camp's relationship with Flaubert. He had him all to himself, without any outside interference, and was his sole companion. Nothing came to disturb their mutual harmony, there was not a cloud in their friendship and they loved one another as never before.[9] Writing many years later, Du Camp said to him: 'That was indeed our real moment, make no mistake about it.'[10]

They visited the châteaux of the Loire, which were then

not as well known as now – Blois, Amboise, Chenonceaux, Tours and so forth – places which we are not nowadays accustomed to think of as in Brittany.

The trip was, however, not intended to be solely one of pleasure and of aimless wandering – Du Camp hardly ever did anything gratuitously – and they planned to compose a book together in collaboration, on their return. Du Camp was to write the even-numbered chapters, and Flaubert the uneven.

They arrived back in Rouen on 7 August 1847, and began immediately to work on their joint book. When the work was completed they had two copies made, one for each author. It is not known what has become of Flaubert's copy, but Du Camp left his, in his will, to the Bibliothèque de l'Institut in Paris, where it is now. It is a beautiful copy, on parchment paper, bound in Morocco leather, tooled in gold; and each chapter is signed by its author. Du Camp never allowed his share to be printed, but, as we have seen, Flaubert's was eventually published posthumously. He also kept his rough copy and made, from time to time, alterations and additions to the text, so that the final published version is very different from Du Camp's copy in the Institut library. Modern publishers have used their discretion and whim as to which text they print, and there is considerable variety.

Flaubert himself published, separately, one section in the periodical *L'Artiste*, on 18 April 1858, the one entitled 'Les Pierres de Carnac et l'Archéologie Celtique'. This is the chapter which he himself preferred, as he thought it scholarly – but not everyone would agree with this preference, and would place other sections very much higher. 'It is one of the things which I think most highly of,' he wrote.[11] 'It is my summary of Celtic archaeology which is truly a complete and critical exposition of the subject.'

The sections by each author are very different in kind. The chapters by Du Camp – like all his work – are factual, written in a pedestrian style, somewhat impersonal and without much individuality. The facts have been carefully

verified but there is little personal reflection on what he has
seen, and this makes his contribution more like a guidebook
than a work of art. He had a photographic mind and was not
much given to vivid description, but he noticed detail. In his
incapacity for description, he believed that it was sufficient
to put a thing in capital letters to make it effective and create
an impression. For instance, he puts the frescoes of the
church at Niort in capitals, and then adds, in a footnote, that
'this is the only way, in our opinion, of expressing the effect
of the said work of art'. He frequently declares that things
are 'difficult to describe'. His favourite device is to go in for
historical allusions, which could be obtained from textbooks,
and which end by being colourless. His style is pedestrian
and cliché-ridden and occasionally he indulges in commonplace aphorisms such as 'roads are like women, they need a
lot of money for their upkeep'.

Flaubert's contribution is very different in the vivacity of
his style. Whereas Du Camp is a photographer, he is a
painter who observes everything with individual eyes. He
always notices the human touch – a soldier brushing his uniform and polishing his buttons; the appalling state of a bedroom which they occupied one night; a woman weeping
because her husband has been washed ashore drowned. He
was interested by the brothel at Brest; and noticed with compassion the terrible poverty of the people. He was able to
draw general reflections from what he saw. Du Camp would
not have been capable of producing Flaubert's moving description of the tomb which Chateaubriand had built for
himself at the Grand Bey:[12]

Il dormira là-dessous, la tête tournée vers la mer; dans ce
sépulcre bâti sur un écueil, son immortalité sera comme sa vie,
déserte des autres et tour entourée d'orages. Les vagues avec les
siècles murmureront longtemps autour de ce grand souvenir;
dans les tempêtes elles bondiront jusqu'à ses pieds, ou les
matins d'été, quand les voiles blanches se déploient et que
l'hirondelle arrive d'au delà des mers, longues et douces, elles
lui apporteront la volupté mélancolique des horizons et la caresse

des larges brises. Et les jours ainsi s'écoulant, pendant que les flots de la grève natale iront se balançant toujours entre son berceau et son tombeau, le coeur de René devenu froid, lentement, s'éparpillera dans le néant, au rythme sans fin de cette musique éternelle.

Nous avons tourné autour du tombeau, nous l'avons touché de nos mains, nous l'avons regardé comme s'il eût contenu son hôte, nous nous sommes assis par terre à ses côtés.

Chateaubriand was only to die the following year.

Nor could he have written Flaubert's reflection at Combourg, where Chateaubriand was born and lived all his youth – *René*, his personal novel, had been one of Flaubert's seminal works when he was composing *Mémoires d'un Fou* and *Novembre*:[13]

La nuit tombait. Le château, flanqué de ses quatre tourelles, encadré dans sa verdure et dominant le village qu'il écrase, étendait sa grande masse sombre. Le soleil couchant, qui passait devant sans l'atteindre, le faisait paraître noir, et ses rayons, effleurant la surface du lac, allaient se perdre dans la brume, sur la cime violette des bois immobiles.

Assis sur l'herbe, au pied d'un chêne, nous lisions *René*. Nous étions devant ce lac où il contemplait l'hirondelle agile sur le roseau mobile, à l'ombre de ces bois où il poursuivait l'arc-en-ciel sur les collines pluvieuses; nous écoutions ce frémissement de feuilles, ce bruit de l'eau sous la brise qui avaient mêlé leur murmure à la mélodie éplorée des ennuis de sa jeunesse. À une mesure que l'ombre tombait sur les pages du livre, l'amertume des phrases gagnait nos coeurs, et nous nous fondions avec délices dans ce je ne sais quoi de large, de mélancolique et de doux.

Prè de nous, une charrette a passé en claquant dans les ornières son essieu sonore. On sentait l'odeur des foins coupés. On entendait le bruit des grenouilles qui coassaient dans le marécage. Nous rentrâmes.

Le ciel était lourd; toute la nuit il y eut de l'orage. A la lueur des éclairs, la façade de plâtre d'une maison voisine s'illuminait et flambait comme embrasée. Haletant, lassé de me retourner sur mes matelas, je me suis levé, j'ai allumé ma chandelle, j'ai ouvert la fenêtre et regardé la nuit.

Elle était noire, silencieuse comme le sommeil. Mon flambeau qui brûlait dessinait monstrueusement sur le mur d'en face ma silhouette agrandie. De temps à autre, un éclair muet survenant tout à coup m'éblouissait les yeux.

J'ai pensé à cet homme qui a commencé là et qui a rempli un demisiècle du tapage de sa douleur.

Very much later Flaubert showed his part of the work on Brittany to Louise Colet, after he renewed his relationship with her in 1851, but she was not impressed by it for she considered that the realism of its detail was vulgar. She did not understand that the value of his contribution came from the fact of his observation of everything and his enjoyment in it. He was deeply interested in people on the trip, whereas Du Camp was more interested in facts and things.

Flaubert and Du Camp returned to political unrest and, at the end of 1847, the situation began to deteriorate rapidly. On Christmas Day 1847 a revolutionary 'banquet' was held at Rouen which Flaubert attended. These banquets were a striking feature of political life just before the Revolution of 1848, and they were considered so dangerous by the authorities that they tried to prohibit them whenever possible.

This banquet was presided over by Sénard, a well-known Rouen lawyer and a friend of the Flaubert family. He was to defend Flaubert ten years later at his trial concerning *Madame Bovary*.

The *Journal de Rouen* summoned its readers to attend the banquet but the conservative paper. *Le Mémorial*, called it the Banquet of Disorder.

Du Camp describes the banquet in his *Souvenirs de l'Année 1848*.[14] He mentions the poor speeches and the indifferent food. 'The fare was certainly not delicious; the eloquence was no better.' He describes Odilon Barrot in a blue coat and grey trousers, using every known cliché. He spoke of 'le char de l'état, la coupe décevante de la popularité, l'hydre de l'anarchie' and so forth. 'Never', added Du Camp, "had such an avalanche of commonplaces, made hideous by ready-made phrases, rolled over us.' He declared that he and his friends were men of letters and that they were horrified. Was this the way to speak to the masses? Are these the stupidities which have an effect? 'It is this kind of rhetoric, more hollow than dangerous, which moves people.' One hears in these words the echo of Flaubert's sentiments.

Flaubert and Bouilhet arrived in Paris, to see what was happening, on 23 February, but one cannot claim that the part that either of them played in the Revolution was very glorious. The Revolution began in earnest on the 24th, and they saw the fighting at the rue Helder and at the Palais Royal. Bouilhet, always slow, vague and timid, got caught in the crowd and separated from his friend. He was seized upon by some revolutionaries and pressed into building a barricade, but a paving-stone fell on his foot and incapacitated him temporarily. They saw the looting and burning of the Palais-Royal, and Flaubert remembered the scene twenty years later, when he described it vividly in the second *Éducation Sentimentale*.

Flaubert did not grieve at the disappearance of Louis-Philippe and the fall of the July Monarchy, for he had always disliked and despised them. In a letter to Louise Colet, he said:[15]

All this is very funny! There are many disconcerted faces which make one very happy to behold. I take a profound delight in the contemplation of all these flattened ambitions. I don't know if the new form of government and the social state which will result from it, will be favourable to Art. That is a question! It can't be more bourgeois nor more worthless. As for being more stupid, is that possible?

In the second Revolution of 1848, that of June, Du Camp was wounded in the knee and was, for a time, in danger of losing his leg. He was, however, decorated for the part he had played, with the cross of Chevalier de la Légion d'Honneur – he generally managed to make capital out of what happened to him – and he was only twenty-six.

Flaubert had returned to Rouen, and thence had gone to Neuville-Champ-d'Oisel, where Alfred Le Poittevin was lying dangerously ill. He had been in failing health for some time – this was due, it is thought, to his dissipated living – and his condition had now become desperate. Shortly before he died, he said in a letter to Du Camp:[16] 'I'm beginning to look at the things of this world, only in the light of that sinister taper which is lit for the dying. I warn you that this sentence isn't mine; it is by Saint-Simon, but he was wrong: this taper isn't sinister.'

Flaubert sat beside Le Poittevin's death-bed for two days and two nights, and, as he watched over him, his love for his friend welled up again as strongly as formerly, and he felt that there was no one in the wide world whom he had ever loved so dearly.

Alfred Le Poittevin died on Monday, 3 April 1848, and he was thirty-two years old. Flaubert once again recorded his obituary feelings in a letter to Maxime Du Camp:[17]

Alfred died on Monday at midnight. I buried him yesterday. I watched beside him for two nights. I wrapped him in his winding sheet, I gave him a farewell kiss, and I saw his coffin soldered down. I spent beside him two whole days. As I watched over him, I was reading *The Religions of Antiquity* by Kreutzer. The window was open, the night was most beautiful, one could hear a cock crowing and a moth was fluttering round the candle. I shall never forget all that, nor the expression on his face nor, the first night, at midnight, the distant sound of a horn which came to me through the woods. On the Wednesday I went for a walk the whole afternoon with a bitch which followed me without my calling her. This bitch had developed an affection for him and used to accompany him always when he went out alone. On the night before he died, she howled terribly, and no one could silence her. I sat down several times on the moss, I smoked, I looked at the sky, I lay down behind a heap of bundles of broom, and I slept. On the last night I read *Les Feuilles d'Automne*. I constantly came across the poems he loved best, or those that had some connection with the present circumstances. Every now and then I went over to lift up the veil they had put over his face, to gaze at him. I was wrapped in an overcoat which had belonged to my father and that he had only worn once, the day of Caroline's wedding. When day broke, at four o'clock, the nurse and I set to work. I lifted him up, turning him over and shrouded him. The feeling of his limbs, cold and stiff, remained all day in my fingertips. He was most terribly decomposed. We put two shrouds on him. When he was laid out, he looked like an Egyptian mummy, bound in his wrappings, and I felt some curious, tremendous, feeling of joy and liberty for him. The mist was pale, the woods were beginning to stand out against the sky, the two candles were burning against that growing whiteness. Birds were singing and I repeated to myself this sentence from his *Bélial*: 'He'll fly away, joyful bird, to greet the rising sun, amongst the pines'; or rather I could hear his voice reciting it to me, and, all day, I was delightfully obsessed by it. They placed him in the hall. The doors were taken down, and the full morning air poured in, with the freshness from the rain, which had begun to fall. They carried him to the cemetery, and the procession took more than an hour. Walking at the back I could see the coffin swaying with a movement like that of a boat rocked by the swell. The service was horribly long. At the cemetery the earth was greasy. I went near to the edge of the grave and I looked at the shovelfuls of earth flung in one after the other. It seemed to me that a hundred thousand fell in. To return to Rouen I sat up on the box with Bouilhet. The rain was falling heavily. The horses were galloping; and I shouted to make them go faster. The air did me a lot of good. I slept all that night and all the following day. This is what I've lived through since Tuesday evening. I've had marvellous revelations, and dazzling conceptions, which I could not translate into words. A heap of things came back to my mind, with choirs of music, and wafts of perfume. Until the moment when it became impossible for him to do anything, he used to read Spinoza until one o'clock in the morning, every night in bed. On one of his last days, as the window was open and the sun was pouring into the room, he said: 'Close it, it is too beautiful, too beautiful!'

There were moments, dear Max, when I thought strangely of you, and when I made sad comparisons of impressions.

Farewell. I embrace you, and I'm longing to see you, for I need to say incomprehensible things.

All the calm and discipline he thought he had gained was shattered at one blow. It was in this state of disarray and emotional intensity that he composed his next work, his first *Tentation de Saint Antoine*.

[13]

La Tentation de Saint Antoine
(1848–9)

THERE may have been some coldness between Flaubert and
Le Poittevin in the period after the marriage of the latter,
but, as soon as he died, all this changed, and he felt that here
was the friend of all others whom he had most dearly loved.
Suddenly he underwent a great change, and Alfred's
influence became more marked on him after his death than
it had ever been during his life-time, and he tried then to
become all the things that Alfred had wanted him to be.
Flaubert was to utilize such a phenomenon later, the post-
humous influence of those whom one had loved and, in
Madame Bovary, he showed how Charles was influenced
from beyond the grave by his dead wife, and how he then
did his utmost to become all the things which she had
wanted, in vain, for him to be when she was alive.

Flaubert now turned temporarily away from the more austere standards of the Art for Art's Sake movement, which he
had tried to follow in his part of the book on Brittany, and
became once more the most extreme Romanticist. He felt
the urge to compose a Romantic work full of eastern exotic
colour and overflowing with personal feeling.

He then remembered the emotion he had experienced
when he had been composing *Smarh* at the height of his
friendship with Alfred Le Poittevin; he recalled also how
excited and moved he had been when he had seen the
Breughel picture of the *Temptation of Saint Anthony* in the
Balbi Palace in Genoa, and all he had written about it to
Alfred in his letters from abroad, and all he had said after
his return.

He had intended, when he got back, to start work immedi-

ately and his first idea had been to make a play on the subject.[1]

But then occurred all the tragic events of 1846 and he still
did not start writing. In August, two years later, in 1847, he
said that he was postponing composition as he did not feel
that he had yet done sufficient reading for it.[2] In October
the same year he said that he might begin his *Saint Antoine*
some time the following year.[3] And he wrote to Laure de
Maupassant that he had discussed his *Saint Antoine* with
her brother Alfred Le Poittevin six months before he had
died, which would have meant that it was in November 1847.[4]

What can, however, be accepted as certain is that *La Tentation de Saint Antoine* was not begun – the writing of it –
until after Le Poittevin had died, and that it was his death
which forced Flaubert to write it when he did, making it
seem urgent. He began the work fifty days after the death of
his friend. He wrote, on the manuscript, that it was begun on
24 May 1848, at a quarter past three, and that it was finished
on Wednesday 12 September 1849, at twenty minutes past
three o'clock in the afternoon, on a sunny and windy day.

Maxime Du Camp had long wanted to travel in the East
with Flaubert, and he had managed to extract from
Madame Flaubert permission for him to accompany him.
Du Camp had wanted to start as early as possible, but Flaubert said that he could not leave until his *Tentation de Saint
Antoine* was finished. It was then decided that, as soon as the
book was completed, Flaubert should read it to his friends,
Louis Bouilhet and Maxime Du Camp, and that they would
after that be able to set out on their journey.

This time Flaubert wrote with excitement and a flow of
inspiration, and he felt that he had regained the fluency of
his youth. Writing later, he said:[5] 'Never again shall I be
able to recapture the abandonment of style which I indulged
in for eighteen long months.'[2]

But, although he wrote with ease and pleasure, the months
of writing cannot all have been joy and happiness. On a
blank page in one of his unpublished *Carnets de Lecture*, he

had written:[6] 'Rouen, 23 November 1848, 9 o'clock in the evening; my dog died yesterday – I am more and more bored.'

The book was finished on 12 September 1849, and the reading began soon afterwards.

Du Camp has given a vivid account of it in his *Souvenirs Littéraires*.[7]

For four days Flaubert read without stopping, from midday until four in the afternoon, and again from eight o'clock until midnight. It had been agreed between them that Du Camp and Bouilhet should keep their opinions to themselves as long as the reading continued, that they would not interrupt, and that, only when he had finished, would they make any comment. Before he began, Flaubert cried excitedly, waving his sheaf of papers:[8] 'If you don't shriek with excitement, it will only mean that nothing is capable of moving you!'

Du Camp, when writing, over thirty years later, said that the memory of the long hours of reading had never faded from his mind, and they remained very painful in retrospect. He said that he and Bouilhet went on expecting the action to begin, but they were always disappointed, for the only unity that they could find was the unity of monotony, which was constant from the beginning. There were nothing but lyric phrases, fine in themselves, but meaning nothing; there was nothing but overwhelming lyricism. They could not grasp what he was aiming at, and they had the impression that three years' work was crumbling away into nothingness. After each reading Madame Flaubert used to ask them what they thought of the work, but they did not dare answer.

Before the reading of the last part started Bouilhet and Du Camp decided between themselves that, at the end, they would tell him the unvarnished truth. They considered the matter urgent and that the whole of his literary future was at stake; they thought it necessary to restrain him before his talent had become completely liquefied. Utter frankness, they agreed, was the only possible policy.

At midnight, after the last reading, when he had ended, Flaubert said to them: 'And now tell me frankly what you think of it.'

Bouilhet, who was by nature gentle and shy, is said to have answered desperately:[9] 'We think you should throw it in the fire and never mention it again!'

We have only Du Camp's testimony for this answer, written thirty years later, and it is hard to imagine that Bouilhet could ever have been so harsh.

Flaubert bounded up, uttering a cry of horror. Then, Du Camp tells us, there began a serious conversation, of the kind only possible between friends who trust and love one another. Every sentence was gone through, word by word, while Flaubert tried to defend his writing. They ended by advising him to choose a commonplace subject like, for instance, *La Cousine Bette* or *Le Cousin Pons* by Balzac. The struggle continued from midnight until eight o'clock the following morning, and the night had gone by in their discussions.

It was a shattering blow to Flaubert, all his hopes destroyed at one fell swoop, and the repercussion of it can be found in his correspondence, in the letters which he wrote during his eastern trip, when he described how depressed and low he was, though he was by then beginning to recover from the shock.[10] Later he was to admit to Du Camp, recognizing the value of the lesson he had received:[11]

I was riddled with the cancer of lyricism; you operated on me, but it was only in the nick of time, and I howled with pain.

Nevertheless, although he accepted, on the whole, the verdict of his friends, he was not convinced that they had been entirely right. Three years later, while composing *Madame Bovary*, he said to Louise Colet that the book had been hastily judged:[12]

And so you're definitely enthusiastic about *Saint Antoine!* Well, I'll have had one person for it, and that's something! Although I don't accept everything that you say about it, I believe that my friends weren't prepared to see what was in it. It was too lightly judged; I don't say unjustly, but too lightly.

Du Camp tells us that, at one moment during the day which followed the sad verdict on the work, as they sat in the garden, Bouilhet suddenly said to Flaubert:[13] 'Why shouldn't you write the story of Delaunay?' And Flaubert raised his head, suddenly overjoyed, and answered: 'What a good idea!'

Du Camp was writing thirty years after the events concerned, and it is not astonishing that there should be errors in his statement. The man he wanted Flaubert to write about was not called Delaunay but Delamare, and he had been an 'officer de santé', one of Dr Flaubert's former students. Also it is certainly not true that, at this time, Flaubert was considering writing about Delamare and his wife, or that anyone had suggested the subject to him. It was only after his return from the eastern trip, when other circumstances brought it to his notice, that it seemed to him a possible topic for him. We now know, from his letters that, all through his eastern trip, and, even on his return, he was very undecided about what subject he should embark upon, and the Delamare story was not mentioned.

Many critics have blamed this verdict, and some have even accused the two friends of jealousy. This could certainly not have been true of Bouilhet, who was incapable of envy, and it is very unlikely to have been true either of Du Camp. He was still very much attached to Flaubert and wanted to help him in his career as a man of letters – his own was very much more advanced than that of his friend. But both men, as minor writers, saw more clearly than a genius could the way literature was going. Both of them realized that the days of Romanticism were over; and they understood that for a man who had literary pretensions to produce a work in the romantic vein of Quinet's *Ahasvérus* or Byron's *Cain*, at that time, was artistic suicide. The day for that kind of lush exuberance was long past in 1849.

Nowadays readers are less scandalized by Du Camp's and

Bouilhet's verdict than were those who read it in the *Souvenirs Littéraires* when it appeared in 1883, and who had not yet had the opportunity to wade through the five hundred and thirty-one pages of the first *Tentation de Saint Antoine*. Many nowadays consider that the verdict was, on the whole, justified and that the work, except in isolated fragments, is unreadable. It is one of the most extreme manifestations of Romantic subjectivity, and Flaubert, according to his own testimony, became Saint Anthony as he wrote. He analysed himself, and the book became a personal confession.[14] 'In the place of Saint Anthony, for instance, it is I who am there; the *Tentation* was for me and not for the reader.' And again:[15] 'Oh! happy time of *Saint Antoine*, where are you now? Then I wrote with my whole being.' And also:[16] 'It was a "déversoir"; I had only pleasure in composing it, and the eighteen months that I spent in writing its five hundred pages, were the most deeply voluptuous of my whole life.'

Bouilhet and Du Camp should, however, have realized the lyric beauty of certain portions – perhaps they did but they did not draw attention to them: as for instance the passage describing Simon the Magician's companion Helen.[17] Or the one where Death exclaims:[18]

Où sont-elles maintenant toutes les femmes qui furent aimées, celles qui mettaient des anneaux d'or pour plaire à leurs maris, les vierges aux joues roses qui brodaient des tissus, et les reines qui se faisaient, au clair de lune, porter près des fontaines? Elles avaient des tapis, des éventails, des esclaves, des musiques amoureuses jouant tout à coup derrière les murs; elles avaient des dents brillantes qui mordaient à même dans les grenades, et des vêtements lâches qui embaumaient l'air autour d'elles. Où sont-ils donc les forts jeunes hommes qui couraient si bien, qui riaient si haut, qui avaient la barbe noire et l'oeil ardent? Où sont leurs boucliers polis, leurs chevaux qui piaffaient, leurs chiens de chasse rapides qui bondissaient dans les bruyères? Qu'est devenue la cire des torches qui éclairaient leurs festins?

Oh! comme il en a passé de ces hommes, de ces femmes, de ces enfants et de ces vieillards aussi. . . .

Plus d'un couple d'amis a causé de moi bien souvent, seuls près du foyer, dont ils remuaient les cendres, tout en se demandant ce qu'ils deviendraient plus tard; mais celui qui s'en est allé ne revient point pour dire à l'autre s'ils s'étaient trompés jadis, et, quand ils se retrouveront dans le néant, rien d'eux ne se reconnaîtra, pas plus que ne se rejoindront les parties du morceau de bois qu'ils regardaient brûler.

This passage might be the prose version of a poem by Victor Hugo in a collection from his first lyric period, between 1830 and 1840.

In *La Tentation de Saint Antoine*, Flaubert returned to the inspiration of *Smarh* of ten years before, to the epic tradition of the nineteenth century, with its symbolical picture of mankind – its miserable state of degradation, its restlessness as it longs for ever for something beyond its grasp. The visions of Saint Anthony fascinated Flaubert, as they gave him the opportunity for philosophic reflections on the world, religion, the infinite, and so forth. Anthony discusses these matters with the vices and virtues; with the heresies; with logic and science; with various historical and legendary characters – Apollonius of Thyana, Helen of Sparta, Juno, Minerva, Zoroaster; with abstractions such as Death and the Earth; and the Devil.

There are here the same influences at play as in the earlier work – Byron's *Cain*, Goethe's *Faust* and especially Quinet's *Ahasvérus*, which, we have seen, was the basis of the first work.

There is here, as there had been in *Smarh*, the summing-up of the universal tragedy of mankind, in all its stages, through all the ages, and Flaubert had intended to give a picture of the evolution of humanity as it passes through all the phases of doubt, and eventually reaches the same state as his Saint Anthony, a return to prayer. This gives a quality of mysticism to the first *Tentation de Saint Antoine* which is absent from the final version, which is more sceptical, more critical and historical. The first possesses some of the religious feeling which is found in Baudelaire, who was writing at the same time what the poet calls 'spleen' and 'idéal', the contrast between the baseness of the instinct in man, his leaning towards the ignoble, and his longing for the ideal.

In form, the work keeps the dramatic structure of *Smarh*, and there is the memory of the medieval mystery puppet play which he had seen as a child at the Foire Saint-Romain.

There is manifest here, in very marked form, the characeristic Flaubertian mixture of the serious and the grotesque, which is seen in his mature works, which we find in the meetings between the pig and the saint.

Although, taken as a whole, *La Tentation de Saint Antoine* is formless and diffuse, and largely unreadable today except for those with specialized knowledge, we have seen that there are fine lyrical passages which redeem it. The prose poem on death has been quoted and there is also the description of the earth as it was before the coming of man:[19]

Moi, j'avais des forêts mystérieuses, j'avais des océans démesurés, j'avais des montagnes inaccessibles. Dans des eaux noires vivaient des bêtes dangereuses, et l'haleine des marécages comme un voile sombre se balançait sur ma figure. J'étais couverte de plantes, je tremblais comme un épileptique aux secousses de mes volcans. Durant les nuits le champignon large poussait au tronc des chênes; sur des mousses d'or, des grands serpents au soleil dormaient le corps plié, des odeurs suaves passaient dans les hautes herbes. Terrible d'énergies, enivrante de parfums, éblouissante de couleurs, immense; ah! j'étais belle, quand je sortis toute échevelée de la couche du Chaos! et que je portais encore sur moi la marque de ses étreintes.

Débile et nu, l'homme alors pâlissait au bruit de mes abîmes, à la voix des animaux, aux éclipses de la lune; il se roulait sur mes fleurs, il grimpait dans mes feuillages pour se gorger de fruits vermeils, il ramassait sur les grèves les perles blondes et les coquilles contournées, il regardait au flanc des collines scintiller les minerais de fer et les diamants qui roulaient dans les ruisseaux; je l'entourais d'étonnements, je l'épuisais de travail, je l'accablais de volupté. A la fois Nature et Dieu, principe et but, j'étais infinie pour lui, et son Olympe ne dépassait point la mesure de mes montagnes.

Flaubert continued in low spirits and was unsure of himself, weighed down by the verdict of his friends. It was hoped that the complete change of the eastern trip might give him back a taste for life and raise him from his deep state of depression.

Maxime Du Camp and Flaubert set out on their journey on 29 October 1849; they were to be away for twenty-one months.

[14]

The Eastern Trip
(1849–51)

WHEN the trip to the East was planned, Maxime Du Camp decided to apply for an official mission, not in order to obtain subsidies, for he was to pay his own expenses, but in order to get government protection in the places that he was to visit. His application is preserved at the Archives Nationales in Paris.[1] The object of his mission is stated to be scientific research in Egypt, Palestine, Syria and Persia. The documents, under his name, comprise: a letter in which he states that he has been given instruction by the Académie des Inscriptions et des Belles Lettres, and he encloses his itinerary, requesting official sanction to help him to carry out his work; a letter of recommendation from a certain Dupont-Delporte, member of parliament, supporting his application; a letter to Du Camp informing him that he has been granted the mission without allowances and that they would gladly receive communications from him; finally an official document granting Monsieur Maxime Du Camp a mission for Egypt, Syria and Persia, to explore the antiquities of these countries. The documents are stamped by the Ministère de l'Instruction Publique et des Cultes. There is also appended a printed document by Du Camp, on fine paper, giving a plan of his itinerary and stating what he hoped to achieve.

Monsieur Napoléon Dupont-Delporte, in his letter of recommendation, declared that 'Monsieur Maxime Du Camp has been engaged for several years, and with great success, on archaeological studies. He is a highly educated man who is frequently consulted by the highest historical authorities. He has published, in various periodicals, articles and commentaries which would suffice to justify the opinion which I have just expressed about him.'

Du Camp, in his application, speaks of his earlier journey to the East and of the book which he wrote on his return, *Souvenirs et Paysages d'Orient;* and he also mentions the part that he played in the Revolution of 1848, that his leg had been fractured and that he had been awarded the decoration of Chevalier de la Légion d'Honneur. He ends his letter: 'These are the qualifications, Monsieur le Ministre, which I can furnish to earn your consideration; I am young, full of energy, I am accustomed to rigorous journeys and I am requesting from you, without incurring to the state any expense, the means of rendering to the science of my country some service.'

There is no application from Flaubert amongst these requests for missions. It seems, however, that Du Camp had tried to obtain for him a mission similar to his own and, in the category of *Missions Commerciales* 1841–63, there is the record of a mission having been granted to Gustave Flaubert, the object of which was stated to be 'A study of the state of commerce and industry' in various countries. Under the heading 'Résultats' there is a blank, which means that Flaubert did not send in a single report.[2] His mission was to deal with Turkey in Asia, Egypt and Persia. There is no application from him amongst the documents but only the very full instructions which were sent to him. But there is a copy of Du Camp's printed itinerary, and one can only wonder what the Ministry of Commerce made of it, for it had no relevance to what they wanted Flaubert to achieve.

These instructions make a long and tedious document – sixteen tightly written foolscap pages – and it is doubtful whether Flaubert ever read them through. He was given a statement of the customs and tariffs in force in the countries he was to visit, and he was instructed to investigate the possibilities of increasing French trade with them. He was expected to take note of the means of commercial communication, navigation and so forth; he was given a list

of the goods which France would like to export to these
countries and those which she would like to import from
them. He was to inquire into the nature of the exchange,
what currency was used, and to make a comparative study of
weights and measures.

There was nothing in the prospect held out to him which
could possibly excite a man of Flaubert's temperament and
tastes, and it was no wonder that he soon abandoned all
interest in the mission entrusted to him, and that he did not
take a single note which he could send to the authorities.

These documents are unpublished. Émile Henriot has
used them in an article in *Le Temps*, but not very accurately. He has mixed up the various instructions in order to
compose a continuous and intelligible narrative.[3]

Flaubert left Croisset on 22 October 1849, and he was seen
off at the station by his sister-in-law, his niece and Louis
Bouilhet. He remarks that the only person of the household
who seemed moved at his departure was his gardener – his
mother was not at home and he was to see her in Paris.[4] He
remained in Paris for a week, except for a short visit to
Nogent where he accompanied his mother who was to stay
there with relations. He had an emotional farewell from her,
as if he were never to come back. It is true that he had
hardly ever been separated from her – only on the journey to
the Mediterranean after he had passed his 'baccalauréat',
and the few months of his student days in Paris, which he
spent longing for home – and never since the death of his
father and sister. He describes it in his *Notes de
Voyages*:[5]

Enfin je suis parti. Ma mère était assise dans un fauteuil, en
face de la cheminée; comme je la caressais et lui parlais, je l'ai
baisée sur le front, me suis élancé sur la porte, ai saisi mon chapeau dans la salle à manger et suis sorti. Quel cri elle a poussé,
quand j'ai fermé la porte du salon! il m'a rappelé celui que je lui
ai entendu pousser à la mort de mon père, quand elle lui a pris
la main.

At the station he encountered a priest and four nuns and

this seemed to him to be an ill-omen; also the fact that a neighbour's dog howled the whole afternoon. In the train from Nogent to Paris he was alone; he shut the windows of the carriage and wept uncontrolledly, stuffing his handkerchief into his mouth. At every station where the train stopped, he was tempted to get out and to return home.[6]

He went immediately to Du Camp's apartment who, returning home later in the evening, found him lying on the floor near the fire. He thought he was asleep but then found that he was sobbing and crying:[7] 'I'll never see my mother again; I'll never see my homeland again; this trip is too long, too far; it is tempting fate; what madness; why are we leaving?' Du Camp, however, made him see that he could not now withdraw, and managed to raise his spirits. The arrival of Bouilhet was also a great comfort to him.

They spent the days in Paris saying farewell to all their friends, especially to Gautier, Pradier and Schlésinger, but he did not see Élisa.

On the last evening they had dinner in a private room at the restaurant in the Palais Royal called 'Les Trois Frères Provinciaux', with Gautier, Bouilhet and Louis de Cormenin, and they talked art, literature and antiquity the whole evening.[8]

Finally they left by the coach on 29 October – there was not yet a railroad to the south – and they took the same route which Flaubert had taken twice before, in 1840 and in 1845. In Marseilles he did not forget Eulalie Foucaud and, as we know, went to look for her, but in vain; he could hardly even recognize the hotel.

They left Marseilles on 4 November, on board a ship called *Le Nil*, and arrived in Malta during the night of 7 November.

They arrived in Alexandria on 15 November and were royally received by Suliman-Pasha, the most powerful man in Egypt, as Flaubert remarked to his mother, called 'the terror of Constantinople'.[9] They went to dinner in Cairo in full regalia and to the opera. They lived in such luxury that

Du Camp's servant, Sassetti, said that for once in his life he had ten slaves to serve him, and one to chase away the flies.[10]

Suliman-Pasha was of great help to them in negotiating the purchase of horses and other necessities for their journey, and he lent them his carriage for trips into the surrounding country.

They spent two months in Cairo visiting the pyramids and other historical monuments, then, on 6 February 1850, they went up the Nile for the more arduous part of their journey. As their ship sped up the river, Flaubert, instead of being full of ardour for the future, for the trip which he was enjoying, was reminiscing about the past, thinking of his departure from France. On the Nile it was of another river that he dreamed, one nearer home, of the house he had left behind him and, like Du Bellay in the sixteenth century, he thought nostalgically of his homeland. In his *Notes de Voyages* he writes:[11]

Là-bas, sur un fleuve plus doux, moins antique, j'ai quelque part une maison blanche dont les volets sont fermés, maintenant que je n'y suis pas. Les peupliers sans feuilles frémissent dans le brouillard froid, et les morceaux de glace que charrie la rivière viennent se heurter aux rives durcies. Les vaches sont à l'étable, les paillassons sur les espaliers, la fumée de la ferme monte lentement dans le ciel gris.

J'ai laissé la longue terrasse Louis XIV, bordée de tilleuls, où, l'été, je me promène en peignoir blanc. Dans six semaines déjà, on verra leurs bourgeons. Chaque branche alors aura des boutons rouges, puis viendront les primevères, qui sont jaunes, vertes, roses, iris. Elles garnissent l'herbe des cours. O primevères, mes petites, ne perdez pas vos graines, et que je vous revoie à l'autre printemps.

J'ai laissé le grand mur tapissé de roses avec le pavillon au bord de l'eau. Une touffe de chèvrefeuille pousse en dehors sur le balcon de fer. A une heure du matin en juillet, par le clair de lune, il y fait bon venir pêcher les caluyots.

To his mother he wrote:[12] 'I see the garden ... the house ... you leaning out of the window ... I hear the sound of the latch of the gate, when the postman comes, and, when there is nothing for you, what a sad day you spend!'

In his *Carnets de Voyages*, there is another prose poem, which is not part of the regular text written consecutively, from page to page, but at the back of the note-book, so that it may have been composed later:[13]

O Nil! ma tristesse est débordante comme tes eaux, et personne, non plus, ne saurait dire d'où elle vient, c'est au coeur (au milieu) de mon été que l'inondation est accourue [?], mais rien ne poussera sur le limon qu'elle y dépose. Aucun voyageur encore n'est remonté jusqu'à sa source. Quand la nuit était venue alors il respirait plus à l'aise – il se couchait sur le dos et, levant ses deux bras, il regardait les étoiles comme des femmes, en regardant couler les eaux pacifiques.

The word queried is difficult to decipher in the manuscript. Dumesnil interprets it as 'assoupie',[14] but it looks more like 'accourue' which makes better sense.

One of the greatest experiences which Flaubert enjoyed in the eastern trip was his encounter with the famous courtesan Kuschiuk Hanem. In the published correspondence her name is always printed 'Ruschiuk Hanem', and Dumesnil declares that Flaubert always spelt her name in this way.[15] This is, however, a misreading of his handwriting, for his capital 'K' and 'R' are very similar and could be confused. Louis Bouilhet, who knew Flaubert's writing well, spells her name correctly in the poem he composed to celebrate her, published in his collection *Festons et Astragales*. The poet's evocation of the courtesan was based on Flaubert's description of her in his letters:

C'est l'heure du soleil et du calme étouffant.
Les champs n'ont pas un cri, les cieux pas une brise;
– Dans ta maison d'Esneh, que fais-tu maintenant,
Brune Kuschiuk Hanem, auprès du fleuve assise?

Le mouton qui te suit, de henné tacheté,
Sur la natte en jouant agace ton chien leste;
Et ta servante noire, accroupie à côté,
Croise ses bras luisants tatoués par la peste!

Le joueur de rebec dort sur son instrument.
Dans ton lit de palmier, maintenant tu reposes!
Ou sur ton escalier tu te tiens gravement,
Avec ton tarbouch large et tes pantalons roses!

L'émeraude, à ton front, allume un rayon vert,
Ta gorge s'arrondit sous une gaze fine,
Et tes cheveux, poudrés par le vent du désert,
Ont une odeur de miel et de térébenthine!

Mais une ombre obscurcit ton regard éclatant.
Tu te sens, dans ton coeur, triste comme une veuve,
Et tu penches la tête, écoutant . . . écoutant
Passer le bruit lointain des canges sur le fleuve.

All men who came to Esneh felt inspired, and obliged, to
visit Kuschiuk Hanem. Many writers and visitors have confused her with the still more famous 'almée', Saphira, who
had been the mistress of Abbas Pasha, who dismissed her,
after having had her severely beaten, because she had sold
some of his presents in the bazaar. She then settled in Esneh
but had no connection with Kuschiuk Hanem. She was a
legendary figure, whereas her rival had no history. Du Camp
was the first to lead his readers astray in his account of the
journey.[16] It is strange that he should have made this mistake, since Flaubert was aware of the difference between the
two women, and mentions it in his *Notes de Voyages*.[17] All
other writers have repeated the error, but Auriant admitted
eventually that he had once confused the two women and he
later corrected his mistake.[18]

Several accounts of Du Camp's and Flaubert's visit to Kus-
chiuk Hanem have come down to us: in Du Camp's *Le Nil,
Égypte et Nubie*, published in 1860; in Flaubert's letters to
Bouilhet from the East; in his *Notes de Voyages*; and in his
Carnets, which are preserved in the Bibliothèque de la Ville
de Paris.

It is interesting to compare the difference between Du
Camp's and Flaubert's relation of the meeting with the
courtesan – and also between Flaubert's various accounts.

The latter is always more direct and more human, whereas Du Camp is merely factual and he has little of the novelist's talent for verbal evocation. His work was published by himself, revised and corrected by himself with an eye on criticism and censorship; while Flaubert's notes were written for himself alone, and he never saw any of them published. In his *Carnets*, in particular, he had no inhibitions of any sort and wrote with complete freedom. This is noticeable in his description of the erotic 'danse de l'abeille', which would not have passed the censor,[19] and which, even in *Notes de Voyages*, is very much cut.[20] He remembered it later when describing Salomé's dance in *Hérodias* from *Trois Contes*.

When Kuschiuk Hanem heard of the arrival of the two travellers in Esneh, she sent her maid Bambeh to their ship to tell them that she would expect them that evening. The servant-girl came accompanied by the courtesan's pet lamb, which, as we have seen in Bouilhet's poem, was spotted with henna and followed her round like a faithful dog.

In the evening they went to Kuschiuk Hanem's house and were ushered in by Bambeh. As they entered the courtyard they saw, at the end, a stairway, on which, outlined against the bright blue sky, stood the courtesan in her pink silk pantaloons, with her torso bare, except for a transparent gauze scarf. She had just come from her bath and smelt very sweetly. She began by perfuming their hands with otto of roses.

They followed her to the upper storey and into a large square room, where there were two divans, and which was lit by two windows, one opening on to a view of the mountains, and the other on to the town; through that window they were shown the house of the famous Saphira.[21]

Kuschiuk Hanem was a tall and beautiful woman, whiter of skin than is usual with Arab women. She was well built and plump, with enormous black eyes and finely drawn brows. She wore jauntily, on her frizzy black hair, a large tarbush with a blue tassel. Her arms were tattooed with blue lettering in Arab characters.

She conducted them into the private apartments of the house and they asked for 'la danse de l'abeille' which she normally danced with Bambeh, and which, as described by Flaubert, seems to have been very erotic and sensual – not to say pornographic.[22] The two young musicians who accompanied the dancers on their instruments had their eyes bound with handkerchiefs so that their youth should not be contaminated.

Flaubert returned to the courtesan later and stayed the night. He declared that the most powerful physical sensations he had ever experienced in his life were those with Kuschiuk Hanem, and he described the whole episode fully in his *Carnets*.[23]

Later she fell asleep, with her hand in his, but he remained awake all through the night, watching over her as she slept, and, as he gazed at her, he thought of all his buried affections. He was touched to hear her snore, and later she coughed so that he was moved to compassion, and care of her, and he covered her with his cloak. Several times during the night she awoke and they came together again, each time with stronger sensations on his part. In the morning they separated, and, as he left, Flaubert reflected sadly to himself, but without much conviction: 'How sweet it would be for one's pride, if one could ever be sure of leaving some memory behind one, be certain that she will think of one more than of all the others, that one will remain in her heart.'[24]

On his return journey, he went back once more to see Kuschiuk Hanem, but he found her sad, ill and depressed, for her pet lamb had died. The second visit did not compare, in intensity, with the first encounter, but it filled him with the bitter and ironic reflections which he appreciated. As he left he assured her that he would return on the following day, but he knew that he would not do this and that he would never see her again: 'It is the end,' he wrote,[25] 'I shall never see her again, and her face, little by little, will fade from my memory.'

They next spent two months travelling up the Nile and stopping at various places; and then decided to cross the desert from Keneh to Qôseir on camel-back. During this journey there occurred a comic quarrel between Du Camp and Flaubert, which might have ended in tragedy and which the former has recounted in his *Souvenirs Littéraires*.[26] They had with them, for the whole trip, only two bottles of poor-quality water, but an accident occurred so that both bottles were broken when they were still three days from their destination. They were able to procure a small quantity of water from other travellers whom they encountered, but they were very short and suffered greatly from thirst, as their mouths were parched. Some madness seized Flaubert and he began to discourse on the ices he had eaten in his life, and especially the lemon ices to be obtained at the Café Tortoni in Paris. 'Do you remember the lemon ices at Tortoni's?' he asked, and, as Du Camp only answered with a nod, he went on: 'Lemon ice is a wonderful thing; now admit that you wouldn't mind one here and now!' And, as his friend gave him no reply, he continued: 'Round the rim of the glass bowl there is a faint haze, like white hoar frost.' For miles he went on extolling the qualities of lemon ice, the pleasure of it on the tongue, and then sliding down the throat. He became quite lyric on the subject so that Du Camp felt that he would go mad and it was only by falling back, on his camel, that he was able to resist the temptation of shooting him down, as he rode ahead of him. Luckily, next day they reached the Nile and slaked their thirst on the water, finer than any wine or lemon ice.

They next came to Beirut and found, to their surprise and pleasure, that the Postmaster General was Camille Rogier, who had been a painter member of the Bouzingo fraternity in the 1830s. They found that they were all of the same spiritual family and they spent three charming days with him and his friends, and could hardly drag themselves away.[27]

From there they moved on to Jerusalem, and Flaubert was

much interested in the contrast between the spiritual associations of the place and the appalling state of decomposition and decay.[28]

> Jérusalem est un charnier entouré de murs; la première chose curieuse que nous y ayons rencontrée, c'est la boucherie. Dans une sorte de place carrée, couverte de monticules d'immodices, un grand trou; dans le trou, du sang caillé, des tripes, des m . . ., des boyaux noirâtres et bruns, presque calcinés au soleil, tout à l'entour. Ça puait très fort, c'était beau comme franchise de saleté. Ainsi disait un homme à rapprochements ingénieux et à allusions fines: 'Dans la ville sainte, la première chose que nous y vîmes, c'est du sang.'

He was also amused, ironically, to see a large portrait of Louis-Philippe hanging in the Holy Sepulchre.[29]

In the church he was much moved when a Greek priest blessed a rose especially for him and handed it to him. He would have liked to have had faith, and he reflected how sweet such a moment would have been for a believer.[30]

In Jerusalem, one evening after dinner with the French Consul, he heard someone playing a sonata by Beethoven, which recalled his dead sister, and the whole scene of his youth came back to him with unbearable poignancy:[31]

> Le soir, sonate de Beethoven qui me rappelle ma pauvre soeur, le père Malenson et ce petit salon où je vois Miss Jane apporter un verre d'eau sucrée. Un sanglot m'a empli le coeur, et cette musique si mal jouée m'a navré de tristesse et de plaisir, ça a duré toute la nuit, où j'ai eu un cauchemar y relatif.

It was on the journey to Beirut that Flaubert contracted syphilis. There is no doubt about this, as he discusses and describes his symptoms in the unpublished portions of his letters to Louis Bouilhet, written at this time, saying that he probably caught the disease from a young Maronite.[32] This illness seems to have been the main cause of the curtailing of their trip. The original plan had been to cross the Syrian desert, to pass through Baghdad, on the way to the Caspian Sea. This project was, however, abandoned. Flaubert said later that this was due to lack of funds, but Du Camp declared that Madame Flaubert was to blame for the decision. It is true that he had written to tell her that her son had been ill, and that he received a letter from her in Beirut, urging them to return home as soon as possible.[33] She also expressed anxiety on the score of the dangers of the journey, which were very real. The country was infested with brigands, and the two young men had been shot at one night, and had been lucky to escape with their lives.[34]

When their trip was finally curtailed, Flaubert does not seem to have been unduly displeased. One of his strongest emotions, all through the journey, had been nagging nostalgia for home, in spite of all his dreams of eastern travel. Similarly, when he had finally reached Paris as a student, after longing for most of his life to get there, he spent his time and energy, to the detriment of his work, yearning for home. He was a man of strong family affections who was never happy for long when separated from those who were near and dear to him.

Du Camp, for his part, abandoned their plans grudgingly, and this is understandable, for he was busy collecting material which was valuable to him and which he knew that he could use to his advantage.

At Beirut they embarked for Rhodes, where they were interned on account of the quarantine for the cholera epidemic. When they were released they went to Smyrna and afterwards to Constantinople, where they were entertained by Baudelaire's mother and step-father, General Aupick, who was French Ambassador at the court of the Sultan. Du Camp tells us that, during the conversation, Aupick had asked him what new writers had appeared on the literary horizon since he had left Paris, and he had answered that Baudelaire was the poet most frequently mentioned.[35] There was, he tells us, immediate embarrassment on the part of the Ambassador and his wife, and the conversation was changed. She, however, he declares, as soon as she could leave her duties as hostess, drew him aside and said to him:

'You do think, don't you, that he's got talent, the young poet of whom you were speaking.'

Flaubert makes no mention of the conversation either in his *Notes de Voyages* or his correspondence. Du Camp was writing thirty-five years after the events, and sixteen years after the death of Baudelaire, when he had become a famous poet – Aupick and his wife were also dead – and it is very likely that he invented the episode. In any case, in 1850, Baudelaire was known as an art critic and not as a poet.

By December 1850 they reached the Piraeus, but they did not have the time to visit Greece as they would have wished. It is, however, interesting to note how Flaubert responded to the Greek scene and landscape as he had not done in the East, and felt as if he had, at last, reached his spiritual home. His descriptions are more easy and natural than when he was depicting the oriental scene.

He was surprised to see that the Greeks were poorer and wilder than the Turks. Then he suddenly saw the Parthenon and realized that here was the country that, above all others, he had wanted to see. He wrote to his mother:[36]

As for me, I am in an Olympian state, and I'm filling my brain full of antiquity. The sight of the Parthenon is one of the things which have most deeply moved me in my life. In spite of what anyone may say, Art isn't a falsehood. Let the bourgeois be happy! I don't envy them their heavy bliss.

And there was also, in Greece, wherever he looked, the sea which had been part of his dreams since he was born, and which he had missed in the East.

By this time Flaubert looked a regular tramp. His clothes were in rags, and he wore a goatskin coat patched with foxes' tails. He had lost a great deal of his hair on account of his illness, but his face was completely covered with a thick beard, and his fair skin was burnt nearly black. He had grown very stout during his travels and he looked far older than his twenty-nine years. His mother was horrified when she met him in Rome shortly afterwards, and she thought that he had grown very coarse during the twenty-one months since she had last seen him.

From Greece they sailed for the south of Italy and there, in Naples, nearer to modern western civilization, Flaubert shaved off his beard.

He was delighted with the museums in Naples and Rome, and their good organization. He describes the exhibits minutely in his travel notes.

Just as in Genoa, five and a half years previously, he experienced an 'illumination' when he was deeply stirred by the picture of a virgin and child by Murillo, in the Corsini Palace in Rome. This was because the woman depicted was the type which always moved him, the prototype of Élisa Schlésinger.[37] He mentions the experience several times in his correspondence. To his mother he wrote:[38] 'I saw, the other day, a *Virgin* by Murillo, which is enough to make one mad.' And to Louis Bouilhet he said:[39] 'I saw a *Virgin* by Murillo which pursues me like a continual hallucination.' and again:[40] 'I'm in love with the *Virgin* by Murillo in the Corsini Gallery. Her head follows me everywhere and her eyes come and go before me like dancing lanterns.'

The obsession with Élisa Schlésinger continued with him and, coming out of the church of Saint Paul, outside the city walls, he suddenly caught sight of a woman, dressed in a red bodice, leaning on the arm of an older woman. With her pale face, her dark brows and black eyes, she brought back to his mind the image of the woman whom he had so deeply loved in his boyhood. The description of this encounter is on a loose sheet in the *Carnets*, headed 'Rome, avril 1851' and it is published in the *Notes de Voyages*:[41]

En tournant la tête à gauche, j'ai vu venir lentement une femme en corsage rouge, elle donnait le bras à une vieille femme qui l'aidait à marcher. . . . J'ai pris mon lorgnon et je me suis avancé, quelque chose me tirait vers elle.

Quand elle a passé près de moi, j'ai vu une figure pâle, avec des sourcils noirs, et un large ruban rouge noué à son chignon et retombant sur ses épaules; elle était bien pâle! . . .

Elle avait un front blanc, d'un blanc de vieil ivoire ou de paros bien poli, front carré, rendu ovale par ses deux bandeaux noirs derrière lesquels fulgurait son ruban rouge (bordé de deux filets blancs) qui rehaussait la pâleur de sa figure. Le blanc de ses yeux était particulier. On eût dit qu'elle s'éveillait, qu'elle venait d'un autre monde, et pourtant c'était calme, calme! sa prunelle, d'un noir brillant, et presque en relief tant elle était nette, vous regardait avec sérénité. Quels sourcils! noirs, très minces et descendant doucement! il y avait une assez grande distance entre le sourcil et l'oeil, ça grandissait ses paupières et embellissait ses sourcils que l'on pouvait voir séparément, indépendamment de l'oeil. Un menton en pomme, les deux coins de la bouche un peu affaissée, un peu de moustache bleuâtre aux commissures, l'ensemble du visage rond . . .

En sortant de l'église, je l'ai revue au loin, assise sur des pierres, à côté des maçons qui travaillaient.

Je ne la reverrai plus.

He visited other churches and other places of interest, and then returned to his hotel:

Déjà ses traits s'effacent dans ma mémoire.
Adieu! Adieu!
Mardi Saint, 15 avril 1851.

Flaubert was home in Croisset by the middle of July 1851, after twenty-one months of absence. He returned very much changed but uncertain of his plans, knowing only that he wanted to begin writing immediately. He had by now recovered from the shock of the rejection of his *Tentation de Saint Antoine*, and, writing to Louis Bouilhet, he said:[42]

I've nevertheless recovered (not without difficulty) from the terrible blow of *Saint Antoine*. I can't claim and boast of not being still a little stupefied by it, but I'm no longer ill from it, as I was during the first four months of the trip. I saw everything through the veil of weariness in which my disappointment had wrapped me, and I used to repeat to myself, the foolish phrase which you send me: 'What is the use of anything?'

We see, from his correspondence, that, during his travels, he had been contemplating several projects, none of which had anything to do with *Madame Bovary*. Writing to Louis Bouilhet, from Constantinople, he said:[43]

Talking of subjects, I've three of them, which are perhaps the same one, and that worries me a great deal. 1. *Une Nuit de Don Juan* which I thought of in the lazaret at Rhodes. 2. The story of *Anubis*, the woman who wants to be loved by God. That is the highest but it presents most terrible difficulties. 3. My Flemish novel, about a young woman who dies a virgin and a mystic, with her father and mother in a little provincial town.

It cannot be true, as Du Camp asserts,[44] that Flaubert suddenly exclaimed, as they were visiting a cataract on the Nile: 'Eureka! I'll call her Emma Bovary!' We shall see that, even if he had thought of composing the novel which was to become *Madame Bovary* – which is highly unlikely – he was not to decide on the names of his characters until he had well embarked on writing the novel.

Flaubert had gone to the East to find Romanticism, but he returned cured of what he had come now to regard as a disease. Before he had left home he had seen the Orient through Byron and Hugo, but, out there, it was the coarse realism of everything which had struck him. He saw, with fascination, the mixture of the filth and the glamour; the lice beneath the jewels and the gold; the contrast between the decay and the luxury. In the East he saw things as they were and not as he wished to see them. Writing to Louise Colet he said:[45]

Up to now the Orient has always been seen as something brilliant, noisy, passionate and violent. Only dancing girls and curved swords were noticed – fanaticism and voluptuousness, etc. In short, people have still remained at the stage of Byron. I felt it differently. On the contrary, what I love in the East is that grandeur which is unaware of itself; that harmony of contrasts. I recall a swimmer who had, on his left arm, a silver bracelet, and, on the other, a plaster. That is the Orient and nevertheless poetic! Scoundrels in gold-braided rags, and covered with vermin. Leave the vermin there, it makes golden arabesques in the sunlight! You tell me that Kuschiuk Hanem's bugs degraded her in your eyes; but that is what delighted me. Their nauseating smell mingled with the perfume of her skin impregnated with the scent of sandalwood. ... It reminds me of Jaffa where, on entering, I smelt, at the same time, the perfume of the lemon trees and the stench of the corpses; the broken-down cemetery revealed skeletons half rotted, whilst the green bushes waved their golden fruit above our heads. Don't you feel how complete is this poetry, and that it is a perfect synthesis?

His view of the world made him grow in humanity, and he felt compassion for the state of suffering mankind. He tried to understand the seething masses and to experience their agony in himself. He saw men as the same everywhere, East or West, but he recoiled from nothing.

The friendship between Flaubert and Du Camp had worn somewhat thin during their travels, and it appeared that they both returned to France a little disillusioned with one another. They realized, at such close quarters together and for so long a time, how different now were their aims and ideals. Flaubert began to see how ambitious was Du Camp and that his love for literature was far from being disinterested, that it was to be a stepping-stone to personal success.

After his return to France Du Camp published the notes and photographs which he had taken on the journey, in book form, in 1853, under the title *Égypte, Nubie, Palestine, Syrie*. He was a very good photographer, and it is the photographs which really constitute the value of the book – Flaubert was very contemptuous of the letter-press.[46] Nevertheless it is a very beautiful book, with very fine pictures for the time – indeed for any time – which do much credit to Du Camp, especially when the rough and unsatisfactory conditions under which he took and developed the plates are remembered.

Like his part of the travel book on Brittany, which he wrote with Flaubert in 1847, this book is also factual, and there is not much more in the letter-press than would be found in a guide book, but the material was new at the time. There are no personal reflections, no individual reactions, nothing that reveals the born writer; it is allusive to other writers rather than original. It is very inferior in quality to the best parts of Flaubert's *Notes de Voyages,* or to his *Carnets,* or to his spontaneous letters to his friends on his journey. Du Camp gives no episode in particular which struck him, nothing of the difficulties which they encountered, or the pleasures which they enjoyed. Nevertheless he must have done a great deal of research to produce his book, and he did carry out the mission with which he had been entrusted, which is more than Flaubert did, for on many occasions, in his letters, he mentions that he is not bothering at all about his assignment.

Du Camp, in January 1852, was raised to the rank of Officier de la Légion d'Honneur for his recent services to learning – he was, as we have seen, already Chevalier for the part he had played in the Revolution of 1848.

He published later a second and fuller book from his travel notes entitled *Le Nil, Égypte et Nubie,* in 1860, and dedicated it to Gautier. Flaubert was again very contemptuous of this production.[47] He talks of the flatness of its style and calls it a 'come-down'. Here, too, Du Camp was factual rather than personal and original; it is narrative rather than critical; historical rather than psychological.

Zola, very unfairly, in *Romanciers Naturalistes,*[48] says that Flaubert's notes on his journey were copied from Du Camp's, but an examination of these notes and his correspondence proves this accusation to be totally unfounded.

Flaubert returned to Croisset in July 1851 very uncertain yet about his plans, knowing only that he wanted to write and that this was the only thing in the world that he wanted to do. He was now almost thirty, but he looked far older than his years, for, after he had contracted syphilis, there was a sudden and serious deterioration in his physical appearance. He had lost most of his hair on account of the mercury treatment; he had grown very stout, and he now seemed well set

in middle age. He looked old, he felt old, and he knew that
he should not waste any more time. He had published
nothing yet, except the two little contributions in the local
Rouen paper, *Le Colibri*, when he was a boy of fifteen. It was
no wonder that the ambitious Maxime Du Camp was forever
urging him to hurry.

BOOK TWO

SUMMER HARVEST

PART ONE

The Workshop

[15]

The Hermit of Croisset
(1851–6)

FLAUBERT was home in Croisset in July 1851, full of energy
and ready to begin work. He was, at first, in a state of great
indecision, and seems to have continued contemplating the
three subjects which he had earlier mentioned in a letter to
Louis Bouilhet, and which were discussed in the previous
chapter.[1] Du Camp inquires about them in a letter of July
that year.[2] We do not know at what moment Flaubert
finally decided to use the story of Delphine Delamare, but
he had certainly thought about it by then since Du Camp
mentions it, saying: 'What are you doing now? What have
you decided? What are you working at? Have you reached a
decision yet? Is it still Don Juan? Or is it the story of
Madame Delamarre (sic) which is so beautiful, and how do
you know about it?'[3] This is proof that he did not know of it
before he went to the East, and could not have thought
about it during the journey.

Du Camp went to Croisset at the end of the month, and it
is probable that they discussed the story of Eugène and Delphine Delamare. It is also very likely that Madame Flaubert had mentioned the death of Eugène to him, which had
occurred during his absence – we know that he had been a
student of her husband at the Hôtel Dieu.[4] What is clear
is that the subject of the novel must have been decided on by
September 1851, for Flaubert, who had a feeling for anniversaries, wrote on the manuscript that he had begun the book
on his name date 'la Sainte Gustave', 19 September. By
August he must have fixed on the title – for the surname at
all events – as Du Camp wrote to him then saying, after a
personal emotional drama:[5]

Yes, certainly I'm going to have a fine trip! I'm leaving sick at heart, and with the desire to throw myself over all the bridges I'll be crossing – well! it could be interesting and I must consider it as a subject for study. I could give you, for your Bovary, everything I've got in me, in this respect; it might be useful to you.

From then on, until he finished the novel, Flaubert remained almost entirely in Croisset, with some excursions away from it. He went to London at the end of September 1851, to see the Great Exhibition, accompanied by his mother and little niece aged five and a half. While he was there he met Henrietta Collier again, and he seems to have felt once more deep affection for her, but he does not seem to have encountered Gertrude, who had been married since 1847. There followed a long correspondence between himself and Henrietta.[6] He also spent three weeks in Paris at the time of the *coup d'état* of 2 December 1851 – and he almost lost his life on several occasions – when the President of the Second Republic, Louis Bonaparte, made himself Emperor. He was to remember that time later, as he was composing *L'Éducation Sentimentale* and needed local colour for his description of the episode.

We have seen that Croisset was a lovely eighteenth-century house, the gardens stretching along the banks of the river and climbing up the hill behind it. From the windows of his study he could see the long stretches of the river, and could view the ships sailing up from the coast, coming from distant lands, for Rouen was one of the most important ports of the country. He liked to see these ships, for they bore his dreams abroad, and he used to inspect them through his telescope. He liked dreaming of distant lands when it was impossible for him to travel. From his windows he had also a view of the thousand spires of Rouen and of the rich pastures where the white and red cows used to graze peacefully. He loved this country which he had known since his earliest childhood.

His study was simply and inelegantly furnished, for he does not seem to have had any taste in house decoration.[7]

The chief features of the room were heavily carved oak bookcases, which covered most of the walls. There were portraits or drawings of his friends, and an enormous oak writing-table on which stood a large supply of goose quills, for he never used anything else, despising steel pens and even blotting-paper, which he said was only for bankers. Beside the table stood the high-backed armchair in which he always sat to write. There are two of these armchairs, identical except for small hardly noticeable details; one in Croisset, in the little summer-house at the river's edge; and the other in the upstairs room at the town hall in the village of Canteleu, where Flaubert's library is preserved, in the bookcases from his study. The librarian, Edmond Ledoux, claims that the chair in his possession is the one in which the novelist wrote.[8] But the drawing of the study made by his niece reveals that the chair there is more like the one now kept in the summer-house.

In the study could also be seen a bronze Buddha and a beautiful bust, in marble, of the author's sister Caroline, by Pradier, executed from her death mask. There were also a divan, on which he rested after his literary exertions, and a bear-skin on the floor. The room had five windows, three opening on to the garden at the back, and two looking out over the river.

At the edge of the river stands the little summer-house, which is all that is now left of the property and which has become a Flaubert museum, though he never worked in it. He used to go there with his friends for coffee after dinner, and sometimes he read to them from the works he was writing.

Croisset had once belonged to the monks of the Abbey of Saint-Ouen, and Flaubert liked to imagine that l'Abbé Prévost had composed part of his *Manon Lescaut* within its walls.[9]

Flaubert adopted at Croisset the kind of existence which he was to lead for the rest of his life when he was working on a book. The house had to be kept quiet until ten o'clock in the morning, for he never stirred until then – he normally wrote for most of the night. Then, when his bell rang, his servant hurried up with the post, the daily papers, a glass of cold water and his first pipe of the day. We know, from the account of all his friends, that he smoked twenty pipes a day and he had a large rack of them in his study. However, when one sees the size of these pipes, in the museum at Croisset, one realizes that his smoking cannot have been excessive, as each held only a pinch of tobacco, and they were the size of a thimble. When he had smoked his first pipe and drunk his glass of water, he called for his mother, bellowing like a spoilt child – all her thoughts were now centred on him, with her husband and daughter dead, and her elder son married, with a family of his own. She sat with him until he rose. Breakfast and lunch were combined in a Gargantuan meal at eleven o'clock; like most Normans, he loved his food, and many are the descriptions of rich meals in his writings. After lunch he walked up and down on the terrace, beneath the canopy of lime trees, for which he had felt such nostalgia during his eastern trip, watching the craft sailing up the river and meditating. At one o'clock he gave his little niece her lessons and he took this task very seriously. Then he read until seven o'clock, when came the second Gargantuan meal of the day; after which he sat with his mother until she retired to bed at nine or ten o'clock. Then began his real work of the day, when he wrote while the house was quiet, often six hours at a stretch, when everyone was asleep. Once, he claims, he worked almost continuously for thirty-six hours and felt a wonderful sensation of serenity afterwards[10]:

What good days I spent on Thursday and Friday! On Thursday night, at two o'clock in the morning, I went to bed, but so lively after my work that, at three o'clock, I got up again and I worked until midday. That night, at one o'clock, I went to bed, and then only to be sensible. I had such a fury of style in my belly that I could have gone on double the time. On Friday morning, when day broke, I went for a walk round the garden. It had rained, the birds were beginning to sing, and large slate-coloured clouds were racing across the sky. I enjoyed there some moments of immense power and serenity which one remembers afterwards and which make one forget much unhappiness. I can still experience a kind of after-taste of these thirty-six Olympian hours, and I remained gay after them, as if from happiness.

My first part is nearly finished.

I feel a great sensation of relief.

I have never written anything with so much care as these last twenty pages.

He led, when he was working, an orderly, disciplined life like that of a bourgeois. Writing to Louise Colet, he said:[11] 'One must make two parts in one's life: live like a bourgeois and think like a God. The satisfactions of the body and of the mind have nothing in common.'

Every Sunday Louis Bouilhet came to spend the day with him, sleeping the night at Croisset; and they used to go over everything which Flaubert had written during the week, discussing each line.

However, in October 1853, after the success of his *Melaenis*, Bouilhet decided to try his luck in Paris and he left Rouen. Flaubert was heart-broken and said that he would miss him more than he could ever say.[12] 'It's all over now! The old Sundays are broken up! I'll be alone now, alone, alone. I'm overcome with boredom and humiliated with intellectual impotence.'

These years of work on *Madame Bovary* were the time of Flaubert's second period of his liaison with Louise Colet,[13] but his mind was not solely occupied with her; his mind – and probably more besides – seems to have wandered towards the English governess of his little niece, whom his mother had engaged when they had gone to London for the Exhibition in 1851, and who arrived in November that year. To allay Louise Colet's jealousy, Flaubert said to her:[14] 'I forgot to tell you that the devout little governess arrived ten days ago. Her physical appearance doesn't impress me.' However Du Camp, writing to him the following April, said:[15] 'Above all be careful not to make the young governess pregnant, whose love seems to flatter you.' This must be Isabella Hutton, who came in November 1851 and left in July 1853.[16] Perhaps Flaubert's attentions to her may have been the cause of her departure – or dismissal – though he himself declared that she was sent away because she ill-treated the child.[17] She was followed by another English governess called Juliet Herbert. Pommier believes that Du Camp, in his letter, is referring to her, but he is mistaken in this, as Isabella was still at Croisset at the time.[18] Flaubert seems to have become particularly attached to Juliet Herbert, and he carried on a correspondence with her even after she had left the family – certainly until after 1870 – and used to go to see her each time that he went to England. His niece stayed with her during the German occupation of France in the 1870 war.

So, while indulging in his affair with Louise Colet, Flaubert seems also to have been occupied, from 1851 to 1853, with his niece's first governess; and, from July 1853, with the second; but it is not known whether his attentions to either were more than flirtatious.

He occasionally left Croisset for odd days and weeks. There was the visit to London in September 1851; to Paris in December the same year; the visit to Mantes, with Louise Colet, in an attempt to recapture some of their former emotion.[19] There was, especially, the significant visit to Trouville in August 1853, when he was dreaming of the past and wishing to relive it. He also needed contact with the sea at certain intervals, as otherwise he lost his courage and his strength. He once said that the three best things that God had ever created were the sea, *Hamlet* and Mozart's *Don Juan*.[20] All the memories of his childhood welled up in him; all his past, his longings, his dreams and his disappointments; all this he was soon to pour into *Madame Bovary*:[21]

All the memories of my youth reverberated under my steps, like the shells of the sea-shore. Each wave of the sea, which I see breaking, awakens in me distant echoes. I hear the rumbling of the by-gone days, and the never-ending sequence of vanished passions, surging like waves. I remember the passion that I felt, the sadness and the longing that I experienced, which whistled like gusts of wind, like storms in the rigging, and imperative desires whirled in the darkness like a flock of wild gulls in the stormy air ...

The other day, in the heat of the day, and alone, I walked eighteen miles at the edge of the sea. It took the whole afternoon. I got back quite intoxicated, for I had imbibed so many smells and so much fresh air. I gathered sea-weed and picked up shells; and I lay, flat on my back, on the sand and on the grass. I put my hands over my eyes and I looked up at the clouds. I got lonely, I smoked, I gazed at the poppies, I slept for five minutes on the sand dunes. A soft rain awoke me. At times I heard the song of a bird cutting across the noise of the sea. Sometimes a little stream, flowing through the cliff, mingled its soft music with the beating of the waves. I went home just as the setting sun was gilding the window-panes of the village. It was low tide. The hammer of the carpenters reverberated on the skeletons of the boats in dry-dock. One could smell the tar, mingling with the smell of oysters.

He was also pondering on his future. He was almost half-way through his allotted three score years and ten, and he decided to cast all this nostalgia for the past behind him and to concentrate on the time that still lay before him. As he wrote to Louis Bouilhet:[22]

This trip to Trouville made me go over my course of personal history. I've dreamt a great deal on the scene of my passions. I take leave of them and forever, I hope. Here am I half-way through my life. It is time to say farewell to youthful sadness. Nevertheless I don't deny that for three weeks they have flowed over me in waves. I've had two or three good afternoons alone, on the sand, in the sunlight, and where I found, sadly, other things than broken shells. I've finished with all that. Thank God. Let's cultivate our garden and not raise our head to listen to the screeching of the rooks.

Flaubert was not progressing very rapidly with the composition of *Madame Bovary*, and his mind seems to have been partly distracted with the idea of another work, in the

vein of his metaphysical writings, a return to the inspiration
of *La Tentation de Saint Antoine* which he had abandoned
in September 1851 when he began writing *Madame Bovary*.

The idea seems to have come to him first towards the end
of April 1852, when he had been at work on his novel for
about eight months, since, in a letter to Louise Colet, he
talks of the 'vague sketch of a tremendous fantastical metaphysical novel, which occurred to me about a fortnight ago.
If I begin work on it, in five or six years' time what will have
happened between this moment, when I'm writing to you,
and the one when the ink will have dried on the last erasures?'[23]

He turned to the subject again at the end of the year[24]
when he had just finished reading *Louis Lambert* by Balzac,
and he was struck by the resemblances between the hero of
the novel and Alfred Le Poittevin – Alfred had always been
associated in his mind with his metaphysical preoccupations.
'I am at the moment,' he wrote,

absolutely terrified, and, if I write to you, it is in order not to be
alone with myself, as one lights a lamp at night when one is
frightened. I don't know whether you'll understand me or not,
but it is most peculiar! Have you ever read a book by Balzac
entitled *Louis Lambert*? I've just finished it five minutes ago; I'm
thunderstruck by it. It is the story of a man who goes mad by
dint of thinking of intangible things. It fastened itself on to me
by a thousand hooks. That Lambert, with a few differences, is
my poor Alfred. I found there our expressions, of that time,
almost literally; the conversations of the two friends at school
were those we used to have, or similar ones. ... Do you remember that I spoke to you of a metaphysical novel, the plan of it,
where a man, by dint of thinking, succeeds in having halluci-
nations, in which the spirit of his friend appears to him, to draw
the conclusion (ideal, absolute) of the premises (worldly, tan-
gible)? Well! that idea is indicated in it, and the whole of the
novel *Louis Lambert* is, as it were, the preface to it.

He mentioned it again a few months later:[25]

My nervous disease has done me good, it has concentrated all that on the physical aspect, leaving my head cool, and it has introduced me to curious psychological phenomena, of which no one has any idea, or rather which no one has yet felt. I'll take my revenge one day by using it all in a book (that metaphysical novel, with apparitions, which I've mentioned to you before). But, as it is a subject which terrifies me, from the health point of view, I must be able to conjure them up artificially, ideally, and hence without danger to myself and to the work.

In August he was still preoccupied with the plan.[26] Writing to Louis Bouilhet, he said: 'How I'm longing to have finished *Bovary*, *Anubis* and my three *prefaces*, to begin a new phase ... I'm dreaming of India, China, of my oriental novel (fragments of which occur to me). I feel the need of tremendous epics.'

He wrote, in identical terms, to Louise Colet three days later.[27]

Amongst Flaubert's unpublished papers, which his niece showed to E. W. Fischer in 1905, there is the rough plan of a text, entitled *La Spirale*, which would seem to correspond with the novel which Flaubert mentioned on several occasions in his correspondence in 1852 and 1853. The title is not mentioned in any of the letters by Flaubert himself, but it is on the folder which his niece showed to Fischer, who published a description of the manuscript, and his interpretation of it, in a French translation in 1908.[28]

There is no date on the manuscript, but there is a strong possibility that it is the work which was preoccupying Flaubert during the early stages of his composition of *Madame Bovary*.

However, Paul Dimoff, in an article entitled 'Autour d'un projet de Roman de Flaubert "La Spirale"', expressed the opinion that it was inspired by Baudelaire's *Les Paradis Artificiels*.[29] He states categorically: 'The real source of *La Spirale* remains certainly *Un Mangeur d'Opium*' – that is an essay in *Les Paradis Artificiels*. If this were true then it could not possibly be the novel which Flaubert discussed in his correspondence, since Baudelaire's work was published only in 1860. It is true that Flaubert might have known his earlier article, 'Du Vin et du Haschich', published in March 1851 in *Le Messager de l'Assemblée*. However, Flaubert was out of France in March 1851, and, moreover, when Baudelaire sent him *Les Paradis Artificiels* in 1860, he did not say that he had ever read the earlier article.

Dimoff does not make out a very good case for his thesis, and his main argument concerns only the title, but Baudelaire uses it with a different meaning. He said:[30] 'La pensée de de Quincey n'est pas seulement sinueuse; le mot n'est pas trop fort; elle est habituellement spirale.'

According to Fischer,[31] Flaubert describes the soaring upwards of the hero's mind 'comme une spirale qui monte à l'infini'. This sufficiently explains the title, and owes nothing to Baudelaire's use of the term.

Only the plan of *La Spirale* exists, which was never carried out. The plot, according to Fischer, can be briefly summarized as follows: The hero is a painter who had lived for many years in the East, where he had formed the habit of indulging in hashish. When he returned to France, he gave up his painting and spent all his days in hallucinatory dreaming, until finally he lived entirely in a state of somnambulism. At his most intense moments he is precipitated back to reality, where he is ill-treated and misunderstood; he is thrown into prison and is finally shut up in a mental hospital, where he reaches complete fulfilment and bliss. The conclusion seems to be that happiness consists in being mad. According to Fischer, the moral of the book would be that 'Tout bonheur repose sur l'illusion, sur l'imaginaire et qu'on peut se sauver par le rêve, en fuyant la vie, l'effroyable vie dont le nom est synonyme de la souffrance.'[32]

This contradicts the conclusion reached by Flaubert when he was writing *Madame Bovary*, that one should learn to know oneself, and that disaster inevitably comes from seeing oneself and reality other than they are.

Flaubert went no further with the project of *La Spirale*. Fischer regrets the abandonment of what he calls 'this conception of genius'.[33] There are, however, many who would not share these regrets. It would have been a return to the extravagant visions of *Smarh* and of the first *Tentation de Saint Antoine*, which he had cast aside, finally deciding not to cut up the latter work for serialization in Maxime Du Camp's new review, *La Revue de Paris*, founded in 1851.

We have seen that, in his correspondence, Flaubert expressed terror of the subject which was probably *La Spirale*, of what it might do to his mental health.[34] He always remained frightened at the thought of drugs and he admitted to Baudelaire, when he received *Les Paradis Artificiels*, that he had never yet tried any because of their possible effect on him, though he was ashamed of this fear.[35]

Whatever may be the reason, we hear no more of *La Spirale*, and, after 1853, Flaubert seems to have allowed nothing to distract his thoughts from the composition of *Madame Bovary*, which continued for a further three years, until 1856.

[16]

The End of the Affair
(1851–5)

SHORTLY after Flaubert returned to Croisset from the East, he renewed his relationship with Louise Colet. His first letter to her is dated 26 July 1851, soon after he got back. It implies that they had met in Rouen – perhaps she wrote to him to arrange a meeting.

Louise Colet was in low spirits at the time, and she was no longer the popular and admired poet she had been six years before, when she had first met him. Since her separation from him, she had been involved in a notorious lawsuit for having published letters of Benjamin Constant to Madame Récamier, of which she had made copies. She had become acquainted with Madame Récamier and, it was alleged at the trial, taking advantage of the lady's blindness, she had obtained from her a declaration, stating that she had been granted the ownership of the letters to do with them what she liked – this document was subsequently declared to be a forgery. Juliette Récamier died of cholera on 11 May 1849, and, the following month, Louise Colet began to make arrangements for the publication of the letters in *La Presse*, where they began to appear on 3 July. Madame Récamier's niece and heir, Madame Lenormand, had the publication stopped on 5 July, and took the matter to the courts, where the lawsuit took place between 25 July and 1 August 1849. It eventually went against Louise Colet, who was also ordered to pay costs, which she could ill afford. She was, moreover, now in 1851, a widow as her husband had died the previous April, while Flaubert was away, and his salary died with him. Hippolyte Colet had returned, at the end, to ask her for shelter and he had died in her house, of tuberculosis. It is impossible to know whether she was sincere, or whether, in her usual manner, she was making copy out of her alleged feelings of grief, but there is a poem entitled *Deuil*, dated May 1851, and published in 1852, in her collection, *Ce qui est dans le coeur des femmes*, which ends:

> Les autres t'oublieront; moi, taisant ma douleur,
> J'évoquerai ton ombre et j'en serai suivie.
> A toi le plus sacré des amours de ma vie!
> A toi le plus sacré des regrets de mon coeur!

She was therefore in great financial difficulties, and in search of any kind of money from literary prizes. Perhaps she was not entirely disinterested in her desire to renew her relationship with Flaubert. She may have thought it possible to marry him, now that she was a widow – Bouilhet certainly believed that three years later.[1]

She may have changed during the six years since she had known Flaubert first, and particularly during the three years since they had last met; but Flaubert, too, had altered greatly; he had gained in confidence in himself, and he knew now where he was going – especially he knew where he did not want to go.

They must have met in Rouen – either by arrangement or by chance – some time in July 1851. He was no longer prepared to sacrifice everything to her, and he was unwilling any more to bear with her tantrums. He told her that he was willing to take up his relationship with her again if only she would be reasonable and calm:[2]

I write to you because my heart urges me to say a few kind words to you, my poor friend. If I could make you happy, I'd do it with joy; it would be only justice. The thought that I've made you suffer so much is a burden to me; don't you understand that? But that doesn't depend (and the rest hasn't depended) on either me or you, but on the things themselves.

You must have found me very cold, the other day in Rouen. All the same I was so as little as possible. I took the greatest pains to be kind; not tender; that would have been scandalous hypocrisy and an insult to the honesty of your heart.

Read a lot and don't dream. Engross yourself in long study;
there's nothing so continuously good as the habit of inveterate
work . . .

I wish you could be in such a state that we could meet one
another calmly. I like your company when it isn't stormy.
Storms, which are so pleasant in youth, become boring in mature
years . . .

You don't say anything about what interests me most, your
plans, you've decided on nothing, I can guess that.

Then he ended in English: 'Farewell! God bless you, poor
child!'

But Louise Colet was incapable of behaving in a calm and
rational manner; she could not cure herself of her pos-
sessiveness and her jealousy; and the struggles and recriminations between them began all over again. There was
some respite while he was in England at the Exhibition, at
the end of September, just after he had begun *Madame
Bovary* – or at least after he had written the title on a sheet
of paper and had added the date of starting the novel.

She wrote a poem to celebrate his return from his trip,
Ressouvenir Païen, dated 1851 and published in her collection *Ce qui est dans le coeur des femmes*, but, after quar-
relling with him, she sent it to Maxime Du Camp pretending
that it had been intended for him. The sentiments, however,
as expressed in the poem, refer to her feelings for Flaubert
rather than for those for Du Camp:

> Dans la lutte et les pleurs vous m'avez rencontrée,
> Inconsolable enfant d'une ardente contrée,
> Et vous vous êtes dit, détournant le regard:
> En elle la souffrance a fait grimacer l'art.

She tried, at first, to ingratiate herself with Flaubert by
showing curiosity about his writings, not realizing that he
lost interest in what he had finished and, on the whole, disliked showing his work to others. Yet, to satisfy her constant
demands to see what he had written, he took out his
Éducation Sentimentale, which he had composed before he
had ever met her, and showed it to her:[3]

I glanced at *L'Education Sentimentale* the day before yesterday evening. You'd have great difficulty in making it out. There are many erasures, hardly indicated. How inexperienced it is in style. Good Heavens! I must indeed love you to make you such confidences at this moment! I'm humbling my literary pride before your wishes.

A few months later, he also showed her his *Tentation de Saint Antoine*, which had been composed after his first separation from her. We have seen that he had not fully agreed with his friends' repudiation of it, but neither did he accept her praise:[4]

And so you're definitely enthusiastic about *Saint Antoine*! Well, I'll have had one person for it, and that's something! ... As for the corrections which you suggest, we'll discuss them; it's an enormous task. ... I'd have great trouble in redoing my Saint. I'd have to absorb myself in it for a long time, to be able to invent anything. I don't say I'll not try it, but it won't be immediately.

But she could not resist the temptation of complaining to him about his character and his conduct, so that he often answered her coldly – as when she accused him of lack of taste, as well as of leaving her without letters:[5]

I've never prided myself, my dear, on being a man of taste, nor of fine manners; the claim would have been too vain. You needn't remind me of that. If your cousin has intuition in matters of the heart, so much the better for her. I haven't even got it in matters of the mind. We each do what we can. Let there be no bitterness between us. What the devil do you want me to write to you about, that you don't know already as well as I? I can't give you any news of society, which I don't see, nor of myself who don't alter, and, as I believe, moreover, as you do, that one should keep one's troubles to oneself without boring others with them, and as I think that I've exaggerated in that respect with you, I've nothing better to do than to do nothing, that is to say, to remain silent. If you only knew in what flat monotony I live, you would be astonished that I can see the difference between winter and summer, and night and day.

She accused him of not loving her sufficiently and he tried to clarify his feelings, but his assurances cannot have been very comforting to her:[6]

You remind me, in your letter, that I promised you your fill of love, I'll send you the truth, or, if you prefer it, I'm going to draw up my sentimental balance sheet, but not on account of bankruptcy. . . . In the highest sense of the word, in the marvellous and dreamt of sense, which makes hearts long for that manna impossible to find; well no! it isn't love! I've delved into these matters so much in my youth that my mind is bewildered for the rest of my life.

I feel for you a mixture of friendship, of attraction, of respect, of tenderness of heart, of excitement of the senses, which make a complicated amalgam of which I don't know the name but which seems to me solid. . . . You're there, in my soul, in a little corner for you alone. If I love others you'll remain, nevertheless, there (it seems to me) you'll be like the favourite wife, the one to whom one always returns; and then, is it not through some sophistry that one would deny the contrary? Examine yourself. Is there a single feeling that you've had which has disappeared? No, everything remains, doesn't it? Everything. The mummies we have in our hearts never fall into dust, and if you look through the window, you see them down below, gazing at you with their eyes wide open, motionless . . .

If I'd loved you as you wanted it, I would no longer love you now so much. The affections which filter, drop by drop, from the heart end by forming stalactites. That is better than the great torrents which sweep it away. That is the truth and I cling to it.

Yes, I love you, my poor Louise, and I would like your life to be sweet in all ways, sanded and bordered with flowers and joys. I love your beautiful and good, frank face, the pressure of your hand, the contact of your skin beneath my lips. If I'm hard to you, believe me, it is the result of all the sadness, the bitter nervousness, the deathly weariness which torture me and swamp me. I've, at the bottom of my nature, the aftertaste of the medieval melancholy of my country. It smells of fog, of plague brought back from the east; and it all subsides to one side, with its carvings, its stained-glass windows, its leaden eaves, like the old wooden houses in Rouen. It is in that niche that you're housed, my beauty; there are many bugs, scratch yourself hard.

Another kiss on your pink mouth.

This reasonable letter, with its artificial imagery, cannot have given her much pleasure and comfort, and it is easy to sympathize with her discomfiture. Nevertheless, he assured her, at the end of a letter of more than ten large printed pages, that she was the greatest affection of his life, and this was indeed true:[7] 'I've not had much voluptuousness in my life, even though I've longed for it. You gave me some. I've not had either many loves (especially happy ones) and I feel for you something calmer, but just as deep, so that you're the best affection I've ever had.'

There were, however, some happy and ecstatic moments, but these were always paid for by hours of anxiety, the constant fear of her pregnancy, and of being caught in family entanglements. He wrote to her on 4 April 1852:[8] 'I'm very anxious about your English troops, though I've nothing to reproach myself with on that score. Me, to have a son! Oh! No! – it would be better to die in the gutter, run over by a bus.'

Luckily the alert proved unfounded, but there was a further one at the end of the year:[9]

If I haven't written to you for the last few days, it is because I was expecting every morning a letter from you, informing me of the event, the delay of which was causing me such hideous anxiety. You don't realize in what a state you put me. I can't understand how I can work in the midst of this worry. I don't cease thinking about you. Look after yourself, and keep me informed. Next Sunday I'll be thirty-one years old. What a cursed birthday it may be!

Two days later he received what he called the best possible birthday gift from her, relief from his anxieties:[10]

I must begin by smothering you with kisses, in the happiness which is sweeping me away. Your letter of this morning removed an enormous weight from my heart. It was time! Yesterday I couldn't work all day. . . . I had to go to bed at eleven, I had a temperature and general lassitude. For three weeks I've suffered most terrible apprehensions; I didn't cease thinking about you for a single minute, but not in an agreeable manner. Oh! that idea tortured me. . . It would need a whole book to elaborate the subject in a comprehensible manner. The idea of giving birth to someone *fills me with horror.* I'd curse myself if I became a father. A son of my own! Oh! no, no, no! Let my flesh perish with me, and let me not transmit to anyone the boredom and the ignominiousness of life.

Then follows an unpublished passage:[11] 'At last, God be praised, there is nothing further to fear, and blessed be the redcoats!' Then he went on:[12]

I'd also a kind of superstitious idea. It's tomorrow that I'll be thirty-one. I've thus passed that fateful year of thirty which classes a man. It's the year when one is set for the future, when one settles down; when one marries and takes a profession. At thirty there are very few people who don't become bourgeois. This paternity would have made me fall into the ordinary conditions of life. My virginity, with respect to the world, would have been wiped out, and I would have sunk into the abyss of common misery. Well! today, serenity overflows in me. I feel calm and radiant. Here is the whole of my youth spent without a blemish or a weakness. From my childhood to the present moment, there is one long straight line. . . . Why did you want this link? No! you don't need, in order to please, to fall into the ordinary conditions of womanhood and, on the contrary, I love you because you're very little a woman, with none of the worldly hypocrisy, nor the weakness of mind. Don't you feel that there is between us a link higher than that of the flesh and independent even of love. Don't spoil for me anything which exists. One is always punished if one leaves one's own path. Let's stay in our own path, separate and for us alone. . . . Time will do nothing to my love because it isn't love as *love might be,* and I'll tell you something which will seem strange to you: It doesn't seem to me that you're my mistress, and that commonplace name never enters my mind when I think of you. You have in me a special place which has never been occupied by anyone else, and, if you weren't there, it would remain empty . . .

I'm not talking literature to you; I'm only just getting over my long anxiety, and my heart is expanding. I'm beginning to breathe again, it's fine, the sun is shining on the river, a yacht is passing with all its sails unfurled; my window is open, and my fire is burning brightly.

Farewell! I love you more than ever, and I smother you with kisses, for my birthday!

Farewell! dear love, much love. Always yours.

Nevertheless there must have been something wrong with her – perhaps a miscarriage or an abortion – for he wrote again, a few days later, with concern:[13]

What is wrong with you my poor darling. What's the reason for all this vomiting, and these abdominal pains, etc. I'm sure that you were near doing something foolish! I'd like to hear that you're completely recovered. All the same I can't disguise from you that the arrival of the *English troops* has been a great joy to me. May the god of coïtus grant that I may never go through such agony again. I don't know how I didn't fall ill.

They returned to Mantes, in an effort to recapture their complete happiness of six years before, in the first stages of their relationship:[14]

Here is what I propose to you: one day, towards the end of next week, towards the 3rd or 4th of June, I'll write to you to arrange a meeting at Mantes, if you'd like it, in our old hotel, and we'd spend there twenty-four hours, far from everyone. A good day, alone the two of us, would be worth five or six visits that I might pay you in Paris, in your house, with crowds around; and it would not break up my work as a pause of a week, at a time when I must not lose the thread of my thought. Tell me whether his plan pleases you.

The visit was a happy one, but there was always, on his side, a withdrawal for the sake of his work, which she did not understand:[15]

You'll remember our forty-eight hours at Mantes, my dear Louise. They were wonderful hours, and I never loved you so much! I had, in my heart, oceans of cream! The whole evening your image followed me round like an hallucination. It's only since yesterday evening that I've begun to work again. Up to then

I spent my time in idleness, in going over the past moments. *I need to grow calm again.*

Courage, a time will come when we'll see one another more frequently. In two or three months time, when my first part is finished, I'll go and spend a few days in Paris and, in October, we'll return to our country house, to see the leaves turn yellow. As soon as my novel is finished I'll take an apartment in Paris. We'll have a solemn house-warming.

Good-bye! I'll write to you at greater length next time, at the end of the week, or at the beginning of the next.

I embrace you! I kiss you everywhere!

Always yours, my love.

In the meantime he had received a letter from her, which she had written on her return home, in which she wrote sadly and regretfully about their separation. He answered in a kind manner, telling her of his own personal sadness at the shortness of their meeting:[16]

This morning I received your kind letter, sad and sweet, my poor dear friend. I'm now going to do as you've done, tell you about my own departure. When I saw your back disappear, I went and stood on the bridge to see the train pass. That's all that I could see. You were in it; I followed the train with my eyes as long as I could, and listened as hard as I could. Towards Rouen the sky was red with even purple streaks. I lit another cigar and walked up and down. Through stupidity or boredom, I went and drank a glass of kirsch in a pub, and then the Paris train came in. ... How good they were, my dear Muse, the days we spent together! I've got very clearly in my mind what I used to understand by *dreams of love*; but what I know clearly is that I don't want anything beyond what you give me and that it seems to me impossible to love as we love one another. Oh! how we melted into one another! how I looked at you! how we embraced one another, and what a penetration there was of all our thoughts! Your good and beautiful face is still there before me; I still have, in front of my eyes, your eyes, and the impression of your mouth on my lips. It will be, for our old age, a warming memory, that walk to Vétheuil, to La Roche, with the wonderful sun that there was. : . . . Poor Mantes! how I love it! We must go there before it is too late, and before the leaves have fallen.

With her letter she had sent him a poem, which she had composed to celebrate their walk to Vétheuil, and which is one of her best. It is entitled *Paysage et Amour*, dated 1853, and published in *Ce qu'on rêve aimant*:

> Oui, pour notre vieillesse, il sera beau, ce jour
> Tout rayonnant de paix, de soleil et d'amour;
> Ensemble nous marchions en face de cette île
> Que le fleuve indolent baigne d'un flot tranquille.
> Les peupliers dans l'air frissonnaient mollement
> Et miraient dans les eaux leur long balancement.
>
> Oh! comme j'étais fière, à ton bras suspendue!
> J'encadrais mon bonheur dans la calme étendue;
> Je mariais les sons adorés de ta voix
> Aux bruits qui s'élevaient des ondes et des bois;
> A la création merveilleuse, infinie,
> J'associais ta force et mêlais ton génie;
> Te sentant grand et bon resplendir sur ce jour,
> Ainsi qu'un Dieu caché visible à mon amour.

In his answer to her letter Flaubert unfortunately forgot to mention the poem and he was obliged to write again to apologize for his carelessness and to praise it. She could not help being hurt at what she considered his indifference. She complained also of his lack of urgency in wishing to see her; and because his letters were so often not love letters at all, but discussions on problems of art, which he could have had with anyone. After she had complained to Bouilhet of the silence of his friend, and Louis had passed on these complaints, he answered that he was working as hard as he could in order to be free to go to Paris to spend some days with her:[17]

What is wrong with you my dear Louise? Bouilhet has shown me a letter from you, which distresses me greatly. What do you mean by my silence? It is, on the contrary, of your silence that I complain. Write to me! Are you sad? . . . So dry your tears. How can you imagine that I could forget you? Where does this mad idea come from, which you've got in your mind?

I'm doing my utmost to hasten my cursed 'agricultural show'

in order to get to you more quickly; but I'm in despair, all my
work this week has had to be done all over again. Bouilhet and
I've just had a discussion of *three hours* about five pages. I ended
by giving in to his arguments. Alas what a slave-galley! It makes
me mad, and it's enough to make one hang oneself.

And so, good-bye, a thousand good kisses, I expect tomorrow
morning a letter from you. I'll write to you in the first days of
next week.

Yours, yours, your G.

She wanted him to come to Paris and to settle there, to take
more part in the literary life of the capital, but he answered
her that his work was not yet sufficiently advanced:[18]

I spent a sad week, and not on account of work, but in connection with you and on account of your idea. I'll tell you later
the personal reflections which arose from it. You believe that I
don't love you, poor dear Louise, and you imagine that you are,
in my life a secondary affection. But I've no human affection
higher than that, and, as for female affections, I swear to you
that you're the first, the only one. I go even further: I've never
had any like it, nor one which lasted so long, none so sweet,
especially so deep. As for the question of my settling in Paris
immediately, I must put that off, or rather settle it at once. *It is
absolutely impossible for me at the moment* (I don't count the
money which I haven't got, and which one must have). I know
myself well, it would be a wasted winter, and perhaps the whole
book.

He told her that he was often tempted to throw up the
whole novel and to go to live with her – this was, however,
not quite sincere – but he promised her that he would pay
her a visit the following month. When the visit finally occurred, it proved a disappointment:[19] 'What a bad parting
we had yesterday! Why? why? The next meeting will be
better. Courage! be of good hope! I kiss your beautiful eyes
which I've so often made weep. At the end of the week, a
long letter.' She wrote, on the back of this letter: 'His first
letter after his visit to Paris from 10 to 22 November. Sad
days! Bouilhet at the Opera. My irritation, its cause, bitterness, disgust at everything.'[20]

He eventually wrote, on 25 November, the promised letter, which has remained unpublished in the *Correspondance*.[21]

Yes, you're right, we weren't enough alone on this trip. Our misunderstandings arose from that, perhaps; for, even if our bodies touched, our hearts didn't have the time to embrace; and if anything could make me long for the end of these eternal partings, the perpetual 'how do you do and farewell', it would be this; I mean the grief always renewed of our separation. Ah! my poor Muse! You judge me wrongly; but I'm not going to give way to recriminations which would only seem hateful to you – and which would perhaps be so? I don't know! I'm always terrified of wounding you, and I wound you the whole time. This humiliates me in my most delicate pretensions. You take up a careless word, an insignificant gesture, indifferent habits. . . . Well! don't think any more about it! Let's kiss, even more tenderly than we kissed on Tuesday at two in the morning. Dry your poor eyes, and keep them not for weeping but for seeing. That is the important thing, to see! The important thing is to understand, and it is especially a question of understanding. If you saw better, you'd suffer less and you'd work better.

Shall I speak to you of Art? Won't you accuse me in your heart, of passing rapidly over the matters of the heart? But everything is connected together, and what troubles your life also troubles your style. For you make a perpetual amalgam of your ideas and your passion, which weakens the one and prevents you from enjoying the other. Oh! if only I could make of you what I dream, what a woman you'd be, what a creature you'd be, and especially what a happy creature. . . . Sleep in peace then, on me, first. Be certain that you are, and always will be the best and the most complete feminine affection I've ever had.

Sometimes, however, he could not keep back his irritation at her incessant demands to meet him and her indifference to the progress of his work:[22]

Don't tell me so often that you want me, don't say these things which hurt me so much. What's the use? Since what is must be, since I can't work otherwise. I'm *a man of excess* in everything. What would be reasonable for another would be fatal for me.

Don't you imagine that I want you also, that I'm not lonely after our so frequent long absences? But I assure you that a three days disturbance makes me lose a fortnight, that I've the utmost difficulty in collecting myself again, and that if I follow the plan which irritates you, it is through repeated and infallible experience. I'm only in the mood for work towards eleven o'clock at night, when I've been working for seven or eight hours; and, in the whole year, only after a sequence of monotonous days, at the end of a month or six weeks, when I've been glued to my writing table.

She was jealous of everyone in his life – even of all those whom he had known before she had met him – of Eulalie Foucaud whom he had only met for two days, when he was eighteen; of Kuschiuk Hanem, the Egyptian courtesan, with whom he had spent two nights and could never hope to see again; or the Collier girls, who had returned to England; and especially of Élisa Schlésinger, who was now living permanently in Germany. She made a scene with him on account of his visit to Trouville, in August 1853, when he had lived nostalgically in the past, in those days when his father and sister had still been alive, and also Alfred Le Poittevin. But he answered her that he had wanted to associate her with these happy days of his youth, when he had been whole, as she had never known him.[23]

She tried, on her side, to make him jealous of her friends, by telling him of her relations with other men, of her affairs – real or imaginary – with Alfred de Vigny, Alfred de Musset. But he was not capable of jealousy, as he never felt possessive of others, and, moreover, his feelings for her no longer had that intensity. She became the mistress of his closest friend at that time, Louis Bouilhet, when he was in Paris for the launching of his poem *Melaenis*. Bouilhet himself does not seem to have felt any guilt in the matter, and, after their first night together, he wrote to her:[24]

Thank you, thank you again and again. That evening was charming; only women can produce these sensitive and sympathetic situations; I'm so much overcome by all that that

I hardly dare write for fear of losing something of it; I'm like a miser, and I clutch my fingers round my memories. . . . Oh! the lovely evening, and the lovely night that we spent together! You'll see, we'll achieve something; we're longing too much to fly not to have wings.

And the letter ends: 'I'm bewildered with happiness and I don't know which way to turn.'

Both Bouilhet and Louise Colet seem to have kept Flaubert informed of the progress of their affair, and Louis showed him letters which Louise had written to him. He had addressed a poem to her, celebrating her 'regards de flamme' her 'bras blancs' and her genius, which she wanted to publish. Flaubert tried to dissuade her from this, for the sake of both of them.[25] He said that it was one of the worst poems that Bouilhet had ever written, and that, otherwise as well, it would cover them both with ridicule, that certain phrases would become proverbial. 'You'll get very angry, I know well, but I beg you to think it over, nay more, I *implore you* to follow my advice.'

By the end of September 1852 she seems to have been treating Bouilhet as she treated Flaubert, expressing doubt of his affection. He wrote to her:[26]

By the way, why do you suppose that I could ever quarrel with you? I know nothing in the world, I repeat nothing in the world, which could bring about such a result. It's not right, my dear Muse, and I feel inclined to scold you. . . . I want you to have as much confidence in me as I've got in you; whatever happens, never have doubts of me. I love you for yourself, and also for him. How could you think that I could ever be angry.

By this time he was telling her that he loved her for his friend's sake as well as for her own.

Flaubert was, however, once moved to jealous rage – and this must have been flattering to Louise's vanity – when she told him that Musset had tried to rape her when she was driving with him, and that she only saved herself by throwing herself out of the moving carriage. Then Flaubert's rage boiled over at the outrage she had endured, and he felt that he could have murdered him:[27]

> No! I shan't reproach you, although you made me suffer a great deal this morning, strangely and in a new way. When, in your letter, I reached the 'tutoiement', it was as if I'd received a slap in the face; I bounded out of my chair. Yes! I had that weakness, and not to own up would be an affectation. That man will pay me for that slap one day or other, and in some way or other. If I made phrases like his, I'd say to you that I feel the need to batter him to death. What is certain is that I'd gladly beat him, and that all this has given me, as it were, a very painful corn. If he ever stamps on my foot, I'll stick that foot in his belly, with something else with it. Oh! my poor Louise, you, you to have been there! I imagined you, at one moment, killed on the pavement, with the wheel going over your body, and the horse's hoof on your face, in the gutter. You, you, and by him! Oh! how I'd like him to come back and that you'd fling him out of the door before thirty people. If he writes to you again, answer him in a tremendous letter of five lines: 'Why do I not want you? Because you fill me with disgust, and because you are a coward!' He was afraid of compromising himself by coming to see whether you hadn't been crushed by the wheel. . . . You lacked 'savoir faire' in the whole matter. . . . Instead of throwing yourself out of the carriage, all you had to do was to stop the coachman and say to him: 'Do me the favour of throwing M. A. de Musset out, who has insulted me.' . . .
>
> Farewell, I embrace you, I hug you, I kiss you everywhere; you, you, my poor outraged love. Once again a long kiss. Your, G.

Although he was enraged at the time, he later disapproved when, in her poem entitled *La Servante*, she painted Alfred de Musset as a lecherous and drunken seducer, and he tried to dissuade her from publishing it:[28]

> That work isn't publishable *as it is*, and I *implore* you not to publish it. . . . *This poem is a bad action,* and you've been punished, for it's a bad work. . . . You've made of art a 'déversoir' for passion, a kind of chamber-pot, in which an overflow of something or other has flowed. It stinks, it smells of hatred. . . . And so I find this work badly intentioned, evil and badly written.

He tells her to ask anyone else's advice – Babinet or Leconte de Lisle for instance – and she will discover that they will agree with him.

'I've now fulfilled my duty,' he added, 'and can you understand that it has been very painful to me?'

He was now becoming more exasperated with her, over the merest trifles. Once, when he was out on a country walk with her, he said to her afterwards:[29] 'Your voice calling to me every moment, and especially your tapping me on the shoulder to attract my attention, caused me real pain. How did I restrain myself from sending you to the devil in the most brutal way.' He added, however, to excuse himself, that he was normally thus on a country walk.

But he was often tempted to do violence to her and he once admitted – as quoted by Frank:[30] 'She is strange this woman; she, who has always been unfaithful, is jealous. Recently she came to make a scene at my house. A log was burning in the grate, and I looked at that log wondering whether I wouldn't soon seize it to strike her over the head with it, burying the embers in her.'

Louise Colet now wished to bring Flaubert to the pitch of marrying her. During his absence abroad, the situation between herself and her accredited lover and protector, Victor Cousin, had become somewhat strained. He was beginning to tire of her and of her succession of lovers, and wished now to make a change in their relationship, on the pretext that he was retiring from the University, and would have to retrench his commitments as he would only have his pension to rely on. He offered her a complete break, when she could find another protector who would take charge of her life – he was probably thinking of Flaubert; or else they should meet, at rare intervals, on a superficially friendly basis. He suggested that she should come to visit him occasionally and spend an odd half-hour or so with the old philosopher. 'Affectionate politeness could then be our link,' he said to her.[31] He offered to make some financial provision for their daughter, Henriette, and promised her a pension of £80 a year for the child until she reached her majority or married, whichever occurred first.[32]

She, however, let it be believed that he had offered her a closer relationship and that he had proposed marriage to her – that was what she told Bouilhet – but that she had refused him. There is no proof of the truth of this assertion, and she may only have been trying to force Flaubert's hand. That was certainly what Bouilhet believed, and he wrote to Flaubert, in January 1854, saying:[33]

Do you want me to give you my opinion? Do you want me to tell you straight out what she wants to achieve? She wants to become your wife, she thinks that she will become your wife. . . . I've believed that for some time without being able to put it into words, but it was said to me, not by herself, but as coming from her, positively. That is why she refused the philosopher [Cousin].

Although he was becoming exasperated with her, Flaubert, nevertheless, had been concerned about her for some time, and he had written to Bouilhet, in December, to ask for news of her:[34]

She makes me very sad, the poor Muse, and I don't know what to do about it. I assure you that it saddens me in every way. How do you think it will all end? I feel that she's tired of me and, for her inner peace, it would be better if she gave me up. . . . In her letter of today she tells me that she is ill. If she is really ill, I count on you to let me know, and I'd rush up to Paris. My mother, in a few days, will be passing through Paris, I hesitate to ask her to call on the Muse. It would be, I think, a kind action, and one should try, as far as possible, to be kind. But . . . but . . . quid? Naturally, don't say anything about this to her!

He tried, for several months, in long letters, to make her see reason, and to answer patiently her objections to his behaviour; her complaints of his miserliness financially towards her; of his meanness in connection with the time he spent with her. He wrote to her:[35]

Finally, my poor Louise, do you want me to open out the

whole of my mind to you, or rather the whole of my heart? I believe that your love is waning. The dissatisfaction that I cause you, the suffering, has no other cause, for such as I am at present, such have I always been. But now you see it all more clearly, and you judge me more logically, perhaps – I don't know. Nevertheless, when one loves completely and utterly, one loves the object of one's love as he is, with his faults and his monstrosities; one adores the mange; one cherishes the hump, one savours with delight the breath which poisons one.

She continued to complain about him in letter after letter. When she accused him of egoism, he answered:[36]

What does that mean, egoism? I'd like to know if you aren't even more egoistic, and in a more complete way. But it appears that my egoism isn't even intelligent! So that I'm not only a monster, but a fool as well. Charming expressions of love! If, for the past year (not a year but only six months) the circle of our affection, as you observe, has shrunk, whose fault is it? I've not changed towards you either in conduct or in language. Never (and go over in your memory my other trips to Paris) have I stayed so long with you as on the last two. Formerly, when I went to Paris, I used still to go out to dine with other people from time to time. But, last November, and a few days ago, I refused all invitations to be free to be more completely with you, and, in all the outings that I made, there wasn't a single one for my own pleasure.

I think that we are growing old and musty; we are growing sour and our vinegars mingle together. When I analyse myself, here is what I feel for you. Firstly great physical attraction, then an attachment of the mind, a virile and calm affection, emotional esteem. I place love beyond what is possible in life, and I never speak of it in connection with myself. Last night in front of me, you mocked, like any bourgeoise, my poor dream of fifteen years, accusing it once more of *not being intelligent*. Oh! I'm sure of it! Haven't you ever understood anything that I write? Didn't you understand that the way I attack sentiment in my works was only the cry of a defeated man – unless it was a cry of victory? You ask for love, you complain that I don't send you flowers. Oh! I've other things to worry about than flowers. I don't like my feelings to be known by the general public, and to have my feelings thrown at me at a party, and that they should be the subject of

conversation. I was past twenty when I still used to blush like a
carrot when anyone said to me 'You write, don't you?' You can
judge from that my modesty with regard to my other feelings. I
feel that I could love you more passionately if no one knew that I
loved you. I'm irritated by Delisle [Leconte de Lisle] because you
said 'tu' to me in front of him, and the sight of him now has
become distasteful to me. That's how I'm made, and I've enough
work on the stocks without undertaking as well the task of my
sentimental reformation.

Her exhibitionism, her parading of her conquests, had
always been distasteful to him but, on the occasion mentioned in the letter, what he had not been able to bear was
her mocking of his ideal and unconsummated love for Élisa
Schlésinger. This letter, however, was not one to ease her
feelings of frustration with him. She must have answered
him, disclaiming what he had said, for he wrote again in
March:[37] 'Yes you're right, my good Muse, let's cease quar-
relling, let's kiss and wipe the slate clean. Let's love one
another each in our own way, according to our own nature.
Let's make an effort not to make one another suffer.'

She could not, however, leave him alone, nor accept the
inevitable, that he would not marry her, and that she must
take him as he was:[38]

How sad you are, my poor Muse! What funereal letters you've
been writing to me for some time. You fight against life, but it is
stronger than we are, and we must follow it. . . . But let's discuss
the moral aspect, since according to you, it is that which is responsible for your ill-health. You say that ideas of voluptuousness don't trouble you any more at all. I've the same confession
to make to you, and I admit that I've no more sex. Thank God!
I'd get it back if I needed it, and that's the main thing. . . . Well
did I tell you that I'd no love left for you? No, no, no more than
I've ever said the contrary. Let's cast away the words to which
people cling, which satisfy them, thinking they are sufficient.
Why be so anxious perpetually about the labels and the phrases.
Put your head in your hands, don't think about yourself but
about me, as I am, nearly thirty-three years old, worn out by
fifteen to eighteen years of incessant toil, more full of experience

than all the moral academies in the world in everything concerning the passions. ... And what does it mean? [love] I don't
understand. If I didn't love you why, firstly, should I write to
you? And why would I see you? What forces me to? What is the
attraction which urges me towards you and draws me back to
you, or rather what keeps me there? ... Why, when I'm in Paris,
do I spend all my time with you, whatever you may say, so much
so that I've given up, on account of that, seeing many people. I
could find other houses to receive me, and other women, how
does it happen that I prefer you to all of them? Don't you feel
that there is, in life, something higher than happiness, than love
or Religion? I mean the Idea. That is where one loves if one lives
by that. I've always tried (but it seems to me that I'm failing in it)
to make you a sublime hermaphrodite. ... God has destined you
to be to be equal to, if not to surpass, what is strongest. No one
was ever *born* like you. Yet you succeed, in perfect good faith, in
producing execrable verses. It is the same in the realm of sentiment. You *don't understand* and then you're capable of injustice, which one doesn't mention, but which, nevertheless,
hurts.

These aren't reproaches that I'm making, my poor dear Muse,
no, and if you're crying, let my lips wipe away the tears. I would
like them to brush away all the old cobwebs. I wanted to love
you, and I love you in a way which may not be that of lovers. ...
One must, I don't say have the ideas of one's time, but one must
understand them. Well! I maintain that one can only live pass-
ably by refusing, as much as possible, to give oneself up to what
is weakest. The civilization in which we live is a triumph (incessant and victorious war) against all perverse instincts. If you wish
to give in to anger, vengeance, cruelty, to unbridled pleasure, to
lunatic love, the desert is there, and the feathers of the savage a
little further on. That is why, for instance, I consider that a man
who hasn't an income of £4,000 a year, and who marries, is a
wretch and a scoundrel who deserves a beating.

But, although he would not marry her, he remained
always interested in her and in her literary career. He and
Bouilhet spent hours of their precious time in correcting her
work for publication, often spending their Sundays on it.
'Bouilhet is there plodding over your work,' wrote Flaubert

to her,[39] 'we'll give you our remarks in writing, and our corrections, which will probably take all our time until six o'clock.'

But he was often irritated, and his integrity as an artist could not accept the rapidity with which she wrote, and her lack of attention to style and questions of aesthetics:[40]

Let's speak, this evening, of ourselves and of others. And firstly, you must abandon forever your system of hasty work which wears out health and thought. One destroys, in this way, all one's intellectual and nervous force. Get into the habit of preparing beforehand, of working more slowly. When I've been with you, when you were making corrections, you can't imagine, my good Muse, how often you irritated me by your haste to pass from one idea to another, by adopting one synonym, then casting it aside . . . etc. One must cling to one thing and stick to it until one has mastered it completely.

As love began to fade, his irritation grew, and the harshness of his criticism. But it seemed to him often that she did not heed his corrections, that she only grew angry at any adverse judgements, and that he might as well have given the time to his own work, which was in arrears:[41] 'My first impulse was to return you your manuscript, without any comment, since our remarks are of no use to you, and that you won't, or can't, understand them. What's the use of asking us our opinion, and of wearing ourselves out, if it is only to end in wasted time and in recriminations on both sides.'

Once, when she had her own paper, *La Librarie Nouvelle*, he even wrote an article for her to sign, which seems to have given him much ironic and satiric pleasure:[42]

I've at last begun your article this evening. It will be a master-piece of bad taste and slickness. *La Librairie Nouvelle* will be moved right into the depths of its entrails of bad literature. Bouilhet is coming back tomorrow, but he's going back to Rouen at once. I'll go on with it and finish it, and I'll bring it to you towards the end of the week. On Friday or Saturday. I don't know yet which day. I'd like to make some corrections in my *Bovary*, the least sentence of which is more trouble to do than all the inflated articles in the world.

Louise Colet also used Flaubert for her own ends, and often to his danger. She was a friend of Victor Hugo and she was trying to enlist his support for a prize. He was, at this time, in exile in Jersey, and his letters to her, and hers to him, could not go direct on account of the censorship. She therefore evolved an elaborate plan of having his letters sent to a friend of the Flaubert family in London, who was to put them in another envelope, redirect them and send them on to him. She had, at first, wanted them to be sent straight to Flaubert, but he had insisted that they should not be sent by Hugo to himself.[43] The letters for her came generally addressed to Flaubert from London.[44] But Hugo was often very careless and sent them direct to Flaubert himself, and they used to arrive in torn envelopes, revealing Hugo's very characteristic writing, which was easily recognizable. It would not have done Flaubert any good if the letters had been discovered. It would also not have done the family any good, as his brother, Achille Flaubert, was a government official as Master of the Hôtel Dieu at Rouen.

Flaubert remonstrated with him and asked him to be more careful in the future:[45] 'I think, Sir, that I must warn you of this: Your missive, dated 27 April, arrived very much damaged; the envelope was torn in several places, and some words of your writing were visible. The second envelope (addressed to Madame Colet) had been torn at the edges, and one could see its contents, that is two other letters and a sheet of printing.'

Flaubert reminded him that he had met him, when he was a student in Paris in the winter of 1843, in the studio of Pradier and he recalled a gold ring which Hugo had worn, engraved with a lion rampant, which had been one of the pledges in a game which they had played. He ended with praise of the work of the poet, which, he said, had been one of the great passions of his youth: 'Receive, Sir, with the homage of all my admiration for your genius, the assurance of all my devotion to your person.' What is strange is that Hugo claimed afterwards that he had no idea who Flaubert was, or that he had ever existed. It is alleged that he said to Jules Clarétie, who reported it in *La Vie à Paris*, that he had only discovered later that he was a writer:[46]

I imagined for a long time that the name 'Gustave Flaubert' was only one of Madame Louise Colet's pseudonyms. During the early years of my exile I never wrote to Madame Colet except under cover to M. Gustave Flaubert at Rouen or at Croisset. I thought that this Gustave Flaubert didn't exist, and when I wrote his name on the envelope, it was of Louise Colet that I was thinking. So much so that I sent the tenderest expressions to 'my dear Flaubert'. It was only when *Madame Bovary* appeared, that I discovered that there really existed someone in the world called Gustave Flaubert. At one moment I thought that Madame Colet was changing her personality and henceforth would sign her novels 'Gustave Flaubert'. However, what they told me of *Madame Bovary* (for I hadn't time to read that book) convinced me that the work wasn't by Madame Colet and that Gustave Flaubert did, in fact, exist in flesh and blood. And in spirit as he is a master.

It is strange that he should know this if he had not read the book. This did not prevent him from praising it to its author, in grandiloquent and fulsome language, when it appeared.

One of Louise Colet's insistent ambitions was to meet Flaubert's mother, to become intimate, as it were, in his home life – this was all part of her plan for marrying him. He frequently promised that he would arrange a meeting some time, when the opportunity arose, but kept on putting her off with excuses.[47] He could not understand, he told her many times, this insistence on her part; he could not see the point of it, especially as his mother nowadays saw so few people – not even her own friends – and there was no reason why she should see his friends.[48]

Finally he decided, once and for all, to put an end to her importunity, to be entirely frank and explicit, and to underline his meaning:[49]

You ask me, in your note of this morning, to answer your letter of last Friday. I've just reread it; it's there, open on my table. How do you expect me to answer it? You must know me as well as I do myself, and you talk to me of things which we've discussed a hundred times, and which aren't any more advanced for all that. You reproach me with being peculiar, even in the expressions of tenderness which I send you in my letters (it seems to me, however, that I don't exaggerate in my use of sentimentalities. I'll deprive myself still more of them since they upset you.) – Let's return to your letter and begin again. I'll be categorical and explicit. 1. About my mother. Well yes! that is the difficulty. You've guessed it! It's because *I'm certain* that, if she met you, she would be very cold with you, and not correct, as you say, that is why I don't want you to meet. Moreover, I don't care for this confusion, this linking together of two affections from different sources (as for her, and you can imagine the woman from this characteristic; she wouldn't go to see her eldest son without an invitation). Then for what reason would she call on you? When I told you that she would go, to please you, I had got over a great obstacle and had discussed it for several days. You didn't take that into account, and you took up again a matter which was irritating to me, which was distasteful to me, and which had given me a lot of trouble. It is you who first broke the silence. So much the worse! But I beg you, once more, don't meddle with it. *When the time and the opportunity* arise I'll know what I've got to do. I find your persistence in this matter most strange. Continually to ask to meet my mother, to call on her, that she should call on you, seems to me as funny as if she wanted, on her part, that I shouldn't be with you, that I should cease seeing you, because, because etc. etc. And I swear to you that if she dared, on her side, to open her mouth on the subject, she wouldn't be long in closing her mouth about it.

Matters came to a head when, in the autumn of 1854, she dared to force her way into the privacy of his retreat at Croisset. He had never wanted her restless and invading presence in his monastery, or hermitage, and he appeared, a prophet of retribution, at the top of the stairs, noble in his grey dressing-gown, to evict her forcibly and to turn her out into the darkness and the rain. She related the episode in her

novel, *L'Histoire d'un Soldat*, published in 1856, which, although exaggerated and highly coloured, rings true.

The mistress of the maid who relates the story is beautiful,
talented and greatly loved by everyone, and she goes, one
evening, when darkness has fallen, to visit her lover in the
country, without warning him beforehand:[50]

Cette maison ressemblait à un cimetière, dont les habitants ne
s'informent pas de ceux qui les visitent.

Enfin il se fit un bruit de portes et de pas. Je vis descendre ma
maîtresse, mais dans quel état, mon Dieu! Elle était plus
blanche qu'un suaire, et ses deux beaux yeux ressemblaient à
deux taches de sang. Une femme habillée de noir l'éclairait par
derrière sans lui dire un mot ni la soutenir, quoiqu'elle chan-
celât. La figure longue et froide de cette femme me rappela les
dames qui sont sur les tombes dans les églises.

Sous sa robe de laine noire droite et plate, on comprenait que
c'était une veuve qui n'avait jamais ri depuis la mort de son mari.
. . . Cette dame paraissait revêche et dure comme quelqu'un qui
se console en voyant souffrir.

Then mistress and maid let themselves out alone into the
dark courtyard and the lady of the house did not accompany
them nor light them on their way:

La pluie tombait de plus belle; on n'aurait pas mis dehors un
pauvre chien, et cependant pas un mot ne fut dit pour nous re-
tenir. Je pris sous mon bras ma pauvre maîtresse, et nous re-
gagnâmes la voiture. Avant d'y monter, je tournai la tête vers
cette maison, et, sans le vouloir, j'appelai sur elle la malédiction
de Dieu. Qu'étaient donc cette mère et ce fils qui laissaient partir,
par une nuit pareille, une pauvre femme désespérée. Et quelle
femme! Vous le savez celle que tout le monde glorifiait comme la
meilleure et la plus belle. Je me souvenais alors de son chez-elle,
toujours ouvert pour Monsieur Léonce, de ce petit salon bleu où
il se chauffait si bien et fumait si joyeux dans un beau fauteuil! et
ma pauvre dame sortait comme une mendiante de cette maison
sans coeur! Oh! ce n'était pas pour elle que j'avais honte, mais
pour ceux qui étaient là-haut auprès d'un feu clair, derrière ces
fenêtres qui brillaient toujours.

That was the end of their affair, and they never met again.

After Ernest Feydeau had published, in 1858, his successful novel *Fanny*, which cashed in on the notoriety of *Madame Bovary*, Louise Colet, always on the lookout for celebrities, wrote to him in praise, but Flaubert warned him to be careful:[51]

As for Widow Colet, she has plots, I don't know what! But she has plans! I know her through and through! The good things which she said to you about *Fanny* were said for a *purpose*. You wrote to her, she'll invite you to come and see her. Go, but beware! She's a pernicious creature. If you want to die laughing, read her *Histoire d'un Soldat* – it's a novel, published in *Le Moniteur*, and what is more comic still, you'll recognize your friend painted in odious colours, in which he's been defamed.

Certainly, by October 1854 Flaubert's affair with Louise Colet was finally over, and he never saw her again. Writing to Louis Bouilhet, in October, he said:[52] 'As for the Muse, it's all over. We can now rest in peace on that score.'

She, however, for her part, did not give up the struggle so easily. Flaubert spent most of the winter of 1854 to 1855 in Paris. He did not go to his usual hotel, Le Bon Lafontaine, in the rue des Saints Pères, because it was too near her apartment in the rue de Sèvres. He moved over to the right bank, to the Hôtel Helder, near the Boulevard des Italiens, but this did not keep Louise Colet away. She somehow found out where he was staying and, on 5 March, she went several times to the hotel to see him, and left messages for him. He wrote her a furious and insolent letter, which is the last word he was ever to write to her:[53]

Madame, I learned that you had taken the trouble to call on me yesterday evening three times. I was not at home and, anxious about the insults which such persistence, on your part, might earn you from mine, courtesy obliges me to warn you that I shall never be at home to you.

I have the honour to greet you.

Flaubert.

She had written on the letter: 'Lâche, couard, et canaille', and had heavily scored under the last word. She also wrote on the envelope: 'Today 13 April, learned from Bab [Babinet] who heard it from Cloquet, of his departure for Croisset.' This gives us the date of the last letter, for Flaubert rarely dates his correspondence.

It appears that Victor Hugo offered his services to intervene with Flaubert on her behalf – it is difficult to reconcile this with his alleged statement that he only knew, on the publication of *Madame Bovary*, that Flaubert really existed. Louise Colet answered Hugo on 19 August 1856:[54] 'I've thought a great deal about what you said to me, about your fatherly offer to intervene with that sick spirit; at first I'd have wished it, then I lost heart. What's the use? I've no more faith left in him, he's destroyed it; he must come back to me of his own accord.' But Flaubert did not choose to return to her, and he never saw her again.

Perhaps the reason for Louise Colet's refusal of Hugo's help was that, in 1856, she was consoling herself with Champfleury, who, as far as his reputation was concerned, was one of the most famous novelists of the day and Flaubert was, as yet, unknown.[55] This may have been the reason for the hostility of Champfleury's paper, *Réalisme*, which published the most unfavourable review of *Madame Bovary* when it appeared.

Thus ended Flaubert's affair with Louise Colet; it had lasted for eight years, with a break of three years in the middle, most of which time Flaubert was abroad – the first period had lasted nearly two years and the second three. It is very likely that the second period would have been cut short sooner if he had not needed the material of her character for the creation of Emma Bovary on which he was engaged at the time. All through this second phase of their relationship there was struggle between Emma and Louise for possession of Flaubert's soul, but it is the fictional character who eventually won the day.

When *Madame Bovary* appeared Louise Colet was very

much hurt when she recognized traits of herself in the heroine, and especially because the author had used satirically a
gift she had once given him, a seal on which she had had
engraved, 'Amor nel Cor'. She drained her wound in a poem
of the same title, published in *Le Monde Illustré* on 29
January 1859, in which she said that he had spurned her
gift in a novel, written in the style of a commercial traveller,
but had, nevertheless, kept the precious seal. The poem
ends:[56]

> C'était pour lui, pour lui, qu'ella aimait comme un Dieu;
> Pour lui, dur au malheur, grossier envers la femme.
> Hélas! elle était pauvre, elle donnait bien peu,
> Mais tout don est sacré quand il renferme une âme.
>
> Eh bien! dans un roman de commis voyageur
> Qui comme un air malsain nous soulève le coeur,
> Il a raillé ce don en une phrase plate,
> Mais il gardé pourtant le beau cachet d'agate.

Louise Colet never forgot Flaubert, but thought about
him bitterly, so much so that, as late as 1872, nearly eighteen
years after the end of their liaison, when Flaubert had written a preface to the *Dernières Chansons* of Louis Bouilhet,
who had died in 1869, she sent him an anonymous letter in
verse, in which she painted him as a 'charlatan thumping
the big drum over the grave of his flat-footed friend'; forgetting that she had been the mistress of both men.[57]

Flaubert himself, according to his own opinion, does not
seem to have suffered permanently from his relationship
with her. Writing to Amélie Bosquet, in December 1859, he
said:[58] 'My liaison with Madame Colet has left no wound in
me, in the deep and emotional meaning of the word; it is
rather the memory (and even still the sensation) of a long
irritation. Her book was the last straw in the affair.' This was
Lui, published in 1859, in which she ridiculed him in the
person of Léonce, who was perfectly recognizable, even
though a caricature – it is true that she also satirized Musset

and Vigny in an equally recognizable manner, but more unflatteringly. Yet Flaubert never forgot her, and, when he heard of her death in 1876, he wrote to Madame Roger des Genettes:[59] 'You guessed correctly the total effect which the death of my poor Muse produced on me. Her renewed memory made me go back over the course of my life. . . . The papers spoke very little of her. Do you remember her little apartment in the rue de Sèvres? and everything else? Ah! unhappy us!'

In spite of its turmoil and stress, Flaubert's relationship with Louise Colet was the greatest emotional adventure of his life. She drew him into the family of human beings and gave him experience he would never have had without her. The relationship ended disastrously, but the blame must not be attributed solely to her. It is doubtful whether he could ever have had a completely satisfactory relationship with any woman. He was always kind to them but was terrified when they tried to encroach upon his private life.

His many close friendships with women came later, after the publication of *Madame Bovary*, when so many wrote to him and said they had found themselves in Emma, and marvelled that he had understood them so well. Élisa Schlésinger, the great and only true love of his life, remained an ideal. His attitude to her was very like that of Baudelaire towards *La Vénus Blanche*, who eventually destroyed that ideal by trying to make love concrete. Flaubert did not persuade his *Fantôme de Trouville* to leave her shrine, and nothing ever tarnished his image of her; she remained, all his life, his *Princess Lointaine*. Except for this ideal veneration, Flaubert professed to despise love for women. Writing to Mademoiselle Leroyer de Chantepie, he said:[60]

As for love, I've never found anything in that supreme happiness except turmoil, storms and despair. Woman seems to me an impossible creature, and I've remained away from her as much as possible; I believe, moreover, that one of the causes of the moral degeneration of the whole of the nineteenth century has been the exaggerated 'poetization' of woman.

His encounters with women in his youth had been casual relationships, like the one with Eulalie Foucaud, in Marseilles, when he was eighteen; and his relationship with bought women, such as Kuschiuk Hanem in Egypt. None of these had meant anything to him deeply, and they merely touched the surface of his nature. Only with Louise Colet had he been deeply stirred, and he had tried to preserve his relationship with her, almost to the end, but she had insisted on going counter to all his deepest feelings and needs.

[17]

The Tribulations of an Artist
(1851–6)

As we have seen, Flaubert began *Madame Bovary* on 19 September 1851, before he went to England with his mother and his niece. On his return he does not seem to have been able to get on with the book. Writing to Louise Colet, in October, he said:[1] 'I'm tormenting myself, I'm scratching myself. My novel has great difficulty in getting going, and the sentences itch without reaching any conclusion. I've only written one page and sketched out three more.'

He then thought of abandoning the book altogether, and embarking on something else. In his state of uncertainty, he went up to Paris to consult Théophile Gautier, whom he admired and whose opinion he valued, but he received from him only cynical advice which disgusted him – Gautier had by now, reached a state of complete disillusionment with literature. When Flaubert questioned him about his theories of art and perfection – he was, after all, the leader of the Art for Art's Sake movement – he is alleged to have answered:[2]

Yes! I know all about that; it's the disease of the beginner; just as measles is the disease of childhood. When we all lived together in the rue du Doyenné, Arsène Houssaye, Camille Rogier, Gérard de Nerval and I . . . we used to cherish these same ideals. . . . You believe in the mission of the writer, in the sacred vocation of the poet, in the divinity of art. Oh! Flaubert, you're only naïf! A writer sells copy, as a draper sells handkerchiefs; only calico fetches a higher price, that's all.

He then considered taking up his *Tentation de Saint Antoine* again, and seeing whether anything of it could be salvaged. In his perplexity he then wrote to Maxime Du Camp on 21 October 1851, begging him to come to Croisset so that they could discuss together the matter, to see which passages, if any, might be published.[3] Bouilhet, however, was of the opinion that he should abandon the project, as he considered that all Flaubert's faults were evident in the work, but none of his qualities, and he did not see how the extracts could be chosen. Flaubert himself was very doubtful, and he did not know what decision to make. As he said in his letter to Du Camp:[4]

Well! in this matter, the most important, perhaps, in the life of an artist, I'm totally lacking in it, alas! [that is an opinion]. . . . I'm doing my utmost to reach some conclusion, but I'm completely devoid of it. The objections for and against seem to me equally good! I might decide heads or tails, and I'd have no regrets in the choice, whatever it might be. If I publish it will be in the most stupid way possible, because I'm told to do so, by imitation, by obedience, without any personal initiative. I don't feel the need, or the desire, for that.

He had spoken to his mother on the matter, but she, too, had no opinion to offer. 'If you've done something you think good,' she said, 'then publish it.'[5]

He was therefore no further on than he had been, and he needed advice. That was why he begged Du Camp to come to his help and he promised to listen to what he said. Critics have usually declared that it was Du Camp who was urging Flaubert, against his wishes and intuition, to publish something, to get his name before the public, but it will be seen that, at this moment, in October 1851, it was Flaubert, on the contrary, who was begging his friend for advice and help:[6]

Then, if I do publish, it won't be in a half-hearted manner. If one does a thing, one must do it properly. I'd go to live in Paris in the winter. . . . I'd have to do a lot of things which would revolt me, and which, beforehand, disgust me. Well! would I be capable of that? . . . Why have I remained in this provincial bog? Do you think I'd not have the strength, that I'd not be happy, to play the part of a fine gentleman there [in Paris]. Yes! I'd enjoy it quite a lot! Study me and tell me whether it is at all possible.

This is a very long letter, and Flaubert gives Du Camp a complete catalogue of his feelings with regard to an active literary life in Paris – his easy boredom, his dislike for action, his discouragement and doubt of himself, his fundamental indifference to success and fame, his weakness now, and his longing to be taken in hand:

I'm giving you all this as a subject for your meditation. Only think carefully and consider me as a whole. In spite of my remark in *L'Éducation Sentimentale*: 'In all our most intimate confidences, there is always something that one doesn't say,' I've told you everything. As far as a man can be honest with himself, it seems to me that I've been honest. I'm revealing to you my innermost depths. I trust you, I'll do everything you want. I put my whole person, of which I'm very weary, in your hands. I'd no inkling, when I started this letter, that I was going to say all this to you. It came of its own accord, but let it stand! Our future conversations will perhaps, thereby, be simplified. Farewell! I embrace you with all sorts of feelings.

By this time Du Camp was in process of becoming an important figure in the literary world in Paris. He had returned from his eastern trip full of energy and ambition. He had come back to France in May 1851, while Flaubert had remained in Italy, and he was determined to get on as quickly as possible. Writing to Flaubert on 27 May 1851, he said:[7] 'I'm like a cupboard of which the key has been lost. One knows that there is something in it, but it's impossible to open it. You'll perhaps also experience that when you get back, and you'll see how it is.' He wrote again on 2 June, before Flaubert returned:[8] 'As far as I'm concerned, I'm going to throw myself into militant literature, come what may, and may God help me! As for political life, I'll not mention that, it's the same old mess as usual.'

Almost immediately he became associated with the project of starting a new literary magazine, *La Revue de Paris*, or rather with taking over a title which had been previously used when, in 1829, Véron had founded a periodical of that name, which enjoyed a high reputation and success in the early years of the July Monarchy. Du Camp, Louis de Cormenin and Théophile Gautier were now to be co-editors. On 30 September, Du Camp wrote to Flaubert to tell him of the project:[9]

My heart is beating very fast. Tomorrow, or the day after tomorrow, I'll be for the literary community either a fool or a scoundrel. Everyone is awaiting the review with excitement. I'm worn out! For the past three days I've spent two nights up, and I've stood today for seven hours at the printing works, correcting some Balzac. It's terrifying!

On 5 October, after the publication of the first number of the magazine, he said:[10] 'Copies are selling; may God grant us life! I'm full of good hope, and, if I've enough to live on this year, I may get by.'

La Revue de Paris was planned to be a special kind of review, as it was intended to be completely free and independent – this was before the *coup d'état* of 2 December 1851, when Louis Bonaparte made himself Emperor, before the days of severe censorship. In the first number, October 1851, the paper set forth its aims. It was to be completely independent, with freedom of expression for all, and no author would be censored. It could happen that different articles might express diametrically opposed opinions. No one would be answerable for anything which he did not sign himself, and each author would have the sole responsibility for his own article. All contributions would be respected and none would be cut. They might, at times, be refused, but none would be altered without its author's leave, and not a word or a sentence would be removed. The editors declared that they wished to encourage and to foster the idiosyncrasies and originality of each writer.

This was bravely said and meant at the time, but the ideal faltered with the passage of time, when Flaubert's *Madame*

Bovary was serialized in the review at the end of 1856, and we shall see what cuts and alterations were made by the editors in his manuscript, against his wishes – and sometimes even without his knowledge.

Du Camp now wished to associate Flaubert with his venture, and it was then that the latter wrote to him for help and advice on 21 October 1851. Du Camp answered him in a very significant letter on 29 October, the same year.[11]

At the beginning of this very long and important document, Du Camp tells Flaubert that it would take him six months, at least, to answer his letter adequately, and he says that he can only concentrate on a few outstanding aspects. He starts with the question of whether Flaubert should publish or not, which seems to him very important:

The question of *publication* is a very complicated matter, in spite of its initial apparent simplicity. Do you want merely to publish? That is easy – do you want to succeed by publishing? – that is not so easy – you know, as well as I do, that we are no longer living at a time when, from one day to the next, one could become famous merely by writing *Les Truands* or *l'Écolier de Cluny* – that moment – or rather the purely literary moment – is past; the present moment is bad for art – philosophy and politics have usurped the whole place. One must resign oneself to spending long years in obscurity, before reaching light. Only the theatre can make one of these meteoric reputations which burst out suddenly, without previous warning.

If one wishes to arrive (I mean at a reputation) one must cut one's seam like a miner, and blow up the citadel, at the moment when one is thinking least of it. And, for that, one needs preparatory work. Will you be capable of that? I very much doubt it. It is the same, in other matters, with you, as in this. You violently desire the means when they are impossible and impracticable. As soon as you've got them, you're disgusted with them, by the very fact that you've got them. Formerly you used to dream of your début, you wanted to play your part, you wanted instantaneous success in rallying round yourself artists and journalists – it seems to me that this was your idea – what you counted on doing with a lot of money, I'm doing now with nothing; and, at bottom, you're shocked by me, and it seems to you that my conduct lacks dignity, that I should have cast my prose on the waters and waited patiently, with folded arms, for admirers to come. No! since I've begun, since I wish to succeed, I'll not fail in my aim. I've started out, good luck to me! My guns are in my pocket, I've studied the route map for a long time, and woe betide those who stand in my way. I know it's a cruel game that I'm playing; my life is the stake on the gaming-table, and it's up to me to win. When you got back from England, you were astonished at the change which was taking place in me, and you dashed off to confide your surprise to Gautier. He gave you a very stupid answer and, if you'd known me more thoroughly, you'd have understood me without having to apply to others. Do you remember what Rastignac said in *Père Goriot*? – well, what he said in a grand way, I've said in a small way. ... I've got something already, I've a circle of artists on whom I can rely, and I can pour out, to my heart's content, the flood of vitality which overflows in me. I've a grim battle to wage, a victory of life and death to win. I must succeed in being, during the two years of literary renaissance which is just beginning, a captain and not a private. A month ago I was full of anxiety, troubled, in a word I was afraid. Today I'm firm and full of confidence. I've won my first battle. I've worked hard, but I've especially made others work under my orders; I've succeeded in blowing up, at my first attempt, that citadel which I've been besieging since 1847.

And what is your place in all this? You always push everything to the wildest extremities; you say, with an absolutely straight face, that you're not made to be a [subordinate?]. Great Heavens! who's talking of that? But what you need, above all, is to learn the truth about life, of which you're totally ignorant, an ignorance which has already done you more harm than you could ever calculate, and which, in the world, will make you the inferior of any fool without talent. You say to me 'do with me what you will, decide for me'. That's impossible! I refuse absolutely! I can't take charge of souls. Even were I to be misunderstood and abused by you, I must leave you in your uncertainty. I could show you the two paths but, with you especially, I would never state which direction you should take. Only, believe me, whatever decision you make, whatever you decide, I'll always be there to save you from the hardest part of the task. The day you wish to publish, you'll find – what doesn't happen to everyone – your place ready and reserved for you.

This was true, and, as soon as *Madame Bovary* was finished, Du Camp serialized it in his *Revue de Paris*: 'Not for one second even, did I separate you from myself. In my mind I worked for the three of us – Bouilhet, you and me. – This has lasted for a long time now and you were never even aware of it.' Du Camp was indeed responsible for helping Bouilhet at the beginning of his literary career and, the following month, in November 1851, he published in *La Revue de Paris*, his *Melaenis*, and ensured its success:

I've made my own success, I'll also make that of Bouilhet and, if you send me something good, I'll make yours also. – All this is very grave and serious, I know, and I can't give you any advice.

Then he analyses Flaubert's life which he considers very un-suitable for a budding writer:

You tell me that it is by choice and after serious deliberation that you've chosen the kind of life that you're leading. You're deceiving yourself greatly – you've submitted to this sort of exist-ence, and it has become second nature to you to endure it. You submitted to it, firstly, through necessity, on account of your illness – then through a sense of duty on account of the death of your relatives; and especially on account of that dislike of change which is in you; and because you were afraid of the silent re-proaches of your mother; in front of her you didn't dare break what had become a habit. What proves this is the joy you've always felt each time you could drag yourself away from it. You like enjoying yourself, make no mistake about that, and you spoke truly when you said to me that you could only be active when you found pleasure in it; this is very true. But this kind of life has two serious disadvantages for you:

(1) It has delivered you, bound hand and foot, into the clutches of your mother. It has given you the pernicious habit of living through others and of being capable only of dealing with your *subjective self* and never with your *objective self*.

(2) It has imprisoned you in the narrow circle of your own personality. You know how you live, but you don't know how others live. However much you look around you, you see only

yourself, and in all your works, you've never done anything but yourself.

These are the two great errors of your life, which, when all is said and done, weigh you down, bore you, and which have made people believe that you hate life, whereas it's only your own life that you hate.

All this isn't incurable, far from it. We're living at a time when one can't isolate oneself from the intellectual movements of the day without serious dangers to oneself. This winter I'll follow classes at the Conservatoire, and, if I was younger, I'd study science to understand what is going on – if only for the sake of the vocabulary – it's useful. Solitude is profitable only to the strong, and only when one is driving oneself to produce a book. Are we strong enough? I don't think so! And knowledge of others would not come amiss to us. If you want to succeed, if you want to arrive – I'd say, moreover, if you want to be *true* – come out of your den where no one will go and find you, and come out into the full daylight – rub shoulders with the world; despise it sufficiently to be alone in it, but through that contempt, learn to live by sharing its company. If you're stronger than it, take advantage of it, listen to what it's saying, so as to get to know it, and talk down to it from your height, so that it must listen to you.

Which of us has ever found himself in a better position than yours? No one! You've had no anxiety about your livelihood, you've had money and the reputation of wealth; you've had the shelter of your mother's house; the certainty that sacrifices would be made to provide for you; you've an illustrious name through your father, to which the general public is already accustomed. What have you done with all this? Absolutely nothing and you're thirty. If you've not started before two years have elapsed, I don't know how it will all end. Nowadays no one believes in the unknown great man. They demand their works mercilessly from those who claim to be strong. If he doesn't produce it they don't believe in him. Beware of behaving like pregnant women who tight-lace in order to appear slim, and then abort. It's fatal!

There's nothing to force you to publish yet, but, if you do, hurry to prepare the ground. I've told you before, your place will be kept for you. I've put my glove on it already, and the day you arrive, you'll do as I did, you'll fling yourself, with such energy and such a fierce look, on the cooking-pot where others are timidly feeding, that they'll give way to you without striking a blow.

But, at the moment, if your life satisfies you and causes you no regrets, if your work makes you happy, if you're content with your work and don't need anything else; if your personality fills your horizon enough so that you can be satisfied with being a great man for yourself alone, I've nothing further to say. . . . So I've no advice to give you and I give you none, and can't give you any, for this is too grave a matter for me to have the right to do so. I can't drag you along a path which may perhaps not be yours, and I don't want to be your tempter. I've been that once already, and that's enough. All that I can say to you is that, if you decide to publish, I'll help you with all my power, with all my heart, with all my intelligence, with all I know about life, with all my connections, with all my friends, with all my might, with all my influence – and, in six months time, I might be able to add, with all my credit. In short, count on me for everything, except to make a decision for you.

Have faith in yourself – you'd be wrong not to. But beware of yourself. Confidence is only fine when legitimized by success; otherwise it's harmful and makes other men laugh and feel modest themselves.

Finally, when you're alone with yourself, with your conscience, you must know better than anyone else what you must do; you should especially know what you want to do, that's what must guide you.

And so, my dear old chap, look round and reach a decision. At the present moment you're between two choices. On the one hand complete burial in yourself, in your own personality. On the other the pride of publishing *something good* within two years.

That, I think, brutally summarized, is your position. Make your own choice and, as soon as you've got an aim, march towards it, without looking back and without leaving your path.

One final word and I'll have finished with this long letter, which has been very painful for me to write, and which I'd never have resolved to write, if you hadn't driven me into a corner. You've found my harshness wounding, and you attributed it to your 'Normandismes' – but you're quite wrong – later when we become real [comrades?] again, we'll discuss it all. All that I can say to you now is that I loved you once as a person that you weren't. When I found that out, I had to adapt my friendship to that new personality, which I discovered in you – and I say it from the bottom of my heart – it caused a grief in my life which upset me for a very long time. Then the harshness, with which you reproach me, escaped from me, and which I regretted as soon as it was expressed; it was then that I felt bitterness rise to my lips, on account of the impetuosity of my nature, and it burst through the restraints which I had raised against it.

Farewell dear child, think about all this, reflect about it calmly; it is almost a medical diagnosis. And, whatever happens, don't forget that I am always yours,

Maxime Du Camp.

This remarkable letter is very revealing – revealing of the character of both the friends – and it explains why their intimate friendship could not last, for there was too radical a difference between their personalities and aims. Du Camp shows himself here, as he had already done in his writings, without much intuition or imagination, relying on diligent work and second-hand material, with a touching faith in the current ideas of the day. What comes out very clearly is his determination to get on in a worldly sense, and to reach the top. There is something comic in his reliance on classes in order to keep up to date. This is very different from the kind of hard work which Flaubert undertook in connection with any book he was writing; very different from his continued gratuitous education of himself all through his life – his constant reading and study of the great French classics, of Shakespeare; of various philosophers and historians; his learning of Greek as an adult, never afterwards, for the rest of his life, abandoning its study. The advice which Du Camp here gives Flaubert is pathetic when one reflects on the way the latter was working. In his defence it must be remembered that, up to this moment, Flaubert's writings had been largely subjective.

But the letter reveals, as well, in spite of some disillusionment, that Du Camp remained deeply attached to Flaubert, wished him well and was determined to do everything in his power to further his career as a writer – even though his aims may not have been very elevated. He was convinced that he could promote him, and he was prepared to do so as he was the more practical of the two. But he also thought – an opinion shared by Louise Colet – that Flaubert was weak in character, was too much under the thumb of his mother – tied to her apron strings – that he needed shaking up and to be torn from his familiar surroundings. There was a great deal of truth in this, but Du Camp did not realize how much there was of instinctive self-preservation in Flaubert's attitude, that it was partly his way of protecting his spiritual privacy for his work, for the only way he could write, and he was prepared to use his mother as a barrier against outside interference. Du Camp thought that Flaubert was wasting himself when, in reality, he was preserving himself.

It would seem that, at this moment at all events – in spite of what all the later critics have written of his jealousy – Du Camp was disinterested in his behaviour towards Flaubert, for he had nothing to gain from him. There was, however, a certain vulgarity in his mind which, in spite of his un-doubted talents, made it difficult for him to understand Flaubert. But he was not very different from most of the men of letters of his day, and critics have usually been too hard on him, for he was, nevertheless, a genuine and good friend, according to his lights and limitations, and as far as Flaubert would allow him.

Flaubert received Du Camp's letter at the end of October 1851 and, the following month, he went to Paris, where he was for the *coup d'état* of 2 December. This gave him a further excuse for postponing work on his novel, on which he did not begin seriously until he got back to Croisset in January. Then he yoked himself to the subject, which he did not abandon until it was finished in April 1856. It became his 'Old Man of the Sea' clamped to his back, leaving him no peace. His niece Caroline, in her *Souvenirs Intimes*,[12] writes that, as a child, she did not know what the word 'Bovary' meant, but imagined that it was a synonym for toil. Every day, when she had finished her lessons with her uncle, he used to say, with a sigh, 'It's time now to return to Bovary', and she imagined that he meant hard work – she had no idea at the time that it was a novel. She was only five when he began writing, and ten when he finished the book.

At first he worked with great energy and he hoped that this would continue. Writing to his old friend Parrain, he said, in January 1852, when he had just started the book:[13] 'I've begun to work again like a rhinoceros. The wonderful time of *Saint Antoine* has returned. May God grant the results will please me better.' This was, however, not to be, and he was soon in the agonizing throes of composition when he felt that he would never be able to finish. We can follow, through his correspondence, for the five years of writing, all his difficulties of composition and his struggles with himself.

We have seen how, in 1852 and 1853, on account of weariness with his novel, or because he could not get on with it, Flaubert was toying with the idea of composing a fantastic, metaphysical tale entitled *La Spirale*, in the same vein as his earlier *Smarh*, or his first *Tentation de Saint Antoine*. But he did not proceed with the project and returned to the tread-mill of *Madame Bovary*. He was, however, unable to make any serious headway with the book, and was often bored with it, longing even to die in order to escape from it.[14] 'Oh, I'll certainly have known the tortures of art,' he cried. He spent all night at work and then produced almost nothing. In five days he had finished only one page.[15] At another time only twenty pages in a month and working more than seven hours a day.[16] At a further time only twenty-five pages in six weeks:[17]

You talk of your discouragement; if you could only see mine; I don't know how my arms don't drop off my body with fatigue, and why my head doesn't turn into pulp. I lead a bitter kind of life, devoid of all external joy, where I've nothing to sustain me except a kind of permanent rage, which shrieks out sometimes with impotence, which is continuous. Yet I love my work, with a frenzied and perverted love, as the ascetic loves the hair-shirt which scratches his belly. Sometimes I find myself completely empty, when the words refuse to come, when, after having scribbled endless pages, I find that I've really not written a single sentence; then I throw myself onto my divan, and I remain stupefied, sunk in an internal swamp of boredom.

What delayed him also was the research he thought it necessary to do for many sections of the book. As, for instance, when he felt obliged to find out everything that could be discovered about the different forms of club-foot and the various operations that were possible. He stayed for long hours discussing the matter with his brother, the Master of the Hôtel Dieu.[18] He also discussed with Louis Bouilhet, who had trained as a doctor, the nature and the symptoms of arsenical poisoning.[19] He consulted him, as well, on what kind of eye complaint he should give the blind beggar whom the chemist Homais was trying to treat.[20] He spent weeks reading all the romantic novels which a girl like Emma might have read, in order to live in her experience. Writing to Louise Colet, whose tastes would have been similar, he said:[21]

For the past two days I've been trying to enter into the dreams of young girls, and for that I'm sailing on the milky oceans of the literature of medieval castles, of troubadours with velvet white-plumed caps. Remind me to talk to you about all this. You could give me, about it, precise details which I lack.

He could not help thinking, with nostalgia and longing, of the happy creative days when he was composing the *Tentation de Saint Antoine* with so much ease and pleasure, when he was engrossed in a subject which, he thought, suited him entirely and which inspired him.[22]

He felt particularly his slowness when he heard that Maxime Du Camp had been made Officier de la Légion d'Honneur for his services to science, literature and learning. He could not then restrain a certain feeling of envy:[23]

News! Young Du Camp is Officier de la Légion d'Honneur!

How that must please him! When he compares himself to me, and considers how far he has advanced since he left me, it's certain that he must think me far behind him, and that he has got on very far (externally). You'll see him one of these days accepting a position, and leaving literature far behind him!

He may have pretended to be indifferent to his separation from Du Camp, he was nevertheless hurt by what he thought was his friend's neglect of him, for having left him a month without news. He wrote to Louise Colet:[24]

Since I left Paris I've had five lines only from Du Camp, that's all. He writes to Bouilhet that he's too busy to write letters. When he wants to come back to me, he'll find his place still there, and I'll kill the fatted calf for him. I believe that that day will be very sweet to him, for he's marching towards disappointments. Well!

Du Camp was not, however, forgetting his friend, and he continued to urge him to get going and start publishing before it was too late, before everyone had got ahead of him and all the places were taken. He considered that there were still vacant places in the ranks of literature to be filled. Chateaubriand and Balzac had recently died; Lamartine was writing nothing, and Vigny had never written much; Hugo was in exile, and Musset was drinking himself to death. He admired Flaubert's talents and potentialities, and he thought that one of the empty places could be filled by him.

What he did not understand was that Flaubert was working very hard and struggling with himself, trying to correct his faults. All he could see was that his friend was being lazy and indolent, sinking into futile domesticity with his mother. He wrote to urge him to bestir himself and again offered his help. Flaubert, whose nerves were upset by his difficulties in progressing with his book, by his lack of success according to his aims, lashed out against his friend in a hard and cruel letter, which reveals clearly how wide the rift had become between them:[25]

My dear friend, you seem to have developed towards me a

nervous habit, a latent defect.[26] It doesn't annoy me in the slightest, don't be afraid of that. My mind has been made up on that score for a long time. I'll only say to you that these words, 'to hurry; now's the moment; it's time; the place is taken; to take a position; beyond the law', are for me a vocabulary totally devoid of meaning. It's as if you were speaking to an Algonquin. Don't understand! *Arrive*, at what? At the position of Messrs Murger, Feuillet, Monselet, etc. Arsène Houssaye, Taxile Delord, Hippolyte Lucas, and seventy others like them? No thank you! *To be known* that's not my main business, that only satisfies very mediocre and vain intellects. Moreover, in that respect, does one ever know what to believe? The most complete fame never satisfies, and one nearly always dies uncertain of one's own name, unless one is a fool. And so, being illustrious doesn't class you any more than being obscure. I aim at something better – to please myself. Success seems to me to be a result and not an aim. Well! I've been marching towards an aim for a long time, it seems to me without faltering a step, without lingering at the side of the road to run after women, or to sleep on the grass. Illusion for illusion, I prefer the one with the noblest stature. May the United States perish rather than a principle; and may I die like a dog, rather than hasten by one second my sentence which is not ripe. I have in my head a way of writing, a niceness of language, which I wish to attain. When I think I've plucked the apricot, I'll not refuse to sell it, nor prevent people from applauding if it's good. Until then I don't want to swindle the public. That's all. If by then it's too late, if everyone's thirst is quenched, that's bad luck! I long for myself, you may be sure, greater facility, and much less labour, and more profit. But I don't see any remedy to it. . . . It's there that you find breath of life, you say to me, speaking of Paris. But for me, your breath of life seems often to stink of dental caries. There arises from that Parnassus where you are summoning me, more miasma than intoxication. The laurels that one gathers there are somewhat covered with shit. By the way, I'm sorry to see a man like you trying to go one better than the Marquise d'Escarbagnac [in Molière's play] who imagined that there was no salvation for decent people outside Paris. That judgement seems to me in itself provincial, that is to say narrow. Humanity is to be found everywhere, my dear Sir, but humbug more frequently in Paris than elsewhere I do agree. Certainly there's one thing that one gains in

Paris and that's cheek; but one loses some of one's hair. .... As for deploring so bitterly my *neutralizing* life, that is the same thing as reproaching a bootmaker with making boots; or a smith for beating his iron; an artist for living in his studio. As I work from one o'clock in the afternoon to one o'clock in the morning, except between six and eight, I don't very well see how I could use the time that is left! If I really lived in the provinces, really in the country, devoting myself to playing dominoes and growing melons, I should reproach myself. If I'm growing stupid, it's Lucian, Shakespeare and writing a novel that are to blame. I've told you that I'd go to live in Paris when my book was finished, and that I'd publish it if I was pleased with it, I've not changed my mind. That's all I can say and nothing more. Believe me, dear friend, let the water flow by. If the literary quarrels surge up or die down, I don't care a tuppenny damn. That Augier should get on I care even less; that Vacquerie and Ponsard should swell out their shoulders and take all my place, I care even less than a damn, and I wouldn't disturb them to get it back from them.

Writing to Louise Colet the same day,[27] he tells her that Du Camp has written to him to show him that his place was between Ponsard and Vacquerie, that it is only in Paris that one can live. He quotes from his letter to him, saying that he does not believe that he will ever broach the subject again, and that he will not dare show the letter to anyone. Although it is clear from his letter to Louise Colet that he had intended to hurt his friend, when the latter showed that he had been wounded he pretended to be surprised, saying that nothing had been further from his intention and he accused him of being very touchy:[28]

I'm very much pained to see you so thin-skinned. Far from having wished to make my letter wounding, I tried my best to keep it the contrary. As far as I could I remained within the limits of the subject – as they say in rhetoric.
But why do you begin all over again the same old story? Why do you advise a diet to a man who believes that he is healthy? I find your concern on my account faintly comic, that's all. Do I blame you for living in Paris, and for having published etc. etc. And when, at one time, you even wanted to come and live in a

house near mine, in the country, did I support your plan? Did I advise you to lead my kind of life? . . .

Anything you can say to me, I've said it to myself, you can be sure – blame or praise, good or bad. Anything you can add over and above that will only be a repetition of an endless monologue which I know by heart.

One word more, nevertheless. The literary rebirth which you prophesy, I deny it, as I don't see, up to now, a new man, nor an original book, nor an idea which isn't worn threadbare. (They go on arse-licking their masters as in the past.) They repeat, over and over again, the old humanitarian and aesthetic theories. I don't deny, in the youth of today, the goodwill to create a school, but I deny its existence. I'll be very happy if I'm wrong; and I'll take advantage of the discovery.

As for my *post* of man of letters, I leave it to you willingly. I'm abandoning the sentry-box, taking my rifle away under my arm. I waive the honour of such a title and such a mission. I'm frankly a bourgeois, living in seclusion in the country, busy with literature and asking nothing of anyone, not consideration, nor honour, nor esteem. They'll have to get on without my lights. I beg them, in return, not to annoy me with their tapers. That's why I keep at a distance. As for *helping them,* I'd never refuse a service, of whatever kind. I'd jump into the water to save a good line of poetry or a good sentence of prose from anyone. But I don't believe, on that account, that humanity has need of me, any more than I have need of it. You must change that idea you've got, namely that I'm turned in on myself. *I'm not satisfied with myself.* It's when I'll be pleased with myself, that I'll leave home where I'm certainly not spoilt by encouragement. If you could only see into my mind, that sentence which you wrote would seem to you a monstrosity.

If your conscience prompted you to give me that advice, you were right to do so, and I thank you for the kind intention. . . .

We're no longer following the same road; we're not sailing in the same skiff. May God lead us each to where he wants to go. I'm not aiming at the port, but the high seas. If I'm ship-wrecked, I dispense you from mourning.

This letter marks an important step in the loosening of the bonds of their friendship. Writing to Louise Colet a few months later, Flaubert said:[29]

As for the good Maxime, I'm incapable, at the moment, of any kind of feeling for him. The place, in my heart, where he used to be, has disintegrated with a slow gangrene, and there is nothing left of it now. Good or bad actions, praise or blame, it's all the same to me. There's no contempt there. It isn't a matter of pride, but I feel a fundamental incapacity of feeling anything with regard to him, or for him, whether it be friendship, hatred, esteem or anger. He has gone, like a dead man, without leaving me even with a regret. God willed it! God be praised! The sweetness that I once experienced in that affection (I remember it with delight) diminishes somewhat, no doubt, the humiliation that I feel now for having experienced it.

There is, however, in this letter more hurt than indifference. It seems as if Flaubert could not bear that the friend, who had once adored him, should think less highly of him, especially when he believed that he was on the right road.

It has always been said that Du Camp was jealous of Flaubert and spiteful about him, but there is no evidence of this at this time. However, there is evidence that Flaubert himself was capable at times of expressing small-mindedness, and perhaps even envy. It was natural in his state of frustration at his failure to finish his book. In a letter to Louise Colet,[30] he even accused Du Camp of suppressing the only photograph of himself which he had taken while they were in the East, in his travel book, *Égypte, Nubie, Palestine, Syrie*. This is manifestly absurd, as the photograph is not a good one of Flaubert, who was taken from a distance and scarcely seen, and he is dressed in native costume which further disguises him. The photograph also was not relevant to the book. 'He would like me not to exist,' Flaubert remarked, 'I weigh on him.' He was also very hard on the book itself, accusing its author of pillaging a German scholar without naming him and he said that, out of twenty-six pages of introduction, there were not three by himself, that it was all borrowed from others.[31]

Du Camp was being very assiduous in getting his works published. His second book, *Le Livre Posthume* (*Mémoires d'un Suicidé*), was published in *La Revue de Paris* in 1852 – his first book, a travel book, had appeared in 1848. It is a novel, but not a very good one, highly Romantic in plot – though intended to be an attack on the Romantic attitude to life – written without much distinction of style. Du Camp was becoming much influenced by the humanitarian view of literature, believing that art should have a moral aim, and this novel is an indictment against those who withdraw from everyday life. The hero, finding nothing, alone with himself, – eventually commits suicide. He is, as the author says, 'un fils naturel de René, élevé par Antony et Chatterton', and before he kills himself, he writes: 'Comme ils sont heureux tous ceux qui ne sont pas moi; tous ceux qui ne sont pas rongés par les dévorantes inquiétudes de rêves impossibles.' He dies because he feels that he is useless. He talks of what brought about his downfall, his isolation and solitude, 'La solitude qui porte à ses deux sinistres mamelles, l'egoïsme et la vanité.' Flaubert realized that Du Camp was thinking of him as he wrote but, at the same time, he had a low opinion of the book.[32]

Du Camp's third book was the book of photographs which he had taken during his eastern trip, with a long introduction by himself, which appeared in 1853. In October, the same year, he began to publish his fourth work, an account of his trip to the Nile, Turkey and Palestine. Flaubert considered this a deterioration on *Le Livre Posthume*, and that there was no hope for him in the future:[33]

Friend Max has begun to publish his journey to Egypt, *Le Nil*, to be a counterpart to *Le Rhin* [Hugo's book]. It is strange in its nothingness. I don't talk about the style, which is exceedingly flat, a hundred times worse than in *Le Livre Posthume*. But, as subject matter, as facts, there's nothing in it at all. The details which he best noticed, the most characteristic in nature, he forgets them. You who've seen my notes you'll be struck by that. What a sudden come-down!

His view of Du Camp's work fortified him in his opinion

that he personally was on the right path. He would not, or could not, join the race for recognition and power. He had no ambitions in that way himself, he would never push himself forward, nor ever seek to belong to any Academy or movement.[34] He declared that he would rather be an usher in a school than ever make money by his writings.[35]

Flaubert suffered greatly at the departure of Bouilhet for Paris in October 1853, when he went to seek fame and fortune in the capital. He had relied on his support and encouragement during the past two years of the torture of composition and he remained very sad without him. 'You can't imagine how lonely I am without you,' he wrote to him,[36] 'and how I think, each Sunday, of my poor Sundays of former times.'

Although he would not lift a finger for the sake of his own advancement, he could give his friend worldly-wise advice, especially after his play *Madame de Montarcy* was twice refused by the Théâtre Français. Flaubert was more upset by this than by any of his own reverses.[37] He realized how prostrated Bouilhet was by his failure, so that his mother was afraid that he might commit suicide, and she went to Paris to persuade him to abandon all thoughts of the stage. Flaubert was very angry with her and he tried to neutralize her action by his encouragement.[38] Although he would never have stirred himself on his own behalf, he urged his friend to go forward, giving him advice very similar to that which he had himself received earlier from Du Camp:[39]

I call on your pride. Remember what you've done, what you dream of doing, and rise up, great Heavens, consider yourself with more respect! and don't lack respect for me at the bottom of your mind, by having doubts of an intelligence which is undisputed.

You'll say to me that you've been for two years in Paris and that you've done everything you could but that nothing good has yet happened to you. Firstly, no: you've done nothing for your own practical advancement and I permit myself to say the contrary. *Melaenis* has had a success, it is spoken about, articles are written about you; but you've not had *Melaenis* yet printed in book form, you don't go to see the people who wrote about you. You're given entries to the Théâtre Français, and you don't put a foot in it, and, in two years, you've not managed, I don't say to make a friend there, but not even an acquaintance. You've refused to see a mass of people, Janin, Dumas, Guttinguer etc. with whom you might have made some friends; and, as for the people you do meet, it might perhaps be better not to see them.

Flaubert now advised him to give up all idea of the Théâtre Français and to concentrate on the second theatre, the Odéon. He showed himself surprisingly adept at intrigue, knowing to whom he should write, what strings he should pull, and advising his friend on his plan of campaign. It was no wonder that Du Camp thought it a pity that some of the talent could not be utilized for his own literary future, but Flaubert continued to be uninterested in that. He worked to such good purpose that Bouilhet's *Madame de Montarcy* was finally accepted by the Théâtre de l'Odéon and eventually produced there.

In 1854, during the last two years of the composition of his novel, Flaubert heard that Champfleury was in process of publishing as a serial a novel on a theme very similar to *Madame Bovary*.

At this time Champfleury was considered the strong hope of fiction, since the death of Balzac in 1850. His main period as a novelist runs at the time when Flaubert was composing *Madame Bovary*. In 1854 his best novel was serialized and it was published in 1855; it is *Les Bourgeois de Molinchart*, the action of which takes place in the little town of Laon where its author was born. It is a sordid account of adultery in the provinces and he had intended, at first, to call it *L'Adultère en Province*. The plot is not of much concern, but what matters is the depiction of the bourgeois provincial atmosphere, which was new. It certainly marks the beginning of the Realist School in the novel and it had a great success when it appeared so that a hundred thousand copies were sold. With its publication Champfleury became the unchallenged leader of the new movement of Realism in literature.

When Flaubert heard of the novel he was anxious for a time as he realized that the subject was very similar to his own, but he was much relieved when he read it:[40]

I've read five issues of Champfleury's novel. Frankly it isn't terrifying. There's similarity of intention rather than of subject or characters. Those of the husband, his wife, and the lover seem to me very different from mine. . . . The only annoying thing is the character of the devout old maid, the enemy of the heroine (her sister-in-law), as, in *Bovary*, Madame Bovary, the mother, is the enemy of her daughter-in-law, and the character, in Champfleury, is promising. That is for me, up to now, the greatest resemblance, and this character of the old maid is far better drawn than that of my good woman, a secondary character by the way in my book. As for the style, not very good, not very good. All the same it is unfortunate that *Bovary* can't be published now. But what can I do?

I've reread *Eugénie Grandet*. That's really beautiful. What a difference with friend Champfleury.

He wrote again four days later and said:[41] 'I've read eleven chapters of Champfleury's novel. I'm more and more reassured; the conception and the tone are very different. No one, except you and me, would draw any comparisons. The only thing alike in the two books, is the *milieu*, and even then!' That Flaubert should feel nervous with regard to Champfleury is flattering to the latter. The commentator of the letters states in a note[42] that the novel by Champfleury in question is *Madame d'Aigrizelles*. This cannot be true, as that novel bears no resemblance whatsoever to *Madame Bovary*, since it tells the story of a mother who fights for the liberty of her son who has been condemned to five years' imprisonment for theft. The novel which it must certainly be – in Flaubert's description of it as well as in its resemblance to his own book – is *Les Bourgeois de Molinchart*, published when he was in process of composing *Madame Bovary*.

In the last month of the composition of *Madame Bovary* Flaubert had a strange experience in a dream.[43] He must have thought it significant for he took the trouble of writing it down, dating it and preserving it, and he also mentioned it in a letter to Louis Bouilhet.[44] He put the title *Un Rêve* on the manuscript, and dated it 'Monday morning, 3 March, 8.30, 1856'. It tells of a terrifying dream he had experienced during the night, when an old woman came to him in his bed, but he felt that his mother was there protecting him. 'At my feet, outside the bed, and lying across it, like the dogs on the tombs, there was (or rather I felt) my mother whose presence was protecting me. I did not see her but I felt her.'

It is a complicated dream, the scene of which then shifts to an evening party at the house of Madame Sabatier. It is difficult to see what its true significance is and what Flaubert thought it symbolized; but he himself thought it had meaning, as he took the trouble of adding a footnote the following day. He wrote that, eight years previously, when he had returned from Le Poittevin's funeral, he had had a similar experience, and he wondered what was going to happen to him during the coming day. The following day he added a note to the effect that it was the anniversary of his sister's wedding day.

Finally, in April 1856, *Madame Bovary* was finished after four and a half years of toil and torture. The manuscript – final draft and rough copies – are preserved in the Municipal Library at Rouen. From them can be seen the extent of his rewriting and corrections. The rough copies comprise 1,788 sheets of foolscap, written on both sides, in the author's minute handwriting; the various scenarios make up forty-two sheets. The final manuscript, in Flaubert's hand, has 487 pages.[45] It is very much corrected and scored over, in spite of all the rough drafts; it is signed by Flaubert on the fly-leaf, and he has written as well:

Madame Bovary
    septembre 1851 – avril 1856.

The definitive manuscript has 489 pages,[46] and it has been transcribed by a professional copyist. The title is written by Flaubert himself, and he has signed the copy at the end of Part One as well as at the end of the book. Although it is supposed to be a fair copy, it is even then very much corrected.

The book is not divided into chapters; this was only done at the last moment, when it was serialized in *La Revue de Paris*.

In May 1856, Flaubert rented an apartment in Paris, at No. 42 Boulevard du Temple, where he was to spend every winter, now that he was to become a published writer. He wanted also to be in the centre for the rapid correction of proofs. His book was supposed to be published in September, in *La Revue de Paris*, but there were endless delays, not this time of his own making, so that it did not finally appear until October.

As soon as he had taken the apartment Flaubert began to regret his action and, writing to Louis Bouilhet in June, he said to him:[47]

I've behaved like a fool, in doing what everyone else does, in going to live in Paris and in wishing to be published. I'd been living in perfect serenity of art as long as I was writing for myself alone. Now I'm full of doubts and worry, and I'm experiencing something new: writing bores me! I feel for literature the hatred of impotence.

I must bore you to extinction, my poor old chap, but I beg you on my bended knees to forgive me, for I've no one else with whom to speak of all this.

While awaiting publication of *Madame Bovary* he occupied himself with revising and rewriting his *Tentation de Saint Antoine* – what is called the version of 1856 – which he hoped he might be able to publish after *Madame Bovary*. He had returned from Paris to the quiet of Croisset in July 1856 and did not expect to return to the capital until the publication of his book in October.

Bouilhet's play, *Madame de Montarcy*, had been finally

accepted by the Odéon; rehearsals began in September, and the first night was expected to take place on 6 November – not much after Flaubert's début in October.

The success of his play was very important to Bouilhet and, if it failed, he might never again be able to have confidence in himself. Flaubert spent nearly the whole of his time trying to ensure its success.[48] He managed to get himself introduced to the main dramatic critics, and he interviewed them on Bouilhet's behalf, extolling the merits of his play.

On the first night, on 6 November, at the Odéon Theatre, Bouilhet, always the most timid of men, was in a distressful state of nerves. He was sure that the play would be a flop; when there was applause, he imagined that the audience was hissing. Half-way through the performance, not being able to stand the suspense any longer, and what he imagined was a fiasco, he left the theatre in company with Flaubert, and they walked round the streets of the left bank, standing on the Pont Neuf to gaze down at the Seine, and it is said that only with difficulty was the unhappy playwright prevented from jumping into the river.

They returned to the theatre and were just in time to hear the thunderous applause which greeted the final curtain. The play had been a definite hit. But, even then, Bouilhet would hardly credit it, and it was only when he read the reviews that he believed in his success. The play was given seventy performances and it is said that the Emperor and the Empress attended one evening.

In the meantime Flaubert himself was enjoying, if not exactly fame, certainly notoriety, during the months of October, November and December while *Madame Bovary* was being serialized in *La Revue de Paris*; this culminated in the trial for blasphemy and immorality the following January.

[18]

Publication
(1856)

FLAUBERT finished *Madame Bovary* in April 1856 and then went to Paris to read it to Louis Bouilhet, who suggested further alterations and improvements. Next he had it transcribed by a copyist, and, at the end of May, he sent the completed manuscript to Maxime Du Camp at *La Revue de Paris*, and then tried to find out what was thought of it at the review.[1] He spent the anxious time of waiting working on his *Tentation de Saint Antoine* and reading the medieval texts which were later to go to the composition of *La Légende de Saint Julien l'Hospitalier*, but he found that he was, for the time being, after the effort of composing *Madame Bovary*, bored with writing.

Du Camp's co-editors at *La Revue de Paris* had changed since its foundation, and he was now associated with Louis Ulbach and Laurent Pichat. They were both anxious about the effect of the publication of *Madame Bovary* and they did not wish to get into difficulties with the government – neither did Du Camp who was, as we have seen, an ambitious man. The difficulties with the authorities were very serious indeed. There was strict censorship under the Second Empire, and *La Revue de Paris* was considered too liberal and advanced in its views. The authorities would have been very glad to find cause and pretext to deal severely with the periodical. Du Camp and his co-editors were afraid that the paper might be suppressed, which would have meant the abandonment of all their hopes. In *Misères et Grandeurs Littéraires*, Ulbach said of the publication of *Madame Bovary*:[2]

First I was very much alarmed when, after a first reading, I recognized that we were about to publish a strange and daring work, cynical in its negation of everything, unreasonable by dint of reason, false on account of too much truth in detail, badly observed on account of the crumbling, so to speak, of observation. *Madame Bovary* offended my artistic taste more than my modesty as a reader, but I was afraid lest it provide a pretext for those who might be looking for one to get the review suppressed.

The editors agreed to publish the novel but Ulbach insisted that, before this happened, certain cuts were necessary:[3]

I explained my reasons to my friends. These reasons still hold good. . . . I demanded corrections. I insisted, amongst other things, on the shortening of the cab-ride. We were all unanimous. The *Revue de Paris* was in opposition to the government. We were spied upon, watched and endlessly menaced. They would have been delighted to catch us red-handed in a charge of immorality.

Du Camp did not explain this fully to Flaubert, but wrote him a clumsy letter on the advice of Pichat, on 14 July:[4]

Laurent Pichat has read your novel and he has sent me the criticism which I enclose herewith. You'll see, when you've read it, how much I must share his opinion, since it reproduces nearly all the remarks which I made to you before you left. I handed your book to Laurent, without doing anything more than recommend it warmly to him. We did not therefore come to any agreement to bore you with the same old arguments. The advice he gives you is good, in fact I should say that it is the only one you should follow. Let us be the *masters* of your novel to publish it in *La Revue*; we shall make the cuts which we consider indispensable; you can publish it afterwards in book form as you like, that will be your own responsibility. My honest opinion is that, if you don't do this, you'll be compromising yourself and you'll be beginning with a muddled work, in which the style isn't sufficient to give it interest. Be courageous, close your eyes during the operation and trust, if not our talent, then the experience which we have acquired in this kind of business and our affection for you. You've buried your novel under a heap of well-made but useless things, and one can't see it clearly, it is only a question of clearing it up. It is an easy task. We'll get it done, under our supervision, by a clever and experienced person; not a word will be added to your text; it will only be a question of lightening it; it will cost you about a hundred francs which will be deducted from your fees, and you'll have published a really good work instead of an incomplete one, which is too padded. You must be cursing me with all your might, but remember that, in all this, I have only your interests in view. Good-bye, old chap, answer me, and know that I am always yours, Maxime Du Camp.

Flaubert wrote, on the back of the letter, 'gigantesque'. He refused, however, to make any of the alterations suggested. There was silence for a time, and then the 1 August 1856 number of *La Revue de Paris* announced the forthcoming publication of *Madame Bovary*, but the author's name was spelt 'Faubert', a grocer in the rue de Richelieu, near the Théâtre Français. The review was still arguing on how and when the novel could be published.[5] September came and there was still no definite news.[6] At last he heard that his book would begin to appear in the issue of 1 October 'without fail, I hope'.[7]

Flaubert's text appeared uncut and untampered with in the issue of *La Revue de Paris* of 1 October 1856, and he wrote immediately to Laurent Pichat to thank him for his generosity:[8]

I've just received *Bovary* and I feel, first of all, the need of thanking you. (If I'm sometimes rude, I'm not ungrateful.) It's a great service you've done me, by accepting it as it is and I shan't forget it. . . . Do you believe that that loathsome reality, the depiction of which disgusts you, doesn't make my gorge rise equally? If you knew me better you'd realize that I hate ordinary life and, personally, I've kept away from it as much as possible. But, aesthetically I wanted, this time, and this time only, to practise it fully. And so I took the matter in a heroic manner – I mean minute – by accepting everything, saying everything, painting everything – an ambitious plan. I can't explain myself very well,

but it's enough for you to understand the *meaning* of my opposition to your criticism, however justified it might be. You were
trying to write another book. . . . I'd believe that I'd be failing in
what I owe myself, and what I owed you, in yielding out of de-
ference to you and not out of conviction. Art doesn't demand
kindness or politeness, but only faith, always faith and liberty.

In November 1856 a friend warned Du Camp that there
would be trouble for *La Revue de Paris* if it continued to
publish *Madame Bovary* in its present form. Du Camp then
tried to persuade Flaubert to be reasonable and to remove
the dangerous passages. Flaubert reminded him that the
novel had been accepted as it was and that the policy of the
review had been to respect each work, to refuse them at
times but never to modify what had been written.

On 18 November Du Camp wrote to Flaubert: 'It's no
joking matter. Your scene in the cab is impossible.'

Flaubert allowed certain alterations to be made, and
Ulbach wrote:[9]

In the following issues I had asked for the deletion of several
passages; as, for instance, the episode of Extreme Unction, and
the coarse wake where the parish priest and the chemist, at the
death-bed of the dead woman, quarrel and become reconciled.
He submitted to the amputations protesting vehemently.

Next, in the number of 1 December, there were cuts about
which Flaubert had not been consulted, on the grounds that
there had not been sufficient time, and he was only informed
by a note printed in the paper: 'The editorial board has
found it necessary to cut a passage here which did not suit
the editors of *La Revue de Paris*. We hereby inform the
author of this.'

Flaubert wrote to Pichat to protest against this treatment
of his work, saying that they should have refused his text
rather than mutilate it, since this was their avowed policy.
There was to be only one further instalment of the novel and
he asked for his manuscript to be returned to him:[10]

Here is what I've got to say to *La Revue de Paris*.

(1) It kept *Madame Bovary* in manuscript, for three months, thus, before publishing a single line, it should have known what it thought of the work. It was take it or leave it. It took it, so much the worse for it!

(2) Once the matter was decided and accepted, I agreed to the deletion of a passage which, in my opinion, was very important, because the *Revue* assured me that there was danger for it in it. I gave in with good grace; but I don't disguise from you (and it is to my friend Pichat that I'm now speaking) that that day I bitterly regretted having had the idea of publishing. Let us say the whole of our thought, or nothing.

(3) I consider that I've already done a lot, and the *Revue* thinks that I should do more. *Well I'll do nothing more,* not a correction, not a deletion, not a comma less, nothing, nothing! But, if the *Revue* feels that I'm compromising it, if it's afraid, there is something very simple, and that is to stop here the publication of *Madame Bovary.* I don't care a bit about that.

And now I've finished speaking to the *Revue,* I'll say this to my friend. In cutting out the passage of the cab, you removed nothing of what scandalized people; and, in omitting from the sixth instalment what they're asking me to, you'll again remove nothing. You attack details but you should go for the whole work. The brutal element is deep down in the work, and not on the surface. One can't whiten Negroes, and one can't change the blood of a book, one can only impoverish it, that is all.

It goes without saying that, if I quarrel with *La Revue de Paris,* I can remain, none the less, friends with its editors.

Du Camp went to see him to try to persuade him to allow the cuts to be made, but Flaubert was adamant and would permit nothing to be altered:[11]

I don't care a jot; if my novel annoys the bourgeois, I don't care a jot; if they take us to the courts, I don't care a jot; if *La Revue de Paris* is suppressed I don't care; you'd only to refuse *Bovary*; you accepted it and must bear the consequences; you'll publish it as it is.

Du Camp tried further arguments but in vain. Then he went to see Madame Flaubert to urge her to persuade her son to be reasonable, but she would do nothing. She remembered vividly still the disastrous reading of *La Tentation de Saint Antoine*, and she made him feel that she considered that he was deliberately trying to destroy her son, that he was jealous of him. Flaubert continued to maintain his refusal, but Du Camp and Pichat would not agree to ending publication of the novel, which, they said, would ruin the paper; they also claimed that they had a perfect right to delete what they considered dangerous to the review, and unsuitable. They suggested, however, that Flaubert should be allowed to publish a note saying that he had no responsibility in the matter. He refused at first, but, the following morning, he yielded and even suggested the terms of the insertion which appeared before the final instalment of *Madame Bovary*:[12]

> Certain considerations into which I need not enter here obliged *La Revue de Paris* to make some deletions in the issue of 1 December 1856. These scruples having been renewed on the occasion of the present number, it has considered it right to remove several passages. Consequently I declare that I accept no responsibility for the text which follows; the reader is therefore requested to consider it only as a fragment and not as a whole. G. Flaubert.

On a copy of the book, which he kept as a memento, he wrote:[13] 'This copy represents my manuscript in the form in which it came from the hands of that gentleman Laurent Pichat, poet and editor, owner of *La Revue de Paris*, 20 April 1857.' In it can be seen that, from page to page, whole lines and paragraphs had been cut out. And, on the last page, the author had written: 'It was necessary, according to Maxime Du Camp, to cut out the *whole* of the wedding; according to Pichat to delete, or to shorten considerably, the agricultural show, to rewrite the whole passage. In the opinion of the *Revue* the episode of the club foot was considerably too long, useless.'

Flaubert, in order to vent his annoyance against *La Revue de Paris*, did something very foolish; he ransacked the review to find passages which he considered as worthy of censure as his own book.[14] Maxime Du Camp declares that he collected any odd sentences, or words, any possibly licentious passages – one came from Du Camp himself – and gave this large dossier to a journalist who made an article from it, in which he asked how it came about the editors who could write such things themselves could be so prudish for others.[15] This was all very unwise as it drew the attention of the government to the review. The article was noticed by the authorities; it was brought to the attention of the Emperor; it was sent to the Minister of the Interior; and finally, it reached the Public Prosecutor. Flaubert's contributions to *La Revue de Paris* were gone through with a fine comb and many things were found in them which made it possible, according to the laws of the day, to charge the author, the editor and the printer of the review with an offence against public morality. Thus Flaubert was, himself, largely responsible for the prosecution of his book.

When *Madame Bovary* had begun to appear in *La Revue de Paris, La Nouvelliste de Rouen* had noticed it with interest and, wishing to serialize a work by one of their own citizens, obtained permission to print it in their own columns. Publication had begun on Sunday 9 November. Later, when there seemed to be the danger of prosecution for *La Revue de Paris*, Du Camp wrote to Flaubert:

Don't you think that it's your duty to write to Claudin of the *Nouvelliste de Rouen*, which is publishing *Bovary*, to warn him of what to expect if he continues. If it bores you to take this step yourself, I'll write. I saw Cavaignac earlier today and, this evening, he's going to see Sénard to discuss the defence with him.

Le Nouvelliste de Rouen later discontinued the publication of the novel, after 14 December, printing the following note to explain their action:[16]

We have reached the decision, after this issue, to cease the publication of *Madame Bovary*, because we could not continue to do so without making certain cuts. The editors of *La Revue de Paris* had thought it necessary to make these cuts, and, moreover, we have learnt that difficulties have arisen between them and the author concerning the last part of the novel. We have even read, in a paper, that, on Friday the parties came under injunction.

Shortly afterwards Du Camp wrote to Flaubert: 'Don't spread this rumour, but nevertheless stir your stumps so that the result shouldn't be too bad. For us it might be suppression and that is what we must try to avoid.'

Preparations for the prosecution went on mercilessly, and Flaubert thought that there must be some indefatigable force at work behind the scenes. 'It is a whirlwind of lies and infamous suggestions,' he said, 'in which I'm completely at sea. I was, at first, only a pretext, and I believe that *La Revue de Paris* itself was only a pretext. I'm now waiting at any minute for the official summons which will inform me on what day I must go and sit in the dock (for the crime of having written in French) with thieves and pederasts.'[17]

The official document finally arrived, and Flaubert was summoned to appear on 24 January 1857 before 'Le Tribunal Correctionnel' for offences against public and religious principles, and against public morality. The editor of the paper, Laurent Pichat, and the printer, Auguste Pillet, were also summoned.

Flaubert was thus justified in his belief that the cuts and omissions would be in vain and that his novel would have been in no greater danger of prosecution if it had been published in its unmutilated form.

[19]

The Trial
(1857)

AFTER the publication of the final instalment of *Madame Bovary*, there were rumours that the paper and the author were to be prosecuted. Flaubert was, at first, not anxious, as he thought that the case would be dropped. He told his brother, on 1 January 1857, that all the mud in the capital was being stirred up to try to catch him:[1]

My affair is a political matter because they want, at all costs, to exterminate *La Revue de Paris*, which irritates the government; it has already had two warnings, and it would be smart to suppress it, at the third warning, for an offence against religion! for what I'm especially reproached with is a scene of *Extreme Unction* copied from *Le Rituel de Paris*. But these good magistrates are such fools that they are completely ignorant of the religion which they are supposed to be defending. . . . I'll become the lion of the week, and all the bitches of the nobility are tearing *Bovary* from each other to try to find obscenities which aren't in it. . . . My affair is very complicated. I'm only a pretext. What is important for us to save (this time) is *La Revue de Paris*, unless the *Revue* drags me to destruction with it. . . . When you receive this my affair will probably be over.

But the danger continued, and Flaubert told his brother that, when he was writing to influential people, he should make a great deal of the position of their father in Rouen, and explain the bad effect it would create on the forthcoming elections in Rouen if such an important family were attacked:[2]

Everything you've done is very good. The important thing is to bring pressure on Paris through Rouen. The information about the influential position of our father is excellent; they thought they were attacking a poor devil, and when they saw that I'd enough to live on, they began to open their eyes wide. They must be got to know, at the Ministry of the Interior, that we are, in Rouen, what is called *a family*, that is to say that we've deep roots in the country, and that, by attacking me, especially for immorality, they would wound a great many people. I'm expecting a great effect from the letter of the *Préfet* to the Ministry of the Interior. . . . It will probably be tonight that it will be decided whether I'm to be prosecuted or not. No matter! look after the *Préfet*, and don't stop until I tell you! . . . Try to get people to say, *cleverly*, that there would be danger in attacking me, in attacking *us*, on account of the forthcoming elections.

According to Finot,[3] the authorities had, at first, intended to make an example of Flaubert and of *La Revue de Paris*; and, according to Dreyfous,[4] it had been decided to condemn him to two years' imprisonment, but his lawyer had gone to the Tuileries to see the Emperor, and had told him what a bad impression it would create if Flaubert were convicted.

It looked then as if the matter were dying down, as if there was not going to be a prosecution after all, and Flaubert told his brother that some grand society ladies had been working for him 'especially la Princesse Beauvau, who is an ardent Bovaryste and who has been twice to see the Emperor to get the prosecution stopped'.[5]

He had thought that he was safe, but the attacks continued nevertheless, and the dangers of prosecution became greater. He had, however, some support in high places, and he was especially pleased and flattered by a letter which he received from Lamartine:[6]

I believe that I have been, all my life, in my literary and other works, the man who has best understood what public and religious morality are. My dear child, it is not possible that there can be found, in France, a court to convict you. It is already very unfortunate that there has been this misunderstanding about the nature of your work, and that prosecution has been decided on. But it is not possible, for the honour of our country and of our age, that there should be a court to convict you.

Flaubert went to see him, spending an hour with him, and
he found that Lamartine claimed to know almost the whole
of the book by heart. The poet promised him a letter, and
support from so noble a man of letters would carry a great
deal of weight.[7] It was indeed surprising that the poet of
Les Méditations, the most romantic collection of poetry,
should admire the realism of *Madame Bovary.* However, he
did not keep his promise, and he must have read the novel
hastily at first, for later, when he saw that he was being
mocked in it, he changed his mind, withdrew and did not
help Flaubert at the decisive moment. As the novelist said to
Maurice Schlésinger:[8] 'On the spur of the moment, he sent
me congratulations, and then he dropped me at the critical
moment. In short he didn't behave towards me like a gentleman; and he even broke a promise he had given me.'

Matters took their course and, writing to his old friend Dr
Cloquet, Flaubert said:[9]

I inform you that tomorrow, 24 January, I'm honouring, with
my presence, the dock of scoundrels at the 'Sixième Chambre de
Police Correctionnelle', at 10 o'clock in the morning. Ladies are
admitted, decent dress and good taste are compulsory.

I don't count on any justice. I'll be condemned, and to the
maximum penalty, perhaps. Sweet reward; a noble encouragement to literature. I cannot even hope to be reminded
for a fortnight, as Sénard can't act for me tomorrow, nor in a
week's time. One thing consoles me for all this stupidity, it is to
have met such sympathy for myself and for my book. ... If my
work has any real value, if you've not made a mistake, I pity
those who are prosecuting it. This book which they're trying to
destroy will survive all the better for their wounds. From the
mouth which they're trying to stifle, they will receive a gob of
spittle in their face. You'll perhaps have the chance, one day or
other, to discuss these matters with the Emperor, and you could,
as an example, quote my trial as one of the most stupid of the
base deeds which are enacted under his reign.

The prosecution was continued because the Public Prosecutor thought it right, as the book had been brought to his

attention, to examine it. He said, much later in his *Mémoires*:[10] 'The Deputy Public Prosecutor, entrusted by the Central Committee with the examination of books and papers, had indicated to me that the novel *Madame Bovary* deserved prosecution.'

He then returned, in imagination, to the famous and notorious trial of 1857, and said: 'The novel *Madame Bovary* reveals real talent, but the description of certain scenes goes beyond all bounds; if we close our eyes to this, Flaubert will have many imitators who will go still further down the same slope.'

Pinard, who is writing in 1892, thirty-five years after the trial, makes many mistakes in his reminiscences. He says, for instance:

The court had just condemned *Les Fleurs du Mal* of Baudelaire; it inflicted a fine on the author and ordered the deletion of certain passages. If we now abstain they will say that we are sparing of those who are strong, and the leaders of a school, that we are accommodating to our own, and merciless to our opponents.

Pinard is wrong here, for Baudelaire's prosecution did not take place until August – in January 1857, his book was not even yet published. Also it is not clear that he was so much less important than Flaubert – his mother, after all, was the widow of a General, Ambassador and Senator.

Pinard said that he had decided on the prosecution of *Madame Bovary* because he was justified by law and because he felt that he could do so without going contrary to his conscience:[11]

To allow someone else to act in my place, because the task was ungrateful, because it would draw on me attacks easy to foresee, that would have seemed to me lacking in dignity. I had never behaved like that and I did not want to begin now. I went to court and I do not repent my action. I have never disowned my prosecution of 1857.

It is interesting that Pinard, the upholder of public virtue in 1857, should later become the poet of a collection of lewd verses.[12] 'Pinard, my enemy,' wrote Flaubert to his niece, 'the author of obscene verses found in the *Prie-Dieu* of Madame Gros. . . . What a joke! What a joke!'

Now that prosecution had been decided on, Flaubert had to consider his means of defence, and he made the same mistake which Baudelaire was to make later – on the advice of the materialistic Sainte-Beuve – that is, to collect all the obscene and blasphemous passages which he could find in others. He asked his friends and acquaintances to collect as many of these obscenities as possible from religious writers, particularly modern authors.[13] Du Camp considered this method a mistake and many would agree with him. He wrote to Flaubert:[14]

If you touch religious writers such as Fléchier, Massillon, and *especially the Bible*, you'll only outrage traditional respect and admiration, and you'll be condemned to the maximum penalty. Take Care! That kind of defence will only do you prejudice. . . . If you believe me, don't use all this. Your book is brutal and its brutality has served to bring out the brutality of certain passages. They are like most bourgeois, those who speak about it, they take brutality for immorality, and one must only prove to them that they are wrong. That's all. . . . You'll find doubtless blacker passages than yours, there's no doubt about that, but not in the aggregate so violent; there's where the real harm lies.

All this is very useless, no doubt, but your preparations for your defence terrify me for you. . . . You're only aggravating your position.

Still Flaubert eventually was acquitted, so perhaps he was more right than Du Camp, but it was in spite of the nature of his defence and was due to his lawyer's eloquence.

Flaubert briefed, as the lawyer to defend him, Sénard, a native of Rouen, who knew his family well, and had known them most of his life. We have seen that he was one of the prime movers in the *Réformiste* banquet of December 1847, in Rouen. Although a liberal and in favour of reform, he, nevertheless, put down the revolution of June 1848 in his native town and restored order. He was known to be a supporter of law, and the fact that he had accepted Flaubert's brief made a very favourable impression, for the defence, on the jury.

On 29 January – not on the 31st as is generally stated[15] – there appeared, in the dock of the Sixième Chambre de Police Correctionnelle, at the Palais de Justice in Paris, Laurent Pichat, editor of *La Revue de Paris*, Auguste Pillet, the printer, and Gustave Flaubert, the author of the novel which was to be prosecuted.

Pinard, the Public Prosecutor, began his indictment by giving an outline of the plot of the novel, underlining what he considered its obscene and blasphemous elements.[16] He quoted passages to prove that the book was an offence against public and religious morality. He even mentioned, irrelevantly, the extracts from *La Tentation de Saint Antoine* which were appearing in *L'Artiste*, to show the anti-religious nature of Flaubert's inspiration. Unfortunately he spoiled his effect by referring to the character as Apollinaire instead of Apollonius of Thyana. He demanded leniency for the printer, whose offence was the smallest; he considered the editor more guilty for he had agreed to publish the novel; he praised him for having deleted the episode of the cab and others, but said that he should have been more ruthless. He asked for the maximum penalty for Flaubert, who had written the book and who had done his best to prevent any deletions in the material.

His conclusion was like a speech from one of Flaubert's most grotesque characters:[17]

Morality stigmatizes realistic literature, not because it depicts the passions: hatred, vengeance and love; the world lives only on these things; and art must depict them; but when it does depict them without restraint, without measure. Art without rules is no longer art; it is like a woman who removes her clothes. To prescribe to art the obligation of public decency as sole law, is not to enslave it, but to honour it. One can only grow within the laws.

Here, gentlemen, are the principles which we uphold; here is the doctrine which we defend with our conscience.

In the opinion of those who heard him speak, Pinard was very feeble in his prosecution. But Sénard was said to have been superb in his defence, and he spoke for four and a half hours. Flaubert wrote to his brother:[18]

Monsieur Sénard's speech was superb! He completely flattened the Public Prosecutor, who was writhing about on his seat, and declared that he would not reply. We crushed him with quotations from Bossuet and Massillon; with smut from Montesquieu etc. The court was packed. It was wonderful and I had a very proud expression on my face. At one moment I took the liberty of contradicting the Prosecutor who, during the sitting, was convicted of dishonesty, and had to withdraw what he had said. You'll see, in any case, all the speeches, word for word, for I had (at the rate of 60 francs an hour) a stenographer of my own. Old Sénard spoke for four hours and a half on end. It was a triumph for him and for me.

He began by speaking of his friendship with the family; of the noble character and high intellectual gifts of the father – qualities which had been inherited by his sons – of whom the elder succeeded his father as Master of the Hôtel Dieu at Rouen, and the younger was a distinguished scholar and writer. He gave his own summary of the novel, emphasizing different aspects from those underlined by Pinard, showing that the book was deeply serious and far from lascivious. He used Lamartine's letter to Flaubert, where he had said that *Madame Bovary* was the finest work that he had read for twenty years, and he quoted him as saying:[19]

At the same time as I read you through, without restraint to the last page, I criticized these last pages. You hurt me, you made me literally suffer! The expiation is out of all proportion with the crime; you created a terrible death, frightful! Certainly the wife who defiles the marriage bed must expect expiation, but this one is so terrible that it is unbearable torture! You went too far; you made me suffer in my nerves; that power of description, applied to the last moments of death, left me with indescribable suffering.

He added, however, that he thought that there could not exist a jury to condemn the author.

Sénard quoted many of the same passages as Pinard, but interpreted them differently; and he read the deleted episode of the cab ride, to show that there were no salacious details in it, and no reason for omitting it. He pointed out that Flaubert had been influenced by Montesquieu and Rousseau, by works which were prescribed reading for school children. He quoted passages from Chénier, Mérimée, and even the religious writer Massillon, to demonstrate that they were more daring than anything written by Flaubert. His trump card was to prove that the passage describing Extreme Unction, which Pinard had castigated, was a softened translation from the Latin of the *Rituel*, which was a religious manual.

The verdict was announced on 7 February, and the result was that the accusation was 'not proven' against all three defendants; and Pichat, Pillet and Flaubert were acquitted, but the Judge considered that they, nevertheless, deserved to be severely reprimanded:

Whereas the indicted work merits a severe reprimand, since the function of literature is to embellish and recreate the mind by elevating the intelligence, and by purifying conduct more than by arousing a disgust of vice by presenting a picture of the delinquencies which may exist in society.

Although the accused were all three acquitted, they were not awarded costs:[20]

Whereas it is not permitted, under the pretext of depicting characters or local colour, to reproduce in their errors, the facts, sayings and gesture of the characters which an author has undertaken to paint; that such a system, applied to works of the mind and of art, would lead to a realism which would be a negation of beauty and goodness, and would give rise to works equally offensive to the eyes and the mind, and would commit continuous offences against public morality.

Whereas there are limits which even the highest literature should not transgress, and which Gustave Flaubert and his co-accused do not seem to have sufficiently taken into account.

Whereas the work of which Flaubert is the author is a work which seems to have been seriously worked on for a long time, from the literary points of view, and the depiction of character; that the passages quoted by the judge's order for adjournment, however reprehensible they may be, are not sufficiently numerous if they are compared with the bulk of the work; that these passages whether in the ideas which they set forth, or in the situations which they represent, are in harmony with the general type of character which the author wished to depict, even while exaggerating them and suffusing them with a vulgar and often shocking realism.

Whereas Gustave Flaubert maintains that he respects morality and everything connected with religious morality; that it does not seem that his book has been, as certain other works have been, composed only for the aim of giving satisfaction to sensual passions, to the spirit of licence and debauchery, or to pour ridicule on matters which should be surrounded by universal respect.

Whereas his only mistake seems to have been to lose sight, on occasions, of the laws which all self-respecting authors must never transgress, and to forget that literature, like art, to accomplish the good which it is called upon to produce, must not content itself with being pure in its form and its expression.

In these circumstances, whereas it has not been sufficiently established that Pichat, Gustave Flaubert and Pillet have been guilty of the offences with which they have been charged, the court acquits them of the indictment brought against them, and dismisses them without costs.

Although he had been acquitted, Flaubert remained discouraged and disgusted and he did not, at first, wish to publish his novel at all, but he allowed himself eventually to be persuaded by the insistence of his mother and friends to agree to publication. Writing to Maurice Schlésinger, he said:[21]

Thank you for your letter. I'll answer it briefly because such a weariness of mind and body has remained with me that I haven't the strength to take a step or to hold a pen. The affair was hard to carry off, but I won a victory.

I received from all my colleagues very flattering compliments and my book will sell in an unprecedented way for a beginner. But, on the whole, I'm angry with the trial. It distorts success, and I don't care for, around art, these things foreign to it; to such an extent that all the noise disgusts me profoundly, and I hesitate to bring out my book. I'd like to return forever to my solitude and my silence, from which I emerged, to publish nothing so that no one will mention me again. For it seems to me impossible to say anything in this kind of age. Social hypocrisy is so terrible. The people in the world best disposed towards me consider me immoral! impious! They say that I'd be wise not to say this and that in the future, or that I must take care etc. etc. Ah! how bored I am dear friend.

Flaubert signed a contract with Michel Lévy, with whom Baudelaire was publishing his translations of Poe. He seems to have exploited Flaubert in the same way as he exploited Baudelaire. Flaubert made very little from his novel, and it must be remembered that he had all the expenses of his trial to find, as he had not been awarded costs.

Madame Bovary appeared in April 1857, and it was Flaubert's first published work although he was thirty-five at the time. He was sad and disillusioned and, after his trial, he was afraid to continue the publication of his *Tentation de Saint Antoine*, as he thought it might earn him a further trial and a prison sentence.[22]

Madame Bovary enjoyed a 'succès d'estime' as well as a 'succès de scandale'. Many who read it in order to discover salacious details were disappointed to find it so unsensational and so pure. Indeed what frightened most people was that it was so ordinary, that the characters could be themselves, and were not separated from themselves by the romantic haze of distance. They had accepted the far greater indecency of *Mademoiselle de Maupin* by Théophile Gautier, because there were no points of contact between themselves and the hero and heroine.

We have seen that Flaubert wrote on the copy which he

sent to Alfred Le Poittevin's mother that the book would have been dedicated to him had he been alive, and that his place in his heart had never been filled.[23]

He also sent a copy to Gertrude Tennant, inscribed as follows:

> To Madame Tennant, née Gertrude Collier,
> a tribute of unfailing affection.
> Gustave Flaubert

We do not know whether he sent one also to Henrietta, as none has come down to us. Gertrude did not, however, appreciate either the gift or the tribute, for she wrote to him:[24] 'I don't understand how you ever came to write this; when there is absolutely nothing beautiful nor good in it, and the day will come when you'll see that I'm right.'

He received praise from various famous writers. Victor Hugo wrote to him grandiloquently from exile in Guernsey:[25] 'You have written a beautiful book, Monsieur, and I am happy to tell you so. *Madame Bovary* is a work! You are, Monsieur, one of the leading minds of the generation to which you belong. Preserve and hold aloft the torch of art!' He was happy, from his exile, for anything with which he could attack the home government. But Flaubert's case, from his point of view, was not as good as Baudelaire's was to be, later in the year, for he had been acquitted, and so the crime of the régime in his case was less heinous. When Baudelaire was convicted, the following August, he wrote to him:[26] 'May I congratulate you! One of the few decorations which the present régime can confer, it has bestowed on you. What it is pleased to call its justice has condemned you in the name of what it calls its morality. That is an added crown for you!'

Champfleury, the leader of the Realist School, wrote to him to express his admiration, but he was, nevertheless, somewhat shocked at some of the descriptions – the scrofulous infection of the blind beggar, the operation for club foot, and the death from arsenical poisoning. 'But,' he said, 'these are minor blemishes which can, nevertheless, do you harm with people of taste.'[27]

Levallois recounts, in his *Mémoires d'un Critique*, how he persuaded Sainte-Beuve to read *Madame Bovary*, and tried to make him review it in his official paper. But the critic, who never liked to write about a controversial book, gave the excuse that it would not be correct, in a government paper, to deal with a book which was being prosecuted on the score of immorality. However, after the publication of the novel, he wrote a private letter to Flaubert which expressed praise, if guarded, of the book:[28]

I waited to thank you for the present you were kind enough to send me, to have finished reading *Madame Bovary*. I had read none of it in its first form in *La Revue de Paris*, and so I had my impression whole and unaltered. It is a beautiful book, a *master* book, by its talent for observation and form. You have, in addition to what is possessed by the writers who observe and describe reality – style. . . . Morality comes as it may and you don't seek it out, but I don't understand how you ever came to be accused of lacking it. . . . Now let me add that I would have been glad if there had been somewhere, in certain details, description less pushed to ultimate conclusions, so that the things to be seen stood out in better relief. I would also have liked, without knowing exactly how it could have fitted into your composition, to see characters with gentler feelings, pure, reserved, deep and equally true. That would have been a rest; that would have reminded one that there is goodness even in the midst of what is evil and stupid. . . . You know everything, Monsieur, but you're cruel! This, it seems to me, is an insult, and it is the second time that I've said it to you. I'm sorry that the only paper to which I contribute, *Le Moniteur*, by the semi-official convention which it imposes upon us, does not permit me to argue with you on *Madame Bovary*; you wouldn't get off so easily.

As we shall see, Sainte-Beuve did eventually write an article on *Madame Bovary* in *Le Moniteur*, on 10 May 1857, and he said to a friend, Madame Gravier, that he had only written on the book because he had been expressly asked to do so by the directors of the paper. He renewed his praise of the novel but said that it was cruel and that he did not advise her to read it. 'I don't advise you all the same to read this book. It is too cruel for most women and it would only offend you. As I've said the fault of the author is cruelty. ... And, once more, don't read it, you've kept too kind a heart.'[29]

There is no doubt that many people are genuinely horrified by Flaubert's novel. In a letter he described the conduct of the parish priest of his village, who had forbidden one of his parishioners to read it:[30]

Speaking about success and fame, did I tell you that the parish priest at Canteleu is fulminating against me? He tears my book from the hands of his women parishioners. I must admit that this gave me great pleasure. No praise has tickled my vanity more deeply. ... And so I'll have been spared nothing – attacks from the government, abuse from the press, and HATRED from the priests.

Sainte-Beuve, in his article in *Le Moniteur*, said, to all intents, the same things as he had said to Flaubert in his letter. He sent him the article, with a covering letter, in which he said, after many compliments:[31] 'Apply this talent for observation and depiction to other subjects equally true, and with that other faculty of observation and composition which you possess, place in them some figures which give peace and comfort and you will not only find admirers but friends amongst all your readers.' The article was favourable, on the whole – though not very sensitive or acute. He described the novel as carefully written and he declared that Flaubert had style – perhaps too much style, for he thought some of the passages were over-written. He considered that the author had been too hard on the heroine, and that certain episodes would have been better omitted. His chief objection was, however, that there was no goodness anywhere in the book.

The article was generally held to be favourable and this was thought to be important, for Sainte-Beuve was considered the greatest critic of the day – the greatest literary figure of the Second Empire.

There were many reviews of *Madame Bovary* but few were satisfactory or favourable. The Catholic papers accused the author of gross immorality and contempt for the Church. Most of the well-known reviewers saw the book as a work of realism, but this did not please Flaubert, who said:[32] 'I loathe what is generally called Realism, although they make me one of its high priests.'

Most of the critics discussed him as the successor of Balzac and the follower of Champfleury, considering him inferior to the latter.

The most unsympathetic notice was the one by Duranty, published on 15 March 1857, in the paper entitled *Réalisme*, the mouth-piece of the Realist Movement, and inspired by Champfleury:[33]

Madame Bovary, a novel by Gustave Flaubert, represents obstinacy in description. The novel is one of those which remind one of a geometrical drawing, as it seems to have been achieved with a compass, to have been minutely calculated and worked out, all in right angles and, finally, dry and arid. They say that it took several years to compose. Indeed all the details seem to have been counted one by one, giving the same importance to each. . . . There is no emotion or feeling in it; no life, but a strong arithmetical force which has calculated and assembled together what it could of gestures, or steps, or irregularities of ground, in the characters and episodes, in the given scenes. This book is a literary application of the calculation of probabilities. . . . The style is uneven, as happens with a man who writes artistically without feeling. Sometimes there are pastiches, sometimes lyrical passages, nothing individual. I repeat there are always materialistic descriptions, but never an impression. It seems to me useless to enter into the point of view of the work, from which the faults already mentioned take away all interest. Before the book appeared one imagined it would be better. A too careful study does not take the place of the spontaneity which comes from true feeling.

The review which gave Flaubert most pleasure was the one by Baudelaire which appeared in *L'Artiste* on 18 October 1857. It was so long delayed because of the poet's trial

in August, which had gone against him and resulted in a
fine and the banning of several of his poems.

Flaubert and Baudelaire had much in common; they
shared the same artistic beliefs – also the same opprobrium –
and each admired the work of the other.

Baudelaire was one of the few critics who understood that
the main interest in *Madame Bovary* was in the psychological insight of the author, and not in the realistic detail.
He also perceived how much there was of Flaubert himself
in the heroine, how much there was of the masculine in her,
in spite of his denials. He had been able to understand her
predicament because of what was feminine in himself – or
perhaps of what he possessed in his character of homosexuality.

An interesting result of the publication of *Madame Bovary*
was the number of women who wrote to Flaubert to say that
they had discovered themselves in his heroine. He himself
was not surprised at this, as he had prophesied, when engaged on the book, that this would happen. Whilst in the
early throes of composition he wrote to Louise Colet and
said:[34]

You mention the tribulations of women. I'm now in that
milieu. You'll see that I've had to dive deep down into that sentimental well. If my book is good it will gently caress many a
feminine wound; and many a one will smile as she recognizes
herself.

I'll have known all your sorrows, poor dim souls, damp with
pent-up melancholy, like your provincial back-yards, the walls of
which are covered with fungus.

After his break with Louise Colet early in 1855, Flaubert
was left without any feminine confidante, and he felt the loss
grievously, as he preferred, on the whole, writing to women
than to men, though, undoubtedly, his most intense friendships were masculine. Bouilhet was the last of his emotional
friendships with men. The epistolary friendships with
women, as far as can be discovered, remained platonic,
though he generally wrote in terms of love – one of them,

Mademoiselle Leroyer de Chantepie, he was never to meet at all.

Most of these feminine attachments occurred in the latter part of his life and were a striking feature of it. They came after the publication of *Madame Bovary*, and Princesse Mathilde and George Sand he certainly met first only in the 1860s.

There were, however, three women whose friendship with him can definitely be said to have come directly out of the publication of *Madame Bovary*: Madame Roger des Genettes, Mademoiselle Amélie Bosquet and Mademoiselle Leroyer de Chantepie.

With Madame Roger des Genettes he was a most faithful correspondent from 1856, when he took a flat in Paris to supervise the publication of *Madame Bovary*, until the day of his death. It is not only that the number of letters which he wrote to her was great, but that he seems to have written more intimately about himself to her than to any of his other correspondents. She was the confidante, particularly of his last sad years and, as she herself made no great demands on him, she did not wear him out as did some of his other women friends. She was three years older than he and belonged to a cultivated military family, for an uncle and her brother were both generals; and she was the niece of a well-known army surgeon at the time of the First Empire, whose grandson she married, Roger des Genettes.

She knew a great many of the literary people of the time, and she used to frequent the salon of Louise Colet, where she was present the evening, in 1852, when the *Melaenis* of Louis Bouilhet was launched, and she read the fourth canto of the poem. She and Bouilhet seemed, at first, to have been attracted to one another, and they were lovers for a short period, although he seems very soon to have grown tired of her. At this time Flaubert seems to have had a low opinion of her. He thought her vain and insincere – 'une infâme coquette' he called her – an intellectual 'poseuse', and he considered that she threw herself at Bouilhet's head in a

disgraceful manner. 'Enfin cette Edma me dégoûte même
de loin,' he said.[35]

Perhaps Flaubert had not yet met her closely at the time,
certainly he did not know her well, and he seems to have
become acquainted with her only when he went to live in
Paris at the end of 1856. Although their relationship probably remained platonic, it was to her that he confided the
most intimate details of his personal life. It was to her that
he bequeathed the desk on which he had written his novels,
and which she, at her own death, left to Pol Neveux; or
rather, a few months before she died, she sent it to his
mother in trust for him:[36]

Everything feels like a departure. The sky is weeping. I'm
sending you back your reviews, and your thoughts, and I send
you also, for your son, Flaubert's desk. From *Salammbô* to *Bouvard et Pécuchet* inclusive, he wrote everything on this desk. It
has been the witness of his rages, his discouragements – no discouragement was more terrible than that when he was composing *L'Éducation Sentimentale*. On that mahogany ledge
there's more than ink – I personally have seen tears.

Amélie Bosquet had been, at one time, the governess of
his little niece, but he does not seem to have known her then.
She had pretensions as a writer, but wrote in the style of a
serial novelette in a provincial paper. She used to address
Flaubert as a fellow-writer, and ask for advice about her
compositions. She was a follower of George Sand, and her
own writings tended to have a social aim and to express fem-
inist ideals – which could not interest Flaubert. Her novels
were all published after *Madame Bovary* – *Louise Meunier,
une Passion en Province* in 1861; *Une Femme bien élevée*
in 1866; *Le Roman des Ouvrières* in 1868; and *Les Trois
Prétendants* in 1874. There is a note, with Flaubert's letters
to her, which she bequeathed to the Bibliothèque Municipale at Rouen, which is interesting as showing his relations with her. It is published as a footnote to the first
letter which Flaubert wrote to her – the first which seems to

have been preserved, for it is unlikely to have been the very
first:[37]

In spite of what there was of fondness in the letters which
G. Flaubert addressed to me, and of their freedom of expression,
to tell the truth, he never, according to the old-fashioned expression, 'paid court to me', and I never wanted it. Moreover all
his friends knew that, from the day when he gave himself up
entirely to literature, from the moment of the publication of
Madame Bovary, he would have feared, to the utmost degree,
any link which would have put any hindrance in the way of his
work. Nevertheless our conversations were very lively, and it happened frequently that we remained talking for two or three hours
alone together. But the intoxication which took hold of us then
was entirely intellectual and, if I judge what was happening in
him by what I was experiencing myself, I would say that the fire
which flared up in our minds absorbed completely all the powers
of our being.

Nevertheless Flaubert's letters to her are tender and intimate, and indicate a warm and loving friendship. What
eventually brought this close friendship to an end was the
clumsy and stupid article which she wrote as a review of
L'Éducation Sentimentale, in *Le Droit des Femmes* in December 1869.[38] Her unpublished *Mémoire* on Flaubert is
preserved in the Bibliothèque Nationale in Paris.[39]

Mademoiselle Leroyer de Chantepie was someone quite
different. For one thing she was twenty-one years older than
Flaubert – though he does not seem to have known that at
first – and he was never to meet her. She was always to him
'My dear correspondent'. What attracted him particularly to
her was the way she seemed to have found herself in Emma
Bovary; and also because she never seemed to have been
happy in her life – he had infinite compassion and understanding for human distress. She had lived all her life in the
provincial town of Angers, and he seems to have continued
writing to her, out of charity, to help her to find something
in her life worth while, and to persuade her to lose herself in
her art. He rarely spoke to her of himself intimately but only

of her. Her unpublished letters to him are preserved in the Bibliothèque Nationale in Paris.[40]

Her first letter is dated 18 December 1856, when she had just finished reading *Madame Bovary*, the last instalment of which had appeared on 15 December:

Monsieur, as I am a subscriber to *La Revue de Paris* and an ardent reader of it, I have been reading, since its first instalment, your drama striking in its truth, entitled *Madame Bovary*. I saw, from the first, that you had composed a masterpiece of truth and naturalness. Yes indeed! these are truly the customs of that province where I was born and where I spent my life! That is sufficient to explain to you how I understood the sadness, the boredom, the unhappiness of that poor Madame Bovary. From the outset I recognized her and loved her as a friend. I identified myself so much with her life that it seemed to me that it was me, that it was her! no that story isn't fiction, it is truth, that woman has existed, you must have been a witness of her life, of her death, of her suffering. As for me, Monsieur, you have made me see all that, almost suffer all that. For the past thirty years I have been reading, during my reading hours, the best authors which are known. Well! I am not afraid to claim that no book has ever left such a deep impression on me as the one I experienced on reading *Madame Bovary*. I have myself written several novels, I'll send you a copy if you like. I read a great deal and I have suffered too much in my life to be able to weep easily, and only in extreme cases. Well! since yesterday I have not ceased weeping over that poor Madame Bovary; I didn't close my eyes all night; I saw her all the time; I cannot comfort myself, nor recover from the violent shock that your drama caused me. This is, perhaps, the highest compliment which I can pay you, no author has ever made me suffer so much, and I'm sorry I've finished the reading. I think that I shall go mad.

Ah! Monsieur, where did you get this perfect knowledge of human nature. It is the operating knife applied to the human heart, to the soul. It is, alas, the world in all its hideousness. The characters are true, too true for none of them elevate the soul, nothing, in this drama, brings comfort, which leaves behind it nothing but infinite despair, but also a severe criticism. That is the moral which comes from all this. Women must remain attached to their duties, whatever it may cost them, but it is so natural to try to be happy. God himself wishes for the happiness of his creatures, only men are against it; finally suffering for suffering, it is better a thousand times to suffer in carrying out one's duty. I needed, Monsieur, to express to you what I felt on reading you. Accept then this feeble tribute of my admiration and believe in the deep sympathy with which I am, Monsieur, your devoted, Marie L. Leroyer de Chantepie (author of *Cécile* and of *Angélique Lagier*).

The spelling, punctuation and grammar are very incorrect for an experienced author. She writes: 'Il relèves; il coûtes; rien ne consoles' and so forth.

Flaubert was, as yet, too inexperienced as a published writer to realize that this was the typical letter of a self-centred author, wishing to draw attention to herself. He was very much touched and, although he could not reply immediately – he was in the midst of the throes of his trial – he answered her as soon as he was acquitted, on 18 February 1857.[41] He offered to send her a copy of his novel when it appeared in book form, and asked for copies of her books. She sent him two of her novels, *Cécile* in one volume and *Angélique Lagier* in two volumes. He thanked her, promising to read the books at leisure, when he had the time. He then went on to answer her question about how it came that he had acquired so deep a knowledge of the human heart, and one feels in him a desire to impress her and to interest her in himself:[42]

For a long time, Madame, I lived your kind of life. I too spent several years completely *alone* in the country, hearing no other sound but the sighing of the wind through the trees, with the cracking of the ice when the Seine was full of drift ice under my windows. If I have attained some knowledge of life it is because I have lived very little in the ordinary meaning of the word, for if I have 'eaten' very little I have 'ruminated' a great deal; I have spent time in various kinds of company, and seen many different countries. I have travelled on foot and on the back of dromedaries. I know the stockbrokers of Paris, the Jews of Damas, the bullies of Italy and the Negro jugglers. I have been a pilgrim in the Holy Land, and I have wandered in the snows of Parnassus, which can be considered as symbolism.

Don't complain of your lot; I have travelled a little round the world and I know thoroughly that Paris you dream of; but nothing is worth a good spell of reading by the fireside . . . to read *Hamlet* or *Faust* . . . on an enthusiastic day. My own dream is to buy a little palace in Venice on the Grand Canal.

Here, Madame, is some of your curiosity satisfied. Add to that to have my complete portrait and biography; that I'm thirty-five years old, that my height is five foot eight inches, that I've shoulders like a porter, and the nervous irritability of a spoilt mistress. I'm a bachelor and solitary.

She must have sent him her likeness, for he says that he will have it framed and hang it amongst other portraits which are dear to him. She must have sent him one representing her when she was younger than her present age of fifty-seven years for he adds: 'I cut short the compliments which rise to my pen, and I beg you to believe me your affectionate colleague.' He seems to have realized that she was morbidly self-centred and he tried to encourage her to forget herself and to lose herself in her art. He took all her scruples very seriously and discussed them with her, but he seems rarely to have confided in her his own doubts and perplexities. He said to her:[43] 'Write to me everything you want, lengthily and often, even if I have to be a long time in answering, for, since yesterday, we are old friends. I know you now and I love you. What you have experienced, I have felt it personally.' She confessed her age to him and, if he was disappointed, he did not show it, but thanked her for her frankness and said that they would now be able to talk like two men together. She probably did not realize how much of a compliment this was. He wrote:[44]

Your letter is so honest, so true and so *intense*; it moved me so greatly that I cannot refrain from answering it immediately. I thank you first for having told me your age. That puts me at ease. We can now talk together like two *men*. The trust which you put in me honours me; I don't think I'm unworthy of it; –

but don't make fun of me, don't call me wise! me who am ashamed of my ignorance.

And then don't compare yourself to Bovary. You're not a bit like her! She was worth far less than you in brains and in heart; for she was a somewhat perverted nature, a woman of false poetry and false sentiments.

He realized that a great deal of her unhappiness came from her brooding on herself. He told her, therefore, to think less of herself, to read, to study and to lose herself in her work.[45]

He tried to encourage her by telling her that he knew, from his own experience, her state of mind, and that he did not like to see a fine nature like her own floundering in grief and idleness. He wrote:[46]

The pleasure that I have in receiving your letters, dear lady, is counter-balanced by the grief which is expressed in them. What an excellent soul you have got! and what a sad existence yours is. I think I understand it and that is why I love you.

I've known, as you have, the intense melancholy which the *Angelus* inspires on summer evenings. However peaceful I may have been on the surface, I too have been *ravaged*, and, need I say it, I am still sometimes. But I'm convinced of that truth that one falls ill as soon as one thinks of oneself, I try to intoxicate myself with art, as others do with brandy. By dint of willpower one ends by losing the notion of one's own individuality. Believe me, one isn't happy, but one doesn't suffer any more.

Later he said to her:[47] 'Why don't you work more? The only way of bearing existence is to drown in literature as in a perpetual orgy. The wine of art induces a long intoxication which is bottomless. It is thinking of oneself which makes one unhappy.' This close and affectionate friendship continued for twelve years and, from the interest of the letters, it is only surpassed by the correspondence with Louise Colet.

In 1865 the theatre in Angers was burnt to the ground. She was much upset by this as she liked going to the opera. She organized a subscription for rebuilding; it went on for years with little result, as the town did not want to spend the large sum necessary. Years went by, and still there was not sufficient money. She then wrote to Flaubert that Angers was now only a village without a theatre. 'I have nostalgia for opera,' she said, 'and I'm afraid that I may die without having seen the theatre again.'

She next thought of asking him to intervene with the Emperor to ask him to order the theatre to be rebuilt. Flaubert was reluctant to do this, as he did not know the Emperor very well – and only recently – and he did not believe in the cause. He replied, advising her to do nothing, saying that one could not force a town to have a theatre, if it did not want one, in spite of itself, that, moreover, there were no funds available, and that the Emperor was powerless in the matter.[48] She answered him, in disgust and anger, addressing him now merely as 'Cher Monsieur':[49]

Your answer is harsh and it hurt me very much indeed. ... You're invited to court, your personal worth, your intellect, your connections with those in high places in political and literary circles, must surely give you great influence. I've never asked anyone for a service which might be disagreeable or boring to them, but the kindly interest, the friendship even, which you have shown me, made me feel that you would be the first person to offer me your support, to assure the success of my modest request. Don't tell me that the Emperor can do nothing, he is the absolute master of all wills, he rules the destiny of Europe, he can do everything, one word from his mouth, one sign from his hand, would be more than sufficient to make all the mayors and municipal councils of France obey. The Emperor is great by his genius and his heart, and I'm sure that if I could implore him myself, in person, he would grant me my poor little request.

Flaubert replied:[50]

I am very much distressed that you misunderstood so much my last letter. I didn't think that you would see in the frank expression of my thought the slightest harshness. You've taken for egoism what is only the truth. . . .

I took no steps to be agreeable to you, because they'd have

laughed in my face. *I give you my word of honour.* Besides I don't possess the authority with which you credit me. For example, last Friday, I had the greatest difficulty in obtaining permission to visit Fontainebleau, and they were on the point of turning me out, very politely, it is true, and, without Octave Feuillet, who is the librarian there, I'd have had to return to Paris like a simple mortal. I assure you, dear Mademoiselle, you've got a totally false idea of the facts. . . .

Don't believe that there was, on my part, any lack of goodwill, and remain assured of the affection which I bear you.

Although he wrote later, to send her his New Year's greetings, the episode marked the end of their friendship, and she did not write again until the death of George Sand, in 1876, when she wrote to him for information of her last days – George Sand had been one of the great admirations of her life. He answered her then:[51] 'No! I've not forgotten you, because I don't forget those whom I love. But I was astonished at your long silence, not knowing what cause to attribute to it . . .' Then he told her of the death of George Sand and of the names of all the friends who had died since he had last written to her – Bouilhet, Sainte-Beuve, Jules de Goncourt, and so forth, and especially of his other mother who had died in 1872. Then he continued:[52]

I live now entirely alone (at least during the summer) and, when I'm not working, I've only, for company, my memories which follow my dreams and so on.

Poor Madame Sand often spoke to me of you, or rather we often spoke of you together; you used to interest her so much. One had to know her, as I knew her, to realize how much there was that was feminine in this great man, the immense depths of tenderness that there were in this genius. She will remain one of the great examples of France, a unique glory.

How is your mind? Do you still read philosophy? I recommend to you the latest book by Renan. It will please you. And don't be so long again without writing to me, for I am always yours.

There were, however, no further letters, and the friendship died.

There was also Jane de Tourbey, who became the Comtesse de Loynes. She arrived in Paris as a young woman, and her literary education was taken in hand by Sainte-Beuve, so that she was able to have one of the most distinguished literary salons of the nineteenth century in France, her salon in the rue de Vendôme, beginning in 1858. We do not know when Flaubert first made her acquaintance but he sent her a copy of *Madame Bovary* when it appeared in 1857. His relationship with her, which seems to have been very close and tender, was largely in the latter part of his life, well after the publication of *Madame Bovary*. His servant Narcisse, who fell in love with her maid, presented her with a copy of *Salammbô*, inscribed as follows: 'To Mademoiselle Jeanne, presented by the servant of the author.'[53]

In 1857, Flaubert reached the summit of his career as a writer. He then brilliantly graduated as an author, at one fell swoop, with his first publication, and everything that he did henceforth would be to fill in the portrait, and to perfect it, of one of the greatest novelists and prose artists of the nineteenth century in France.

PART TWO

The Masterpiece

[20]

The Novel in the
Second Empire

STENDHAL died in 1842, and Balzac in 1850; and their disappearance left a great void in fiction, for there remained only George Sand with a claim to serious consideration. Stendhal had not been appreciated in his own day, but Balzac had dominated the forties and was considered the greatest novelist of the time, as well as having introduced realism into French literature – though Baudelaire considered him chiefly as a great visionary.[1]

The most characteristic form of literature at the time when Flaubert was composing *Madame Bovary*, during the early years of the Second Empire, was the Realist School. That is indeed why he was judged as a Realist when he published his novel, which was considered by many to be the long-awaited masterpiece of the movement. The critics did not realize how much he disliked Realism:[2] 'They imagine I'm in love with reality,' he said, 'whereas I loathe it; for it is in hatred of realism that I began writing this book.'

During the Romantic Movement the literary ideals had been generally the same whether they referred to poetry, fiction or drama; and the movement was monolithic. During the Second Empire, on the contrary, everything was different, and there was opposition, and even antagonism, between verse and prose. On the one hand there were the Art for Art's Sake ideals in poetry, with admiration for work well done and artistic idealism. On the other, in prose, there was Realism, everyday triviality, and contempt for fine writing. Flaubert had far more in common with the Art for Art's Sake poets than with the Realists, and it is with Baudelaire that he has most resemblance of all, in his views of art.

Some critics have considered Murger, with his *Scènes de la Vie de Bohème*, as the originator of Realism, though he really represents the elements of dying Romanticism and also the new form of Bohemianism which was typical of the last years of the July Monarchy and the early years of the Second Empire. A characteristic feature of Bohemianism was that the members were very poor and low-born, without much education. They came from the working class or the lower-middle-class. Murger was the son of a poor concierge; Champfleury was a clerk in a bookshop, in the provincial town of Laon; and Barbara's father was a salesman in a shop for musical instruments.

Murger's parents were extremely poor and he was intended for a working-class life, but his mother had ambitions for her delicate boy, who was so fond of reading, and she managed to procure for him a secondary education. He was not grateful for this privilege, and he did not profit from it in the way that his mother had hoped and wished. However, his schooling permitted him to avoid starting work at an early age, and allowed him to continue to read in a desultory manner. He left home at nineteen, after a quarrel with his parents, and then he began to collect the material for his most famous book. He learned also all the subterfuges and devices needed for obtaining free meals and free lodging. The Bohemians were all desperately poor, and one of them, Charles Bataille, once wrote:[3]

> Joyeux enfants de la Bohème,
> Rions du sort et de ses coups!
> La Société qui nous aime,
> Nous garde, pour l'heure suprême,
>   Quand même,
>   À tous,
> Un lit à l'hôpital des fous.

It was in 1842 that Murger met the group of friends amongst whom were Champfleury and Courbet. They belonged to a society which called itself 'les Buveurs d'Eau', and they chose the name because they could afford nothing stronger than water. Murger described them later in his novel entitled *Les Buveurs d'Eau*, as well as in his sketches, *Scènes de la Vie de Bohème*.

Champfleury, although he was one of the Bohemians, was more provident and careful than the rest; he was, as well, generous and kind-hearted, and he invited Murger to come to live with him, to give him at least a roof over his head. He was, however, himself a respectable bourgeois at heart who liked to live within his means. He had ideas of what modern literature should be and he persuaded Murger to abandon the influence of Musset, which had been, up to then, the strongest on him, and whose poetry was his favourite reading. Champfleury encouraged him to notice the vivid scenes of everyday life round him and to make sketches from them. He depicted the scenes, and they were published in the *avant-garde* literary periodical entitled *Le Corsaire-Satan*. These sketches – scenes they were called – appeared in the paper between 1845 and 1848. They were later collected and published as a book in 1851, under the title *Scènes de la Vie de Bohème*, and they were considered, by most of the critics, as a distinguished work of realism. However, when the book is read today, it is not the realism which strikes the reader, but the romanticism and sentimentality. In fact Murger's romanticism, which earlier had found outlet in his Musset-like poems, now found it in these sketches; and, moreover, it is this disguised romanticism which has prevented the book from dying long ago. These sketches express a very romantic view of what La Bohème was really like, what people imagine – or like to imagine – it is. Murger has talked of himself and of his dreams in the person of Rodolphe, and what he tells us is escapist wishful thinking. In real life the Mimi of the *Scènes* was far nearer to the Sapho of Alphonse Daudet's novel of the same name than to the heroine of his book. The truth is that Murger's unconscious aim was not really to paint realistically the life he saw around him. If we wanted a realistic picture of the Bohème of the late forties and early fifties, we would go to

Champfleury's novel, *Les Aventures de Mademoiselle Mari-ette*. Its characters are the same people who are described in *Scènes de la Vie de Bohème* but they are depicted realisti-cally with realistic details. Yet Murger's book, in spite of its romanticizing, is still read, while Champfleury's, in spite of its truth, has long ago been forgotten. *Scènes de la Vie de Bohème* was later made into a play which enjoyed success, and, later still, it became the libretto for Puccini's opera, *La Vie de Bohème*, which has ensured its immortality.

After the Revolution of 1848 it was clear that Realism had come to stay, and it soon developed its own doctrine. Un-doubtedly the most important novelist in the field was Champfleury, but Henri Monnier should not be forgotten, although he was writing already in 1830, when he was com-posing his *Scènes de la Vie Populaire*, but these were only fully known and appreciated after 1850. He was the creator of one of the best known characters – caricature really – of the nineteenth century, Joseph Prudhomme, who became the epitome of the canting and pompous person, just as Tartuffe became synonymous for the hypocrite. This lasted until the end of the century – and even beyond – so that Rimbaud, writing in 1873, in *Une Saison en Enfer*, and rail-ing against the cant of his own age, could say: 'Monsieur Prudhomme est né avec le Christ', meaning that cant arose at the same time as Christianity. Monsieur Prudhomme is one of the ancestors of Flaubert's Homais in *Madame Bovary*.

In his *Scènes de la Vie Populaire*, Henri Monnier has created a kind of *Comédie Humaine* in miniature – in the Balzacian sense – of simple everyday life, and his gift for caricature – he was a well-known caricaturist of the time – permitted him to see what was comic and ludicrous in life. It is not the harsh and bitter side of bourgeois life that he saw, but the comic. He has chosen his characters amongst the petty clerks and the petty functionaries. It is a valuable col-lection of types that he gives us, and they possess a great deal of the irony which will later be found with a more acrid quality in Flaubert.

His greatest works are his play, *Grandeur et Décadence de Joseph Prudhomme* of 1853, and his *Mémoires de Joseph Prudhomme* of 1857.

Joseph Prudhomme was a man of private means, a captain in the National Guard, also a member of a jury, and on many public committees. He was a good father, a good husband, and was altogether the epitome of the bourgeois in the reign of Louis-Philippe. Many of his pompous and grandiloquent sayings have become proverbial and are still recognizable. 'Je l'ai toujours dit, je le dis encore, et je le dirai toujours, ce sabre est le plus beau jour de ma vie.' Or 'Otez l'homme de la société, vous l'isolez.' Or again, one of his better efforts: 'Le char de l'état navigue sur un volcan.' At a dinner party he once met an Englishman and he said in a kindly way: 'Alors Monsieur est d'Albion. Il n'y a pas de mal à cela, tous les hommes sont faits pour s'estimer.' He was also given to platitudinous philosophizing and, when his taper went out as he crossed the courtyard to his apartment, he said, in noble and reflective style: 'Dame! que voulez-vous, tout finit pars s'éteindre dans la nature. Le rat' – a nineteenth-century colloquial expression for a taper – 'le rat c'est l'image de la vie.' His pomposity is very like that of Homais, and his sayings are worthy of Flaubert's *Dictionnaire des Idées Reçues*.

Joseph Prudhomme, the bourgeois, 'ce type monstrueusement vira' as Baudelaire called him,[4] analysed himself in his *Mémoires*, and we can understand Flaubert's diatribes against the class:[5]

On a dit que j'étais le type du bourgeois; je ne repousse pas cette qualification, bien au contraire; qui donc a plus de droit de parler à ce siècle de bourgeois que le bourgeois lui-même? Car vous avez beau faire et beau dire, tout est bourgeois aujourd'hui. L'aristocratie n'existe plus, la démocratie n'existe pas encore, il n'y a que la bourgeoisie. Vous n'avez que des idées, des opinions, des moeurs, une littérature, des arts, des instincts de transition: saluez donc Joseph Prudhomme, l'homme de la transition, c'est à dire de la bourgeoisie! Fils de Monsieur Prudhomme, voilà votre vrai titre, et non pas fils de Voltaire!

One of the most significant influences on the Realist Movement was undoubtedly the painter Courbet. Before him a
large group of painters had talked about 'le nu harmonieux'
and had admired such works as Ingres's *La Source*. They
claimed that the true aim of art was to inspire beautiful
thoughts by the contemplation of beautiful pictures; or
again that any image which aroused in those who gazed at it
a vulgar thought, or low feelings, was, by this very fact, evil,
however true it might appear.

Courbet had great difficulty in getting his work accepted
by the general public, and the more he progressed, the more
difficult this became. At the International Exhibition in
Paris in 1855, which was attended by Queen Victoria, the
Prince Consort and their two elder children, his work was
not represented, as it was said – probably with truth – that
the Queen would disapprove of it and might be shocked.
Since 1848 he had fought against the idealized tradition in
art, and he painted deliberately coarsely – he used to sign his
paintings 'Courbet without ideals and without religion'.

His successive exhibitions mark the progress of Realism –
and opposition to it. In 1849 seven of his pictures were accepted by the *Salon* – his *Après-Midi à Ornans* and *Vend-
anges à Ornans* amongst them. They were not admired but
they did not yet arouse violent criticism. *La Revue des Deux
Mondes* declared that *L'Après-Midi à Ornans* had trivial
truth in it. Three years later only three of his pictures were
accepted by the *Salon*. They were: *Les Paysans de Flagny
revenant de la Foire*, *Les Casseurs de Pierres* and
L'Enterrement à Ornans. This last picture shocked the
public as they said that death and religion, instead of arousing noble thoughts, were used as a pretext for depicting
local peasant types in ridiculous costumes. The following
year only one of his pictures was present, *Les Demoiselles de
Village*, which was described as merely vulgar. A wag published a comic poem intended to set forth Courbet's aesthetic
ideals:[6]

> Faire vrai ce n'est rien, pour être réaliste
> C'est laid qu'il faut! Or, Monsieur, s'il vous plaît,

Tout ce que je désire est horriblement laid,
Ma peinture est affreuse, et, pour qu'elle soit vraie,
J'en arrache le beau, comme on fait de l'ivraie.
J'aime les teints terreux, les nez de carton,
Les fillettes avec de la barbe au menton,
Les durillons, les cors aux pieds, et les verrues.
Voilà le vrai!

In 1853 his picture *Les Baigneuses,* which depicted realistically naked women, was refused by the *Salon* with con-
tumely. The official critics were indignant at what they
called the 'nudités grosses' which they considered repulsive.
There were also patriotic articles in defence of French
beauty, which had been insulted, they declared, by these
lumps of flesh which were a libel on French womanhood.

As has been previously stated, at the Exhibition of 1855 all
Courbet's pictures were refused, and he held a private one-
man show of his own, to which hundreds came to scoff and
to be scandalized, but many remained to admire and to
praise. The Introduction to his catalogue became a kind of
manifesto of the new Realist School, not only in painting but
in literature as well. The essential points of the programme
were that the artist had the right to choose any subject; that
he had the right to choose a contemporary subject if he so
wished; and that he had the right to represent contemporary
life realistically.

When the Goncourt brothers were composing their novel
Manette Salomon, dealing with an artistic milieu, and
wished to represent a modern painter, they copied him from
Courbet, and used his artistic views.

By 1855 the Realist battle was in full swing in painting,
and it was taken up in literature by Champfleury, the friend
and supporter of Courbet – indeed he was to be called the
Courbet of literature, and his aim was to do for fiction what
his friend had done for painting. He started as a follower of
Courbet but, by degrees, he liberated himself and declared
that painting, as an art, was inferior to literature, as the
novelist had, at his disposal, methods which were more
varied and subtle than those available to the painter.

In 1856 he founded *La Gazette* to set forth his literary
ideals, but it had only two numbers and then failed through
lack of funds – the fate of most of such papers. But he had
followers and admirers, and another periodical, *Réalisme*,
was founded by his rich friend Duranty, who was said to be
the illegitimate son of Mérimée, to give him another platform for his ideas. It had no greater luck than its predecessor
and failed after a few numbers. We have already seen that it
was in *Réalisme* that the fiercest article in condemnation of
Madame Bovary was published, accusing it of being too well
written.

By this time the word 'Realism' was accepted by the general public as a term of abuse and a criticism. Flaubert was
accused of Realism at his trial in January 1857; so too was
Baudelaire at his trial later in the year, in August.

The main principle of Champfleury's criticism was that
the author must write only of what he had seen personally,
and that no prejudice – social or moral – should restrain him.
'One should not,' he said, 'forbid oneself such and such a
character, such and such a scene, because it might shock
certain sections of the public. One must show everything
without any palliative of politeness or prudence.'

He also insisted on great simplicity in art, and considered
that there should be no descriptions, no portraits, no lyric
passages, and that the subject of the novel should deal with
little people.

Champfleury was certainly the most important exponent
of Realism in fiction in the Second Empire.

Champfleury was not his true name, but a pseudonym
which he adopted for literature. He was Jules Fleury Husson
and his father was a poorly paid clerk, while his mother
worked in a toy-shop. He did not do particularly well at
school, but he was always a great reader of modern fiction
and stories of all sorts. His father thought that this love of
reading was the indication of a literary vocation, and he sent
him to Paris to become a messenger in a book-shop. There
he had further opportunities for reading, in the books which

he borrowed from stock. Then he met the members of the 'Buveurs d'Eau'.

It is fashionable nowadays to make fun of Champfleury, to call him a petty bourgeois; yet there was much to be said in his favour – if not much nowadays for his novels – for his intellectual energy and the way he educated himself. This elementary schoolboy made himself a nation-wide authority on caricature, at a time when caricature was beginning to be considered as a serious art; he also studied music theoretically and became a sound musical critic. He was one of the few people at the time to appreciate Wagner, when he was mocked at, and he even became one of his friends; he also made himself an authority on painting.

He used to spend the morning in a library, the afternoon attending public lectures – at the Sorbonne or the Collège de France – and he also followed courses at the medical schools. At the end of his life he reached comparative affluence but, in the 1850s, he was only one of the poor 'Buveurs d'Eau'.

He published, as did most of the young writers at the time, in the *Corsaire-Satan*, and later in *L'Artiste*. Hugo noticed his first collection of stories, published in 1847, and declared that one of them, *Chien Caillou*, was a masterpiece.

His period as a novelist runs from 1850 to 1865, but, after that, he devoted himself to literary and art criticism. He then became nervous on account of the large number of books taken to the courts by the authorities under the Second Empire.

Although Champfleury was a member of the Bohemian circle, he was not a Bohemian by temperament. His association with these writers was on account of his poverty rather than by choice. On the contrary, he himself admired bourgeois qualities and virtues. He liked to owe nothing to anyone and to be able to pay his way himself. His ambition was not so much to produce a work of art – indeed nothing was further from his mind – as to earn, by his pen, a regular and comfortable living, to have security, simple bourgeois security. Literature was for him a trade and not an art, a trade which was to fulfil his modest ambition to provide him with a living and security – a better living than his father had been able to acquire for himself. He used to say at the age of twenty-five:[7]

I only want one thing, and that is to earn a little sum of money, just sufficient to live honestly, and to try to find a wife very stay-at-home, willing to live a quiet life. The greatest happiness for me would be to live a provincial life in Paris; that is to say a quiet and disciplined life, with, over and above, all the advantages of connections and acquaintanceship with people of intelligence.

His taste in literature was commonplace and he admired the poetry of Béranger who was anathema to the members of the Art for Art's Sake Movement. He used also to be amazed that anyone could find anything to admire in Racine. 'If someone finds beauty in the line "Fille de Minos et de Pasiphaé",' he said of one of the lovely lines in Racine's *Phèdre*,[8] 'I honestly believe that he's pulling my leg.'

His mediocre aesthetic ideal comes out clearly in his novels, not only in the subject matter – an author can write nobly about trivial matters, as Flaubert did – but in his attitude to his art. He considered art not as a mission – as did the Romantic writers – not as a vocation or a priesthood – as did Flaubert – but merely as a job – not even a craft. No real artist could have written the words of advice which he gave his friend Duranty, and they should be compared with the advice which Flaubert gave to Louise Colet:[9]

Refuse any party today, which might encroach on five minutes of tomorrow. I permit you all the passions from the age of eighteen to twenty – to depict love one must have loved. But we must be careful lest our passions fasten on to us for the whole of our life. Your food must be simple and regular. If you work a lot, you must walk a lot. Every day give a look at the papers and the reviews; it is good to know what is being produced in literature, art and science. Be discreet in your use of stimulants. There is very much more I could say.

His last word is, however, a masterpiece: 'I've only one more piece of advice to give you; keep your bowels loose and your feet warm.'

Champfleury's three best novels are *Les Bourgeois de Molinchart*, *La Succession le Camus* and *Le Aventures de Mademoiselle Mariette*. It is sufficient to mention *Les Bourgeois de Molinchart*, as it is the novel which most nearly corresponds with *Madame Bovary*. It takes place in the provincial town of Laon, where the author was born, and the local colour is well depicted. It is the sordid account of adultery in the provincial town, and we have seen that the first title of the book was *L'Adultère en Province*. Louise Tilly, the heroine, is bored with her bourgeois lawyer husband; she is the only pretty woman in the neighbourhood and her boredom and her emotions are very like those of Emma Bovary, in her adulterous relationship with the Comte de Vorges.

The plot is not important, but what is significant is the depiction of the bourgeois milieu, which had not yet been studied in fiction. There is some irony here, which recalls Flaubert, and is truly comic – the prize-giving at the local school for instance, and the meeting of the local literary academy.

We know that Flaubert heard of his novel when he was in the throes of composing *Madame Bovary* and that, until he had read it, he was nervous lest he should have been forestalled in his conception, but, when he was able to see it, he realized that it was only the subject which had some resemblance to his, and that the treatment was very different in both cases; he said also that the style of Champfleury's novel was very poor.

Les Bourgeois de Molinchart, in the opinion of the critics, certainly marks the rise of Realism in fiction. It enjoyed an immense success – in excess of that of *Madame Bovary* – and, as we have seen, it sold a hundred thousand copies in a short time, going into four separate editions. With the publication of the book, in 1855, Champfleury became the undoubted leader of the Realist School, the great hope for literature. Even the publication of *Madame Bovary*, the following year, did not oust him from this position, as he was generally considered superior as a novelist to Flaubert.

Champfleury's novels are all built on careful documentation, collected with great diligence and, in so doing, he thought he was following Balzac closely, but he imagined that the whole of Balzac's value lay in the external description of the vulgar details of everyday life.

If Champfleury is still remembered in histories of literature – he is certainly very rarely read at all – it is because he marks an important stage in the novel from Balzac to the Goncourt brothers, and he is the chief exponent of Realism in the 1850s. His aesthetic doctrine – if indeed it can be honoured with the name aesthetic – forced him to describe only what he had seen with his own eyes, and the mediocrity of the life that he had chosen to lead allowed him to see almost nothing at all. He held, erroneously, the view that realism was *terre à terre* triviality, that it must never rise above that, and that is why his novels are never read today, except by specialists in nineteenth-century fiction.

Veron, the mid-nineteenth-century critic, once said of him:[10]

When I was a little boy I used to gaze, with passionate interest, in at the window of a pork-butcher's shop, where one of the assistants, who had artistic leanings, used to model every day in lard some artistic conception of his own invention. Champfleury's literature is precisely that, he models and sculpts mediocrity.

In the 1860s, Champfleury decided to give up writing novels. Then, for the rest of his life, he devoted himself to criticism. He produced books on caricature, on Henri Monnier, on Wagner, on Dumas; and, finally, he became an authority on china when he was appointed Director of the manufactory of Sèvres.

The year after the publication of Flaubert's novel, in 1858,

Ernest Feydeau's *Fanny* appeared, a book which was written to cash in on the success and notoriety of *Madame Bovary*. Its author trusted that, since the case against Flaubert had failed, he would be able to publish what he liked with impunity. He had become known in 1856 for his historical and archaeological popular work, *Histoire des Usages Funèbres et des Sépultures des Peuples Anciens,* which was to be the source of much material for Hugo's *La Légende des Siècles* and Gautier's *Histoire de la Momie.* Then Feydeau thought that he should try his hand at a modern topic, and he chose the fashionable subject of adultery which had been a success in Champfleury's *Les Bourgeois de Molinchart* and in Flaubert's *Madame Bovary.* His *Fanny* was considered deliciously scandalous, but everybody read it, though most women used to pretend that they knew it only through hearsay. Many said that it was the best work of the Realist School, better than anything that Champfleury had written, because it was more poetic. Sainte-Beuve gave it great praise in an article in *Le Moniteur* on 14 June 1858, more praise than he had given to *Madame Bovary* the previous year.

The original feature in *Fanny,* psychologically, is that it is the lover who is jealous of the husband. He fears that the woman who has become his mistress does not dislike her husband as much as she professes, nor keep him at a distance. One night he climbs up to her balcony and, peeping through the gaps in the blinds, he watches everything that goes on in the room, except the final culmination which takes place in the bed, beyond his line of vision. He recounts all that he is seeing, and all his emotions, in the first person. This is the scene which delighted many readers, but scandalized many more. The critic Émile De Montégut said that *Madame Bovary* was immoral but that *Fanny* was indecent.

There is no doubt that Feydeau wanted a *succès de scandale* as soon as possible while the going was good. He had his moment of glory and notoriety with *Fanny* in 1858, which was one of the greatest popular successes of the nineteenth century.

This then was the position of fiction in France in the 1850s, when Flaubert burst on the scene with his *Madame Bovary*. The main trend was realism, trivial realism, and there was neglect, and even contempt, for any distinction of writing. In subject matter writers tried to be as daring as they could without incurring censure – their ideal was to write about everything, without being restrained by fear of offending conservative susceptibilities. Champfleury was considered the greatest novelist of the day, the man on whom the mantle of Balzac had fallen, and other writers were judged by comparison with him.

The Theme

Madame Bovary is first and foremost a psychological novel, and Baudelaire was right when he said so in his review of the book. The character of Emma, her psychological development, is the subject of the novel; it is not primarily an analysis of manner and customs, or any other kind of realistic study. It is true that its sub-title is *Moeurs de Province,* but this did not figure in the earliest versions, being a later addition, and is not a true description of the work. It is interesting, in this respect, to compare the novel with Stendhal's *Le Rouge et le Noir, Chronique de 1830,* which is very definitely the account of a period, a restricted period, right at the end of the reign of Charles X, at the end of the Restoration; it could not have taken place at any other time. Flaubert's period remains deliberately vague and unspecified, and could be a picture of provincial life in any age – almost in any country. He has not been exhaustive in his treatment of the life of the locality as Balzac had been in *Eugénie Grandet,* and he has given only what is necessary for the unfolding of the characters. If one considers what one has learnt about the district it boils down to very little in the long run. But he has somehow conveyed the essence, the quintessence, of provincialism in general, rather than given the picture of any given period, and it is as true today, after more than a century, as it was in his day, since it is not tied down by any passing or local characteristics. There are no temporary details of local colour, no contemporary tittle-tattle, all of which would have been out of date in a short time, when the conditions had altered. This gives the work a classical and universal character which is not present in the Realistic novel of his day.

Madame Bovary is divided into three uneven parts.[1]
They were intended, at first, to be evenly balanced, but
much new material eventually accrued to the second part.
The first, ninety-four pages, sets the characters, so to speak,
before us. It shows them in the present and in the past, and
establishes the point they have reached at the beginning of
the tale. It is a duet between the two main characters,
Charles and Emma, and it ends when we know them
thoroughly and can see that they are well set on the road for
tragedy, though we do not yet see in what direction. At the
end of Part One Emma burns her wedding bouquet, when
she fully realizes her disillusionment with her present
plight; when the ball at the castle of La Vaubyessard has
shown it up, by contrast, in all its petty meanness. She sees
this act as symbolical of all she has lost. This is just when
they are leaving Tostes, where they had spent the first period
of their married life, when Charles hoped that the move
would bring back his wife's health and strength:[2]

Un jour qu'en prévision de son départ elle faisait des range-
ments dans un tiroir, elle se piqua les doigts à quelque chose.
C'était un fil de fer de son bouquet de mariage. Les boutons
d'oranger étaient jaunes de poussière, et les rubans de satin, à
liséré d'argent, s'effiloquaient par le bord. Elle le jeta dans le feu.
Il s'enflamma plus vite qu'une paille sèche. Puis ce fut comme un
buisson rouge sur les cendres, et qui se rongeait lentement. Elle
le regarda brûler. Les petites baies de carton éclataient, les fils
d'archal se tordaient, le galon se fondait; et les corolles de papier,
racornies, se balançant le long de la plaque comme des papillons
noirs, enfin s'envolèrent par la cheminée.
Quand on partit de Tostes, au mois de mars, Madame Bovary
était enceinte.

The second part, which has grown during the composition,
two hundred and twenty-four pages, deals with the life of
Charles and Emma in their new little provincial town of
Yonville, the centre part of which is Emma's affair with Rodolphe Boulanger, which fails in the end; and we have, as
well, all her other vain efforts at giving meaning to her life.

This part ends with the meeting, once again, at the opera, with Léon, and her hope of a new rebirth in her affair with him. In an earlier draft of the novel she has an affair with him before she meets Rodolphe, but, in the final text, her relationship with him, at first, is purely platonic and romantic, and this is very much more effective. There is only one love affair in this part. This is the main portion of the book; in it we fully learn about the two chief characters, and everything is set for the final tragedy.

The third part, one hundred and sixty-five pages, balances the first part; it gives Emma's final love affair with Léon; it winds up everything and finishes off the story. All the characters are now accounted for, as in a classical play; it is all rounded off and we know what has happened to everyone.

Flaubert saw his novel as a succession of scenes – he called them *tableaux* – this may be the remains of his early interest in the stage, and the fact that his first literary efforts were mostly in the form of plays. He liked big set pieces – *scènes montées* – and he usually saw them in contrasting pairs; the rich coarseness of the wedding feast is contrasted with the refined luxury of the ball at the castle of La Vaubyessard. There is the orchestrated seduction scene at the agricultural show, where Rodolphe's and Emma's exchange of love platitudes alternates with the differently platitudinous speeches of the officials; this scene is contrasted with the other seduction scene, in the Cathedral at Rouen, where Léon's remarks are heard against those of the verger, detailing the beauties and interest of the church. There are the two death scenes, so to speak. In the first Emma imagines that she is dying – or wishes to think that – and she is surrounded by flowers, candles, and prayers, as she lies on her carefully arranged couch, and sees herself dying like one of the heroines in the romantic novels she had read in her youth. In the second she is in reality dying of arsenical poisoning, and there is nothing elegant or beautiful about it. She asks for a mirror but she cannot bear the look of her face. There is no possibility of romanticism in this real dying, only hideous reality.

Another of these orchestrated scenes is the arrival of Charles and Emma Bovary at the Lion d'Or at Yonville, where all the inhabitants are gathered together to greet them, and we see them in all their characteristic idiosyncrasies. It is a wonderful scene of visual depiction. Then there is, perhaps the greatest *tour de force* of all, the cab drive through all the streets of Rouen of Léon and Emma when she finally yields to him. It is a kind of mad ride of the fates. Nothing that occurs in the cab is described to us and we only guess the intensity of the emotion by the rapidity of the pace, and the indifference of the occupants to the road they are taking. Finally, there floats out of the windows the torn-up scraps of the farewell letter which Emma had intended to give Léon. That is all we are shown but we know that she has fallen.

Flaubert worked on many successive scenarios, as he called them, which helped him to make clear to himself what he wanted to say. He composed his novel as strictly as any five-act play, removing everything, or rewriting, which did not contribute to the central idea, to the scheme, which had the inevitability of an architectural plan. This is in the final published version. Jean Pommier and Gabrielle Leleu have published what might be considered the original novel, made up from all the rough drafts which were amongst Flaubert's notes. There is, however, no evidence that all the passages which they have included in their version were intended to be part of the same novel.[3] To this writer, at least, the final text seems, in every way, a nobler one than the other, which is very much more diffuse – though not everyone is of this opinion, and some consider that the pruning has cut off many valuable shoots. In the Pommier and Leleu version the people talk and reflect too much, which is not in character, while Flaubert wanted to leave more to the imagination. One striking example is when Charles looks at Emma, after she is dead, in her coffin. In the final version the reader is allowed to imagine what he is feeling, what his incoherent feelings are, which he would never have been able to exteriorize in words. In the other text there are too many reflections which could not possibly have been those of a man of such limited intelligence and sensibility, and are clearly those of the author himself; they are the feelings which he had experienced at the death-bed of his beloved sister and of his friend Le Poittevin, and which he had described in his letters to Du Camp.

The novel starts in the first person, told by an unknown narrator, continues thus for nearly five pages, then the narrator fades from the scene, in the middle of a chapter, and is never heard of any more. The third-person author now takes over. Some readers have thought that this first-person narrator adds vividness to the scene, that it helps to see Bovary more clearly at the outset. If this is true here, at the opening, then it should be true of other parts as well. The opening scene certainly has vividness but it is different in tone from the rest of the novel, and the first-person narrator takes from the impersonality of the book, while the transition to the third person, without any warning, is somewhat clumsy, and one cannot help feeling that there has been here an error in technique – though it is certainly presumptuous, and probably incorrect, to accuse so meticulous and scrupulous an artist of error. It is, however, difficult to discover what has been the gain from this method.

Du Camp said – though he said it over thirty years later, when Flaubert was dead – that, after the reading of *La Tentation de Saint Antoine* in 1849, he and Bouilhet had suggested to Flaubert that he should write the story of Delphine Delamare, who had died the previous year. Her husband had been the local 'officer de santé', and she was alleged to have taken lovers and to have ruined her husband by her extravagance. He also declared that when he and Flaubert had been in the East together his friend had suddenly exclaimed, one day: 'I'll call her Emma Bovary.'[4] Neither of these stories has any truth in it, and we have seen that

Flaubert, right up to the moment when he began composing *Madame Bovary*, was doubtful of what he would write.
Moreover, in the earliest drafts of the novel the heroine is
called Maria and not Emma – Maria was one of his favourite
names, and he had already used it in *Mémoires d'un Fou*
and in *Novembre*.

He assured Mademoiselle Leroyer de Chantepie that his
first idea of the novel had been to make the heroine a virgin,
living in a provincial setting, growing old in the midst of
frustration and eventually reaching the last stages of imagined mysticism and passion.[5] He had kept, he said, the
general sombre background but had later chosen a heroine
more in keeping with life as we know it.

In spite of Flaubert's declarations: 'No model sat for
me,'[6] and 'There is nothing in *Madame Bovary* that is
true,'[7] it seems clear that he did, in fact, take his subject, in
embryo, from real life. He admits it himself, by implication,
when he says that he fears that the ending, which was much
fuller in reality, will be somewhat thin in his version.[8]
Nevertheless he was certainly always much irritated when
people wrote to him to say that they recognized real people
in the novel.[9]

The story of Delphine Delamare seems, then, to have been
the starting point of *Madame Bovary*, and her name, as we
have seen, was mentioned by Du Camp to Flaubert in his
letter of 22 July 1851,[10] and the name Bovary in the letter
of 2 August 1851.[11]

A curious thing then happened: as Flaubert was alleged to
have taken his plot from the story of Delphine and Eugène
Delamare, the real life of the characters was now coloured by
the facts in his novel, which were used as evidence of their
adventures. Her life was now told as if the facts related by
Flaubert were strictly true. But this is far from being the
case. There is no proof whatsoever that Delphine Delamare
committed suicide, though all accounts now state that she
did. The death certificate was published in *La Normandie
Médicale*,[12] and no cause for her death was given. It is

dated 7 March 1848 and merely states that she had died at
Ry at 3 a.m. on the previous day, at the age of twenty-seven.
There was no inquest; no paper mentions the possibility of
suicide; and the priest allowed the body to be buried in con-
secrated ground. When Emma Bovary committed suicide,
Flaubert was very particular to make the chemist write an
article to appear in the local paper, saying that she had acci-
dentally poisoned herself through mistaking the arsenic for
sugar; otherwise she could not have been buried in the
churchyard.

The Delamare theme is, however, only the very small
nucleus of the novel, the grain of sand at the centre of the
pearl in the oyster; it is only a handful of Japanese paper
flowers, which need to be cast into water – the mind of the
genius – to blossom like the gardens of Babylon. Eugène
Delamare had died while Flaubert had been in the East in
1849; he had been a student under Dr Flaubert, and had
been known to the family. It is very likely that Madame
Flaubert had discussed his untimely death with her son on
his return, and it was probably only then that the idea of
using the subject for his novel occurred to him.

It is not, however, the only possible source of the novel:
there are others as well. Flaubert had been much interested
in Louise Pradier, the wife of the sculptor, since he met her
when she was a student in Paris. She was a very unfaithful
wife, and her husband finally divorced her in January 1845.
We have seen that Flaubert continued to visit her after she
had separated from Pradier, and that he had written to
Alfred Le Poittevin that he had been able to make a wonderful psychological study of her.[13]

In 1947 the then librarian of the Municipal Library at
Rouen, Gabrielle Leleu, had the sudden idea of investigating a manuscript in an uneducated hand[14] – that was
probably why it had escaped examination for so long –
which, for some unknown reason, is kept amongst the *Bouvard et Pécuchet* notes.[15] It is entitled *Les Mémoires de
Madame Ludovica* – Louise Pradier was always known as

Ludovica amongst her intimates – and it was probably written by her maid. It is not known why it was written, and it
may even have been commissioned by Flaubert himself, for
authors are like that, even to their closest friends. If he did
commission it, it is not known at what moment, whether
very early, intending to use it one day, or at the time of
composing *Madame Bovary*. It only goes as far as her separation from her husband. It is an illiterate document, badly
written and full of grammatical mistakes. The writer begins
by pretending that she is a friend of Ludovica, but she says
many spiteful things about her. It is a merciless indictment
of the life and loves of Ludovica, her promiscuity, her extravagance and her debts which were ruining her husband.
Flaubert certainly used the document and underlined the
passages which were useful to him. There was the description of a dream in Italy which recalls those of Emma Bovary.
Ludovica, like Emma, tried to borrow money from her
lovers, and Flaubert has underlined the sentence: 'Not one
of these men even put politeness in his refusal.'

The writer of the *Mémoires* expressed anxiety lest she
should attempt to commit suicide on account of her desperate financial straits. It is largely her money difficulties and
her plans for solving them which Flaubert has used in his
Madame Bovary.

One must also not forget that Flaubert, from his earliest
years, had been interested in the kind of woman whom he
later depicted in *Madame Bovary*, and we have seen that he
used her in his boyhood works, *Quid Quis Volueris*, and especially in *Passion et Vertu*, which, even in the circumstances of the plot, could be considered as a first sketch for
Madame Bovary. The similarities between the two compositions have already been mentioned in an earlier chapter.

There was also the law case, in Rouen in 1845, in which a
woman called Esther de Bovery was implicated, and of
which Jean Pommier has written.[16] A man called Loursel
was alleged, at the trial, to have murdered his wife and the

servant-girl, in order to marry a young woman called Esther de Bovery with whom he had fallen in love, and who had also fallen in love with him. Her passionate letters to him, written after his arrest, showing a character very like that of Emma Bovary, were read in court. They were greatly censured by the judge, but Loursel's lawyer – the Sénard who was to defend Flaubert twelve years later at his own trial – declared that their extravagant style was the result of the romantic literature current at the time. The death of the servant-girl, as described at the trial, is very like that of Emma. She was looked after by an inexperienced and incompetent 'officier de santé' who called in the qualified doctor too late to save her. Loursel was eventually acquitted through lack of evidence.

It is possible to believe that Flaubert, in the name of his heroine, and in some of the details of his plot, was inspired by this law case.

There was also *Les Mémoires de Marie Cappelle* by Veuve Lafarge, published in 1842, who was accused and convicted of murdering her husband through arsenical poisoning. Flaubert is very likely to have read this book, since he mentions it twice in his letters to Louise Colet.[17] The editor of the *Correspondance* states in a note[18] that the book in question is *Heures de Prison*, but this cannot be true, as it was published only in 1854 and Flaubert mentions the book in 1852; also there is nothing in *Heures de Prison* which could have served him when he was composing *Madame Bovary*. But the description of a ball at the Palais Royal, in the other book, might have inspired the ball which Emma Bovary attends at the Château de la Vaubyessard.[19] There is, too, a country wedding very similar to Emma's.[20] And the lengthy account of her husband's death from poisoning, which could have served for the death of Emma.[21] Also Marie Cappelle, writing to a friend about the child which she was carrying, recalls Charles Bovary's dream for his little daughter Berthe:[22] 'Déjà je ne vois, je ne rêve, que ma petite Jacqueline. Quand je ne dors pas la nuit, je la vois d'abord têtant, puis marchant, puis plus grande, puis plus belle. Enfin je la marie, et me préoccupe excessivement de son bonheur intérieur.'

All these references to possible sources of Flaubert's novel are only intended to show that there are many possibilities for the plot and circumstances of *Madame Bovary*, that none is more likely than the other, and that none of them are of any real significance or importance. Critics have usually allowed their imagination to run riot in their search for possible sources and parallels. For instance, most of them claim that he obtained the idea for Charles Bovary's cap – the one he wore at school on his first day – from a lithograph by Gavarni, published in *Le Charivari* on 21 June 1833, and he is alleged to have consulted the complete set of the paper in a hotel in Constantinople in 1850. It may be true that he looked through the complete set of *Le Charivari* while he was in Constantinople in 1850, and the cap depicted in the lithograph is certainly strange, but it bears not the slightest resemblance to Bovary's cap as described by Flaubert in the novel.[23] The cap in the illustration looks like an ordinary round cap fitting tightly to the head, and going down to the ears and brow. But what is strange is that, on top of this, at the back, there is a square like that of an English university mortar-board, with a tassel. In fact the cap looks like a mortar-board with a soft head-piece covering most of the head. It requires a great deal of imagination to see it as the counterpart of Bovary's eccentric cap.

Why did Flaubert choose this subject, which he kept on repeating was so distasteful to him? One must, of course, not take too seriously what an artist says when he is in the throes of gestation; and he was to express the same difficulty in writing, the same dislike for his other books, when in the process of composition, whether they were exotic or realist.

He chose the subject because he wanted to study clinically the disease of Romanticism. He knew, from the effects of himself, its deliquescing nature, how it prevented any clear thinking, any clear and objective view of self, and how it led to senseless dreaming which impeded all action. He considered that romantic reading was most dangerous to the human personality. Amongst his papers, in the Municipal Library at Rouen, there are notes on the danger of romantic reading.[24] One passage is copied from *Le Dictionnaire des Sciences Med.-Art. Nymphomanie:*

The evils of the education adopted for our young people, the preference given to the arts of pure pleasure, the reading of novels, offer to young people a precocious activity in premature desires, ideas of imaginary perfection which they will be unable to find anywhere.

And another from *Dict. des Sciences Médicales:*

The reading of novels is still more dangerous for women, because it puts before them man in an exaggerated form and with exaggerated characteristics; it prepares them for inevitable disgust and an emptiness which they cannot reasonably hope to fill.

Romanticism had idealized adultery – as had Flaubert also when he had been composing *Novembre* – and all the authors whom he had read in his youth, whom Emma was also to read, had glorified it – and the supreme rights of passion had been set forth in the novels of George Sand, *Indiana* and *Lélia.* Flaubert wished now to puncture this theory and to show it up in all its sordid reality; he wanted to strip it of its glory and to put it in its place. Emma Bovary still regarded it romantically and considered that it raised those who practised it above the common herd. When she was seduced by Rodolphe her feelings were not that she loved him and that he loved her, but that she was now the equal of all these glamorous adulteresses of whom she had read in Romantic literature:[25]

Elle se répétait: 'J'ai un amant! un amant!' se délectant à cette idée comme à celle d'une autre puberté qui lui serait survenue. Elle allait donc posséder enfin ces joies de l'amour, cette fièvre du bonheur dont elle avait désespéré. . . . Alors elle se rappela les héroïnes des livres qu'elle avait lus, et la légion lyrique de ces femmes adultères se mit à chanter dans sa mémoire avec des voix de soeurs qui la charmaient. Elle devenait elle-même comme une partie véritable de ces imaginations et réalisait la longue rêverie de sa jeunesse, en se considérant dans ce type d'amoureuse qu'elle avait tant envié.

Flaubert used the slender plot – wherever he obtained it – on which to hang his real study. When he had begun writing, as a youth, in the middle thirties, Romanticism had been at its height, and the years of its fullest flowering were between 1830 and 1840 – the failure of Hugo's play, *Les Burgraves*, in 1843, is generally taken as the death-blow to the movement. Twenty years afterwards, in the fifties, Romanticism had become debased and outworn, and had sunk, in taste, to the lowest intellectual classes. Bouilhet and Du Camp realized this, and this was why they had been so hard on the explosion of Romanticism in Flaubert's *Tentation de Saint Antoine*, and had told him that all he had to do was to burn the manuscript and to think no more about it. After reflection he had eventually come round to their opinion.

He had been reading Montaigne for a long time, and he now took seriously the essayist's avowed plan of learning to know himself fully, and he considered that all the misfortunes of mankind came from imperfect knowledge of self. All the characters in his novels fail through not knowing themselves, through seeing themselves other than they are, and not realizing their capabilities and possibilities. It is possible to believe that he intended to show, in *Bouvard & Pécuchet*, his last novel – unfinished when he died – that these two ludicrous Charlie Chaplinesque characters had embarked on studies and research for which they were unsuited and unequipped by their intelligence and education, but that they eventually reached wisdom when they realized that all they were really suited for was copying, and they returned to that former humble occupation.

Emma Bovary does not know what her possibilities are nor what she is capable of achieving, and that is her tragedy. A philosophic term has been coined by the critic Jules de Gaultier from this characteristic in her, Bovarysme, that is to say the capacity of seeing oneself other than one is. All Flaubert's characters, major and minor, to a lesser or to a greater degree, possess this failing; and their view of themselves and their ambitions is far beyond their possible powers of achievement, so that they can never attain happiness or content. Although he recognized this, he could, nevertheless, not withhold his grudging admiration from them, and especially his understanding compassion. He saw the same characteristic in Don Quixote whose adventures had been, since his childhood, one of his favourite books. He had admired his idealism and heroism, while seeing clearly their falseness. Don Quixote might be called the first victim of Bovarysme. He could never adapt himself to real life as it is lived in the world, and he always saw it through the haze of literature as something romantic, which inevitably led him to disaster. All Flaubert's characters create for themselves tastes and sentiments at variance with their real nature, and they fix their eyes on an ideal which they are incapable of attaining and which hides reality from their view.

Although the psychology is the main interest in *Madame Bovary*, it is not the only one. Flaubert had deeply reflected on life and its problems, on human nature, but, instead of setting down his conclusions in abstract form, in a treatise, he created characters and situations which would exemplify and incarnate them. He had certain decided opinions with regard to life, and his philosophy influenced his choice of characters and situations, so that we can deduce from them what his views were on human destiny.

When he reached maturity, and had grown beyond the youthful stage of animal optimism, his view of life was pessimistic. He did not believe in happiness and he wrote to Louise Colet:[26] 'Be assured that happiness is only a myth invented by the Devil to drive us to despair.' He thought that man had been dealt a raw deal by a jealous God, and that there was little that he could do. Even in *Un Coeur*

Simple, a tale written to please George Sand and to be consoling; even here the good, simple servant-girl, Félicité the heroine, in spite of all her goodness, is gradually stripped of everything until, at the end, she is left with only a moth-eaten stuffed parrot to represent the Holy Ghost. The fact that she does not realize her plight does not alter the matter, and the tale is basically as pessimistic as anything that he ever wrote. In his view, all of us here below, metaphorically speaking, have only a moth-eaten stuffed parrot to represent the Holy Ghost.

Flaubert saw man in general as mean, conventional, insensitive and selfish. Yet, in his personal relationship he remained, to the end of his life, full of illusions about those whom he loved. But he believed intellectually that those who were gross, insensitive and self-interested always prospered, and were left in command at the final curtain; while the gentler and self-forgetful were always the victims. When he was only twenty-four, he wrote in *L'Éducation Sentimentale* of Henry, who had become a self-seeking climber:[27] 'L'avenir est à lui; ce sont ces gens-là qui deviennent puissants.'

In our moments of depression we are inclined to agree with him; nevertheless, it is not necessarily a realistic or true view of life, and it is not the universal experience that the Homais of this world are always successful. Flaubert seemed incapable of believing that anyone of intelligence, of complexity and subtlety, could possibly be, morally speaking, worthy of admiration. Dr Larivière, in *Madame Bovary*, drawn from his father, is a notable exception, and he hardly counts in the novel. Otherwise goodness is found only in the simple and inarticulate – the chemist's assistant, little Justin; in Catherine Leroux, who, dumbly and faithfully, has served in one farm for fifty-four years and who is given, as a reward, a little silver medal costing twenty-five francs; or Félicité in *Un Coeur Simple*. This has led critics to claim that he was cynical and cruel, but this is far from the truth. He was a man of great sensibility and compassion – especially towards the lowly and the victims of life – and, in the materialistic milieu of the July Monarchy, and later in the Second Empire, he was frequently bitterly hurt by the lack of idealism in the jungle of the men of letters of the day. It was not a hard man who understood the overwhelming and inarticulate grief of Charles Bovary beside the death-bed of his wife. It was not a cruel man who depicted movingly the humble figure of Catherine Leroux standing before the pompous judges at the agricultural show; nor who described old farmer Rouault arriving at Bovary's house to find his daughter dead and fainting at the sight of the black hangings over the hall-door; nor who noticed his tears after the funeral:[28]

En rentrant, Charles se déshabilla, et le père Rouault repassa sa blouse bleue. Elle était neuve, et, comme il s'était, pendant la route, souvent essuyé les yeux avec les manches, elle avait déteint sur sa figure; et la trace des pleurs y faisait des lignes dans la couche de poussière qui la salissait.

It was not a hard man who described young Justin weeping, at dead of night, when everyone was asleep, over the grave of Emma Bovary:[29]

Sur la fosse, entre les sapins, un enfant pleurait agenouillé, et sa poitrine, brisée par les sanglots, haletait dans l'ombre, sous la pression d'un regret immense, plus doux que la lune et plus insondable que la nuit. La grille, tout à coup, craqua. C'était Lestiboudois; il venait chercher sa bêche qu'il avait oubliée tantôt. Il reconnut Justin escaladant le mur, et sut alors à quoi s'en tenir sur le malfaiteur qui lui dérobait ses pommes de terre.

Flaubert could not, however, resist the temptation to put, as a contrast to Justin's entirely innocent and disinterested grief, the selfish and mean reflection of the grave-digger, that the boy had only come to the churchyard at night to steal his potatoes; in the same way as he contrasted the twenty-five francs given to Catherine Leroux for her half-century of service with the sixty francs given to a competitor, at the agricultural show, for a prize example of 'la race porcine'.

He understood particularly the depth of feeling which could exist in the inarticulate, in those who could not exteriorize their emotion. He also understood how much sincerity there could be in those who could only express themselves in clichés. When Rodolphe Boulanger is bored with the emotional conventionalities which Emma utters, for he has heard them so often before, Flaubert remarks:[30]

Il ne distinguait pas, cet homme si plein de pratique, la dissemblance des sentiments sous la parité des expressions. Parce que des lèvres libertines ou vénales lui avaient murmuré des phrases pareilles, il ne croyait que faiblement à la candeur de celles-là; on en devait rabattre, pensait-il, les discours exagérés cachant les affections médiocres; comme si la plénitude de l'âme ne débordait pas quelquefois par les métaphores les plus vides, puisque personne, jamais, ne peut donner l'exacte mesure de ses besoins, ni de ses conceptions, ni de ses douleurs, et que la parole humaine est comme un chaudron fêlé où nous battons des mélodies à faire danser les ours, quand on voudrait attendrir les étoiles.

Flaubert believed in fatality, in inexorable fate, but this did not preclude a belief in free will and in a certain amount of free choice. The fatality of each of us is in his character, and no man can go beyond his nature, so that he must learn what it is to take it into account, and to make his peace with his limitations. His character is, as it were, the chain by which a dog is attached to its kennel. It is completely free to move as it likes, or not to move at all, but it must take into account the length of its chain, and it cannot move beyond that. It is wisdom to learn what is its length and not to waste energy in pulling against it. Nearly all Flaubert's characters are destroyed because they do not take into account their character, the length of their chain, and they never get to know themselves, since they cannot be altered. Only one of his characters does alter himself radically and redeem his past life completely, and that is Julien in *Saint Julien l'Hospitalier* from *Trois Contes*.

There are two episodes in *Madame Bovary* which have

given rise to much controversy and criticism. One is Emma's suicide, and the other the appearance of the blind beggar beneath her window as she is dying. Professor F. C. Green believes that this suicide is entirely wrong and out of character.[31] He considers that the motive is not sufficiently established and that, as long as there was one unattached male left, she would not have taken her life, but would have continued to get round her besotted husband, and the money would have been found somehow. He does not believe that the money motive is sufficient to explain her killing herself.

It is true that the question of money would not have explained anything, but it is not likely that Flaubert intended it to be the main motive, and Professor Green has been somewhat insensitive, and has not understood Emma's character. She would not take her life for lack of money – she was not a woman who thought much about the future and she lived in the present – but she had certain ideals and a fixed view of herself; if these were damaged, then, in momentary despair, she might do violence to herself.[32]

The episode occurs when Charles is about to be sold up for the debts incurred by his wife. She tried to obtain the money from Léon to settle the most urgent accounts, tried to persuade him to borrow from the till in his office – she was certain of her authority over him and she was prepared to turn him into a criminal for her own ends. But he was no longer the weak youth whom she had known at first, and he stood firm against all her blandishments.

Then she thought of Monsieur Guillaumin the lawyer, and even toyed with the idea, for a moment, of giving herself to him to obtain the money she needed – he had often made advances to her and had insinuated that she could have anything that she wanted if she would be nice to him. When it came to the point she could not do it. There was too much refinement in her and also – though this may seem strange at this stage – too much idealism. She could not make this final sacrifice, for she had never yet sold herself for money – and neither had the heroines in the romances, whom she had admired. Cheap as she was, she had kept her kind of sincerity, her own nobility. She could not accept it and, after Monsieur Guillaumin had attempted to paw her, nausea seized her and she could not go through with it. 'Vous profitez impudemment de ma détresse, Monsieur,' she said. 'Je suis à plaindre mais pas à vendre.' She then swept out on this last noble line.

She next thought of Rodolphe, not as a lover but as a friend, who had always – even when he was leaving her – protested the permanence of his friendship and goodwill towards her. She went to see him with no ulterior motive – no motive of love, that is – but to obtain a loan. But, in his presence, she was once more overwhelmed by her love, particularly the memory of her love for him; it would not be wrong or indiscreet, she said to herself, to accept money from him, since she loved him still so deeply, and he would not refuse her, since he had always said to her – in his ready-made phrases – that she had only to call on his friendship and he would always be ready to help her.

He started again with his empty compliments, his expert clever words, which, once more, bewitched and charmed the stupid and vain little provincial. She believed him; she plucked up her courage and asked for a loan. This had the effect which the mention of money always has in life; it was a damper on all emotion. 'Une demande pécuniaire, de toutes les bourrasques qui tombent sur l'amour, étant la plus froide et la plus déracinante.' 'Je ne les ai pas, chère Madame,' he answered. 'Tu ne les as pas,' she asked in amazement and repeated it, 'tu ne les as pas! J'aurais dû m'épargner cette dernière honte. Tu ne m'as jamais aimée. Tu ne vaux pas mieux que les autres!' She was giving herself away, she was destroying all her chances. Then, as many another woman in similar circumstances, she drove him into the wrong, and there is nothing as fatal. She pointed to all the rich things in the room around him – the furniture, the cigarette case, the decanters of wine, his watch, his cuff-links and so forth. 'Ah!

je te plains,' she said contemptuously. 'Oui considérablement!':

> Mais, lorsqu'on est si pauvre, on ne met pas d'argent à la crosse de son fusil! On n'achète pas une pendule avec des incrustations d'écailles! ... ni des sifflets de vermeil pour ses fouets ... ni des breloques pour sa montre! Oh! rien ne lui manque! jusqu'à un porte-liqueurs dans sa chambre; car tu t'aimes, tu vis bien, tu as un château, des fermes, des bois; tu chasses à courre, tu voyages à Paris. ... Eh! quand ce ne serait que cela ... que la moindre de ces niaiseries! on en peut faire de l'argent! ... Oh! je n'en veux pas! garde-les.

And she seized a pair of cuff-links from the mantelpiece and threw them against the wall:

> Mais, moi, je t'aurais tout donné, j'aurais tout vendu, j'aurais travaillé de mes mains, j'aurais mendié sur les routes, pour un sourire, pour un regard, pour t'entendre dire 'Merci!' Et tu restes là tranquillement dans ton fauteuil, comme si déjà tu ne m'avais pas fait assez souffrir! Sans toi, sais-tu bien, j'aurais pu vivre heureuse! qui t'y forçait? Était-ce une gageure? Tu m'aimais cependant, tu le disais. ... Et tout à l'heure encore. .. Ah! il eût mieux valu me chasser! J'ai les mains chaudes de tes baisers, et voilà la place sur le tapis où tu jurais à mes genoux une éternité d'amour. Tu m'y as fait croire: tu m'as pendant deux ans traînée dans le rêve le plus magnifique et le plus suave! ... Hein! nos projets de voyage, tu te rappelles? Oh! ta lettre, ta lettre! elle m'a déchiré le coeur! ... Et puis, quand je reviens vers lui, vers lui, qui est riche, heureux, libre! pour implorer un secours que le premier venu rendrait, suppliante et lui rapportant toute ma tendresse, il me repousse, parce que ça lui coûterait trois mille francs.

But Rodolphe only repeated coldly: 'Je ne les ai pas!'

What Professor Green has not understood is the romantic quality which was still there, in Emma, in spite of her failings, and her pride in herself. Now that Rodolphe had humiliated her and let her down, everything else was forgotten. He had denied love, love as she had always seen it. Rodolphe's letting her down became the symbol, the syn-

thesis of all the humiliations and disillusionment which
women have suffered at the hands of men since the beginning of time. Nine women out of ten would have felt at that
moment that death would be preferable to anything else, to
ease the intolerable agony. Luckily most women have not
the means at their disposal to assuage this sudden craving,
and later the impulse is gone as grief is deadened. It was not
a reflected act on Emma's part, any more than it would have
been with any other woman at such a moment, but a violent
temporary urge. This is clear from the passage which
follows, when she has left Rodolphe's house:

Elle resta perdue de stupeur, et n'ayant plus conscience d'elle-
même que par le battement de ses artères, qu'elle croyait entendre s'échapper comme une assourdissante musique qui em-
plissait la campagne. Le sol sous ses pieds était plus mou qu'une
onde, et les sillons lui parurent d'immenses vagues brunes, qui
déferlaient. Tout ce qu'il y avait dans sa tête de réminiscences,
d'idées, s'échappaient à la fois d'un seul bond, comme les mille
pièces d'un feu d'artifice. Elle vit son père, le cabinet de Lheu-
reux, leur chambre là-bas, un autre paysage. La folie la prenait,
elle eut peur, et parvint à se ressaisir, d'une manière confuse, il
est vrai; car elle ne se rappelait point la cause de son horrible état,
c'est à dire la question d'argent. Elle ne souffrait que de son
amour, et sentait son âme l'abandonner par ce souvenir,
comme les blessés, en agonisant, sentent l'existence qui s'en va
par leur plaie qui saigne.
   La nuit tombait, des corneilles volaient.
   Il lui semblait tout à coup que des globules couleur de feu
éclataient dans l'air comme des balles fulminantes en
s'aplatissant, et tournaient, tournaient, pour aller se fondre sur la
neige, entre les branches des arbres. Au milieu de chacun d'eux,
la figure de Rodolphe apparaissait. Ils se multiplièrent et ils se
rapprochaient, la pénétraient; tout disparut. Elle reconnut les
lumières des maisons qui rayonnaient de loin dans le brouillard.

Then she remembered that she knew where the arsenic was
kept in Homais's shop. She went there and persuaded Justin
to give her the key of the attic where it was locked up: she

seized the jar of poison and swallowed a full handful. Then she was overcome by a feeling of peace as if she had accomplished some duty.

Even if we did not have this passage as evidence, we have further proof in the rough notes of the novel, in the Municipal Library at Rouen, which makes it clear that it is disillusioned love that has driven her to take her life.[33] The attempt with Rodolphe – like a blow from a pick-axe – she goes to him – or rather a failed attempt – then, on a mad impulse, she commits suicide. Calm returns to her when she knows she is going to die.'

The other episode is in connection with the appearance of the blind beggar beneath Emma's window when she is dying, and the singing of his alleged obscene song.[34] Incidentally this song, which was accused of being indecent, was, said Ulrich Guttiguer, one that his mother used to sing to him, when he was a baby in his cradle.[35] Flaubert himself mentions in his notes that it came from Rétif de la Bretonne.[36] Steegmuller sees this episode as a Romantic trait which had escaped the vigilance of Louis Bouilhet.[37] But the singing of the blind beggar at this point did not slip in by accident; it was very carefully contrived. In his correspondence we realize that Flaubert had worried very much about this detail, and he explains that it was essential that the beggar should be there at the end, and he had to devise a legitimate reason for his presence.[30] He needed him there as a final touch for Emma's characterization. The blind beggar was a figure whom she had so often encountered when she was off on her adulterous meetings with her lover, and he had become symbolical to her of her sin. It was to him that she had flung her last crown piece, in a final gesture of bravado. Then, when she heard him singing beneath her window, his licentious little song, after she had fully realized that she was dying criminally through her own hand, then all her other sins rose up before her and she imagined the beggar as a figure of damnation, the Devil coming to fetch her soul. After all, that was what had always happened in the Romantic books which she had read in her youth, about those who had made pacts with Satan, selling their souls and their future eternal salvation for the temporary pleasures of this world; and finally, at the day of reckoning, they were obliged to fulfil their pledge, when he came to fetch them away to Hell. This conception is in Emma's mind, and not in Flaubert's; and, when she heard the beggar singing beneath her window, she imagined that she saw his hideous face rising out of the eternal darkness as a symbol of retribution. This was the last trait needed for her final characterization.

[22]

Characters and
Characterization

WE have seen that it is in the understanding and depiction of character that the main interest of *Madame Bovary* lies. Flaubert himself said:[1] '*Bovary* ... will be the sum total of my psychological knowledge.' He was interested in people in general, and could not see any of them without speculating on their personalities and their lives. In his *Notes de Voyages* he wrote:[2]

I have the habit of composing a whole set of books on the people whom I encounter. An invincible curiosity makes me wonder, in spite of myself, what can be the life of the passer-by whom I meet. I would like to know his profession, his country, his name; what is preoccupying him at the time, what he is regretting, what he is hoping for – forgotten loves, present dreams – I want to know everything, even to the borders of his flannel waistcoats, and what he looks like when he is purging himself. And, if it is a woman (of a certain age especially) then the itch becomes burning. How one longs to see her naked – let's admit it – naked to the depths of her heart! How one tries to find out where she comes from, where she is going, and why she happens to be here rather than elsewhere. As you look her over, you imagine adventures for her, and feelings. One thinks of the kind of room which she must inhabit, of a thousand others things, and what have you! Of the down-at-heel slippers into which she thrusts her feet on rising from her bed.

Flaubert saw most of his characters as ultimate failures because they were incapable of seeing themselves as they really were. Nevertheless his main characters possess something which raises them above the ordinary. In boorish Charles Bovary it was his overwhelming and disinterested love for Emma. She, too, had something which lifted her above the lowest. She was vulgar, stupid, lazy and vain – indeed one could make a whole catalogue of her deficiencies – but she had something which raised her above material considerations. Flaubert said:[3] 'A soul is measured by the extent of its aspirations!' The extent of Emma's dreams was great even if their quality was shoddy. She had all the characteristics of a Romantic heroine, but in doubtful taste. That is one of the miracles of Flaubert's art, his portrayal of character, so that we can sympathize with Emma while realizing her vulgarity. She is a Woolworth's or bargain-basement Isolde, but her feelings are none the less genuine for all that.

We have seen that it was Flaubert's philosophy of life which dictated his choice of characters, those whom he was urged to depict. He believed that most people were egoistic and self-seeking, and that genuineness and goodness were normally only to be found in the very simple and unpretentious. On the whole, his characters tend to be unlovable. Yet if one is going to spend so much time with fictitious people, as one must when one reads a novel, there is something to be said for liking them as people and as friends, as one does Anna Karenina in Tolstoy's novel of the same name, or Natasha in *War and Peace*. It would, however, be difficult to imagine oneself as intimate with Charles or Emma; or with Rodolphe; or Léon, or Homais; and little Justin and Catherine Leroux are too undeveloped as characters for intelligent frequentation. One should not, however, quarrel with an author on the score of his subjects; one must only see whether he has carried out his intention.

In his depiction of character Flaubert revolted against the Romantic conception and tradition of individual man, the exception. Rousseau had said, at the beginning of his *Confessions*, that he considered that he was like no one who had ever existed, in fact unique, a monster. All the Romantic writers followed him in describing exceptional beings. Flaubert thought that art should not deal with heroes or monsters. 'Art is not intended to depict exceptions,' he said.[4] It must generalize. 'What characterizes the great geniuses,' he wrote,[5] 'is their power of generalization and creation. They manage to resume, in one type, scattered personalities, and bring new beings to the knowledge of the human race.'

The aim of the writers of the Realist School of his time was to be locally and chronologically true to their own age, so that the characters they created could not have lived at any other time or in any other place. Flaubert, on the contrary, wished to depict what did not pass, what was the same for every age, what was eternal. Writing to Hippolyte Taine, to dispute the critic's view that the only value in a work of art was its importance as a historical document, he said:[6] 'Indeed a work has significance only in respect of its eternity; that is to say that the more it represents humanity of all times, the more beautiful it is.'

In Emma he has painted a woman of all ages, not merely a provincial adulteress of the 1840s. We have all known our Emma Bovarys. Today she would read fewer novels, but view many films and see herself in terms of a film star. She would call her daughter Marlene instead of Galswinde. Flaubert said of her:[7] 'My poor Bovary is no doubt weeping and suffering in twenty villages of France at the present moment.' That is as true today as it was a century ago.

Flaubert's methods of characterization were very different from those of his great predecessors, Stendhal and Balzac. What is important in Stendhal – and this has become the source of his popularity in the twentieth century – is his subtle analysis of motive, his subtle understanding of shades of character. Without the aid of the modern psychoanalyst's methods, he has reached, by his powers of observation and deduction, many of the conclusions of modern psychiatrists. There had never been seen in fiction before him such understanding of men's hidden motives. Stendhal is an analyst who creates characters in order to pull them to pieces to show how they work. The cartoon which represents Flaubert standing, with a scalpel in his hand, over Emma Bovary lying on the dissecting-table before him would be far more true of Stendhal. Flaubert carries out his laboratory work beforehand, in order to obtain his ingredients *before* he creates his characters. He does not cut them up *afterwards*.

Stendhal analyses his characters from the point of view of the omniscient author who has them there in front of him and knows how they work. Although his affinities with the eighteenth century have usually been noticed, he has really more with the seventeenth century, in that he is concerned with moral problems and the manner in which human beings react to them.

Balzac's method was very different. He was very much interested in the scientific discoveries of his age. He considered man as a kind of higher animal of which there were many breeds, and he proceeded to study them zoologically. He used to say 'give me the glove and I'll build you the man from it' as if it were a piece of bone. He considered his function as a novelist to be that of a scientist and not of an artist, a scientist studying this curious animal called man. Thus he puts down every detail which he notices about him, without artistic selection, as a scientist would. That is why he spares us no detail, however insignificant, in the appearance or surroundings of any character he is investigating, for everything may be scientific data, and a scientist does not pick and choose in what he records, he includes everything. For Balzac all these details were scientific facts. In the process his novels have now become a scientific document for the study of the nineteenth century, and they are the raw material for further work. Anyone wishing to write about nineteenth-century France cannot ignore Balzac's writings, as there is no richer source of material to be found anywhere.

The scientist, when studying a frog, is not concerned with giving a psychological picture of it, but only with recording its behaviour. In the same way, it is the behaviour of his characters which interests Balzac rather than their motives, and it is their behaviour that he studies. This makes his characters less subtle than those of Stendhal. He normally assumes knowledge of what can be deduced from the outward appearance of his characters, and that is why description plays such an important part in his novels. He was confirmed in his method by his study of the eighteenth-century physiognomist Lavater, who believed that all internal characteristics were revealed outwardly. Balzac proceeded in the same way, and this has made him a wonderful portrait painter – what one remembers best in his novels are his portraits, and these are unforgettable. The method has, however, the disadvantage of being limited, as there are many qualities – often amongst the most interesting and subtle – which never reach surface expression at all. It means also that the method will be more successful with the obvious, with those of mature years on whose countenance life has written much; it will not be successful with the young and undeveloped. There are in fact very few good portraits of the young in Balzac, or the inexpressive. It also means that it is difficult to show development and modification of character through events.

In his methods of characterization Balzac made great use of conversation, and only Marivaux before him, in the eighteenth century, realized what could be made of realistic conversation in bringing a character to life. In Balzac speech is made one of the most revealing qualities of the person portrayed. The conversation is realistically expressed; he goes to great lengths in verbal contortions to render it phonetically, and it has all the vulgarity and incoherence of real speech.

Flaubert's methods of characterization are very different, both from those of Stendhal, and those of Balzac. He is not the omniscient author, like Stendhal, who knows what goes on in his characters and imparts this knowledge, himself, to his readers. On the contrary, he becomes, unconsciously, the characters whom he is depicting. Writing to Taine, he said:[8]

My imaginary characters *affect* me, pursue me, or rather it is I who am in them. When I was describing the death from poisoning of Emma Bovary, I had the *taste of arsenic* in my mouth *to such an extent*, I was so much poisoned myself, that I gave myself two separate attacks of indigestion, one after the other, two very real attacks, for I threw up the whole of my dinner.

Or again to Louise Colet:[9]

All the same, good or bad, it is a wonderful thing to write, to be no longer *oneself*, but to move about in the whole of the creation one is talking about. Today, for instance, man and woman together, I rode on horseback, in a forest, on an autumn afternoon, under the golden leaves, and I was the horses, the leaves, the wind, the words they were saying to one another, and the red sun which made their eyes, drowning with love, blink. Is it pride, or piety, is it the foolish overflow of exaggerated self-satisfaction? Or is it a vague and noble instinct of religion? But when I reflect on these joys, after having experienced them, I'm almost tempted to send up a prayer of thanks to God Almighty, if I thought that he could hear me.

As an author he did not wish to appear at all himself. 'The artist must manage,' he said,[10] 'to make posterity believe that he never existed.'

He used very little conversation in his novels – astonishingly little if one compares them with those of Balzac – because he could not bring himself to write French which was not correct, and he could never have written the kind of realistic dialogue which is found in Balzac. Writing to Louise Colet, he said:[11] 'How can one write trivial dialogue which is well written.' And to Louis Bouilhet about a modern novel he wrote:[12] 'I reproach the beginning with having too much dialogue. (You know the dislike I have for dialogue in a novel.)'

But he made great use of indirect speech, and this becomes one of the miracles of his characterization, as it permits him to give expression to the unexpressed thoughts of incoherent people. This, subsequently, was to become the interior monologue of the modern novel.

A striking example in *Madame Bovary* is the evocation of

the day-dreams of Charles and Emma, which run on parallel lines which never meet.

Charles, coming in one night from a patient, sees his wife, as he thinks, asleep in their bed and the baby in the crib beside her. Then, as he gazes down at the two sleepers, he dreams of the future and this reveals the naïve – if boorish – goodness of his nature. Already he could see the child growing up: she would go to school and would return with ink-stains on her pinafore, and her little basket on her arm. Later he would have to find the money to send her to a convent to finish her education. He turned over the problem in his mind and planned to rent a small farm near enough to keep an eye on it as he went about his rounds. He would save and the child would grow up beautiful, she would resemble her mother and everyone would say that they were like two sisters. He could imagine her sitting with them, in the evening, when the lamp was lit, doing her work. She would embroider slippers for him and fill his home with sweetness and gaiety. Then he would have to find a husband for her, a good reliable fellow, and they would live happily for ever and ever after.

Emma's dream is different and reveals her equally. It is only of herself that she thinks, of her romantic love, of her elopement with Rodolphe, and never a thought for her husband and child. She would go to a new country whence she would never return. She fills her dream from the rag-bag of her romantic novel reading. It is a strange and splendid land she will inhabit, all domes and bridges, with harbours filled with shipping, amid groves of lemon; cathedrals of white marble, with storks nesting on pointed gothic spires. There is the sound of guitars beneath the palm trees, as she floats along in her gondola, and comes to rest in the oases; the sea spreads to the horizon, still, blue and sun-drenched, and she is happy at last for ever more.[13]

These passages give a better knowledge of the characters than would pages of description and analysis.

Flaubert does not build up his characters, as did Balzac, by objective, external description; in fact, so careless is he of their outward appearance that on one occasion he gives Emma brown eyes;[14] on another deep black eyes;[15] and, on another, blue eyes.[16] Léon, when we first encounter him, is described as having golden hair;[17] and later as having chestnut locks.[18]

We see the characters not in the absolute sense but through what they notice of one another. Thus all we know at first of Emma is what impinges on the consciousness of Charles: a cloud of dark hair and well-kept hands, so different from the work-worn hands of the women whom he had known hitherto. She is for us then only a pretty young girl who is rather silent, and we know nothing of what goes on inside her. The first inkling we have of her romanticism is when she expresses the longing to be married by torch-light.[19] Then we begin to wonder what sort of a woman she really is. It is only in chapter six, when she is beginning to be disillusioned with Charles and with married life, that we are told of the dreams which fill her mind.[20]

The characters in *Madame Bovary* are of various kinds, and the method of characterization is different for each. There are the main characters, the secondary characters, the minor characters and the host of little characters who make short and infrequent appearances but are drawn with a few deft and moving traits.

The main characters – Charles and Emma – are drawn fully, in the round, with no irony and always with compassion. The secondary characters – Rodolphe and Léon – are depicted with subtle irony; while the minor characters – Homais and Bournisien – are drawn through the external method of Balzac, and they tend to be caricatures – clever caricatures, it is true.

In the earlier drafts of the book the secondary and minor characters were inclined to be too important, but Flaubert finally diminished their significance so that they should not usurp too much of the interest.

The novel begins and ends with Charles – though Emma

gives her name to the work – and this is deliberate, for she cannot be fully understood unless her influence on Charles is realized; she influences him from beyond the grave, more than when she was alive, so that, after she has died, he tries to become all the things, which, in her lifetime, she had tried, in vain, to make him. In the notes for the novel, Flaubert wrote:[21] 'He becomes like her. He signs promissory notes; he makes debts, in imitation of her. She was corrupting him from beyond the grave. He curled his hair; wore patent-leather boots; and the embroidered collars of the National Guard.' Flaubert understood such a phenomenon, for had he not, himself, been influenced by Alfred Le Poittevin after he had died.

Charles is all the things most abhorred by Flaubert: a bourgeois, heavy, stupid and, in the ordinary sense, boorish, insensitive and lacking in imagination. He had had the greatest difficulty in passing his examinations, so that he had become only an 'officier de santé' and not a doctor. Thus Flaubert is wrong in making him perform an operation without a fully qualified doctor being present, as this was illegal. However, Charles, who was a weak character, easily led by others, may only have been persuaded by Homais for his own ends, for the sake of publicity.

We can understand and sympathize with Emma's irritation, when she reflects:[22] 'La conversation de Charles était plate comme un trottoir de rue, et les idées de tout le monde y défilaient, dans leur costume ordinaire, sans exciter d'émotion, de rire ou de rêverie.' We can only smile ironically when Rodolphe offers to take Emma riding, and Charles writes to him that 'sa femme était à sa disposition, et qu'ils comptaient sur sa complaisance.[23] Also when, after the death of Emma, he hears of the engagement of Léon, and writes to him, saying: 'Comme ma pauvre femme aurait été heureuse.'[24]

Charles may have been the epitome of all the bourgeois characteristics which Flaubert abhorred – indeed his character is mercilessly described – nevertheless he possessed that quality possessed by all Flaubert's main characters, that is of having dreams beyond his powers of attainment. What raised him above the ordinary was his love for Emma. She was his exoticism, his romantic dream, the woman least suited to be his wife, but without her he would have sunk into total materialism. He loved her fine clothes, her delicate hands; he was charmed by her idleness and her useless accomplishments – he paid out hard-earned money on music lessons for her. It is easy to see his uncouth and grotesque side, but the converse has received less attention. In the earlier drafts of the novel this romantic characteristic was more marked than finally, and Charles tended to become somewhat like Frédéric in *L'Éducation Sentimentale*, but Flaubert eventually softened it to make him a better foil to Emma. However, it bursts out when she dies and he wishes her to be buried with all the trappings which would have appealed to her, but which scandalize the neighbours by their extravagance, and his mother when she arrives for the funeral. He cannot trust himself to speak as his sobs are shaking him, but he withdraws to his study and writes out his instructions, which he insists should be obeyed:[25]

Je veux qu'on l'enterre dans sa robe de noces, avec des souliers blancs, une couronne. On lui étalera ses cheveux sur les épaules; trois cerceuils, un de chêne, un d'acajou, un de plomb. Qu'on ne me dise rien. J'aurai de la force. On lui mettra par-dessus tout une grande pièce de velours vert. Je le veux. Faites-le.

There is also his last visit to see Emma, as she lay ready for burial, when the chemist and the priest had fallen asleep, one on each side of the bed:[26]

Charles, entrant, ne les réveilla point. C'était la dernière fois. Il venait lui faire ses adieux.

Les herbes aromatiques fumaient encore, et des tourbillons de vapeur bleuâtre se confondaient au bord de la croisée avec le brouillard qui entrait. Il y avait quelques étoiles et la nuit était douce.

La cire des cierges tombait par grosses larmes sur les draps du lit. Charles les regardait brûler, fatiguant ses yeux contre le rayonnement de leur flamme jaune.

Des moires frissonnaient sur la robe de satin, blanche comme un clair de lune. Emma disparaissait dessous; et il lui semblait que, s'épandant au dehors d'elle-même, elle se perdait confusément dans l'entourage des choses, dans le silence, dans la nuit, dans le vent qui passait, dans les senteurs humides qui montaient.

Puis tout à coup il la voyait dans le jardin de Tostes sur le banc, contre la haie d'épines, ou bien à Rouen, dans les rues, sur le seuil de leur maison, dans la cour des Bertaux. Il entendait encore le rire des garçons en gaieté qui dansaient sous les pommiers; la chambre était pleine du parfum de sa chevelure, et sa robe lui frissonnait dans les bras avec un bruit d'étincelles. C'était la même celle-là!

Il fut longtemps à se rappeler ainsi toutes les félicités disparues, ses attitudes, ses gestes, le timbre de sa voix. Après un désespoir, il en venait un autre, et toujours intarissablement, comme les flots d'une marée qui déborde.

In spite of his ludicrous stupidity and boorishness, his goodness shines through, all the same, so that even Emma recognizes it at the last, when he says to her:[27] 'N'étais-tu pas heureuse? Est-ce ma faute? J'ai fait tout ce que j'ai pu pourtant!' And she answers: 'Oui! ... c'est vrai ... tu es bon, toi!' remembering how the men whom she had loved had finally let her down.

Charles is heartbroken at her death but lives on in a certain degree of happiness with her memory. In the rough notes, he makes the maid wear her dresses, to try to pretend to himself that she is still alive.[28] Then, one day, as he sorts her effects, he comes across Rodolphe's and Léon's letters. After that a decline sets in at this hideous awakening from his dream; he was as incapable as Emma of accepting reality, and he no longer has any desire to live, so that, soon afterwards, he dies. But, before that, he too had his moment of greatness.[29] After he has read the love letters, he meets Rodolphe one day, and they sit together in a café. Rodolphe is condescending because he thinks that Charles is only a common cuckold who does not even know that he was deceived. As they drink their beer together Charles is thinking only of Emma, and how she must have looked at Rodolphe, in a way he knows that he himself has never seen, and he feels a longing to be this man. In the early drafts and notes, Charles asks Rodolphe what they did together, and he persists in his questioning, but the inarticulate silence of the final version is more effective. Suddenly as he meditates, anger surges up in him and he feels that he must strike his rival. Rodolphe senses this instinctively and is afraid, for he does not want a public brawl in a café with the injured husband. But Charles recovers and slumps down in his chair; he has learnt understanding and compassion in his great grief. Suddenly he realized how little we can do and how – as Madame de Lafayette used to say – there are many more unhappy people in the world than truly guilty ones. This was Charles' moment of greatness, which redeemed all, and he came out of the encounter more nobly than did Rodolphe. He did not strike his rival but only said very sadly: 'Non! je ne vous en veux pas' and he repeated, in a dull voice, bowing his head into his hands, 'avec l'accent résigné des douleurs infinies: "Non, je ne vous en veux plus!" ' And he added, the only generalization of his life, which, nevertheless, was one of his great clichés: 'C'est la faute de la fatalité.'

After this there was nothing further for him to do, and he died of a broken heart, for no cause for his death could be found at the autopsy:[30]

Le lendemain, Charles alla s'asseoir sur le banc dans la tonnelle. Des jours passaient par le treillis; les feuilles de vigne dessinaient leurs ombres sur le sable, le jasmin embaumait, le ciel était bleu, des cantharides boudonnaient autour des lis en fleur, et Charles suffoquait comme un adolescent sous les vagues effleuves amoureux qui gonflaient son coeur chagrin.

His little daughter Berthe found him in the evening, dead in the arbour where Emma had so often waited for Rodolphe, and he was clutching in his hands a lock of dark hair.

Emma is a more complex character but fundamentally she is no more intelligent than Charles, though she is more refined and she suffers more fully from the romantic disease. She has no positive character herself, but sees herself in various parts, at different times – as the great lover, the devoted mother, the mystic – and all these parts are built up artificially and are inspired by her reading of romantic novels, so that she is incapable of living life directly, but only through some fanciful idea. From her reading she took only what could be incorporated into her picture of herself. The literature of the time encouraged this concentration on self and she borrowed from it only what could feed this obsession. In her own, more artistic, way she was just as conventional and cliché-ridden as Charles – but they were different clichés. In her dreams Flaubert has shown their shoddiness, as they are made up of 'idées reçues', and they are very different from the more complicated similar dreams of the more sophisticated Frédéric in *L'Éducation Sentimentale*. She is not capable of discrimination and she is taken in by the obviousness of Rodolphe and Léon, whom she considered out of the ordinary.

Her favourite view of herself was as the romantic lover, and we have seen that her first reaction, after she had been seduced by Rodolphe, is delight and pride because she now has joined that family of famous lovers and adulteresses in literature, whom she had hitherto envied. 'J'ai un amant,' she said to her reflection in the mirror. She had now reached the rank which she deserved.[31]

In an earlier version of the novel her mother-in-law says to Charles that she was cut out to be a kept woman in Paris.[32] This would not have seemed to Emma an insult – though it was intended to be so – it would, on the contrary, have delighted her. Homais recognized her unusual talents and the lack of opportunity she enjoyed in the kind of life which fate had decreed for her. 'C'est une femme de grands moyens,' he said, 'qui ne serait pas déplacée dans une sous-préfecture.'[33]

All she could do was dream of other possibilities, those of
the heroes and heroines in the novels she had read, of other
countries which surely must produce happiness, but it only
brought her dissatisfaction:[34]

Elle songeait quelquefois que c'étaient là pourtant les plus
beaux jours de sa vie, la lune de miel, comme on disait. Pour en
goûter la douceur, il eût fallu, sans doute, s'en aller vers ces
plays à noms sonores où les lendemains de mariage ont de plus
suaves paresses! Dans les chaises de poste, sous des stores de soie
bleue, on monte au pas des routes ecarpées, écoutant la chanson
du postillon qui se répète dans la montagne avec les clochettes
des chèvres et le bruit sourd de la cascade. Quand le soleil se
couche, on respire au bord des golfes le parfum des citronniers;
puis, le soir, sur la terrasse des villas, seuls et les doigts con-
fondus, on regarde les étoiles en faisant des projets. Il lui semblait que certains lieux sur la terre devaient produire du
bonheur, comme une plante particulière au sol et qui pousse
mal toute autre part. Que ne pouvait-elle s'accouder sur le balcon
des chalets suisses ou enfermer sa tristesse dans un cottage écos-
sais, avec un mari vêtu d'un habit de velours noir à longues
basques, et qui porte des bottes molles, un chapeau pointu et des
manchettes!
Peut-être aurait-elle souhaité faire à quelqu'un la
confidence de toutes ces choses. Mais comment dîre un in-
saisissable malaise, qui change d'aspect comme les nuées, qui
tourbillonne comme le vent?

Emma had always been pretty and refined, and her father, a
small farmer, gave her a convent boarding-school education
above her station in life. This fed her natural dissatisfaction,
her Bovarysme, so that, when she returned to the farm, she
spent her time dreaming romantic situations for herself. She
married Charles to escape from the narrowness of her life,
and she thought that she could mould him to her wishes,
but he could do nothing but disappoint her, and he could
never respond to her mood:[35]

Si Charles l'avait voulu cependant, s'il s'en fût douté, si son
regard, une seule fois, fût venue à la rencontre de sa pensée, il

lui semblait qu'une abondance subite se serait détachée de son coeur, comme tombe la récolte d'un espalier, quand on y porte la main. Mais, à mesure que se serrait davantage l'intimité de leur vie, un détachement intérieur se faisait qui la déliait de lui.

She could not turn him into anything romantic. His clothes were coarse and common – suitable for the country, he used to say. He did not know how to fence, swim or shoot; and his conversation consisted only of talk about the dull patients whom he had seen during his rounds, and of the prescriptions he had written.

Then once, in view of the coming elections, the local Marquis had given a ball for his electors, to which he had invited Charles and Emma – he had seen her and had thought her very presentable for her station. This taste of luxury gave her still greater dissatisfaction with her commonplace life, and it remained for her as a vision of the kind of existence which she felt was her due. She listened wide-eyed to the conversation; heard the gossip of life at court, and how the father-in-law of her host, the old Duc de Laverdière, was rumoured to have been the lover of Marie Antoinette. There was talk of Italian trips, of all the things which, hitherto, had only been her dreams as she read her romantic novels. It seemed to her that her past life on the farm, and now in her poor little house at Tostes, had never really existed and that this was real life.

She danced with a viscount and this remained forever afterwards as the symbol of her dream, so that she never forgot him. Towards the end of her life, when she had gone to Rouen to try to obtain the money from her lover to save her husband from being sold up, and had failed, then, as she was going to get the coach for her homeward journey, she thought she saw him pass in his carriage and she could not prevent herself from comparing her meeting with him at the ball and her present plight:[36]

Elle s'arrêta pour laisser passer un cheval noir, piaffant dans les brancards d'un tilbury que conduisait un gentleman en fourrure de zibeline. Qui était-ce donc? Elle le connaissait. . . . La voiture s'élança et disparut.

Mais c'était lui, le Vicomte! Elle se détourna; la rue était déserte. Et elle fut si accablée, si triste, qu'elle s'appuya contre un mur pour ne pas tomber.

After they got home from the ball next day, all Charles could say, as they sat down to their evening onion soup, was how good it was to be home again. But Emma knew that a deep gulf had been blasted in her life, in her heart, as if by a raging torrent. As if performing an act of devotion, she put away her beautiful new dress and her dancing slippers, 'dont la semelle s'était jaunie à la cire glassante du parquet. Son coeur était comme eux: au frottement de la richesse, il s'était placé dessus quelque chose qui ne s'effacerait pas.'[37]

The memory of the ball gave Emma such a disgust for the life she was leading that she seemed to fall into a decline, and she persuaded Charles that it was the climate of Tostes which was affecting her, so that he sold up his practice, which was beginning to prosper, and bought another at Yonville l'Abbaye. As she was packing to leave she came upon her wedding bouquet and she burnt it, to indicate a break with the past.

Yonville seemed, at first, to offer more possibilities than Tostes, for she met on arrival, at the inn, the handsome – pretty rather – young lawyer's clerk, who was of the same spiritual family as herself, who had the same romantic dreams, and shared her love of Lamartinian quotations and suggestions.

In an earlier version of the novel Emma and Léon have an affair before he goes to Paris to finish his studies, but, in the final text, their relationship remains platonic and sentimental, and this is more interesting for her psychological development.

When Léon finally went to Paris, Emma felt the same emptiness as after the ball, and she regretted not having yielded to him, for, in absence, he seemed to her everything that she had ever dreamt of and wanted. Again she seemed

to fall into a decline, and she was ready to be vanquished by
the first man who laid siege to her. It was then that Rodolphe appeared on the scene. He came one day to have his
servant bled by Charles. He was temporarily at a loose end
and he noticed the pretty refined wife of the country 'officier
de santé'. He was experienced in matters of the heart, very
different from shy and diffident Léon, and he was prepared
to enjoy himself for a time with the pretty little woman. She,
on her side, was completely overcome by his handsome appearance, by his elegant clothes – his velvet coat, white
riding-breeches, his soft leather boots – clothes she had read
about and had only seen at the ball. His expert words took
her in as they have taken in women since the beginning of
time. She believed him and fell. She had her time of ecstasy
which made her feel that all her life was redeemed, and
joined the company of the great lovers of literature. She felt
that the whole of nature participated in her joy:[38]

Les ombres du soir descendaient; le soleil horizontal, passant
entre les branches, lui éblouissait les yeux. Çà et là, tout autour
d'elle, dans les feuilles ou par terre, des taches lumineuses trem-
blaient, comme si des colibris, en volant, eussent éparpillé leurs
plumes. Le silence était partout; quelque chose de doux semblait
sortir des arbres; elle sentait son coeur, dont les battements rec-
ommençaient, et le sang circuler dans sa chair comme un fleuve
de lait. Alors, elle entendit, tout au loin, au delà bu bois, sur les
autres collines, un cri vague et prolongé, une voix qui se
traînait, et elle l'écoutait silencieusement, se mêlant comme
une musique aux dernières vibrations de ses nerfs émus.

Emma soon became possessive, expecting him to come at the
slightest wish from her; she also went to his house in the
early morning, or late at night, when Charles was out on his
rounds; she even received him in the living-room in her
house, when Charles was asleep in bed upstairs; or he came
late at night to the arbour in the garden, when she made a
sign from the window to call him. She bored him with her
melodramatic romanticism and once, when she heard steps
outside, she said to him: 'As-tu tes pistolets?' and when he

asked, in amazement: 'Pourquoi?' she answered, 'Mais ... pour te défendre.' And he replied: 'Est-ce de ton mari? Ah! le pauvre garçon.'[39]

She, also, was growing too sentimental. She insisted on their exchanging locks of hair; she insisted on his giving her his likeness; and a wedding-ring to symbolize their eternal union. She gave him presents which he did not want and which embarrassed him, amongst others the seal engraved with the words 'Amor nel Cor'.

After six months he began to grow weary of her intensity and kept away from her. She turned then towards her husband and wondered whether she could love him better, but he was very unpromising material. Then Homais, in order to advertise himself, conceived the idea of persuading Charles to perform a difficult and new operation on the hotel servant to cure his club foot. If Charles had been successful at this, if he could have had his name in the papers as someone famous and distinguished, she might have endured him, and even admired him. Charles allowed himself to be persuaded, but he bungled the operation and it failed. Gangrene developed. another doctor had to be called in, and the unfortunate young man lost his leg. Emma had no sympathy with her husband's grief and remorse, and all she felt was the humiliation to herself:[40]

Emma, en face de lui, le regardait; elle ne partageait pas son humiliation, elle en éprouvait une autre; c'était de s'être imaginé qu'un pareil homme pût valoir quelque chose, comme si vingt fois déjà elle n'avait pas suffisamment aperçu sa médiocrité.

Her disappointment in Charles caused her to turn once more to Rodolphe, and they took up their affair again. This time nothing less than an elopement would satisfy her, and Rodolphe, not wishing to go counter to her passionate entreaties, seemed to acquiesce.

She made luxurious preparations for her elopement, in clothes and accessories, but so little practical sense did she possess that she did not realize that she would need a pass-port and that she could obtain this only if she went with her husband to apply for it.

At the last moment, when she was expecting to meet him the following day at a hotel, he let her down, sending her an insincere, romantic farewell letter, with a basket of apricots, telling his servant to say that he had gone away on a journey for a long time. Emma carried the letter away to read it in solitude in the attic. The shock for her was very great, and she was tempted to kill herself, to throw herself out of the window. And she was very conscious of the scene below her:[41]

En face, par-dessus les toits, la pleine campagne s'étalait à perte de vue. En bas, sous elle, la place du village était vide; les cailloux du trottoir scintillaient, les girouettes des maisons se tenaient immobiles; au coin de la rue, il partit d'un étage inférieur une sorte de ronflement à modulations stridentes. C'était Binet qui tournait ...

Le rayon lumineux qui montait d'en bas directement tirait vers l'abîme le poids de son corps. Il lui semblait que le sol de la place oscillant s'élevait le long des murs, et que le plancher s'inclinait par le bout, à la manière d'un vaisseau qui tangue. Elle se tenait tout au bord, presque suspendue, entourée d'un grand espace. Le bleu du ciel l'envahissait, l'air circulait dans sa tête creuse, elle n'avait qu'à céder, qu'à se laisser prendre; et le ronflement du tour ne discontinuait pas, comme une voix furieuse qui l'appelait.

This was Binet at his lathe, working at his never-ending napkin rings. Then she heard the maid calling from below that lunch was ready, and she had to take up ordinary life again.

Then she fell ill and she saw herself romantically dying of love, as one of the heroines in her Romantic novels.[42] She lay on her couch, with flowers and candles around her, with prayers at the foot of the bed. This scene should be placed beside the real death scene, where she is truly dying, of arsenical poisoning, and there is nothing elegant or romantic in that. As we have seen, she asks for a mirror, but she cannot bear the look of her face. There is no possibility of romanticism in this real dying, only stark reality.

She next thought of becoming a saint; she bought a Gothic prie-dieu on which she used to kneel in prayer:[43] 'Elle voulait devenir une sainte. Elle acheta des chapelets, elle porta des amulettes; elle souhaitait avoir dans sa chambre, au chevet de sa couche, un reliquaire enchâssé d'émeraudes, pour le baiser tous les soirs.' Her religious ardour was no more realistic or rational than her romantic love. Instead of seeing herself as one of the great adulter-esses, she saw herself now as one of the great penitents of history:[43] 'Qui, traînant avec tant de majesté la queue chamarrée de leurs longues robes, se retiraient en des soli-tudes pour y répandre aux pieds du Christ toutes les larmes d'un coeur que l'existence blessait.' She gradually recovered, and Charles, on the advice of Homais, to distract her, took tickets for a performance of *Lucia de Lammermoor* by Don-izetti, at the opera house in Rouen. It was not by chance that Flaubert chose this particular opera for her to attend. It was taken from Scott's novel, *The Bride of Lammermoor*, which she had read in her youth, telling of a young woman who had greatly loved handsome young Edgar, but is married, against her will, by a subterfuge, to Henry whom she does not love, and, in a fit of madness, murders her unloved hus-band on her wedding night.

Emma found in the opera all her early dreams and aspir-ations, her despairs and her present plight. She was ready again for experience of love, and it was then that Léon crossed her path once more. During the interval, when Charles goes to the bar to buy drinks, he encounters Léon, who comes back with him to pay his respects to her. It was inevitable that they should become lovers, and it seemed to her a new rebirth.

Emma's affair with Léon had three different phases. At first she had sweet and innocent happiness – innocent, that is, according to her ideas – and it seemed to her perfect. The second stage was violent and sensual, when she greatly

altered, and finally there was the long boredom and lassitude, as adultery took on all the platitudes of marriage,[45]
'elle était aussi dégoûtée de lui qu'il était fatigué d'elle.
Emma retrouvait dans l'adultère toutes les platitudes du
mariage.'

With him she renewed, at first, her Lamartinian experience; as they boated on the river by moonlight, she sings a
line from *Le Lac*, knowing that he will understand and appreciate the reference, and she gazes upwards in the attitude
of Corinne, in the novel by Madame de Staël, in the famous
Romantic picture, *Corinne au Cap Misène*, by François
Gérard.[46] We know that *Corinne* was one of Emma's
favourite books in her youth.

Emma Bovary's two love affairs were in great contrast.
With Rodolphe she had been young and submissive and it
was he who had been the leader. He was an experienced
man of the world, and, when she had tried to take up too
much place in his life, he had separated from her.

Léon was weak and sentimental, and Emma ruled him,
trying to alter him to her wishes. Rodolphe still remained
her ideal, and she tried to make Léon like him in the clothes
he wore and in the furnishing of his apartment.

With him she eventually became very corrupt and sensual, with nothing of the fresh young woman whom Rodolphe had seduced – witness the scenes in the hotel in Rouen
where they used to meet. This change in her was carefully
thought out as we see from Flaubert's notes.[47] In other
notes we are told that during her affair with Rodolphe
Emma had not slept with her husband but that now she
sought him out as if she could not have too much sexual
experience.[48]

This sophisticated corruption ended by frightening Léon,
who had formerly regarded her as an ideal far above him.
He did not understand where she could have gained so
much experience:[49]

Emma revenait à lui plus enflammée, plus avide. Elle se
déshabillait brutalement, arrachant le lacet mince de son corset,

qui sifflait autour de ses hanches comme une couleuvre qui glisse. Elle allait sur la pointe de ses pieds nus regarder encore une fois si la porte était fermée, puis elle faisait d'un seul geste tomber ensemble tous ses vêtements; – et pâle, sans parler, sérieuse, elle s'abattait contre sa poitrine, avec un long frisson.

Cependant il y avait sur ce front couvert de gouttes froides, sur ces lèvres balbutiantes, dans ces prunelles égarées, dans l'étreinte de ces bras, quelque chose d'extrême, de vague et de lugubre, qui semblait à Léon se glisser entre eux, subtilement comme pour les séparer.

She was not any happier; she could never be happy for the dissatisfaction was in herself, firmly rooted in her. Even if her life could have been changed, and made over as she wanted it, she could never have found peace and happiness. Some readers think that if she could have lived in Paris, if she could have eloped with Rodolphe and had a fuller life, she would have found content. She herself certainly imagined that she could have been happy in Paris. After the ball she used to imagine the Viscount there and the kind of life he led. She bought a map of the town, subscribed to several women's papers; and she found out which were the fashionable places to shop at, and to be at during the various seasons of the year:[50]

Paris, plus vague que l'Océan, miroitait donc aux yeux d'Emma dans une atmosphère vermeille. La vie nombreuse qui s'agitait en ce tumulte y'était cependant divisée par parties, clasées en tableux distincts. Emma n'en apercevait que deux ou trois qui lui cachaient tous les autres, et représentaient à eux seuls l'humanité complète. Le monde des ambassadeurs marchait sur des parquets luisants, dans des salons lambrissés de miroirs autour de tables ovales couvertes d'un tapis de velours à crépines d'or. Il y avait là des robes à queue, de grands mystères, des angoisses dissimulées sous des sourires. Venait ensuite la société des duchesses; on y était pâle; on se levait à quatre heures; les femmes, pauvres anges! portaient du point d'Angleterre au bas de leur jupon, et les hommes, capacités méconnues sous des dehors futiles, crevaient leurs chevaux par partie de plaisir, allaient passer à Bade la saison d'été, et, vers la quarantaine enfin, épousaient des héritières. Dans les cabinets des restaurants où l'on soupe après minuit, riait, à la clarté des bougies, la foule bigarrée des gens de lettres et des actrices. Ils étaient, ceux-là, prodigues comme des rois, pleins d'ambitions idéales et de délires fantastiques. C'était une existence au-dessus des autres, entre ciel et terre, dans les orages, quelque chose de sublime.

Flaubert had first intended a trip to Paris for Emma, after her disappointment with Rodolphe.[51] But he eventually took it out, probably believing that it would not make any difference to her state, and that the provincial milieu showed up her dissatisfaction to better advantage. As she is depicted it would have been impossible for her to find happiness anywhere.

Faguet said that the misfortune of Madame Bovary came from the fact that she had not married Homais.[52] Although he might have given her a better life than Charles had been able to achieve, although she might have appreciated his ambitions and furthered them, and his grandiloquent language, it is hard to believe that he would have satisfied her romantic cravings or her conviction of what was due to her.

Emma Bovary's last conscious act, as we have seen, was a passionate reiteration of her belief in love, and her conviction of the vanity of life if its image is destroyed. In the midst of all her falseness and contradictions, that is Emma at her most characteristic.

The main characters are drawn, so to speak, in the round, from the inside out, with understanding and compassion, and Flaubert does not hold them up to ridicule, nor treat them with satire. He does not make fun of them – not even of Charles. The secondary characters, Rodolphe and Léon, are treated with subtle irony and he loses no occasion of mocking at them. The beginning of the seduction of Emma by Rodolphe, at the agricultural show, is a masterpiece in which the irony is so subtle as to be almost invisible, except to the experienced and clever. He utters the emotional platitudes which the attractive and expert seducer has used since the beginning of time, which the women have always believed, and Emma was lost.[53] Trying to rouse her compassion, he said:[54] 'Que de fois, à la vue d'un cimetière au clair de lune, je me suis demandé si je ne ferais pas mieux d'aller rejoindre ceux qui sont à dormir.' There is also the scene, with more obvious irony, when he writes the seemingly touching letter, to break off his relationship with her, and sprinkles what he intends her to believe are tears, from his glass of water, on the pages.[55] She was indeed moved by it:[56] 'Oh! ta lettre, ta lettre! m'a déchiré le coeur,' she said to him later. Flaubert, as we see from his notes, intended Rodolphe to be coarse and insensitive, in spite of his breeding, charm and sophistication, and all his sympathy goes out to Emma.

Léon is also depicted ironically, and Flaubert was afraid that his readers might not understand his subtlety, might take it seriously. Writing to Louise Colet, he said:[57]

I'm composing a conversation between a young man and a young woman on literature, the sea, the mountains, music, in fact all the poetic subjects. One might take it seriously and yet it is intended to be grotesque. It will be the first time, I believe, that one will see a book making fun of its leading lady and juvenile lead. The irony doesn't diminish the pathos, on the contrary it enhances it.

The scene occurs when Charles and Emma arrive at Yonville, and meet Léon for the first time at the inn, and she is charmed by his romantic appearance and poetic conversation, which expresses preoccupations in harmony with her own:[58]

— Avez-vous, du moins, quelques promenades dans les environs? continuait Mme Bovary parlant au jeune homme.

— Oh! fort peu, répondit-il. Il y a un endroit que l'on nomme la Pâture, je vais là, et j'y reste avec un livre, à regarder le soleil couchant.

— Je ne trouve rien d'admirable comme les soleils couchants, reprit-elle, mais au bord de la mer surtout.

– Oh! j'adore le mer, dit M. Léon.

– Et puis ne vous semble-t-il pas, répliqua Mme Bovary, que l'esprit vogue plus librement sur cette étendue sans limites, dont la contemplation vous élève l'âme et donne des idées d'infini, d'idéal.

– Il est de même des paysages de montagne, reprit Léon. J'ai un cousin qui a voyagé en Suisse l'année dernière, et qui me disait qu'on ne peut se figurer la poésie des lacs, le charme des cascades, l'effet gigantesque des glaciers. On voir des pins d'une grandeur incroyable, en travers des torrents, des cabanes suspendues sur des précipices, et, à mille pieds sous vous, des vallées entières quand les nuages s'entr'ouvrent. Ces spectacles doivent enthousiasmer, disposer à la prière, à l'extase! Aussi je ne m'étonne plus de ce musicien célèbre qui, pour exciter mieux son imagination, avait coutume d'aller jouer du piano devant un site imposant.

Neither of them realized the grotesqueness of a musician having a piano handy at the edge of a precipice. This passage contains all the platitudes of Romantic inspiration, especially of the poetry of Lamartine, and this poet was, in fact, the favourite author of both Emma and Léon.

Léon was weak and easily led, and Emma tried to turn him into someone from her Romantic reading. She suggested what kind of clothes he should wear, how he should dress his hair and the cut of his beard; what furnishings he should have in his apartment – this was when they became lovers on their second encounter. He found her difficult to live up to and, when she insisted that he should compose poems in her honour, he could not get beyond the first line, and was obliged to copy a sonnet from a *keepsake*.[59] As Flaubert said: 'Il ne discutait pas ses idées; il acceptait tous ses goûts; il devenait sa maîtresse plutôt qu'elle n'était la sienne.'

Then they both began to grow tired of each other but did not know how to separate. Emma continued to write long love letters to him, because it was in the tradition, but it was someone else whom she saw as she wrote, some ideal imagined man who became more real than Léon:[60]

Elle n'en continuait pas moins à lui écrire des lettres amoureuses, en vertu de cette idée qu'une femme doit toujours écrire à son amant.

Mais, en écrivant, elle percevait un autre homme, un fantôme fait de ses plus ardents souvenirs, de ses lectures les plus belles, de ses convoitises les plus fortes; et il devenait à la fin si véritable, et accessible, qu'elle en palpitait émerveillée, sans pouvoir néanmoins le nettement imaginer, tant il se perdait, comme un dieu, sous l'abondance de ses attributs. Il habitait la contrée bleuâtre où les échelles de soie se balancent à des balcons, sous le souffle des fleurs, dans la clarté de la lune. Elle le sentait près d'elle, il allait venir et l'enlèverait tout entière dans un baiser.

Neither Rodolphe nor Léon went to Emma's funeral, nor did they send wreaths, and this shows hardness and aridity of heart in both of them. She was the wife of the local 'officier de santé' and both had received hospitality from the hand of the bereaved husband, even if he had not known their true relationship with her. They could, at least, and should, have sent flowers, and it is strange that they did not, considering the important part played by floral tributes in French life. Rodolphe had spent the day out shooting, had gone home to his manor house, tired out, in the evening, and had slept peacefully the whole night through. Léon, also in his lodgings, had slept soundly. Neither had given a thought to the woman to whom each had meant, for a time, the whole of life.

Next there are the minor characters, who are depicted from the outside, in the external method of Balzac, and they tend to be caricatures, but in them is seen Flaubert's talent for the grotesque. At first these minor characters tended to usurp too much space in the novel, because he enjoyed so much portraying them, and could pour into them his bile and his anger at their ideas and values. He realized, however, the artistic mistake in giving them too much importance and, in the final version, he curtailed them.

There is Binet, endlessly turning out napkin rings on his lathe. Father Bournisien, with his parody of religious advice

and comfort; and especially Homais, the greatest caricature
of all. Whenever he appears on the stage there are always
scenes of the highest comedy, and we realize how much
Flaubert must have enjoyed depicting him.

Homais is a descendant of Henri Monnier's Joseph Prudhomme, typical of the ignorant, self-confident, anti-clerical
'esprit fort' of the day; he is a true representative of the
lower-middle-class bursting upwards, after the Revolution of
1830, semi-educated, with little understanding of what true
learning is, but whose grandiloquent clichés, taken largely
from eighteenth-century philosophers, are, nevertheless, a
tribute to learning:[61]

– Taisez-vous donc, monsieur Homais, vous êtes un impie!
vous n'avez pas de religion!

Le pharmacien répondit:

– J'ai une religion, ma religion, et même j'en ai plus qu'eux
tous, avec leurs mômeries, et leurs jongleries! J'adore Dieu, au
contraire! Je crois en l'Être Suprême, à un Créateur, quelqu'il
soit, peu m'importe, qui nous a placés ici-bas pour y remplir nos
devoirs de citoyen et de père de famille; mais je n'ai pas besoin
d'aller, dans une église, baiser des plats d'argent, et engraisser de
ma poche un tas de farceurs qui se nourrissent mieux que nous!
Car on peut l'honorer aussi bien dans un bois, dans un champ,
ou même contemplant la voûte éthérée, comme les anciens.
Mon Dieu à moi, c'est le Dieu de Socrate, de Franklin, de Voltaire et de Béranger! Je suis pour *La Profession de foi du Vicaire
savoyard* et les immortels principes de 89! Aussi je n'admets pas
un bonhomme de bon Dieu qui se promène dans son parterre, la
canne à la main, loge ses amis dans le ventre des baleines, meurt
en poussant un cri, et ressuscite au bout de trois jours: choses
absurdes en elles-mêmes et complètement opposées, d'ailleurs, à
toutes les lois de la physique; ce qui nous démontre, en passant,
que les prêtres ont toujours croupi, dans une ignorance turpide,
où ils s'efforcent d'engloutir avec eux les populations.

Then Homais looked round for applause, forgetting that he
was not speaking in the municipal council, but only at the
inn where no one was listening to him for they had heard it
all before. But he could never resist the temptation of using

his grandiloquent vocabulary, or his pompous exhibitionism, even on the most inopportune occasions, as when
he tried to impress Dr Larivière with his superior knowledge
when the latter had been called in, at the last moment, in a
vain attempt to save the dying Emma:[62]

> Il jugea bon, après les premiers morceaux, de fournir quelques
> détails sur la catastrophe:
> – Nous avons eu d'abord un sentiment de siccité au pharynx,
> puis des douleurs intolérables à l'épigastre, superpurgation,
> coma.
> – Comment s'est-elle donc empoisonnée?
> – Je l'ignore docteur, et même je ne sais pas trop où elle a pu
> se procurer cet acide arsénieux. . . .
> – J'ai voulu, docteur, tenter une analyse, et *primo*, j'ai
> délicatement introduit dans un tube. . . .
> – Il aurait mieux valu, dit le chirurgien, lui introduire vos
> doigts dans la gorge. . . .
> Homais s'épanouissait dans son orgueil d'amphitryon, et
> l'affligeante idée de Bovary contribuait, vaguement à son plaisir,
> par un retour égoïste qu'il faisait sur lui-même. Puis la présence
> du docteur le transportait. Il étalait son érudition, il citait pêle-
> mêle les cantharides, l'upas, le mancenillier, la vipère.

His love of grand language gave him the ambition of shining in literature as well as in what he would have called his
science, witness the article, describing the agricultural show,
which he published in the local paper, *Le Fanal de Rouen*,
which is a collection of wittily chosen noble platitudes:[63]
'Pourquoi ces festons, ces fleurs, ces guirlandes? Où courait
cette foule, comme les flots d'une mer en furie, sous les torrents d'un soleil tropical qui répandait sa chaleur sur nos
guérets?' The article ends with a gibe at the clergy which, as
a matter of fact, consisted only of Father Bournisien:[64] 'On
y a seulement remarqué l'absence du clergé. Sans doutes les
sacristes entendent le progrès d'une autre manière. Libre à
vous messieurs de Loyola!' By dint of strenuous effort
Homais eventually managed to make himself the most
important citizen in Yonville – and most talked of anyway.

His ambition grew and, in order to advance his interests, he, the former republican and democrat, paid court to the authorities and compared the King, Louis-Philippe, to Henri IV.[65]

With importance and power he became snobbish and did not allow his children to consort with little Berthe Bovary, after the death of her mother, on account of the differences in their present social position.

His great ambition was eventually to be decorated and he brought his qualifications to the knowledge of the authorities. In fact if anyone in the district was to be elevated it would certainly have been he for he was the best known citizen, the one who most pushed himself forward. Every day he looked in the papers for news of his award, but in vain. In the end, in desperation, he planned a flower-bed, in his garden, to represent the cross of the Légion d'Honneur:[66]

Enfin, n'y tenant plus, il fit dessiner dans son jardin un gazon figurant l'étoile de l'honneur, avec deux petits tordillons d'herbe qui partaient du sommet pour imiter le ruban. Il se promenait autour, les bras croisés, en méditant sur l'ineptie du gouvernement et l'ingratitude des hommes.

Finally his efforts were rewarded, he reached his ambition and was decorated. The last line of the novel states: 'Il vient de recevoir la croix d'honneur.'

In the notes of the novel, at the Municipal Library in Rouen, there is the sketch for an *Épilogue* which shows Homais, after he has obtained his award, trying on his decoration before a mirror, and dreaming of all the further promotions which will be conferred on him. He saw himself as becoming 'officier', then 'commandeur', and finally 'Grande Croix'. 'Homais s'absorbait dans le soleil d'Austerlitz.'[67]

Flaubert was wise to omit this *Épilogue*, thinking, probably rightly, that it went too far in the matter of the grotesque.

We have seen that the kindest portraits are in the small

characters who play little part in the action, and merely pass on occasions across the stage – such characters as Dr Larivière; the peasant woman, Catherine Leroux; Emma's father, Rouault; and especially little Justin, who had loved Emma so greatly, in his boy's way, from a distance, so that he was heartbroken at her death. As he depicted him Flaubert must have remembered his own feelings in front of Élisa Schlésinger, when he was the same age as Justin, with the same shyness and idealism.

Martin Turnell considers that the minor characters, such as Homais and Bournisien, are the successful ones, and not the main characters.[68] He declares: 'They are successful because there is identity between the character and the symbol. Bournisien stands for the inadequacy of the rural clergy in Normandy, as Homais stands for the limitations of progressive thought.' Flaubert would have denied that they stood for anything of the kind. He was not concerned with the inadequacies of the rural clergy, nor with the limitations of progressive thought. If he shows anything in Homais it is the grotesqueness of the 'idées reçues', the clichés, of whatever kind they might be, and he makes grim comedy with them.

Few nowadays would agree with Martin Turnell as he declares further:[69] 'When he turns from his successful minor characters to his principals, his hand falters.' Many on the contrary believe that, in Emma Bovary, Flaubert has created one of the greatest – best drawn – women characters in French literature – perhaps in any literature – and whether we like or admire her has nothing to do with the case. What is certain is that he has succeeded in making her arouse our sympathy and compassion.

What we find in Flaubert, in his characterization, is sorrow and pity for man, for his condition; not criticism of what he is or does, but compassion for what he is called upon to endure.

Flaubert's Aesthetic
Doctrine

FLAUBERT'S first novel was published when he was thirty-five, after he had been writing for about twenty-five years. As he wrote this first novel which he was willing to print, he crystallized his literary doctrine and his method of composition, which he altered little thereafter, except in increased mastery and quintessence of vision.

Few writers have written so much about the craft and art of fiction as Flaubert, and we can follow his arguments on the subject with himself, in his correspondence; his experiments and alterations; his solution of the problems which preoccupied him. There are also nearly four thousand pages of scenarios, plans and rough notes which are preserved in the Municipal Library at Rouen.

Flaubert was one of the few prose writers of the middle of the nineteenth century in France who were interested in the ideals of the Art for Art's Sake Movement, and followed its precepts. Otherwise most of them belonged to the Realist persuasion and had no concern for artistic values – indeed they thought that fine writing was an affectation. Flaubert, as we have seen, disliked Realism as it was understood by the School. 'Please note', he wrote to George Sand,[1] 'that I loathe what is generally called *realism*.'

He believed that the Realists perceived only the exterior of things and did not concern themselves with the interior; while he considered that what an external phenomenon meant was more important than its appearance. He thought that the Realists merely copied without choice, as a photograph registers things, and he had the same contempt for photography as Baudelaire had.[2] The camera is incapable of choice, and he considered that the value of an artist lay in his power of choice. Writing to Huysmans, he said:[3] 'Art is not reality. Whatever one may do, one is obliged to choose amongst the elements which it provides.'

This did not mean that he disliked reality or was unaware of it, for he was, in fact, a very careful observer of it; he liked humble reality and was always very much moved by it – we have seen that in his travel notes on his journey to the East, and we know how much Louise Colet was disgusted by his description of it. He always saw the touching side of poor reality, especially when seen against the background of the complacent and self-satisfied bourgeois – we have seen that in connection with the small and humble characters in *Madame Bovary*, such as Catherine Leroux. He possessed great violence and intensity of feeling so that his encounters with reality were always deeply burnt into his being. Writing to Louise Colet, he said that nothing was ever wiped from his memory.[4] One must feel deeply, he thought, then reflect on it in tranquillity, to try to make it permanent and universal, to see its profound significance. He could not bear that deep emotion should ever evaporate and be lost forever, and that was why he described, in his letters to Maxime Du Camp, the death and funeral of his beloved sister and of his dearest friend Alfred Le Poittevin.

Art for him was the power of communicating his passionate experience to his readers.

He was one of the few prose writers of the middle of the nineteenth century in France to be concerned with beauty, to think that the aim of the novel should be the creation of beauty. Before him novelists had written well if they happened to write well – like Mérimée – but no one considered it adverse criticism to say of Balzac that his style was clumsy and his planning confused. Flaubert said of him: 'What a man Balzac would have been if only he'd known how to write!'[5]

This admiration for beauty did not, however, imply writing only about so-called beautiful subjects – which was the

aim of the Art for Art's Sake Movement. Writing to Louise
Colet, he said:[6] 'It is on that account that there are neither
beautiful nor ugly subjects, and one could state, as an axiom,
from the point of view of art, pure Art, that there is none,
style alone being an absolute way of seeing things.'

Poetry he thought – and by poetry he meant beauty –
could arise from anything:[7]

Let us try to see things as they are, and not wish to be wiser
than God. Formerly they thought that only the cane could produce sugar; one can get it now from almost anything. It is the
same with poetry. Let us extract it from anything, for it exists in
everything and everywhere; there isn't a single atom but what
contains thought; and let us grow accustomed to considering the
world as a work of art, of which we must reproduce the methods
in our works.

And again:[8]

There aren't in literature beautiful subjects of art, and Yvetot
is as good as Constantinople, and so one can write 'sur n'importe
quoi aussi bien que sur quoi que ce soit'. *The artist must raise
everything up*. He is like a pump, he has in him a big tube which
penetrates down into the heart of things, into the deepest layers.
He draws it out and makes burst out into the full sunlight, in
enormous sheaves of light, what was hidden underground and
was invisible.

Beauty was not in the subject but in what the artist
brought to it. He would have agreed with Baudelaire who
said, addressing the town of Paris: 'Tu m'as donné ta boue et
j'en ai fait de l'or.'[9]

Although Flaubert hated Realism – the realism of the
Realists, not reality – he did not in maturity like Romanticism any better, and saw the danger of it.

The question has often been asked whether Flaubert was a
Romantic or a Realist. Émile Faguet enunciated the theory
of the two warring brothers to him – 'les deux frères
ennemis' – struggling for ascendancy, sometimes one, sometimes the other, being victorious.[10] The argument is not

very profitable, and many books have been written on the Classicism of the Romantics; the Romanticism of the Classicists; the Realism of the Romantics; the Romanticism of the Realists. It generally happens that the richly gifted artists, creatively, tend, by their very nature, to be Romantics, otherwise they would not feel the overwhelming urge to create, for creation is fundamentally a Romantic activity in all forms of life. It depends, however, on the age in which the artist is creating whether the form of the creation will be objective or subjective – that is, Classical or Romantic. Certain writers have had the good fortune to live in an age which exactly suited their kind of genius; but others have had to do violence to themselves to fit in with the ideals of their age. Heredia was a poet who was thus lucky to be writing at the time of the Parnassian School, and he would not have felt at home if he had been writing during the Romantic Movement. Vigny, on the other hand, felt uncomfortable and out of place amongst the Romantics and he would have been happier amongst the poets of the Art for Art's Sake Movement, when it was unfashionable to write about oneself. He used to declare, very differently from what his contemporaries used to say: 'Le mot de la langue le plus difficile à prononcer et à placer convenablement, c'est *moi.*'[11]

It seems to be an established fact that a writer who is a novelist or a dramatist is all the better for Classical discipline. Flaubert might have been happier, and have composed more fluently, had he written at the height of the Romantic Movement, but his work might then not have stood the test of time, and he would probably not have produced the novels which have not dated. He might merely have become another Quinet.

He did violence to himself to reach discipline and forgetfulness of self. By nature he possessed great fluency – to realize this, one has only to read the immensely long letters, which he wrote to Louise Colet, mostly written in the early hours of the morning after a heavy night of composition –

but he learnt to restrain this natural flow and desire for self-expression, for the sake of the perfection of the finished work of art.

It must also be remembered that, after 1850, it was impossible for a serious writer to remain a Romantic writer, for the products of the movement had become perfectly discredited and out-worn and were only imitated by the poorest writers. Louis Bouilhet and Maxime Du Camp, as secondary writers, understood this – it is often thus with minor writers, for they can see more clearly what is happening, as they are not blinded by the radiance of vision – and they eradicated in Flaubert his Romanticism of form.

Those who, like Faguet, talk of the Romanticism of Flaubert, base their opinion largely on his so-called exotic and oriental themes. But they forget that Romanticism does not consist in the choice of subject, but only in the use made of it. Exoticism is not exclusively – nor even largely – a Romantic topic. When one has mentioned *Les Orientales* of Victor Hugo one has almost shot one's bolt and that work, in any case, is the least Romantic of Hugo's works, and it would not have been out of place amongst the writings of the Parnassian School – it was indeed greatly admired by the poets of that School. There is, in fact, far more exoticism amongst the poets of the Art for Art's Sake Movement than there ever was amongst the Romantics – witness the poetry of Leconte de Lisle and Heredia. Their exoticism was, however, treated objectively.

Flaubert's attitude to composition was the same whether he was writing on a modern, oriental or historical theme. He was a Romantic by nature, but a Realist or a Classicist by discipline. *Salammbô* is treated with the same objectivity as *Madame Bovary* – indeed, paradoxical as this may seem, it is a more objective and realistic work, for he had become more expert and more practised in his ideals as a writer in his second book than in his first, and his technique was more sure. There are, in *Madame Bovary*, many more traces of Romanticism in style, not merely where the author is evoking the feelings of his heroine, but also when he is writing in his own person.

Flaubert was, however, a man of many facets, and there was some clash of temperament in him; there were in him 'deux frères ennemis', but not between the Classicist or Realist and the Romantic. He himself talked of the 'deux bonshommes distincts' in himself,[12] but these were the creator, and the scholar or scientist. It might be claimed that he had been bred for science – it has been seen that he had scientific blood on both sides of his family – and he had a burning passion for the pursuit of learning and truth. His researches were always vastly in excess of what was needed for the mere documentation of his books, and were undertaken largely for themselves alone. To realize this one need only compare his documentation with that of Victor Hugo, who had a totally unscholarly and unscientific mind; he collected and preserved only what he needed for his immediate purpose – all the rest he ignored or forgot – and he did not mind whether his material was accurate or not so long as it was highly coloured and vivid. Hugo was a pure creator with no vestige of the scholar or the scientist in his make-up; and critics have had a fine time pointing out all his errors. But Flaubert, if he had not been a great creative artist, could easily have become a great scholar, for he had the necessary selfless devotion to research. Had he possessed only his passion for learning, or had he been only a creator, there would have been no clash in him, but the two enemy brothers were the scholar and the creator, and each held the other back.

Like all great psychologists, interested in the workings of the human mind, Flaubert would have liked, in his novel, to dispense with the tyranny of plot, which is an artificial thing, and to write about nothing. This was the dream also of Racine, as he declares in the Preface to his play *Bérénice*. Flaubert chose the most ordinary subject he could find, which was almost devoid of plot. He said to Louise Colet:[13]

What seems to me beautiful, and what I would like to achieve is a book about nothing, a book with no external links, which would stand by itself by the internal force of its style, as the earth, without being supported, remains in the air, a book which had almost no subject, or at least where the subject was almost invisible, if that were possible. The most beautiful works are those which have least material.

All his books – all those which he consented to publish – were written with great pain and tribulation, whatever the subject. He imagined that when he had finished *Madame Bovary* he would write *Salammbô* with ease and pleasure, but it took him the same amount of time – almost five years – and cost him the same blood, sweat and tears. This was due to his high ideal of art. He was first and foremost an artist and he had a strong feeling for the structure and composition of his novels.

Flaubert thought that the novel should have a strict and well-jointed plan, to which nothing could be added and from which nothing could be deducted without endangering the structure. 'When I change a word,' he said,[14] 'I must sometimes upset several pages.' His scheme was so clear, while he was writing, that he planned beforehand how many pages he could allot to each episode. 'My book', he wrote,[15] 'will be 450 to 480 pages long and I am now only at page 204.' And again: 'My conclusion, which will be the account of the death of my little woman, her funeral and the sadness of the husband, will be sixty pages at least. That means that I've left, for the body of the action, 120 to 160 pages at most.'

His plan was as strict as that of a five-act play, and he sacrificed everything which would take from its unity. There are very few of the literary '*hors d'oeuvre*', interesting in themselves, found in such writers as the Goncourt brothers. He removed all these from earlier versions of the novel – as, for instance, long passages concerning Bovary's school days; or the long digression describing the strange toy which Charles had wanted to give the Homais children as an expression of gratitude for the chemist's care of Emma during her illness. He intended nothing to be left in the novel, except what would contribute to the whole, to the central plan. He said to Sainte-Beuve, discussing *Salammbô*, but it would be as true of *Madame Bovary*:[16] 'There is not in my whole book one single separate and gratuitous description; all of them are useful to my characters, and have an immediate or distant influence on the action.'

He considered that there should be complete objectivity of approach on the part of the novelist, who was not to use his work as a vessel to contain his emotion and his confidences – as was common with the Romantic writers. Writing to Louise Colet, he said:[17] 'I don't want to consider Art as a safety-valve (a "déversoir" he called it), a chamber pot':

... No! poetry must not be the foam of the heart. That isn't serious or right. Your child deserves a better fate than to be shown off in verse between the covers of a book, to be called an angel etc. All that is romantic literature, more or less well written, but which has the same fault, of a weak foundation. One can no longer permit oneself these whims, not even for fun. The *sentimental personality* will be what will later cause a large part of contemporary literature to be condemned as puerile and foolish. How much sentiment, how much sentiment, how much fondness, how many tears!

He is here attacking the personal outpourings of the Lamartines and Mussets which had been copied *ad nauseam* by their successors. It was the natural reaction of the Art for Art's Sake Movement against the excessive subjective manifestations of its Romantic predecessors. He said:[18]

The public must know nothing about us. It must not take its enjoyment from our eyes, our hair, or our loves. ... It's enough to give it our heart, which we've diluted in ink without its being aware of the fact. Personal prostitution in art revolts me.

The author must be completely absent from his work, and it should be no more possible to know what he thinks of his creations than to know what God thinks of his own.[19] 'The author, in his work, must be like God in the universe, present everywhere but visible nowhere.' And again:[20] 'He must imitate God in the midst of his creation, that is to say act and remain silent – "faire et se taire".'

The author also must not express his personal opinion on anything; not on his characters nor on the meaning of the works; he must never take sides, nor ever give any solution or conclusion, that must arise quite naturally out of the work itself:[21]

I consider that the novelist *hasn't the right to express his opinion* on anything. Has God ever given his opinion on anything? That is why, although I've a fair amount of things which are choking me, and which I'd like to spit out, I swallow them down. Indeed, what is the point of saying them? Anybody is more interesting than M. Gustave Flaubert, because he's more *general* and so more typical.

And again:[22] 'I don't want there to be, in my book ... one single observation by the author.'

Many readers have found this disconcerting, for they like to be given a lead, to be shown who is worthy of admiration, of whom the author himself approves. But Flaubert refuses to help him and to take up any moral attitude. He considered that the reader should be allowed to make up his own mind. If the author has done his work properly, then the thought should come through without any underlining:[23]

As for showing my personal opinion of the people I put on the stage. No! no! a thousand times no! I don't consider that I've any right to do so. If the reader doesn't draw from a book the moral which it must contain, it is because the reader is a fool, or the book is *false* from the point of view of truth. For, as long as a thing is true it's good. Obscene books aren't even immoral, because they lack truth. Life isn't like that!

The author, according to Flaubert, must not be pledged to any particular idea or creed, any particular belief; he must not be, as they say today, 'engagé'. This has been one of the reasons for his lack of popularity during the period since the 1930s when the writers were very much concerned with the affairs of the age and determined to remedy them. This was true of the writings of most of the poets at the time.

Art must be as impersonal as a science, he thought, and science does not take sides, nor pronounce on the morality of its discoveries.

In the mid-nineteenth century the authors, especially the Realists, talked a great deal about using science as an ally and an aid. But they understood science very differently from the way that Flaubert understood it. They used the jargon of science, the vocabulary, the external details. The Goncourt brothers, in their novels, used science very much in the same way as the Romantics had used history, that is to say as local colour, to add vividness to their narrative, but never with accuracy. In *Renée Mauperin* it is impossible to state scientifically what the heroine dies of. The authors wanted her to die romantically and movingly on the stage and, in fact, she dies, most unscientifically, of a nineteenth-century decline, on a sofa. Flaubert would have known exactly what she had died of, her symptoms and their effect on her actions and character. Although he did not use scientific jargon in the same way, he thought nevertheless that the method of the novelist should be scientific, in the true sense; that characters should be treated with the objective impartiality of science, with its lack of preconceived ideas and prejudices. He complained that Lamartine did not possess what he called 'le coup d'oeil médical' and that this had made his novel, *Graziella*, completely false.[24]

We do not find in Flaubert's novels any arbitrary statement about his characters, who are allowed to develop naturally before our eyes, from the early embryo to their final state; all the changes are shown as inevitable, given the characters as depicted. His own later criticism of his first *Éducation Sentimentale* was that the first causes had been shown and also the final results, but not what he called 'l'enchaînement', that is the path taken to reach the final point. He said that the book needed to be rewritten in order to add what was lacking:[25]

To show how, inevitably, the same trunk must have divided in two; that is to say how such and such an action has caused such and such a result in a character, rather than another. The causes are shown, the results also, but the logical sequence, 'l'enchaînement', from the cause to the effect, has not been demonstrated. That is the great fault of the book.

Sometimes, even as late as *Madame Bovary*, the 'enchaînement' is clumsily and inexpertly achieved, and seems somewhat forced. For instance, when he wants Emma, at a later point, to know where the arsenic is kept, in the chemist's shop, he prepares this many pages beforehand, and there is a great deal of comic palaver – amusing in itself – when Homais pompously scolds Justin for his carelessness with regard to the key of the 'Capharnaum' where the poison is kept. The conversation is very lengthy and every point is made several times. Emma is present so that she cannot fail to know, when the occasion arises, where to find the arsenic. At the time the reader wonders why so much effort is expended on this unimportant point, to make sure that no one fails to notice the whereabouts of the poison. It is only when she suddenly commits suicide that one realizes the point of the elaborate preparation. In his later novels the 'enchaînement' is better disguised and more subtly achieved.

We have seen that Flaubert's aim was to paint for eternity what would not pass, but would remain true always, and fit in with any age and any locality. He did not want to depict any special characteristics of landscape, and he deliberately chose, for *Madame Bovary*, a vague locality with no particular features, which could be anywhere in France, or anywhere else – that is, of course, north of the Loire; he did not wish to be a regional writer. He said in his novel:[26] 'On est ici, sur les confins de la Normandie, de la Picardie, et de l'Ile de France, contrée bâtarde où le langage est sans accentuation comme le pays sans caractère.' He did not want to copy any definite or known landscape or district. The efforts which critics have made to identify the locality and its feat-

ures have, therefore, been pointless – pictures of Bovary's
house and garden; of Homais' shop; of Rodolphe's manor
house have even been published. Pierre Lambert declares
that he was born in Charles Bovary's house at Tostes.[27] He
was the son of the notary who had the deeds of a farm which
Dr Flaubert once bought in the district, and which Lambert
alleges is the farm of Emma's father. He does, however,
admit that Flaubert must have made many changes in his
description of the house. Although things he knew might be
the starting point of his work, he did not want to copy accurately and, writing to George Sand, he said:[28] 'I consider of
very secondary importance technical details, local information, in fact the historical and exact side of things.' This
was in great contrast with the excessive amount of local and
scientific detail to be found in the writings of his contemporaries.

Because he did not want anything to be too precise, to be
tied down by particular external characteristics, he refused
to allow the book to be illustrated:[29]

Never, as long as I live, shall I allow myself to be illustrated!
the most beautiful literary description is destroyed by the most
wretched drawing. As soon as a type is fixed by the pencil it loses
generality, that harmony with a thousand known objects, which
makes the reader exclaim: 'I've seen that' or 'that must be so'. A
woman who is drawn is like one woman, that's all. The idea is
then fixed, closed, complete and all writing is then useless; whilst
a woman who is described in writing makes one dream of a thousand women. Thus, this being a question of aesthetics, I absolutely refuse any sort of illustration.

When his publisher tried to insist on having a novel of his
illustrated he said:[30]

The persistence with which Lévy insists on demanding
illustrations puts me into a rage impossible to describe. . . . There
was no point in expending so much art, in an effort to leave
everything vague, for an old fool to come along and destroy my
dream with his inept precision.

He must have weakened later, for an illustrated edition of *Madame Bovary* was, in fact, published by Lemerre in 1874, though Flaubert said that the illustrations had as much connection with the book as with the moon.[31]

Flaubert always insisted that it was style which gave value and beauty to a work of art, but, when he talked of style, he did not only mean beauty and harmony of language, and musicality of phrase. Critics have often made the mistake of merely talking of his language when discussing his style. Style for him was a way of seeing things, and it was closely allied to inspiration, forming one unity with it:[32]

You tell me that I pay too much attention to form. Alas! it is like the body and soul; form and the idea, for me, are one and the same thing, and I don't know what the one is without the other. The more beautiful an idea is, the more melodious is the language, make no mistake about that. Precision in thought makes (and is in itself) that of the expression.

Style and thought were then only two facets of the same essence, the two sides of the same medal.

Flaubert did not consider that style consisted solely in beautiful language and harmonious periods, but that a fine style was part of fine vision. Like the Symbolists after him he believed that there was only one way of saying a thing and that was the perfect way, which exactly fitted the subject as the skin fits the body. When the perfect expression is found – and the artist always knows it – there is perfect fusion, as when the two parts of an electric machine meet, and then there is light, but only if the two fit perfectly.

Maupassant quotes him as saying:[33]

Whatever may be the thing that one wants to express, there is only one word to express it, only one verb to animate it, only one adjective to qualify it. One must then look for them until one finds them: that word, that adjective, that verb, and never be satisfied with the approximate.

It would be impossible, he thought, to render the vision without the perfection of expression which fitted it. He also considered that the style should exactly suit the subject, that each theme demanded its own style, and that it should not be something which was idiosyncratic to the author himself, something which was stamped with his own hall-mark. Maupassant said of him:[34]

He did not think of styles as a series of particular moulds, each of which belonged to one writer, and into which he poured all his thoughts; but he believed in 'style', that is to say in a unique way of expressing a thing in all its colour and intensity. For him the form was the work itself, in the same way, as, in human beings, the blood nourishes the flesh and determines even its shape, its external appearance, according to his race and family, thus, with him, the work, the inner meaning of it, inevitably imposes the unique and correct expression, the measure, the rhythm, the whole finish of the form.

Where this characteristic feature of Flaubert's way of writing is seen to best advantage is in *Trois Contes*, where each tale has a different style and each appropriate to each particular subject. It is a nosegay of his different styles, tied together in one bouquet.

He considered that a writer's style should have no trick, no idiosyncrasies peculiar to himself – language should have nothing which could tie it down to one period, or class, or locality. He aimed at a style clear as water, which would hide nothing and distort nothing. One did not, he thought, need a peculiar and eccentric vocabulary, or complicated turns of phrase. He was here thinking of the affected 'écriture artiste' of the Goncourt brothers. He said to Maupassant:[35] 'Let us try to be excellent stylists rather than collectors of rare terms.'

He was also very anxious that there should be musicality and harmony of style. We know the trouble he took to take out everything which clashed unpleasantly on the ear. He submitted all his writings to the experiment of the 'gueuloir', that is to say that they were shouted, at the top of his voice, to test their harmony. For him a piece of prose should be like a piece of verse, and this musicality is one of the great features of his style. 'I was born a lyricist,' he said,[36] 'and I don't write verse!' He thought that a good piece of prose should be like a piece of verse. Writing to Louise Colet, he said:[37]

A good sentence of prose must be like a good line of verse, that is to say impossible to change, and with as much rhythm, melodious. That, at least, is my ambition (there's one thing of which I'm sure, that no one has ever had in view a kind of prose more perfect than I have; but as for carrying it out, how much weakness, how much weakness, good heavens!).

Maupassant quotes him as saying:[38]

In verse the poet has fixed rules. He has metre, caesura, rhyme and a host of practical hints, a whole lore of learning, of the trade. In prose one needs a deep feeling for rhythm, a rhythm which evades one, without rules, without certainty; one needs inborn qualities, and also reasoning powers, an artistic sense infinitely more subtle and sharper, to sing, at every instant, movement, colour, a different kind of style according to what one wants to say. If one knows how to handle that fluid thing which is French prose, when one knows the exact value of the different words, and when one knows how to modify that value according to the position one gives them, when one knows how to stir a soul, and fill it suddenly with joy or fear, enthusiasm or grief, then one is really an artist, really a prose artist.

Flaubert himself did become such a prose artist and he was especially fine as a nature artist. For him nature was, as it was to be for the Symbolists, an 'état d'âme', that is to say that it is not described in an absolute sense, as it is with the Goncourts, in such novels as *Manette Salomon*. The Goncourts describe nature in the abstract, independently of the characters, which are later placed against the background. These passages, in connection with the art of fiction, are literary '*hors d'oeuvre*'. The landscapes in Flaubert's novel are described only because they reflect the moods of the characters. We have seen that after Emma has been seduced by Rodolphe the whole of nature participates in her feeling of ecstasy. It is the same in her love affair with Léon:[39]

Ce n'était pas la première fois qu'ils apercevaient des arbres, du
ciel bleu, du gazon, qu'ils entendaient l'eau couler et la brise
soufflant dans le feuillage, mais ils n'avaient sans doute jamais
admiré tout cela, comme si la nature n'existait pas auparavant,
ou qu'elle n'eût commencé à être belle que depuis l'assouvisse-
ment de leurs désirs.

A la nuit, ils repartaient. La barque suivait le bord des îles. Ils
restaient au fond, tous les deux cachés dans l'ombre, sans parler.
Les avirons carrés sonnaient entre les tolets de fer; et cela mar-
quait dans le silence comme un battement de métronome, tandis
qu'à l'arrière la bauce qui traînait ne discontinuait pas son
petit clapotement doux dans l'eau.

Une fois, la lune parut; alors ils ne manquèrent pas à faire des
phrases, trouvant l'astre mélancolique et plein de poésie; même
elle se mit à chanter:

> 'Un soir, t'en souvient-il? nous voguions etc.'

This is a quotation from *Le Lac* by Lamartine.

Flaubert's chief element of style is the image, the metaphor, and these are very frequent, especially in his earlier
works. He saw everything in the form of an image, but often,
especially when he was young, the image tended to take over
and to become more important than the idea symbolized. In
his later works, after *Madame Bovary*, these very long metaphors became more restrained and largely disappeared. In
his correspondence the images are usually spontaneous and
natural and arise easily out of what he was saying. But often
in *Madame Bovary* one loses sight of the idea expressed and
one considers the image separately in itself. There is a particularly long metaphor which is intended to suggest
Emma's sadness at the departure of Léon to Paris which
becomes an independent piece of narrative which is artificial
in its context:[40]

Dès lors, ce souvenir de Léon fut comme le centre de son
ennui; il y pétillait plus fort que, dans une steppe de Russie, un
feu de voyageurs abandonné sur la neige. Elle se précipitait vers
lui, elle se blottissait contre, elle remuait délicatement ce foyer
près de s'éteindre, elle allait cherchant tout autour d'elle ce qui

pouvait l'aviver davantage; et les réminiscences les plus loin-
taines comme les plus immédiates occasions, ce qu'elle éprouvait avec ce qu'elle imaginait, ses envies de volupté qui se
dispersaient, ses projects de bonheur qui craquaient au vent
comme des branchages morts, sa vertu stérile, ses espérances
tombées, la litière domestique, elle ramassait tout, prenait tout,
et faisait servir tout à réchauffer sa tristesse.

Cependant les flammes s'apaisèrent, soit que la provision d'elle-
même s'épuisât, ou que l'entassement fût trop considérable.
L'amour, peu à peu, s'éteignit par l'absence, le regret s'étouffa
sous l'habitude; et cette lueur d'incendie qui empourprait son
ciel pâle se couvrit de plus d'ombre et s'effaça par degrés. Dans
l'assoupissement de sa conscience, elle prit même les
répugnances du mari pour des aspirations vers l'amant, les
brûlures de la haine pour des réchauffements de la tendresse;
mais, comme l'ouragan soufflait toujours, et que la passion se consuma jusqu'aux cendres, et qu'aucun secours ne
vint, qu'aucun soleil ne parut, il fut de tous côtés nuit complète,
et elle demeura perdue dans un froid horrible qui la traversait.

Madame Flaubert once said to her son:[41] 'It's your passion
for phrases which has dried up your heart.'

Flaubert was often coarse and licentious in his language,
in his correspondence, in his private notes and in the rough
drafts for his novel. Examples of this can be seen in *Madame
Bovary, Ébauches et Fragments Inédits*. In his published
writing his corrections were always made with the view of
making the final text more pure in language, leaving the
implications to come out in the actions. His published writings always show great delicacy and restraint; it is the meaning which is often daring but never the expression. One
could compare, for instance, the seduction scenes in
Madame Bovary, in the woods, or in the cab, with the love
scenes in *Lady Chatterley's Lover* to realize Flaubert's restraint. He always used silence and suggestion rather than
description. The position of the sun in the scene of Rodolphe's seduction of Emma in the woods indicates the passage of time and we realize what has happened. In the
seduction by Léon in the cab we imagine, without a word

being uttered, what is happening, in the mad flight, behind drawn curtains, and finally the fluttering out of the window of the cab of the fragments of the letter which Emma had intended to give him, but which she now tore up. That is all.

Writing to Louise Colet, while he was composing the seduction scene of Emma by Rodolphe, he said:[42] 'I've a piece of love-making which is worrying me quite a lot and which I mustn't shirk, although I want it to be pure, that is to say literary, without any spicy details or licentious images. What is lustful must be in the emotions.'

Flaubert believed in the celibacy of the writer, not for reasons of chastity, but so that there should be no divided loyalties; so that, like a priest, he should owe allegiance to one thing only, and have no family ties to encroach on his energies or preoccupations. We have seen the horror that he felt when he feared, on several occasions, that he might have a child by Louise Colet and have to take on other responsibilities but those of art. 'For me,' he said, 'the true poet is a priest. As soon as he takes holy orders and puts on his cassock, he must leave his family.'[43] He also said to George Sand:[44] 'Artists (who are priests) lose nothing in being chaste – on the contrary.' Zola once said of him that he had entered literature as formerly one entered a religious order, to experience all its joys and to die in it. Mauriac declared, in an essay on Flaubert, in *Trois Grands Hommes*, that he had substituted Art for God and that, in so doing, he had been guilty of idolatry, sinning greatly, for he had fallen into a more dangerous plight than if he had been merely cynical. He reached a mystical state in the practice of his art which took the place of every other kind of activity – pleasure or devotional state. Art brought him the same joy, mingled with pain, as religious experience might. He himself said:[45] 'I love my work with a frenzied and perverted passion as the ascetic loves the hair-shirt which scratches his belly.'

Life did not exist for him except as the substance for art, and he came to think of it solely as something which could be turned into literature. He spent his life in trying to reach the quintessence of his experience and then in crystallizing it eternally in a permanent work of beauty, and he sacrificed to it everything which stood in the way of this aim – love, friendship, and every kind of pleasure.

This sacrifice was purely disinterested and he had great contempt for those who made money from their writings. He said that he would rather be a master in a school than write four lines for gain;[46] and, again, that he would prefer to be a cabby than to write for money.[47]

We have seen that his view of life was a pessimistic one; this was true with regard to art as to everything else, and he believed that the rewards generally went to the egoistic and the time-servers. He himself, however, was able to find peace and oblivion with the opiate and intoxicant of art. Writing to Mademoiselle Leroyer de Chantepie, he said:[48] 'I try to get drunk on art as others do on brandy'; and again to her:[49] 'I get drunk on ink as others do on wine.'

His love of art and his search for perfection were an activity which lasted him to the end of his life, without the disillusionment which he inevitably found in everything else.

Conclusion

IN the meantime, after his acquittal in January 1857, and the
publication of his first book in April the same year, Flaubert
enjoyed, for about thirteen years, until the Franco-Prussian
War in 1870, a period of comparative success and appreciation, when he was highly considered by people of taste and
discrimination, and held by them to be the foremost novelist
of the day.

He had rented an apartment in Paris in 1856, to be at hand
for the correction of his proofs, and the publication of his
novel in *La Revue de Paris*. He lived there, at No. 42 rue du
Temple, for some years, an almost fashionable life, going to
parties, and himself entertaining literary, and even fashionable people in his own modest apartment. Previously he had
remained in Paris only for odd days at a time, and had then
stayed in some hotel, but now he was there for weeks or
months on end. He became a member of Princesse Mathilde's *Salon* – indeed his feelings for her seem to have been
warmer than those of mere friendship – and he kept up his
association with her until the day of his death, being a frequent visitor at her house at Saint-Gratien; and, through
her, he became acquainted with her cousin, the Emperor. It
was she who, in 1866, obtained for him the decoration of
Chevalier de la Légion d'Honneur, which he accepted grate-
fully in spite of his ironic remarks when Maxime Du Camp
was made Officier in 1852. On being decorated he wrote to
Princesse Mathilde:[1] 'And so the red ribbon is for me more
than a mere favour; it is almost a souvenir; but I did not
need that to think of Princesse Mathilde.' Like many rec-
ipients of honours, he claimed that the chief pleasure he
derived from it came from the delight it gave his friends.
'What gives me most happiness in the red ribbon,' he said,[2]

'is in the joy it gives to those who love me; that is the best aspect of the matter I assure you.'

He now wore fine clothes, always expensive and made to measure, though of a somewhat provincial cut and fashion. For a time he was a sophisticated Parisian, and almost a man about town.

His life during these thirteen years belies the opinion generally held of him as the hermit of Croisset, the bear of Croisset. It is true that, when he was engaged on a work of composition, he would retire to the solitude of his country house, but he made more frequent visits to Paris than formerly, and he seemed to enjoy the companionship of his new literary and fashionable friends.

His mother eventually rented an apartment in the same house as himself, and looked after him there as well as at Croisset.

Although, during these years, he enjoyed a 'succès d'estime', he was not yet unquestionably accepted by the established critics. Émile de Montégut, writing in 1861 about the novel of the time,[3] said that he did not wish to appear unduly pessimistic, nor blind to the qualities which undoubtedly existed in those writing then; he did not wish to claim that the present age was inferior to all previous ones; and certainly, if one looked round carefully, one would find some talent – it is true, of a minor kind – but he thought that the contemporary imaginative literature in France was the poorest that the country had ever known. He said this at a time when Baudelaire and Flaubert had published their works. He declared that George Sand was the most distinguished novelist still writing; and he also discussed Erckman and Chatrian, but made no mention of Flaubert. He devoted more than eighty pages to Octave Feuillet, and the same to Victor Cherbuliez, but none to Flaubert. He ended by saying:[4] 'Our harvest is completed; it is scanty you will say, but nevertheless it is all that we have been able to glean, in twenty-odd volumes; all that we considered worthy of presenting to the reader and of recommending to his attention.'

In 1876 he studied the novel once more.[5] Again he discoursed on the weakness of contemporary fiction, though by this time Flaubert had published all the works he was going to print in his lifetime – except *Trois Contes*. This time he does mention him and 'the solid country house which he has erected. like a farm house in his native Normandy'. He gives some praise to *Madame Bovary* – the only work he mentions – as 'l'oeuvre déplaisante peut-être, mais si forte de Gustave Flaubert', and he praises it especially as the work which gave the 'coup de grâce' to the dangerous influence of Romanticism. But he gives far more importance to the novels of Alphonse Daudet and Gustave Droz.

Although Flaubert had many friends and acquaintants, and went out a good deal when he was in Paris, he was often lonely, especially after the death of his friend and mentor – his literary conscience – Louis Bouilhet, in 1869. He wrote to George Sand:[6] 'When I lost my poor Bouilhet, I lost my midwife, the man who saw more clearly into my mind than I did myself. His death left a void in my life which I notice more and more each day.'

Towards the end of his life he drew near again to Maxime Du Camp, but the former intimacy could not be fully renewed. He had many close women friends, to whom he wrote long letters – this was one of the striking features of his later life – Princesse Mathilde, Mademoiselle Leroyer de Chantepie, Amélie Bosquet, Madame Roger des Genettes, the Comtesse de Loynes, George Sand – in fact, on the whole, he preferred writing to women than to men – but none seems to have been more than affectionate friendships, and there is no proof that he had sexual relationships with any of them. He may have been the lover of Juliet Herbert, the second English governess of his niece, for he seems, on several occasions, to have gone to see her in London for some weeks at a time.

On the whole he was not successful in love, and none of his relationships are known to have been completely satisfactory.

As well as the other obstacles which have already been mentioned, perhaps he was too self-conscious, too self-ana-lytical. Writing to Louise Colet, a few days after they first became lovers, he said:[7] 'The grotesque side of love has always prevented me from indulging in it. I've sometimes wished to please women, but then the vision of the peculiar appearance I must have presented on these occasions, has made me laugh too much, has made my will melt under the fire of the interior irony, which sang in me the hymn of bitterness and derision. It's only with you that I've not yet laughed at myself.'

He was only twenty-four when he wrote these lines, and the following: 'You'll believe that I'm an egoist and that I'm afraid of you. Well yes! I'm terrified of your love, because I feel that it is devouring us both.'

A Swiss bibliographer, some time ago, acquired a presen-tation copy of *Madame Bovary* on the fly-leaf of which the author had written the inscription:[8] 'L'amour est comme l'opéra. On s'y ennuie, mais on y retourne.' There is no indi-cation concerning the recipient of the volume.

The great love of his life remained Élisa Schlésinger, in what he called his bricked-up room, in his 'chambre murée'. 'Each of us possesses, in his heart, a royal chamber. I've bricked up mine, but it isn't destroyed.'[9]

As long as her husband was alive, he remained distant and respectful to her, but, when he died, he seems to have drawn nearer to her, and to have expressed his affection more openly; he then addressed her as 'Vieille amie, toujours chère, oui, toujours!'[10] He tells her then that he had hoped that the end of his life would be spent near her, but this was not to be, as he could not bear the thought of visiting Ger-many after the end of the War. When she came to Trouville, in the summer of 1871, to look after her property there, he was not able to see her on account of the illness of his mother, but he begged her to come and visit him at Crois-set:[11]

Do come, we have so many things to say to one another, these

T–O

things which cannot be said, or can only be said badly, with a pen.

What is preventing you? Aren't you free? My mother would receive you with the greatest pleasure, in memory of the good old days. We can offer you at least a bed and dinner. Don't refuse me. Good-bye. I embrace you very hard, and am always yours.

She was not, however, able to visit him then. The following year, after the death of his mother, he wrote again:[12]

My dear old friend, my dear old affection. I can't see your writing without being deeply moved, and so, this morning, I tore open your envelope avidly. I hoped it would announce your visit. Alas no! It will be when? Next year? I'd like so much to entertain you in my own home, and to have you sleep in my mother's bedroom.

He told her that the scenes which stood out most clearly in his past were those of Trouville, with which she was connected:[13]

The future for me has no more dreams, but the days gone by stand out before me, bathed in a golden haze. On that bright background, where dead ghosts hold out their arms towards me, the image which stands out most splendidly is yours. Ah! poor Trouville!

But, no more than Frédéric in the final *Éducation Sentimentale*, did he make her his mistress. There is, in this work, an episode which must have had its counterpart in real life, and it is the finest passage which Flaubert ever wrote. It is the final scene when Madame Arnoux comes, unexpectedly, to see Frédéric, when she has grown old and they have not met for close on twenty years. Then, as they recall the past, they discover that their love has not grown cold. She seems now at last ready to be his, but he does not take her – they have waited too long for this moment; he is afraid of destroying his illusion; also it would have seemed, after all this time, almost like incest; and he lets her go. She understands that this is now the end, and, before leaving, she removes her hat and he sees with a stab of pain, that she is now quite white. She cuts a lock of the white hair, gives it to him and then leaves. With great intensity of emotion and economy of phrase, Flaubert makes us feel the dead weight of the vanished years, and the poignancy of the woman who has grown old. This is the most moving scene in the whole of Flaubert.[14]

Flaubert spent the largest part of his life at Croisset, with his aged mother, who was beginning to lose her memory, and his niece Caroline, who reminded him of his dead sister. As he grew older he lived more and more with his memories. Even as a young man, he had said:[15] 'I like to surround myself with memories and souvenirs. In the same way, I don't sell my old clothes. I go and look at them sometimes, in the attic where they are kept, and I think of the time when they were new, and everything that I used to do when I wore them.'

When his mother died in 1872 he said that he then realized that she was the human being whom, in his whole life, he had most loved.

Flaubert was a man of deep and passionate emotions, particularly for his immediate family and his close friends, and we have seen that he was never really happy when he was far from them – when he was a student in Paris, and on his trip to the East. It is possible to believe that he would have been a sympathetic and kind father – he was both father and mother to his niece and sacrificed everything which made life precious to him, for her sake. But he refused paternity and was always afraid that his duties to a family might encroach on his duties as an artist. Writing to Louise Colet, when he was only twenty-four, he said:[16] 'I understand, as well as anyone, what one must feel on looking at one's child sleeping. I wouldn't have been a bad father.' And, eight years later:[17] 'I've got a human heart, and if I don't want children of my own, it is because I feel that I would be too paternal. I love my little niece, as if she were my own daughter, and I look after her enough to prove that these are not idle phrases.'

He was always devoted to his friends and much moved by

them. He suffered greatly in his sorrows on their account – at the death of Alfred Le Poittevin, of Louis Bouilhet, of George Sand, at whose funeral he wept openly and uncontrolledly. He thought very highly of the faculty for love and affection. 'We are only worth something through our power for affection,' he said to Mademoiselle Leroyer de Chantepie.[18] And, to Louise Colet:[19] 'No! we're not really good; but this faculty of assimilating in oneself all the unhappiness of others, and of imagining having it oneself, that is, perhaps, the truest form of human charity.'

He believed only the best of his friends, and he, so clear-sighted about those who were not connected with himself, was gullible in ordinary life, and he saw all his geese as swans. He spent himself in the service of his friends, as he would never have done for himself – witness his efforts on behalf of Bouilhet in the matter of the production of his plays; and his labour in correcting Louise Colet's poems.

He was good and generous towards those in his *intimacy*, and for those who worked for him. He lavished devoted care on his mother until the day of her death, and she was always the first of his preoccupations. He was the same towards those who served him. He looked after the old family servant until his death; he was also good to his personal servant Narcisse. There is a story of his helping him to bed one night, when he was drunk, and the servant saying to him: 'Monsieur would put the finishing touches to his kindness if he would only consent to take off my boots.' This Flaubert willingly accomplished.

But deep feelings inevitably lead to pain, and there was a great deal in his life. He had been obliged to endure too many griefs, too much suffering, in too short a time. At twenty-two he was struck down by the first attack of his nervous disorder, which maimed him forever, and took him out of the ordinary life of a young man. At twenty-four he lost his father whom he loved and revered, and his adored sister; and, at twenty-six, he lost his closest friend, who was also his guide in literature.

Flaubert considered suffering highly and did not believe in the value of happiness. When he was only twenty-four, he said to his friend Emmanuel Vaisse:[20] 'I've seen what is commonly called happiness from close quarters, and I've turned it inside out; it's a dangerous delusion to want to possess it.'

He would not sacrifice anything in favour of happiness. But he believed in the importance of suffering and he would have echoed Baudelaire's belief in 'la fertilisante douleur' and 'l'indispensable douleur'. He believed that the higher one climbed up the ladder of humanity, the greater the power of suffering, and that the value of the human heart was measured by its faculty for suffering.[21] 'The human heart,' he said,[22] 'becomes deeper through the sharp knife which cuts into it.'

Even as a young man he felt all the unhappiness which lay hidden beneath the fairest exterior, all the misery of the human condition. His escape from this was in what he called 'rêverie', and this made possible for him the contemplation of reality. His aim was the pursuit of beauty, which he could create from suffering, and he did not believe that one could seek both happiness and beauty at the same time without running the risk of losing both.[23] He said:[24]

I loathe that search for worldly happiness. It seems to me a mediocre and dangerous delusion. Long live money, love, wine, family, joy and sentiment! Let's seize hold of all that, as much as we can, but don't let us believe in it. Let's believe that happiness is a myth invented by the devil to drive us to despair. It's the people who are certain that Heaven exists who have no imagination.

He did, however, believe that a certain strength could be derived from despair when it is accepted:[25]

People like us must have the religion of despair. One must be equal to one's destiny, that is to say impassive like it. By dint of saying: 'That is so! That is so! That is so!' and of gazing down at the deep black hole at one's feet, one reaches calm.

Nevertheless, in spite of his many references, in his correspondence, to strong men and the need for strength, he was far from being a decisive man himself. He had the weakness and wavering characteristics which he was later to pour into the character of Frédéric in his final *Éducation Sentimentale* – which we have seen that Maxime Du Camp deplored. Frédéric was what Flaubert might have been if he had not possessed genius and an overwhelming passion for art. Writing to Du Camp and begging him to help him in his state of indecision, he said:[26]

You know that I'm a man of passion and weakness. If you could only know the invisible nets of inaction which enmesh my body and all the mists which befog my mind. I sometimes feel so much weakness that I could die of weariness when I've got to do anything, and it is only by the greatest effort that I can grasp even the clearest idea. My youth drugged me with some kind of opium of boredom for the rest of my life. I hate life! That has escaped me in spite of myself – well let it stand! Yes, life, and everything which reminds me that I must endure it. It is a torture to eat, to dress, to be up and about. I've dragged this burden round with me, in everything, through everything; at school, in Paris, in Rouen, on the Nile, on our trip. Like the snail who is afraid of soiling himself on the sand, or of being squashed under the feet of passers-by, I creep back into my shell. I don't say that I'm incapable of all kinds of action, but it must be for a short time and have some pleasure in it for myself. Even if I've the strength, I've no patience, and patience is everything.

As an individualist and a solitary, Flaubert hated mass movements and any kind of collectivity. Writing to Louise Colet, he said:[27]

I hate the crowd, the herd. It seems to me always atrociously stupid or vile. It's on that account that collective generations, philanthropic charities, subscriptions etc. are so antipathetic to me. They destroy charity, that is to say the compassion of man towards man, the spontaneous communion which arises between you and the supplicant. The populace has never pleased me except on days of revolt, and even then! And if one could see into the heart of the matter, one would find many ringleaders and agitators – it is perhaps more artificial than one thinks.

Yet he had a liking for people individually and was good to them. He would probably have made a good university teacher. He enjoyed educating his niece, and spent much time on it. He spent hours in criticizing the poor efforts in fiction of Mademoiselle Leroyer de Chantepie; in correcting Louise Colet's verse and in preparing it for publication. He would probably have been happy as a Professor at the Collège de France, or in an Oxford or Cambridge college. Men liked his conversation, which was outspoken and passionate, and enjoyed discussing matters with him. His pessimism was more through conviction than in practice. His daily life was like that of any ordinary citizen and he was far from being a boor or a bear – this only happened when he was in the midst of the birth pangs of a book. He thought that one should live like a bourgeois so as to be able to think like a god. It is true that he was helped in this by having private means and not being obliged to earn his living. He said that paid employment, of whatever kind it might be, seemed to him a degradation.[28] Martin Turnell says that 'his life was indeed the life of a typical nineteenth century writer – uninteresting, uneventful and drab'.[29]

The opinion that one needs to move about the world to be exciting is the kind that would have interested Flaubert, and he might well have included it in his *Dictionnaire des Idées Reçues*. He did, in fact, move about and travel – and not so little either for the period – especially when it was needed for creation. He travelled to the south of France, in the days before railways; to Corsica; to Italy; to England on several occasions; to North Africa; and there was especially his long trip to the East with Maxime Du Camp, which lasted for almost two years. He was involved in the Revolution of 1848 – he saw the sack of the Palais Royal – in the *coup d'état* of December 1851; he was a member of the National Guard; he was taken to the courts on the score of the obscenity and

immorality of his first published work. It was not an un-
adventurous life. However, most of his wanderings and
adventures were in the realms of his own mind.

It is true that, in ordinary life, many of his values were
those which he fundamentally deplored in others. He married his niece in the most bourgeois way possible, and said
that he would prefer her to marry a rich Philistine than a
poor artist. He married her thus in an effort to ensure her
future safely; yet it was this bourgeois marriage which,
eventually, ruined him financially, for he sacrificed most of
his money in a vain effort to save his nephew-in-law, a
lumber merchant, from bankruptcy. So the bourgeois finally
ruined Flaubert and eventually killed him. This would sec-
retly have struck his grim sense of irony.

Flaubert was fascinated by evidence of bourgeois crassness
and inanity, and he collected examples of it. One can collect
anything – even match-boxes – so why not examples of bourgeois foolishness. If the bourgeois had suddenly been completely reformed, he would have been deprived of his most
valued occupation. Amongst his papers in the Bibliothèque
Municipale in Rouen, there is a printed card, of the kind
sent out to friends to announce the arrival of a baby – except
that this one records the birth of a litter of puppies:
'Madame Cora Chardon, née Cora Desgranges, est heureuse-
ment accouchée d'un chien et de trois chiennes. La mère et
les enfants se portent bien. Monsieur Dick Chardon a
l'honneur de vous en faire part.' He must have kept this as
evidence of inanity, and have felt justified in his diatribes
against the crass stupidity of human nature.

The depths of Flaubert's nature were suffused with mysticism and religion – whatever he might say otherwise.
When giving an account of his life to Mademoiselle Leroyer
de Chantepie, he said:[30]

What attracts me above all else is religion. I mean all religions,
not one more than another. . . . I consider that the feelings which
engendered them are the most natural and the most poetical in
humanity. I don't care for the philosophers who have seen in

them nothing but deceit and foolishness. As for me I find in them necessity and intuition.

And he had said earlier to Louise Colet:[31]

I'm turning towards a kind of aesthetic mysticism (if the two terms can be linked together), and I would like it to be stronger. When one receives no encouragement from others, when the external world disgusts one ... corrupts one, stupefies one, honest men of taste are forced to seek in themselves, somewhere, a cleaner place in which to live. If society continues in the way it is now going, we shall see mystics arising again, I believe, as there always have been in dark ages.

He once said of Alfred de Musset: 'He's an unfortunate young man! One can't live without religion.'[32]

In another milieu or age, Flaubert might well have been an ascetic and a mystic – perhaps even a Pascal, for he would have appreciated his austerity. But, in the scientific milieu in which he was reared and lived, orthodox religion did not have a chance, and he developed scepticism, while all his religious feeling went into literature. His fanatical feeling for literature was, in fact, mysticism. Claudel called Rimbaud 'un mystique à l'état sauvage', but, in many ways, this would also be true of Flaubert. There are many examples in his work of aspirations towards beauty which take on religious fervour – as, for instance, right at the end of his travel notes, on his journey to Africa, his prayer:[33]

Que toutes les énergies de la nature que j'ai aspirées me pénètrent et qu'elles s'exhalent dans mon livre. A moi, puissance de l'émotion plastique! résurrection du passé, à moi! à moi! Il faut faire, à travers le Beau, vivant et vrai quand même. Pitié pour ma volonté, Dieu des âmes! donnez-moi la force – et l'espoir!

Nuit du samedi 12 au dimanche 13 juin, minuit.

Father Didon write to Flaubert's niece, after his death: 'I loved your uncle. His wide-seeing eye saw further and higher than what was visible. Certainly that gaze encountered what is divine.'[34]

His mysticism is particularly seen in his attitude to his art. He was prepared to sacrifice everything on the altar of that jealous god. He would have agreed with Mallarmé when he said: 'Le monde est fait pour aboutir à un beau livre.'[35]

When he was only twenty he wrote to his friend Ernest Chevalier: 'We must accustom ourselves to seeing in people nothing but books.'[36]

He used events concerned with his friends – he planned to use the feelings of a dear and close friend at the burial of his wife as copy for Charles Bovary's grief at Emma's funeral; and yet he had loved both husband and wife, and had much compassion for the widower.[37] We have seen how he used the material provided for him by the spiteful maid of one of his closest friends, *Les Mémoires de Madame Ludovica*. This behaviour horrified many people, yet it is the way that artists work, and everything must serve the cause of art.

Madame Bovary remains Flaubert's most popular book, and there are good reasons for that. It is his warmest book, less cerebral than his later novels, and, in spite of what he might say, it is the book into which he has put most of himself.

The publication of *Madame Bovary* is one of the key dates in the history of the novel in France – indeed not only in France but in the rest of the world as well. A French critic has said: 'One says the year of *Madame Bovary* as one says the year of *Le Cid*.' Corneille's play had been the formulation of the French Classical ideal in the theatre, the stabilizing of it, and there is all the difference in the world between French drama before and after *Le Cid*. *Madame Bovary* is the same for the French novel. It is the coming-of-age of the novel, the attainment, for the first time, of an aesthetic, based on perfection.

Flaubert is the creator of the modern novel, not only in France but also in the rest of the world, and a large part of the most interesting innovations come from him – especially in the realm of psychology. When, towards the end of the nineteenth century, Henry James in America, and George

Moore in England, wished to renovate the novel in their own countries, it was to Flaubert that they turned for example and inspiration.

One can say that Flaubert used the novel, what one might call inevitably, that is to say that he uses it to render what could not be expressed in any other way, and what he says cannot be translated into any other medium without sacrificing most of its value. He always refused to have *Madame Bovary* dramatized, saying, quite rightly, that it was not the right kind of subject for the theatre. He persisted in his refusal in spite of financial inducements, and he always declared that, when he entered the theatre, it would be through the front door.[38] After his death his wishes were not respected and there were several attempts at dramatization, most of which were unsuccessful. The best of these was the one by Baty, produced at the Théâtre du Montparnasse, in 1936, which was very well done, if one thinks that such a thing should be done at all, which is very doubtful; but, even this was all wrong; it was not what Flaubert had conceived, and the emphasis was quite different. Nevertheless, to attend the performance was not sheer waste of time, for much was learnt critically by realizing what the producer had been obliged to omit and to alter. The first thing which came as a surprise was to see the characters in the clothes and the interiors of the 1840s, when the author had not intended to tie the action down to one period or one place, but wanted it to be true of all times.

Also, in the play, the only means at the disposal of the producer to bring his characters to life was dialogue. Charles and Emma had to speak, make concrete in speech, their complicated feelings which, in the novel, remain unexpressed and never reach the surface. We have seen that, in the novel, there is very little conversation – astonishingly little if one compares it with one by Balzac. Charles and Emma would have been incapable of saying the things which were in the dialogue of the play, and the emphasis was completely altered, so that one did not recognize them.

The wonderful parallel day-dreams of Charles and Emma, so revealing psychologically, in which not a word is uttered, had to be omitted altogether in the dramatic version of the novel, to the great impoverishment of the psychological depiction. The most successful scene in the play was the Balzacian one, the arrival at the Lion d'Or at Yonville, where the characters are built up visually and through conversation.

Flaubert came to regard Romanticism as a disease which destroyed the human fibre and he undertook his first published novel in order to cure himself of the malady. He believed that everything which came from the North was weak and that, on the contrary, what came from the South was healthy, strong and noble. While composing *Madame Bovary* he said to Louise Colet:[39] 'At heart, I'm a man of fogs, and it's only by dint of patience and hard work that I've divested myself of the whitish fat which was clogging my muscles.' And again the following year: 'It's through hard labour that I've got rid of my northern mists.'

In 1849, under pressure from his friends and mentors, Flaubert turned away from the exuberant Romanticism of *La Tentation de Saint Antoine* to the disciplined form of *Madame Bovary*. For him this had been a confession of defeat, even though it might eventually lead to victory. There are certain critics who regret the curbing and pruning of his genius, but the present writer is not one of them. Before the shock which changed him radically, he seemed like some uncouth figure, though hewn with genius: some statue excavated from a bog or river-bed, its true lineaments still hidden beneath its coating of slime. By degrees, and with immense patience and labour, he cleansed the statue of its defiling mud, and revealed the clear nobility of its austere lines, in their eternal and immutable harmony; or, as Mallarmé said of Edgar Allen Poe, in *Le Tombeau de Poe*, 'Tel qu'en lui-même enfin l'éternité le change.'

Bibliography

A

THE fullest edition of Flaubert's works is the one published by Conard in twenty-eight volumes and is the one used throughout this book. It is not entirely satisfactory, especially in the matter of the correspondence, which is very faulty.

It does not include *Souvenirs, Notes et Pensées Intimes* which was published by Buchet-Chastel in 1965, edited by L. Chevalley-Sabatier.

Nor *Madame Bovary, Nouvelle Version*, published by José Corti in 1949 and edited by J. Pommier and G. Leleu. This is an enlarged version of the novel, compiled from the rough notes and scenarios preserved in the Municipal Library at Rouen.

A useful edition for those who only want the novels published by Flaubert himself is the *Édition de la Pléiade* published in two volumes by Gallimard.

B

Only books useful for a study of Flaubert's early life and writings, and of *Madame Bovary*, are listed below.

Albalat, A. *Gustave Flaubert & ses Amis.* 1927.

Auriant, —. *Koutchouk-Hanem, l'Aimée de Flaubert.* 1943.

Bertrand, G. E. *Les Jours de Flaubert.* 1947.

Bertrand, L. *La Première Tentation de Saint Antoine.* 1908.

Bertrand, L. *Gustave Flaubert avec des Fragments Inédits.* 1923.

Bollème, G. *La Leçon de Flaubert.* 1964.

Bonwit, M. *Gustave Flaubert et le Principe d'Impassibilité.* California, 1950.

Bopp, L. *Commentaire sur Madame Bovary.* Neufchâtel, 1951.

Bruneau, J. *Les Débuts Littéraires de Gustave Flaubert.* 1962.

Bouquel, F. *Souvenirs du Collège de Rouen par un Élève de Pension.* Rouen, 1895.

Bouquet, F. *L'Enseignement Supérieur à Rouen pendant le XIXe Siècle, 1808–1896.* Rouen, 1896.

Cassagne, A. *La Théorie de l'Art pour l'Art en France chez les Derniers Romantiques et les Premiers Parnassiens.* 1906.

Castex, P. G. *Le Conte Fantastique en France de Nodier à Maupassant.* 1951.

Champfleury, J. *Les Bourgeois de Molinchart.* 1855.

Coleman, A. *Flaubert's Literary Development in the Light of his 'Mémoires d'un Fou', 'Novembre' and 'Éducation Sentimentale' (1845).* Baltimore, 1914.

Colling, A. *Gustave Flaubert.* 1947.

Commanville, C. *Souvenirs sur Gustave Flaubert.* 1895.

Degoumois, L. *Flaubert à l'École de Goethe.* Geneva, 1925.

Demorest, D. *L'Expression Figure et Symbolique dans l'Oeuvre de Gustave Flaubert.* 1931.

Descharmes, R. *Flaubert, sa Vie, son Caractère, et ses Idées avant 1857.* 1909.

Descharmes, R., and Dumesnil, R. *Autour de Flaubert.* 1912.

Du Camp, M. *Souvenirs de l'Année 1848.* 1876.

Du Camp, M. *Souvenirs Littéraires.* 1883.

Dumesnil, R. *Madame Bovary.* (No date.)

Dumesnil, R. *En Marge de Flaubert.* 1928.

Dumesnil, R. *Gustave Flaubert, l'Homme et l'Oeuvre.* 1932.

Dumesnil, R. *Le Grand Amour de Flaubert.* Geneva, 1945.

Dumesnil, R. *La Vocation de Flaubert.* 1961.

Dumesnil, R., and Demorest, D. *Bibliographie de Gustave Flaubert.* 1937.

Durry, M. J. *Flaubert et ses Projets Inédits.* 1950.

Estève, E. *Byron et le Romantisme Français.* 1907.

Faguet, E. *Flaubert.* 1899.

Fairlie, A. *Madame Bovary.* 1962.

Ferrère, E. *L'Esthétique de Flaubert.* 1913.

Finot, A. *Maxime Du Camp.* 1949.

Fischer, E. *Études sur Flaubert Inédit.* Leipzig. 1908.

Frejlich, H. *Flaubert d'après sa Correspondance.* 1933.

Frejlich, H. *Les Amants de Mantes.* 1936.

Gaultier, J. de. *Le Bovarysme.* 1892.

Gaultier, J. de. *Le Génie de Flaubert.* 1913.

Gérard-Gailly. *Flaubert et les Fantômes de Trouville.* 1930.

Gérard-Gailly. *Les Véhémences de Louise Colet.* 1934.

Gérard-Gailly. *Le Grand Amour de Flaubert.* 1944.

Gothot-Mersch, C. *La Genèse de 'Madame Bovary'.* 1966.

Herval, R. *Les Véritables Origines de 'Madame Bovary'.* 1957.

Jackson, J. *Louise Colet et ses Amis Littéraires.* New Haven, U.S.A., 1937.

Lafarge, —. *Mémoires de Marie Cappelle.* 1842 and 1843.

Laumet, L. *La Sensibilité de Flaubert.* 1951.

Leleu, G. *Madame Bovary. Ébauches et Fragments Inédits* 1936.

Le Poittevin, A. *Oeuvres Inédites.* 1909.

Le Poittevin, A. *Lettres Inédites à Gustave Flaubert.* 1910.

Le Poittevin, A. *Une Promenade de Bélial et Oeuvres Inédites, Précédées d'une Introduction sur la Vie et le Caractère d'Alfred Le Poittevin.* 1924.

Le Sidanar, L. *Gustave Flaubert.* 1930.

Martino, P. *Le Roman Réaliste sous le Second Empire.* 1913.

Maupassant, G. *Études sur Gustave Flaubert (Oeuvres Posthumes, II).* 1930.

Maynial, E. *La Jeunesse de Flaubert.* 1913.

Maynial, E. *Flaubert.* 1943.

Maynial, E. *Flaubert et son Milieu.* 1927.

Mestrel-Combremont, J. de. *La Belle Madame Colet.* 1913.

Monnier, H. *Grandeur et Décadence de M. Joseph Prudhomme.* 1853.

Moreau, P. *Madame Bovary.* (No date.)

Naaman, A. *Les Débuts de Gustave Flaubert et sa Technique de la Description.* 1962.

Proust, M. *Chroniques.* (No date.)

Richard, J. *Littérature et Sensation.* 1954.

Seillère, Baron E. *Gustave Flaubert.* 1914.

Seznec, J. *Les Sources de l'Episode des Dieux dans la Tentation de Saint Antoine (Première Version 1849).* 1940.

Seznec, J. *Nouvelles Études sur la Tentation de Saint Antoine.* London. 1949.

Shanks, L. P. *Flaubert's Youth.* Baltimore, 1927.

Spencer, P. *Flaubert.* 1952.

Steegmuller, F. *Flaubert and Madame Bovary.* 1947.

Suffel, J. *Gustave Flaubert.* 1958.

Thibaudet, A. *Gustave Flaubert.* 1935.

Thorlby, A. *Gustave Flaubert and the Art of Realism.* 1956.

Tillett, M. *On reading Flaubert.* 1961.

Weill, G. *Histoire de l'Enseignement Secondaire en France (1802–1920).* 1921.

C

Here are listed some of the chief articles dealing with Flaubert or his writings, which have appeared in reviews or papers. Only those which throw some special light on the novelist are given here, and those not used by their authors in subsequent works.

Bulletin des Amis de Flaubert, No. 12. Barron, J. 'La Première Éducation Sentimentale de Flaubert'.

French Studies, April 1954. Spencer, P. 'New Light on Flaubert's Youth'.

Lettres Françaises, Les, 11 April 1947. Pommier, J. 'L'Affaire Loursel'.

Mercure de France, Le, 1 May 1952. Pommier, J., and Digeon, C. 'Du Nouveau sur Flaubert et son Oeuvre'.

Progrès Médical, Le, August 1947. Pommier, J. 'Les Maladies de Flaubert'.

Publications of the Modern Language Association, The, June 1947. Bonwit, M. 'The Significance of the Dog in Flaubert's "Éducation Sentimentale" '.

Revue de Littérature Comparée, 1936, pp. 63–81. Bardon, M. 'Don Quichotte et le Roman Réaliste en France'.

Revue de Paris, June 1948. Audiat, P. 'Maxime Du Camp ou le Médisant Scrupuleux'.

Revue des Deux Mondes, 15 July 1910. Bertrand, L. 'Les Carnets de Gustave Flaubert'.

Revue d'Histoire Littéraire de la France, July–September 1947. Leleu, G. 'Une Source Inconnue de "Madame Bovary" '; Leleu, G., and Pommier, J. 'Du Nouveau sur "Madame Bovary" '.

December 1948. Dimoff, P. 'Autour d'un Projet de Roman de Flaubert'.

January–March 1957. West, C. 'Flaubert and Harriet Collier'.

October–December 1959. Cattin, M., and Bruneau, J. 'Sur le Manuscrit de "Passion & Vertu" '.

Revue Hebdomadaire, 12 December 1936. Chevalley-Sabatier, L. 'Gustave Flaubert et sa Soeur Caroline d'après leur Correspondance Inédite'.

Notes

INTRODUCTION

1 Jean Bruneau: *Les Débuts Littéraires de Gustave Flaubert.*
Antoine Youssef Naaman: *Les Débuts de Gustave Flaubert et sa Technique de la Description.*

2 *Correspondance*, vol. III, p. 181, letter to Louise Colet, 26–7 April 1852.

3 *Correspondance Supplément*, vol. III, p. 215, letter to George Sand, 3 October 1875.

4 It is correctly dated in the Descharmes documents.

5 *Nouvelle Revue Française*, April 1913.

6 Spoehlberch de Lovenjoul Collection, in the Institut Library, at Chantilly, Flaubert's letters to Louis Bouilhet, A.V.

15 jan. 1850.

Ce matin à midi, cher et pauvre vieux, j'ai reçu ta bonne et longue lettre tant désirée, elle m'a remué jusqu'au fond des entrailles. *J'ai mouillé.* Comme je pense à toi, va, inestimable bougre, combien de fois par jour je t'évoque et que je te regrette. Si tu trouves que je te manque, tu me manques aussi et marchant le nez en l'air dans rues et regardant le ciel bleu, les marchandises des maisons et les minarets couverts d'oiseaux, je rêve à ta personne . . .

Quand nous nous reverrons il aura passé beaucoup de jours, je veux dire beaucoup de choses. Serons-nous toujours les mêmes, n'y aura-t-il rien de changé dans la communion de nos êtres . . .

Ici c'est très bien parlé, on avoue sa sodomie et on en parle à table d'hôte. Quelquefois on nie un petit peu, tout le monde alors vous engueule et cela finit par s'avouer. Chargés d'une mission par le gouvernement nous avons regardé comme de notre devoir de nous livrer à ce mode d'éjaculation. . . . Pauvre cher bougre, j'ai bien envie de t'embrasser. Je serai content quand je reverrai ta figure . . .

Le soir, quand tu es rentré, que les strophes ne vont pas, que tu penses à moi, et que tu t'ennuyes, appuyé debout du coude sur la table, prends un morceau de papier et envoie moi tout, tout. J'ai mangé ta lettre et je l'ai relue plus d'une fois. En ce moment j'ai l'apperception de toi en chemise auprès de ton feu, ayant trop chaud et contemplant ton vi. . . .

13 mars 1850.
   Dans l'absorption de tout ce qui précède, mon pauvre vieux, tu n'as pas cessé d'être présent. C'était comme un vésicatoire permanent qui me démangeait mon esprit et en faisait couler le jus en l'irritant davantage. Je regrettais (le mot est faible) que tu ne fusses pas là. Je jouissais par moi de par toi – je m'excitais pour nous deux et tu en avais une bonne part, sois tranquille.

Once, when Louise Colet had tried to make him jealous by saying that Louis Bouilhet was about to leave him, he wrote to him, in December 1853:

   Sais-tu que dans son avant dernière lettre elle *m'insinuait*, et même me disait, que tu pensais bien d'ici à peu me lâcher, ou du moins 'en préférer d'autres amis' et elle chantait un grand éloge de Quérard que tu aimais. . . .

Once, accusing Louis Bouilhet of his indifferent letters, he wrote to him, on 12 August 1856:

   Mais tu as adopté un genre de correspondance si expéditif, que tu demandes des détails sur n'importe quoi, c'est se casser le nez contre le mur. Je te ferai seulement observer que voilà *trois fois* que la présence du poète Philoxène te sert de prétexte. – Cherche maintenant d'autres moyens dramatiques ne serait-ce que par amour propre. Oh! vieux! vieux! il fut un temps où nous passions chaque semaine vingt-quatre heures ensemble. Puis – non je m'arrête, j'aurais l'air d'une garce délaissée.

One of his letters to Bouilhet, 2 October 1860, begins 'Vieux Pédéraste' but this might only be a joke.

7   *Correspondance Supplément*, vol. IV, p. 287, letter to Mme Brainne, 10–11 December 1879.
8   *Souvenirs, Notes et Pensées Intimes*, p. 105.
9   *Correspondance*, vol. III, p. 76, letter to Louise Colet, 22 December 1852.
10 ibid., vol. VI, p. 368, letter to George Sand, 16 April 1872.
11 Du Camp: *Souvenirs Littéraires*, vol. II, p. 466.

BOOK ONE: SPRING SOWING

Part One: The Child Father to the Man

CHAPTER 1: THE FAMILY BACKGROUND (1821–31)

1   *Feuilles d'Automne.*
2   G. Dubosc: *Trois Normands*, p. 102.
3   *Souvenirs Intimes* by Mme de Commanville: *Correspondance*, vol. I, p. xi.
4   *Correspondance*, vol. I, p. 347, letter to Louise Colet, 30 September 1846.
5   *Journal de Rouen*, 21 December 1921.
6   *Correspondance*, vol. III, p. 269, letter to Louise Colet, 7–8 July 1853.
7   *Bulletin des Amis de Flaubert*, No. 7.
8   *Flaubert à Paris.*
9   *Correspondance*, vol. II, p. 442, letter to Louise Colet, 12 June 1852.
10 Bibliothèque Nationale, N.A.F. 23,825.
11 *Correspondance*, vol. I, p. 3, letter to Chevalier, 15 January 1832.
12 Bibliothèque Nationale, N.A.F. 23,827.
13 *Correspondance*, vol. I, p. 2, letter to Chevalier, 4 February 1831.

CHAPTER 2: ERNEST CHEVALIER (1831–6)

1   Maynial: *Flaubert*, p. 25.
2   *Souvenirs du Collège de Rouen.*
3   *Bulletin des Amis de Flaubert*, No. 10, *L'Élève Gustave Flaubert au Collège Royal de Rouen.*
4   Bibliothèque Nationale, Paris, N.A.F. 23,827.
5   *Correspondance*, vol. I, p. 7, letter 23 August 1832.
6   ibid., vol. I, p. 11, letter 26 August 1834.
7   ibid., vol. I, p. 7, letter 23 August 1832.
8   ibid., vol. I, p. 3, letter 15 January 1832.
9   ibid., vol. I, p. 11, letter 11 September 1833.
10 ibid., vol. I, p. 14, letter 29 August 1834.
11 *Oeuvres de Jeunesse Inédites*, vol. I, p. 6.

12 ibid., p. 523.

13 ibid., p. 524.

14 *Revue d'Histoire Littéraire de la France*, January–March 1957.

15 As I knew Caroline's letters to her brother, I have always been convinced that the English girls in *Mémoires d'un Fou* could not have been the Collier girls. I have tried for years to discover who might have been Caroline's schoolmates, but I could not find a school where she had been a pupil. I could not see the manuscript of *Mémoires d'un Fou* and so could not find out for myself whether it had been added to later – the episode of the English girls – but all the evidence is against such a view.

16 Jean Bruneau: *Les Débuts Littéraires de Flaubert*, p. 244.

17 *Bulletin des Amis de Flaubert*, 23 December 1963.

18 *Correspondance*, vol. IV, p. 444, letter 24 August 1861.

19 *Oeuvres de Jeunesse Inédites*, vol. I, p. 106.

20 ibid., p. 107.

21 *Correspondance*, vol. I, p. 22, letter 14 August 1835.

CHAPTER 3: ÉLISA SCHLÉSINGER (1836–7)

1 *Correspondance*, vol. IV, pp. 126–7, letter to Èlisa Schlésinger, 2 October 1856.

2 *Oeuvres de Jeunesse Inédites*, vol. I, p. 506.

3 It has generally been thought that the first *Éducation Sentimentale* also refers to her, but this has always seemed to me impossible. The problem will be discussed in a later chapter.

4 Steinhardt-Leins: op. cit., pp. 39–40.

5 *Notes de Voyages*, vol. I, p. 161.

6 *Correspondance*, vol. II, p. 177, letter to Louis Bouilhet, 13 March 1850.

7 Jean Bruneau: op. cit., p. 495.

8 *Correspondance*, vol. IV, p. 3, letter to Louise Colet, January 1854.

9 ibid., vol. III, p. 130, letter to Louise Colet, 25–8 March 1853.

10 *Oeuvres de Jeunesse Inédites*, vol. I, p. 166.

11 ibid., p. 197.

12 This is Flaubert's second published work, as an earlier tale,

Bibliomania, composed in November 1836, was also printed in *Le Colibri*, on 12 February 1837.

13 *Oeuvres de Jeunesse Inédites*, vol. i, pp. 199–200.
14 Vide Maigron: *Le Romantisme et les Moeurs*, p. 443.
15 *Oeuvres de Jeunesse Inédites*, vol. i, p. 252.
16 ibid., p. 252.
17 ibid., pp. 256–7.
18 *Madame Bovary*, p. 285.
19 *Oeuvres de Jeunesse Inédites*, vol. i, pp. 243–4.
20 *Correspondance*, vol. i, p. 27, letter 24 June 1837.

CHAPTER 4: ALFRED LE POITTEVIN (1837–8)

1 *Correspondance*, vol. v, p. 72, letter to Laure de Maupassant, January 1863.
2 Le Poittevin: *Une Promenade de Bélial*, p. xxxv, Note 6.
3 ibid., p. 177.
4 *Correspondance*, vol. i, p. 165, letter to Le Poittevin, April 1845.
5 ibid., vol. i, p. 190, letter to Le Poittevin, August 1845.
6 ibid., vol. v, p. 72, letter January 1863.
7 *Oeuvres de Jeunesse Inédites*, vol. i, p. 406.
8 ibid., vol. i, p. 408.
9 ibid., vol. i, p. 411.
10 ibid., vol. i, p. 422.
11 ibid., vol. i, p. 464.
12 Bibliothèque Nationale, Paris, N.A.F. 23,825.
13 Le Poittevin: *Une Promenade de Bélial et Oeuvres Inédites, Précédées d'une Introduction sur la Vie et le Caractère d'Alfred Le Poittevin par René Descharmes.*
14 op. cit., p. 187.
15 *Correspondance*, vol. i, p. 29, letter 13 September 1838.
16 Bibliothèque Nationale, Paris, letter to Chevalier, N.A.F. 23,827, unpublished in *Correspondance*.
17 *Correspondance*, vol. i, p. 29, letter to Chevalier, 23 September 1838.
18 ibid., vol. i, p. 33, letter to Chevalier, 28 October 1838.
19 op. cit., p. 263.
20 *Oeuvres de Jeunesse Inédites*, vol. i, p. 496.
21 op. cit., p. 206
22 *Oeuvres de Jeunesse Inédites*, vol. ii, pp. 20–1.

23 ibid., vol. ii, p. 56.
24 ibid., vol. ii, p. 85.
25 *Correspondance*, vol. i, p. 44, letter 18 March 1839.
26 ibid.
27 *Oeuvres de Jeunesse Inédites*, vol. ii, pp. 106–16.
28 ibid., vol. ii, p. 112.
29 *Correspondance*, vol. i, p. 38, letter 26 December 1838.
30 *Oeuvres de Jeunesse Inédites*, vol. ii, p. 117.

CHAPTER 5: MÉMOIRES D'UN FOU (1838–40)

1 *Oeuvres de Jeunesse Inédites*, vol. i, p. 538.
2 *Correspondance*, vol. iii, p. 30 letter to Louise Colet, 25 September 1852.
3 *Une Promenade de Bélial*, p. 162.
4 *Correspondance*, vol. i, pp. 30–1, letter to Chevalier, 11 October 1838.
5 ibid., vol. i, p. 36, letter to Chevalier, 30 November 1838.
6 ibid., vol. i, pp. 30–1, letter to Chevalier, 30 November 1838.
7 ibid., vol. i, p. 39, letter to Chevalier, 26 December 1838.
8 ibid., vol. i, p. 37, letter to Chevalier, 26 December 1838.
9 ibid., vol. i, p. 39, letter to Chevalier, 26 December 1838.
10 *Oeuvres de Jeunesse Inédites*, vol. i, p. 483.
11 Bibliothèque Nationale, Paris, N.A.F. 23,839.
12 Vide Chapter Two.
13 *Oeuvres de Jeunesse Inédites*, vol. i, p. 484.
14 ibid., vol. i, p. 497.
15 ibid., vol. i, p. 502.
16 ibid., vol. i, p. 504.
17 ibid., vol. i, p. 505.
18 ibid., vol. i, p. 515.
19 ibid., vol. i, p. 540.
20 ibid., vol. i, p. 526.
21 *Correspondance*, vol. i, p. 54, letter to Chevalier, 23 July 1839.
22 ibid., vol. i, p. 40, letter to Chevalier, 24 February 1839.
23 ibid., vol. i, p. 54 letter to Chevalier, 23 July 1839.
24 ibid., vol. i, p. 61, letter to Chevalier, 19 November 1839.
25 *Bulletin des Amis de Flaubert*, No. 10.
26 ibid.

27 *Correspondance*, vol. 1, p. 62, letter to Chevalier, 18 December 1839.
28 ibid., vol. 1, p. 69, letter to Chevalier, 22 June 1840.
29 ibid., vol. 1, p. 67, letter to Chevalier, 21 April 1840.
30 *Souvenirs, Notes et Pensées Intimes*, pp. 58–9.
31 ibid., p. 57.
32 ibid., p. 56.
33 ibid., p. 66.
34 ibid., p. 49.
35 ibid., p. 60.

CHAPTER 6: EULALIE FOUCAUD (1840–41)

1 Unpublished letter quoted by Bruneau: op. cit., p. 285.
2 *Par les Champs et par les Grèves*, p. 478.
3 ibid., pp. 362–3.
4 ibid., p. 381.
5 *Souvenirs, Notes et Pensées Intimes*, p. 83.
6 *Correspondance*, vol. 1, p. 71, letter to Caroline Flaubert, 29 September 1840.
7 *Par les Champs et par les Grèves*, p. 478.
8 ibid., pp. 424–5.
9 op. cit., p. 304, Note 185.
10 *Souvenirs, Notes et Pensées Intimes*, p. 78.
11 Bruneau: op. cit., p. 315, Note 38.
12 *Correspondance*, vol 1, p. 166, letter to Le Poittevin, April 1845.
13 ibid., vol. IV, p. 256, letter to Louis Bouilhet, c. April 1858.
14 From C. West's notes on the Tennant papers.
15 *Souvenirs Littéraires*, vol. 1, pp. 219–20.
16 *Correspondance*, vol. 1, p. 79, letter to Chevalier, 29 March 1841.
17 ibid., vol. 1, p. 76, letter to Chevalier, 14 November 1841.
18 ibid., vol. 1, p. 78, letter to Chevalier, 14 January 1841.
19 *Souvenirs, Notes et Pensées Intimes*, p. 94.
20 *Correspondance*, vol. 1, p. 89, letter to Chevalier, 31 December 1841.
21 ibid., vol. 1, p. 93, letter to Gourgaud-Dugazon, 22 January 1842.

Part Two: The Apprentice

CHAPTER 7: NOVEMBRE (1841–2)

1   *Correspondance*, vol. I, p. 93, letter to Gourgaud-Dugazon, 22 January 1842.
2   ibid., vol. I, p. 96, letter to Chevalier, 23 February 1842.
3   ibid., vol. I, p. 106, letter to Chevalier, 25 June 1842.
4   ibid., vol. III, p. 216, letter 1 June 1853.
5   ibid., vol. I, p. 106, letter to Caroline, 3 July 1842.
6   ibid., vol. III, p. 287, letter to Louise Colet, 9 August 1853.
7   *Oeuvres de Jeunesse Inédites*, vol. II, p. 190.
8   *Revue Hebdomadaire*, 12 December 1936. Chevalley-Sabatier: *Gustave Flaubert et sa Soeur Caroline d'après leur Correspondance inédite*.
9   Bibliothèque Nationale, Paris, N.A.F. 23,825. 'J'ai admiré ta froideur à l'égard de la femme que tu fais baigner. Le repos de ton membre viril ne tiendrait-il pas au froid de l'eau? Ou encore à l'age? Peut-être à la figure de ta baigneuse? Ou n'es-tu pas épuisé par *l'on ne peut plus fréquente* habitude de la masturbation?'
10 Bibliothèque Nationale, Paris, N.A.F. 23,825.
11 I am indebted to Dr C. West for the use of her notes. Philip Spencer used the papers for his biography of Flaubert.
12 West notes, *Mémoire*.
13 *Revue Hebdomadaire*, 12 December 1936.
14 ibid.
15 *Correspondance*, vol. I, pp. 332–3, letter to Louise Colet, 22 September 1846.
16 *Revue de Littérature Comparée*, 1957, p. 277.
17 West notes, *Mémoire*.
18 *Correspondance*, vol. II, p. 359, letter to Louise Colet, 25 January 1852.
19 G. P. Coleman: *Flaubert's Literary Development* etc.
20 L. P. Shanks: *Flaubert's Youth*.
21 *Correspondance*, vol. III, p. 379, letter 28–9 October 1853.
22 ibid., vol. IV, p. 381, letter 3 July 1860.
23 Goncourts: *Journal*, 1888–92, p. 157.
24 *Correspondance*, vol. I, p. 403, letter 17 November 1846.
25 *Oeuvres de Jeunesse Inédites*, vol. II, p. 181.
26 ibid., vol. II, p. 186.

27 ibid., vol. ii, p. 198.

28 ibid., vol. ii, p. 202.

29 ibid., vol. ii, p. 204.

30 ibid., vol. ii, p. 213.

31 ibid., vol. ii, p. 255.

32 *Correspondance*, vol. i, p. 410, letter to Louise Colet, 2 December 1846.

CHAPTER 8: MAXIME DU CAMP (1842–4)

1 *Correspondance*, vol. i, p. 118, letter to Caroline, 18 November 1842.

2 Du Camp: *Souvenirs Littéraires*, vol. i, p. 220.

3 *Correspondance*, vol. i, p. 336, letter to Louise Colet, 24 September 1846.

4 Durry: *Flaubert et ses Projets Inédits*, p. 403.

5 Letter to Bouilhet in the Spoehlberch de Lovenjoul Collection in the Institut Library at Chantilly, A. V. (Unpublished.)

6 *Correspondance*, vol. i, p. 133, letter March 1843.

7 Le Poittevin's letters, in *Promenade de Bélial*, p. 168.

8 *Correspondance*, vol. i, p. 144, letter August 1843.

9 ibid., vol. i, p. 161, letter to Le Poittevin, April 1845.

10 ibid., vol. i, p. 162, letter to Le Poittevin, 2 April 1845.

11 ibid., vol. i, p. 127, letter to Caroline, January 1843.

12 *Correspondance Supplément*, vol. i, p. 8, letter to Caroline, April 1842.

13 *Correspondance*, vol. iv, p. 127, letter 2 October 1856.

14 Wagner: *Histoire de ma Vie*, vol. i, translated in 1911.

15 ibid.

16 *Correspondance*, vol. i, p. 282, letter 30 August 1846; also p. 363, letter 8 October 1846. Pommier & Digeon: *Mercure de France*, 1 May 1952: *Du Nouveau sur Flaubert et son Oeuvre*, Bruneau: *Les Débuts Littéraires de Gustave Flaubert*, pp. 365–71.

17 Durry: *Flaubert et ses Projets Inédits*, p. 151.

18 *Correspondance*, vol. iv, pp. 351–2, letter November or December 1859.

19 ibid., vol. i, p. 135, letter to Caroline, April 1843.

20 ibid., vol. i, p. 139, letter to Caroline, 11 May 1843.

21 *Revue Hebdomadaire*, 12 December 1936.

22 *Correspondance*, vol. i, p. 143, letter to Caroline, August
    1843.
23 Le Poittevin: *Une Promenade de Bélial*, p. 178.
24 *Correspondance Supplément*, vol. iii, p. 319, letter 3 March
    1877.
25 *Souvenirs Littéraires*, vol. i, p. 218.
26 ibid., vol. i, p. 254.
27 Unpublished letter in the Spoehlberch de Lovenjoul Col-
    lection, in the Institut Library at Chantilly, B. II.
28 *Souvenirs Littéraires*, vol. i, p. 177.
29 Letter in the Spoehlberch de Lovenjoul Collection in the
    Institut Library at Chantilly, B.II. Also, published by Pom-
    mier & Digeon, *Mercure de France*, 1 May 1952: *Du Nou-
    veau sur Flaubert et son Oeuvre*.
30 *Correspondance*, vol. ii, p. 343, letter to Louise Colet, 16
    January 1852.
31 Gérard-Gailly: *Flaubert et les Fantômes de Trouville*, pp.
    110–12.
32 *Correspondance*, vol. i, pp. 243–4, letter 11 August 1846.

CHAPTER 9: L'ÉDUCATION SENTIMENTALE–(1844–5)

1   *Correspondance*, vol. i, p. 146, letter January or February
    1844.
2   ibid., vol. i, p. 148, letter 9 February 1844.
3   ibid., vol. i, p. 150, letter 7 June 1844.
4   Unpublished letter 13 May 1845, Spoehlberch de Lovenjoul
    Collection in the Institut Library at Chantilly, A. VI.
5   *Correspondance*, vol. i, p. 277, letter 27 August 1846.
6   ibid., vol. i, p. 187, letter 13 August 1845.
7   ibid., vol. i, p. 205, letter April 1846.
8   *Souvenirs, Notes et Pensées Intimes*, pp. 66–7.
9   *Correspondance*, vol. i, p. 160, letter 2 April 1845.
10 Bibliothèque Nationale, Paris, N.A.F., 25,825, unpublished
    letter.
11 *Promenade de Bélial*, p. xxxvi.
12 *Correspondance*, vol. i, 190, letter to Le Poittevin, August
    1845.
13 *Souvenirs Littéraires*, vol. i, p. 234.
14 Unpublished letter 31 October 1844, Spoehlberch de Loven-
    joul Collection in the Institut Library at Chantilly, A.I.

15 ibid.
16 Letter 5, 22 June 1844. ibid.
17 Letter 14 August 1844. ibid.
18 Letter 12 June 1844. ibid.
19 Letter 22 June 1844. ibid.
20 *Correspondance*, vol. I, p. 185, letter to Le Poittevin, June–July 1845.
21 ibid., vol. II, pp. 343–4, letter to Louise Colet, 16 January 1852.
22 Note, in Bruneau: *Les Débuts Littéraires de Gustave Flaubert*, and in Barron: *La Première Éducation Sentimentale* in *Bulletin des Amis de Flaubert*, No. 12, for the influence of various philosophers, including Spinoza, on Flaubert.
23 *Oeuvres de Jeunesse Inédites*, vol. III, p. 255.
24 *Correspondance*, vol. I, pp. 385–6, letter to Louise Colet, 23 October 1846.
25 *Oeuvres de Jeunesse Inédites*, vol. III, p. 255.
26 ibid., vol. III, p. 267.
24 *Correspondance*, vol. I, pp. 385–6, letter to Louise Colet, 23 October 1846.
28 ibid., vol. III, p. 336, letter 7 September 1853.
29 *Oeuvres de Jeunesse Inédites*, vol. III, pp. 12–13.
30 ibid., vol. III, p. 26
31 ibid., vol. III, p. 150.
32 L. P. Shanks: *Flaubert's Youth*, p. 196.
33 Demorest: *L'Expression Figurée et Symbolique dans l'Oeuvre de Gustave Flaubert*, p. 531.
34 *The Significance of the Dog in Flaubert's 'Éducation Sentimentale'*, *P.M.L.A.*, June 1947.
35 *Les Débuts Littéraires de Gustave Flaubert*, p. 428.
36 *Oeuvres de Jeunesse Inédites*, vol. III, pp. 251–2.
37 ibid., vol. III, p. 253.
38 ibid., vol. III, p. 310.
39 *Souvenirs Littéraires*, vol. I, p. 301.
40 *Correspondance*, vol. I, p. 373, letter 14 October 1846.

CHAPTER 10: THE TRAGIC YEAR (1845–6)

1   *Correspondance Supplément*, vol. 1, p. 25, Note.
2   Letter 26 November 1844, Spoehlberch de Lovenjoul Collection at the Institut Library at Chantilly, B. II.
3   *Correspondance*, vol. 1, p. 161, letter to Le Poittevin, 2 April 1845.
4   ibid., vol. 1, p. 164, letter to Le Poittevin, end April 1845.
5   ibid., vol. 1, p. 165, letter to Le Poittevin, end April 1845.
6   ibid., vol. 1, p. 163, letter to Le Poittevin, 2 April 1845.
7   ibid., vol. 1, p. 166, letter to Le Poittevin, end April 1845.
8   ibid., vol. 1, p. 172, letter to Le Poittevin, 13 May 1845.
9   *Notes de Voyages*, vol. 1, p. 13.
10 *Correspondance*, vol. 1, p. 173, letter to Le Poittevin, 13 May 1845.
11 *Notes de Voyages*, vol. 1, pp. 36–7.
12 *Correspondance*, vol. 1, p. 173, letter to Le Poittevin, 13 May, 1845.
13 ibid., vol. 1, p. 180, letter to Chevalier, 13 June 1845.
14 ibid., vol. 1, p. 189, letter to Le Poittevin, August 1845.
15 *Souvenirs Littéraires*, vol. 1, pp. 305–8.
16 *Correspondance*, vol. 1, p. 199, letter to Chevalier, 5 April 1846.
17 ibid., vol. 1, p. 195, letter 20 March 1846.
18 ibid., vol. 1, pp. 196–8, letter to Du Camp, 23–4 March 1846.
19 *Correspondance Supplément*, vol. 1, p. 59, letter 31 May 1846.

CHAPTER 11: LOUISE COLET (1846–8)

1   J. F. Jackson: *Louise Colet et ses Amis Littéraires*.
2   Gérard-Gailly: *Les Véhémences de Louise Colet*, pp. 16–99.
3   Jackson op. cit., pp. 66–9.
4   *Les Chroniques, Revue du Monde Fashionable*, May 1842.
5   Sainte-Beuve: *Correspondance Générale*, tome IX, pp. 294–7, letters 4 and 7 June 1853.
6   E. Henriot: *D'Héloïse à Marie Bashkirtseff*, p. 180.
7   *Correspondance*, vol. III, p. 428, letter 18 April 1854.

8   *Correspondance*, vol. I, p. 226, letter 8 August 1846.
9   *Correspondance*, vol. I, pp. 211–12, letter 4 August 1846.
10 ibid., vol. I, p. 217, letter 6 August 1846.
11 ibid., vol. I, pp. 346–7, letter 23 August 1846.
12 ibid., vol. I, p. 286, letter 2 September 1846.
13 ibid., vol. I, p. 293, letter 5 September 1846.
14 Bibliothèque Nationale, Paris, N.A.F. 23,830, unpublished letter.
15 *Correspondance*, vol. I, p. 243, letter 11 August 1846.
16 ibid., vol. I, p. 263, letter 23 August 1846.
17 ibid., vol. I, pp. 264–5, letter 23 August 1846.
18 Bibliothèque Nationale, Paris, N.A.F. 23,830, unpublished letter 24–5 August 1846.
19 *Correspondance*, vol. I, p. 286, letter 25 September 1846.
20 ibid., vol. I, p. 290, letter 4–5 September 1846.
21 ibid., vol. I, p. 292, letter 5 September 1846.
22 ibid., vol. I, p. 296, letter 6 September 1846.
23 ibid., vol. I, p. 299, letter 10 September 1846.
24 ibid., vol. VII, p. 2, letter January 1873.
25 ibid., vol. I, p. 298, letter 10 September 1846.
26 Bibliothèque de la Ville de Paris, *Carnet V*.
27 *Correspondance*, vol. I, p. 309, letter 14 September 1846.
28 ibid., vol. I, p. 318, letter 18 September 1846.
29 ibid., vol. I, p. 357, letter 4 October 1846.
30 Bibliothèque Nationale, Paris, N.A.F. 23,830, unpublished letter 13 September 1846.
31 *Correspondance*, vol. I, p. 311, letter 15 September 1846.
32 Bibliothèque Nationale, Paris, N.A.F. 23,830, unpublished letter 8 December 1846.
33 *Correspondance*, vol. I, p. 306, letter 13 September 1846.
34 ibid., vol. I, p. 233, letter 9 August 1846.
35 ibid., vol. II, p. 64, letter, undated, 1846.
36 Louise Colet: *L'Art et l'Amour* in *Ce qui est dans le Coeur des Femmes*.
37 *Correspondance*, vol. II, p. 63, no date, 1847.
38 ibid., vol. II, p. 64, no date, 1847.
39 Du Camp: *Souvenirs Littéraires*, vol. II, p. 364.
40 *Correspondance*, vol. I, p. 396, letter 15 November 1846.
41 ibid., vol. II, p. 1, letter, no date, and p. 19, letter 30 April 1847.
42 ibid., vol. I, p. 431, letter end of 1846.

43 ibid., vol. I, p. 422, letter 16 December 1846.
44 ibid., vol. I, p. 432, letter end of 1846.
45 Bibliothèque Nationale, Paris, N.A.F. 23,830, letter March 1847, unpublished.
46 *Correspondance*, vol. II, pp. 45–6, letter August 1847.
47 ibid., vol. II, p. 50 letter, no date, and p. 55, letter, no date, 1847.
48 ibid., vol. II, pp. 80–1, letter March 1848.
49 ibid., vol. II, p. 68, letter 21 August 1848.

CHAPTER 12: LOUIS BOUILHET (1846–8)

1 *Souvenirs Littéraires*, vol. I, p. 320.
2 Vide Introduction, Note 5.
3 *Correspondance*, vol. VI, p. 39, letter to Jules Duplan, 22 July 1869.
4 Bibliothèque Municipale, Rouen, g 226^g. Bibliothèque Nationale, Paris, N.A.F. 14,155, 14,156, and 14,249–54.
5 *Correspondance*, vol. II, p. 390, letter 15 April 1852.
6 ibid., vol. II, p. 384, letter to Louise Colet, 3 April 1852.
7 ibid., vol. II, p. 53, letter to Louise Colet, October 1847.
8 *Souvenirs Littéraires*, vol. II, p. 353.
9 ibid., vol. II, p. 364.
10 Letter 8 May 1843, Spoehlberch de Lovenjoul Collection, Institut Library at Chantilly, B.II.
11 *Correspondance*, vol. II, p. 384, letter to Louise Colet, 5 April 1852.
12 *Par les Champs et par les Grèves*, p. 295.
13 ibid., pp. 324–5.
14 p. 41 et seq.
15 *Correspondance*, vol. II, p. 80, letter March 1848.
16 *Souvenirs Littéraires*, vol. I, p. 372.
17 *Correspondance*, vol. II, p. 81, letter 7 April 1848.

CHAPTER 13: LA TENTATION DE SAINT ANTOINE (1848–9)

1 *Correspondance*, vol. I, p. 173, letter to Le Poittevin, 13 May 1845.
2 ibid., vol. II, p. 33, letter to Louise Colet, August 1847.

3 ibid., vol. II, p. 54, letter to Louise Colet, October 1847.

4 ibid., vol. VI, p. 443, letter 30 October 1872.

5 ibid., vol. II, pp. 344–5, letter to Louise Colet, 16 June 1852.

6 *Carnets de Lecture No. 3*, in Bibliothèque de la Ville de Paris.

7 vol. I, p. 427 *et seq.*

8 ibid., p. 428.

9 ibid., p. 450.

10 *Correspondance*, vol. II, p. 146, letter to his mother, 5 January 1850.

11 *Souvenirs Littéraires*, vol. I, p. 433.

12 *Correspondance*, vol. II, p. 364, letter 8 February 1852.

13 *Souvenirs Littéraires*, vol. I, p. 435.

14 *Correspondance*, vol. II, p. 462, letter to Louise Colet, 6 July 1852.

15 ibid., vol. III, p. 92, letter to Louise Colet, 29–30 January 1853.

16 ibid., vol. III, p. 156, letter to Louise Colet, 6 April 1853.

17 *La Tentation de Saint Antoine*, pp. 264–5.

18 ibid., pp. 437–8.

19 ibid., p. 457

CHAPTER 14: THE EASTERN TRIP (1849–51)

1 No. F[17] 2957[1].

2 No. F[12] 2593(A-B).

3 *Le Temps*, 9 October 1923.

4 *Notes de Voyages*, vol. I, p. 65.

5 ibid., vol. I, p. 67.

6 ibid., vol. I, p. 68.

7 Du Camp: *Souvenirs Littéraires*, vol. I, p. 439.

8 ibid., vol. I, p. 440.

9 *Correspondance*, vol. II, p. 108, letter 17 November 1849.

10 ibid., vol. II, p. 110, letter 22 November 1849.

11 *Notes de Voyages*, vol. I, p. 74.

12 *Correspondance Supplément*, vol. I, p. 110, letter to Mme Flaubert, 7 November 1850.

13 Bibliothèque de la Ville de Paris, *Carnet No. 5*, p. 81.

14 Flaubert: *Voyages* (Société les Belles Lettres), Tome I, p. xliv.

15 ibid., Tome I, p. xlv.
16 *Le Nil, Egypte, et Nubie*, p. 129.
17 *Notes de Voyages*, vol. I, p. 155.
18 *Koutchouk-Hanem, l'Aimée de Flaubert*, p. 15.
19 Bibliothèque de la Ville de Paris, *Carnet No. 4*, p. 63 *et seq.*
20 *Notes de Voyages*, vol. I, pp. 156–60.
21 ibid., vol. I, p. 155.
22 Bibliothèque de la Ville de Paris, *Carnet No. 4*, p. 63 *et seq.*
23 ibid., *Carnet No. 4*, p. 63 *et seq.*
24 *Notes de Voyages*, vol. I, p. 160.
25 ibid., vol. I, p. 212.
26 *Souvenirs Littéraires*, vol. I, pp. 492–3.
27 *Correspondance*, vol. II, p. 225, letter to Mme Flaubert, 10 August 1850.
28 *Notes de Voyages*, vol. I, pp. 291–2.
29 ibid., vol. I, p. 297.
30 ibid., vol. I, p. 306.
31 ibid., vol. I, p. 319.
32 Spoehlberch de Lovenjoul Collection at the Institut Library at Chantilly, unpublished letters to Louis Bouilhet, A.V.
33 *Souvenirs Littéraires*, vol. I, pp. 510–11.
34 *Notes de Voyages*, vol. I, pp. 318–39 and p. 333.
35 *Souvenirs Littéraires*, vol. II, p. 78.
36 *Correspondance*, vol. II, p. 282, letter to Mme Flaubert, 24 December 1850.
37 Reproduction of the picture in *Nouvelles Études sur la Tentation de Saint Antoine* by Jean Seznec, plate VIII.
38 *Correspondance*, vol. II, p. 302, letter to Mme Flaubert, 8 April 1851.
39 ibid., vol. II, p. 305, letter to Bouilhet, 9 April 1851.
40 ibid., vol. II, p. 313, letter to Bouilhet, 4 May 1851.
41 *Notes de Voyages*, vol. II, pp. 257–8.
42 *Correspondance*, vol. II, p. 237, letter to Bouilhet, 4 September 1850.
43 Bruneau: op. cit., p. 516. Also *Correspondance*, vol. II, p. 253, letter to Bouilhet, 14 November 1850.
44 *Souvenirs Littéraires*, vol. I, p. 481.
45 *Correspondance*, vol. III, pp. 136–8, letter to Louise Colet, 27 March 1853.
46 ibid., vol. III, p. 254, letter to Louise Colet, 28–9 June 1853.

47 ibid., vol. III, p. 364 and p. 366, letters to Louise Colet, 7 and 12 October 1853

48 Zola: *Les Romanciers Naturalistes* (Bernouard), p. 170.

BOOK TWO: SUMMER HARVEST

Part One: The Workshop

CHAPTER 15: THE HERMIT OF CROISSET (1851–6)

1 *Correspondance*, vol. II, p. 253, letter 14 November 1850.

2 *Bulletin des Amis de Flaubert*, No. 14, 1959, letter 23 July 1851.

3 Most of those who write on Flaubert, and those who have edited the *Correspondance*, confuse the two names 'Delamarre' and 'Delamare'. There was a wealthy family in Rouen called Delamarre – with two 'r's' – a mother and two sons, frequently mentioned in Flaubert's correspondence and in Alfred Le Poittevin's letters to him. The two sons, Ernest and Jules, seem to have been rich and smart men about town; and the richness of their clothes, their clubs in Paris, their horses and their duelling, were far from the life of the unfortunate 'Officier de Santé', Eugène Delamare – with one 'r' – and he had no money for their kind of extravagance. The Madame Delamarre in Flaubert's letters was certainly not his mother, but that of the other two young men. Even René Descharmes, with his profound knowledge of Flaubert, is wrong in his edition of the correspondence, *Édition du Centenaire*, vol. I, p. 26, when he states that Jules Delamarre, whom Flaubert mentions, is Eugène Delamare, the future 'Officier de Santé', the model for Charles Bovary. Flaubert tells Louise Colet – *Correspondance*, vol. III, p. 348 – that Ernest Delamarre gave him the little gilt statue which he possessed, and certainly Eugène Delamare would not have been able to afford such a gift. There is no proof at all that Flaubert had ever known Eugène Delamare, and there is no mention of him in any of the letters.

4 The question of the sources of *Madame Bovary* will be fully discussed in a later chapter.

5 Spoehlberch de Lovenjoul Collection in the Institut Library

T–P

at Chantilly, Du Camp's unpublished letters to Flaubert, B.II.

6   Published in *Correspondance Supplément,* vol. I.

7   *Correspondance,* vol. I, p. xix.

8   In conversation with the present author.

9   *Correspondanc*e, vol. I, p. xxv.

10 ibid., vol. II, p. 467, letter to Louise Colet, 18 July 1852.

11 ibid., vol. III, p. 305, letter to Louise Colet, 21–2 August 1853.

12 ibid., vol. III, p. 369, letter to Louise Colet, 17–18 October 1853.

13 This episode will be discussed in the following chapter.

14 *Correspondance,* vol. II, p. 329, letter to Louise Colet, November 1851.

15 *Mercure de France,* 1 May 1952.

16 *Correspondance,* vol. III, p. 272, letter to Louise Colet, 7–8 July 1853.

17 This will be discussed in the following chapter.

18 *Correspondance,* Vol. III, p. 265, letter to Louise Colet, 2 July 1853.

19 *Mercure de France,* 1 May 1952.

20 *Correspondance,* vol. I, p. 352, letter to Louise Colet, 3 October 1846.

21 ibid., vol. III, pp. 308–9, letter to Louise Colet, 21–2 August 1853.

22 ibid., vol. III, p. 316, letter to Bouilhet, 23 August 1853.

23 ibid., vol. II, p. 407, letter 8–9 May 1852.

24 ibid., vol. III, p. 76, letter to Louise Colet, 27 December 1852.

25 ibid., vol. III, p. 146, letter to Louise Colet, 31 March 1853.

26 ibid., vol. III, p. 317, letter 23 August 1853.

27 ibid., vol. III, p. 321, letter 26 August 1853.

28 E. W. Fischer: *Études sur Flaubert Inédit.*

29 *Revue d'Histoire Littéraire de la France,* October–December 1948.

30 Chapter IX, *Conclusion.*

31 op. cit., p. 128.

32 ibid., p. 137.

33 ibid., p. 128.

34 *Correspondance,* vol. III, p. 146, letter to Louise Colet, 31 March 1853.

35 ibid., vol. IV, p. 408, letter to Baudelaire, 22 October 1860.

CHAPTER 16: THE END OF THE AFFAIR (1851–5)

1   Unpublished letters in the Spoehlberch de Lovenjoul Collection in the Institut Library at Chantilly, C.I.

2   *Correspondance*, vol. II, p. 313, letter to Louise Colet, 26 July 1851.

3   Bibliothèque Nationale, Paris, N.A.F. 23,831, unpublished letter October 1851.

4   *Correspondance*, vol. II, p. 364, letter 8 February 1852.

5   ibid., vol. II, p. 330, letter 1 November 1851.

6   ibid., vol. II, pp. 346–7, letter 16 January 1852.

7   ibid., vol. II, p. 403, letter 24 April 1852.

8   Bibliothèque Nationale, Paris, N.A.F. 23,831, unpublished portion of letter 4 April 1852.

9   ibid., N.A.F. 23,831, unpublished portion of letter 9 December 1852.

10 *Correspondance*, vol. III, pp. 62–3, letter 1 December 1852.

11 Bibliothèque Nationale, Paris, N.A.F. 23,831, unpublished portion of same letter.

12 *Correspondance*, vol. III, p. 63, letter 1 December 1852.

13 Bibliothèque Nationale, Paris, N.A.F. 23,831, unpublished.

14 *Correspondance*, vol. II, p. 419, letter 23 May 1852.

15 ibid., vol. II, pp. 430–1, letter 9 June 1852.

16 ibid., vol. III, p. 194 *et seq.*, letter 17 May 1853.

17 *Correspondance*, vol. III, p. 279, letter July 1853.

18 ibid., vol. III, p. 377, letter 28 October 1853.

19 ibid., vol. III, p. 385, letter 22 November 1853.

20 ibid., vol. III, p. 385, Note.

21 Bibliothèque Nationale, Paris, N.A.F. 23,831, unpublished letter 25–6 November 1853.

22 *Correspondance*, vol. III, p. 28, letter 25 September 1852.

23 ibid., vol. III, p. 308, letter 21–2 August 1853.

24 *Revue de Paris*, 1 November 1908, letter 16 March 1852.

25 *Correspondance*, vol. III, p. 6, letter to Louise Colet, 1 September 1852.

26 *Revue de Paris*, 1 November 1908.

27 *Correspondance*, vol. II, pp. 464–5, letter 7–8 July 1852.

28 *Correspondance Supplément*, vol. I, p. 172, letter 10 January 1854.

29 *Correspondance*, vol. iii, p. 154, letter 31 March 1853.

30 Bibliothèque Nationale, Paris, N.A.F. 23,827.

31 Jackson: *Louise Colet et ses Amis Littéraires*, pp. 142–3.

32 ibid., op. cit., p 215.

33 A. Albalat: *Gustave Flaubert et ses Amis*, pp. 31–3.

34 H. Frejlich: *Les Amants de Mantes*, p. 137. This portion of
    the letter is unpublished in the *Correspondance*, vol. iii,
    p. 395, letter 10 December 1853, which is the date of the un-
    published fragment, though there is no indication in the
    published version that anything has been omitted.

35 *Correspondance*, vol. iv, p. 9, letter 13 January 1854.

36 ibid., vol. iv, p. 29, letter 25 February 1854.

37 ibid., vol. iv, p. 29, letter 25 February 1854.

38 *Correspondance*, vol. iv, p. 56 *et seq.*, letter 12–13 April
    1854.

39 ibid., vol. ii, p. 382, letter March 1852.

40 ibid., vol. iii, pp. 106–7, letter 5–6 March 1853.

41 ibid., vol. iii, p. 117, letter 1 March 1853.

42 *Revue des Deux Mondes*, 1 June 1954, letter not in *Cor-
    respondance*.

43 *Correspondance*, vol. iii, pp. 132–3, letter 27 March 1853.

44 ibid., vol. iii, p. 127, letter 24 March 1853.

45 ibid., vol. iii, p. 219, letter 2 June 1853.

46 Published in *Bulletin des Amis de Flaubert*, No. 10.

47 *Correspondance*, vol. ii, p. 428, letter 30 May 1852; vol. iii,
    p. 363, letter 7 October 1853.

48 ibid., vol. iii, p. 366, letter 12 October 1853.

49 ibid., vol. iv, pp. 6–7, letter 13 January 1854.

50 *Histoire d'un Soldat*, pp. 129–31.

51 *Correspondance*, vol. iv, p. 325, letter 21 August 1859.

52 *Correspondance Supplément*, vol. i, p. 186, letter 16 Oc-
    tober 1854.

53 Published in *Le Bulletin des Amis de Flaubert*, No. 6, not in
    Correspondance.

54 H. Frejlich: *Les Amants de Mantes*, p. 59.

55 Gérard-Gailly: *Les Véhémences de Louise Colet*, p. 95.

56 Discovered by Jackson and discussed in op. cit., pp. 232–3.

57 *Correspondance*, vol. vi, p. 353, letter to George Sand be-
    tween 20 and 29 February 1872.

58 ibid., vol. iv, pp. 350–1, letter November or December
    1859.

59   ibid., vol. VII, p. 291, letter to Mme Roger des Genettes, 13 to
     18 March 1876.
60   ibid., vol. IV, p. 356, letter 18 December 1859.

CHAPTER 17: THE TRIBULATIONS OF AN ARTIST
(1851–6)

1   *Correspondance*, vol. II, p. 326, letter October 1851.
2   A. Houssaye *Confessions*, Tome VI, p. 95.
3   *Correspondance*, vol. II, p. 319, letter 21 October 1851.
4   ibid., vol. II, pp. 320–1, letter to Du Camp, 21 October
     1851.
5   ibid., vol. II, p. 323, letter 21 October 1851.
6   ibid., vol. II, pp. 321–4, letter 21 October 1851.
7   Spoehlberch de Lovenjoul Collection in the Institut Library
     at Chantilly, B.II.
8   ibid., B.II.
9   ibid., B.II.
10   ibid., B.II.
11   ibid., B.II.
12   Published in Introduction to *Correspondance*, vol. I.
13   *Correspondance*, vol. II, p. 339, letter January 1852.
14   ibid., vol. II, p. 339, letter January 1852.
15   ibid., vol. II, p. 350, letter to Louise Colet, 17 January
     1852.
16   ibid., vol. II, p. 383, letter to Louise Colet, 3 April 1852.
17   ibid., vol. II, p. 394, letter to Louise Colet, 24 April 1852.
18   ibid., vol. III, p. 92, and vol. IV, p. 52, letters 29 January 1853
     and 7 April 1854.
19   ibid., vol. IV, p. 99, letter 2 October 1855.
20   ibid., vol. IV, p. 88, letter 17 September 1855, and p. 90,
     letter 20 September 1855.
21   ibid., vol. II, p. 371, letter to Louise Colet, 3 March 1852.
22   ibid., vol. II, p. 344, letter to Louise Colet, 16 January 1852,
     and vol. III, p. 92, letter to Louise Colet, 30 January 1853.
23   ibid., vol. II, p. 351, letter to Louise Colet, 17 January
     1852.
24   ibid., vol. II, p. 368, letter to Louise Colet, 16 February
     1852.
25   ibid., vol. II, p. 442, letter 26 June 1852.
26   A term which Flaubert remembered from his legal studies.

27   *Correspondance*, vol. II, p. 445, letter 26 June 1852.
28   ibid., vol. II, p. 451, letter July 1851.
29   ibid., vol. III, pp. 109–10, letter 5–6 March 1853.
30   ibid., vol. III, pp. 253–4, letter 28–9 June 1853.
31   ibid., vol. III, p. 260, letter to Louise Colet, 2 July 1853.
32   ibid., vol. III, pp. 56–7, letter to Louise Colet, December 1852.
33   ibid., vol. III, p. 364, letter to Louise Colet, 7 October 1853.
34   ibid., vol. IV, p. 17, letter to Louise Colet, January 1854.
35   ibid., vol. IV, p. 316, letter to Ernest Feydeau, May 1859.
36   ibid., vol. IV, p. 114, letter to Louis Bouilhet, 1 September 1856.
37   ibid., vol. IV, pp. 91–3, letter to Louis Bouilhet, 30 September 1855.
38   ibid., vol. IV, pp. 92–6, letter to Louis Bouilhet, 30 September 1855, and p. 99, letter 2 October 1855.
39   ibid., vol. IV, pp. 92–3, letter to Louis Bouilhet, 30 September 1855.
40   ibid., vol. IV, pp. 64–5, letter to Louis Bouilhet, 5 August 1854.
41   ibid., vol. IV, p. 66, letter 9 August 1854.
42   ibid., vol. IV, p. 64, Note 2.
43   Published in *Candide*, 22 September 1932.
44   *Correspondance Supplément*, vol. I, p. 198, letter 3 March 1856.
45   Bibliothèque Municipale de Rouen, g 221.
46   ibid., g 222.
47   *Correspondance*, vol. IV, p. 107, letter 17 June 1856.
48   Vide Steegmuller: *Flaubert and Madame Bovary*, pp. 285–6. He does not, however, say where he has obtained his material.

CHAPTER 18: PUBLICATION (1856)

1   *Correspondance*, vol. IV, p. 103, letter to Louis Bouilhet, 1 June 1856.
2   As quoted by Finot: *Maxime du Camp*, p. 39.
3   ibid., p. 41.
4   *Madame Bovary*, p. 512.
5   *Correspondance*, vol. IV, p. 111, letters to Bouilhet, 15 August 1856, and p. 113, letter 25 August 1856.

6   ibid., vol. IV, p. 115, letter to Bouilhet, 1 September 1856.
7   ibid., vol. IV, p. 118, letter 9 September 1856.
8   ibid., vol. IV, pp. 124–5, letter 2 October 1856.
9   Finot: op. cit., p. 41.
10 *Correspondance*, vol. IV, pp. 136–8, letter between 1 and 15 December 1856.
11 Du Camp: *Souvenirs Littéraires*, Tome II, pp. 200–1.
12 *Madame Bovary*, p. 513.
13 ibid., p. 507.
14 Finot: op. cit., p. 42.
15 Du Camp: *Souvenirs Littéraires*, Tome II, pp. 203–4.
16 Descharmes and Dumesnil: *Autour de Flaubert*, vol. I, p. 22, Note.
17 *Madame Bovary*, p. 514.

CHAPTER 19: THE TRIAL (1857)

1   *Correspondance*, vol. IV, pp. 139–41.
2   ibid., vol. IV, pp. 141–3, letter 3 January 1857.
3   *Maxime du Camp*, p. 44.
4   *Ce qu'il me reste à dire*, p. 271.
5   *Correspondance*, vol. IV, p. 145, letter to Achille Flaubert, 6 January 1857.
6   Descharmes and Dumesnil: *Autour de Flaubert*, vol. I, p. 31.
7   *Correspondance*, vol. IV, pp. 150–1, letter 18 January 1857.
8   ibid., vol. IV, pp. 160–1, letter February 1857.
9   ibid., vol. IV, p. 155, letter 23 January 1857.
10 Quoted by André Pasquet: *Ernest Pinaud et le Procès de Madame Bovary*.
11 ibid., pp. 12–13.
12 *Correspondance*, vol. VIII, p. 255, letter to his niece, 16 April 1879.
13 ibid., vol. IV, p. 157, letter to Eugène Crépet, c. 26 January 1857.
14 Spoehlberch de Lovenjoul Collection at the Institut Library at Chantilly, letters from Du Camp to Flaubert, B.II.
15 Suffel: *Gustave Flaubert*, p. 51, Note.
16 The speeches and the verdict are printed at the back of *Madame Bovary*, pp. 558–630.
17 *Madame Bovary*, pp. 577–8.

18 *Correspondance*, vol. IV, p. 158, letter to Achille Flaubert, 31 January 1857.

19 *Madame Bovary*, p. 587.

20 *Madame Bovary*, pp. 629–30.

21 *Correspondance*, vol. IV, pp. 159–60, letter to Maurice Schlésinger, February 1857.

22 ibid., vol. IV, p. 160, letter to Maurice Schlésinger, February 1857.

23 Descharmes: *Le Poittevin* etc., p. lxxxvi, Note 5.

24 *Revue de Littérature Comparée*, 1957, p. 277.

25 Descharmes and Dumesnil: op. cit., Tome I, p. 45.

26 Crépet: *Baudelaire*, p. 113.

27 Descharmes and Dumesnil: op. cit., p. 51.

28 ibid., op. cit., p. 53.

29 ibid., op. cit., p. 55, Note.

30 *Correspondance Supplément*, vol. I, pp. 232–3, letter to Bouilhet, 8 October 1857.

31 Descharmes and Dumesnil: op. cit., p. 55.

32 *Correspondance*, vol. VII, p. 285, letter to George Sand, 6 February 1876.

33 Descharmes and Dumesnil: op. cit., pp. 43–4.

34 *Correspondance*, vol. III, p. 11, letter 1 September 1852.

35 *Correspondance*, vol. III, p. 23, letter to Louise Colet, 19 September 1852. Also p. 100, letter 23 February 1853, and p. 391, letter 24 November 1853.

36 *L'Oeuvre*, 20 November 1931. Deffoux: *Le Pupitre de Flaubert*.

37 *Correspondance*, vol. IV, p. 350, Note.

38 Dumesnil: *Gustave Flaubert, l'Homme et l'Oeuvre*, p. 200.

39 Bibliothèque Nationale, Paris, N.A.F. 23,824, unpublished.

40 ibid., N.A.F. 23,825, unpublished.

41 *Correspondance*, vol. IV, p. 163, letter 19 February 1857.

42 ibid., vol. IV, p. 165, letter 18 March 1857.

43 ibid., vol. IV, p. 169, letter 30 March 1857.

44 ibid., vol. IV, p. 168, letter 30 March 1857.

45 ibid., vol. IV, p. 182, letter 18 May 1857.

46 ibid., vol. IV, p. 194, letter June 1857.

47 ibid., vol. IV, p. 277 letter 4 September 1858.

48 ibid., vol. V, p. 386, letter 15 July 1868.

49 Bibliothèque Nationale, Paris, N.A.F. 23,825, unpublished.
50 *Correspondance*, vol. v, pp. 394–5, letter August 1868.
51 ibid., vol. vii, p. 304, letter 27 June 1876.
52 ibid., vol. vii, p. 305, letter 27 June 1876.
53 Charles Lapierre: *Esquisse sur Flaubert Intime*.

Part Two: The Masterpiece

CHAPTER 20: THE NOVEL IN THE SECOND EMPIRE

1 *L'Art Romantique* (Conard), p. 168.
2 *Correspondance*, vol. iv, p. 134, letter to Mme Roger des Genettes, October or November 1856.
3 Maillard: *Les Derniers Jours de la Bohème*, p. 85.
4 *Curiosités Esthétiques* (Conard), p. 419.
5 Mayniad: *L'Époque Réaliste*, p. 37.
6 Emile Bouyier: *La Bataille Réaliste*, p. 247.
7 Martino: *Le Roman Réaliste sous le Second Empire*, p. 112.
8 Champfleury: *Préface* to *Le Réalisme*.
9 Martino: *Le Roman Réaliste sous le Second Empire*, p. 115.
10 Boisson: *Les Compagnons de la Vie de Bohème*, p. 106.

CHAPTER 21: THE THEME

1 All references are to the Conard edition of *Madame Bovary*.
2 *Madame Bovary*, p. 94.
3 Pommier and Leleu: *Madame Bovary, Nouvelle Version* (José Corti).
4 *Souvenirs Littéraires*, vol. i, p. 481.
5 *Correspondance*, vol. iv, p. 168, letter to Mlle Leroyer de Chantepie, 30 March 1857.
6 ibid., vol. iv, p. 191, letter to Cailleteaux, 4 June 1857.
7 ibid., vol. iv, p. 164, letter to Mlle Leroyer de Chantepie, 18 March 1857.
8 ibid., vol. iv, p. 70, letter to Bouilhet, 10 May 1855.
9 ibid., vol. vi, p. 107, letter to Mme Hortense Cornu, 20 March 1870.

10   Spoehlberch de Lovenjoul Collection at the Institut Library at Chantilly, B.II, unpublished.

11   ibid., letter 2 August 1851.

12   15 April 1910.

13   *Correspondance*, vol. I, p. 162, letter to Le Poittevin, 2 April 1845.

14   *Revue d'Histoire Littéraire de la France*, 1947, July–September, pp. 211–26.

15   Bibliothèque Municipale, Rouen, Ms. g 226(4).

16   *Les Lettres Françaises*, 11 April 1947. Pommier: *L'Affaire Loursel*.

17   *Correspondance*, vol. II, p. 372 and p. 382, letters of 20 and 27 March 1852, to Louise Colet.

18   ibid., vol. II, p. 372, Note.

19   *Les Mémoires de Marie Cappelle*, vol. II, p. 173.

20   ibid., vol. II, p. 118.

21   ibid., vol. III, pp. 168–95.

22   ibid., vol. III, p. 272.

23   *Madame Bovary*, pp. 2–3.

24   Bibliothèque Municipale, Rouen, Ms. g(226[7]), unpublished.

25   *Madame Bovary*, pp. 225–6.

26   *Correspondance*, vol. III, p. 403, letter 18 December 1853.

27   *Oeuvres de Jeunesse Inédites*, vol. III, p. 305.

28   *Madame Bovary*, p. 468.

29   ibid., p. 469.

30   ibid., p. 265.

31   *French Novelists from the Revolution to Proust*, p. 232.

32   The whole episode is in *Madame Bovary*, pp. 426–34.

33   Bibliothèque Municipale, Rouen, Ms. gg[9].

34   *Madame Bovary*, pp. 448–9.

35   Descharmes and Dumesnil: *Autour de Flaubert*, vol. I, p. 49.

36   Bibliothèque Municipale, Rouen, Ms. g 223[5].

37   *Flaubert and Madame Bovary*, p. 304.

38   *Correspondance*, vol. IV, p. 90, letter to Louis Bouilhet, 20 September 1855.

CHAPTER 22: CHARACTERS AND CHARACTERIZATION

1   *Correspondance*, vol. ii, p. 457, letter to Louise Colet, 3–4
    July 1852.
2   *Notes de Voyages*, vol. i, pp. 80–1.
3   *Correspondance*, vol. iii, p. 201, letter to Louise Colet, 21–2
    March 1852.
4   ibid., vol. v, p. 253, letter to George Sand, 5–6 December
    1866.
5   ibid., vol. iii, p. 31, letter to Louise Colet, 25 September
    1852.
6   *Correspondance Supplément*, vol. ii, p. 118, letter 14 June
    1867.
7   *Correspondance*, vol. iii, p. 291, letter to Louise Colet, 14
    August 1853.
8   ibid., vol. v, p. 350, letter 1868.
9   ibid., vol. iii, p. 405, letter to Louise Colet, 23 December
    1852.
10 ibid., vol. ii, p. 380, letter to Louise Colet, 27 March 1852.
11 ibid., vol. iii, p. 20, letter to Louise Colet, 3 September
    1852.
12 ibid., vol. v, p. 294, letter 8–9 April 1867.
13 *Madame Bovary*, pp. 270–1.
14 ibid., p. 19.
15 ibid., p. 69.
16 ibid., p. 324.
17 ibid., p. 110.
18 ibid., p. 130.
19 ibid., p. 34.
20 ibid., pp. 48 and 56–7.
21 Bibliothèque Municipale, Rouen, Ms. gg⁹.
22 *Madame Bovary*, p. 57.
23 ibid., p. 218.
24 ibid., p. 471.
25 ibid., p. 452.
26 ibid., pp. 458–9.
27 ibid., p. 438.
28 Bibliothèque Municipale, Rouen, Ms. gg⁹.
29 *Madame Bovary*, pp. 479–80.
30 ibid., pp. 480–1.
31 ibid., p. 225.

32 Bibliothèque Municipale, Rouen, Ms. g 223[6].
33 *Madame Bovary*, p. 149.
34 ibid., p. 56.
35 ibid., p. 57.
36 ibid., p. 413.
37 ibid., p. 78.
38 ibid., pp. 223–4.
39 ibid., p. 235.
40 ibid., p. 255.
41 ibid., p. 285.
42 ibid., p. 295.
43 ibid., p. 296.
44 ibid., p. 298.
45 ibid., p. 401.
46 ibid., pp. 354–5.
47 Bibliothèque Municipale, Rouen, Ms. gg[9].
48 ibid., Ms. gg.
49 *Madame Bovary*, p. 390.
50 ibid., p. 81.
51 Bibliothèque Municipale, Rouen, Ms. gg[9].
52 *Flaubert*, p. 90.
53 *Madame Bovary*, pp. 196–209
54 ibid., p. 192.
55 ibid., pp. 280–2.
56 ibid., p. 431.
57 *Correspondance*, vol. III, pp. 42–3, letter 9 October 1852.
58 *Madame Bovary*, pp. 112–13.
59 ibid., p. 383.
60 ibid., p. 401.
61 ibid., p. 106.
62 ibid., p. 443.
63 ibid., p. 212.
64 ibid., p. 214.
65 ibid., p. 478.
66 ibid., p. 478.
67 Bibliothèque Municipale, Rouen, Ms. gg[9].
68 *The Novel in France*, p. 252.
69 ibid., p. 254.

CHAPTER 23: FLAUBERT'S AESTHETIC DOCTRINE

1   *Correspondance*, vol. VII, p. 285, letter 6 February 1876.
2   ibid., vol. III, p. 295, letter to Louise Colet, 14 August 1853.
3   ibid., vol. VIII, p. 224, letter February–March 1879.
4   ibid., vol. II, p. 468, letter 18 July 1852.
5   ibid., vol. III, p. 68, letter to Louise Colet, 17 December 1852.
6   ibid., vol. II, p. 345, letter 16 January 1852.
7   ibid., vol. III, p. 138, letter to Louise Colet, 27 March 1853.
8   ibid., vol. III, p. 249, letter to Louise Colet, 25–6 June 1853.
9   Pléiade Edition of *Oeuvres Complètes*, vol. I.
10   *Flaubert*, p. 35
11   *Journal d'un Poète*, p. 98 (Michel Lévy).
12   *Correspondance*, vol. II, pp. 343–5, letter to Louise Colet, 16 June 1852.
13   ibid., vol. II, p. 345, letter 16 January 1852.
14   ibid., vol. III, p. 223, letter to Louise Colet, 3 June 1853.
15   ibid., vol. III, p. 92 and p. 247, letters to Louise Colet, 29 January and 29 June 1853.
16   ibid., vol. V, pp. 60–1, letter 22 April 1854.
17   ibid., vol. IV, pp. 61–2, letter 22 April 1854.
18   ibid., vol. III, p. 7, letter to Louise Colet, 1 September 1852.
19   ibid., vol. III, pp. 61–2, letter to Louise Colet, 9 December 1852.
20   ibid., vol. V, pp. 227–8 letter to Amélie Bosquet, 20 August 1866.
21   ibid., vol. V, p. 253, letter to George Sand, 5–6 December 1866.
22   ibid., vol. II, p. 365, letter to Louise Colet, 8 February 1852.
23   ibid., vol. VII, p. 285, letter to George Sand, 6 February 1876.
24   ibid., vol. II, p. 398, letter 24 April 1852, to Louise Colet.
25   ibid., vol. II, p. 344, letter to Louise Colet, 16 January 1852.
26   *Madame Bovary*, p. 96.
27   In conversation with the present author.

28 *Correspondance*, vol. VII, p. 281, letter end of December 1875.

29 ibid., vol. V, pp. 25–6, letter to Duplan, 12 June 1862.

30 ibid., vol. V, p. 24, letter to Duplan, 10 June 1862.

31 *Correspondance Supplément*, vol. IV, p. 292, letter to his niece, 26 December 1879.

32 ibid., vol. IV, p. 243, letter to Mlle Leroyer de Chantepie, 12 December 1857.

33 *Préface* to *Pierre et Jean*, p. 21 (Garnier edition).

34 *Nouvelle Revue*, January 1881, *Flaubert dans sa Vie Intime*.

35 Maupassant: *Préface* to *Pierre et Jean*, p. 21 (Garnier edition).

36 *Correspondance*, vol. III, p. 375, letter to Louise Colet, 25 October 1853.

37 ibid., vol. II, p. 469, letter July 1852.

38 *Préface* to *Lettres à George Sand*, 1884, p. lvii.

39 *Madame Bovary*, p. 354.

40 ibid., p. 172.

41 *Correspondance*, vol. IV, pp. 78–9, letter to Bouilhet, 28 June 1855.

42 ibid., vol. III, p. 264, letter 2 July 1853.

43 ibid., vol. III, p. 215, letter to Louise Colet, 1 June 1853.

44 ibid., vol. V, p. 253, letter 3–6 December 1866.

45 ibid., vol. II, p. 394, letter to Louise Colet, 24 April 1852.

46 ibid., vol. IV, p. 316, letter to Ernest Feydeau, May 1859.

47 ibid., vol. IV, p. 311, letter to Ernest Feydeau, February 1859.

48 ibid., vol. IV, p. 194, letter June 1857.

49 ibid., vol. IV, p. 356, letter 18 December 1859.

CONCLUSION

1 *Correspondance*, vol. V, p. 223, letter 16 August 1866.

2 ibid., vol. V, p. 227, letter to Mlle Leroyer de Chantepie, 20 August 1866.

3 *Dramaturges et Romanciers*, pp. 25–8.

4 op. cit., p. 67.

5 op. cit., pp. 224–62.

6 *Correspondance*, vol. VI, p. 102, letter 12 January 1870.

7 *Correspondance*, vol. I, p. 236, letter 9 August 1846.

8   *Sunday Times,* 27 June 1954.
9   *Correspondance,* vol. IV, p. 352, letter to Amélie Bosquet, November or December 1859.
10 ibid., vol. VI, p. 237, letter 22 May 1871.
11 ibid., vol. VI, p. 278, letter 6 September 1871.
12 ibid., vol. VI, p. 427, letter 5 October 1872.
13 ibid., vol. VI, p. 428, letter 5 October 1872.
14 *L'Éducation Sentimentale,* pp. 600–6.
15 *Correspondance,* vol. I, p. 233, letter to Louise Colet, 19 August 1846.
16 ibid., vol. I, p. 355, letter to Louise Colet, 4 October 1846.
17 ibid., vol. IV, p. 61, letter to Louise Colet, 22 April 1854.
18 ibid., vol. V, p. 255, letter 13 December 1866.
19 ibid., vol. III, p. 225, letter 6 June 1853.
20 ibid., vol. I, p. 200 letter 5 April 1846.
21 ibid., vol. III, p. 358, letter to Louise Colet, 30 September 1853.
22 ibid., vol. I, p. 218, letter to Louise Colet, 6 August 1846.
23 ibid., vol. III, p. 306, letter to Louise Colet, 21 August 1853.
24 ibid., vol. III, p. 403, letter to Louise Colet, 18 December 1853.
25 ibid., vol. IV, p. 341, letter to Ernest Feydeau, October–November 1859.
26 ibid., vol. II, pp. 321–3, letter 21 October 1851.
27 ibid., vol. III, p. 150, letter 31 March 1853.
28 *Correspondance Supplément,* vol. III, p. 218, letter to Commanville, 7 October 1875.
29 op. cit., p. 253.
30 *Correspondance,* vol. IV, p. 170, letter 30 March 1857.
31 ibid., vol. III, p. 16, letter 4 September 1852.
32 ibid., vol. II, p. 446 letter to Louise Colet, 26 January 1852.
33 *Notes de Voyages,* vol. II, p. 347.
34 Guillaumin: *Flaubert devant la Vie et devant Dieu,* p. 234.
35 Mallarmé: *Oeuvres Complètes* (Pléiade Edition), p. 872.
36 *Correspondance,* vol. I, p. 97, letter 23 February 1842.
37 ibid., vol. III, pp. 224–5, letter to Louise Colet, 6 June 1853.
38 ibid., vol. IV, p. 246, letter to Mlle Leroyer de Chantepie, 23 January 1858.
39 ibid., vol. III, p. 3, letter 27 July 1852.

Index

MORE ABOUT PENGUINS
AND PELICANS

Penguinews, which appears every month, contains details of all the new books issued by Penguins as they are published. From time to time it is supplemented by *Penguins in Print*, which is a complete list of all available books published by Penguins. (There are well over three thousand of these.)

A specimen copy of *Penguinews* will be sent to you free on request, and you can become a subscriber for the price of the postage. For a year's issues (including the complete lists) please send 30p if you live in the United Kingdom, or 60p if you live elsewhere. Just write to Dept EP, Penguin Books Ltd, Harmondsworth, Middlesex, enclosing a cheque or postal order, and your name will be added to the mailing list.

Note: *Penguinews* and *Penguins in Print* are not available in the U.S.A. or Canada.

Penguin Classics

FLAUBERT

MADAME BOVARY

Translated by Alan Russell

With *Madame Bovary* (1857) Flaubert established the realistic novel in France. Yet he always refused to ally himself with any literary movement, devoting himself in splendid isolation to his art, with that intense concern for stylistic perfection which has made him a legendary figure among novelists.

SENTIMENTAL EDUCATION

Translated by Robert Baldick

In this story of a young man's romantic attachment to an older woman, the modern English reader can appreciate the accuracy, the artistry and the insight with which Flaubert reconstructed in one masterpiece the very fibre of his times.

THREE TALES

Translated by Robert Baldick

Each of these tales reveals a different aspect of Flaubert's creative genius and fine craftsmanship. In *A Simple Heart* he recounts the life of a pious and devoted servant-girl. A stained-glass window in Rouen cathedral inspired him to write *The Legend of St Julian Hospitator* with its insight into the violence and mysticism of the medieval mind. *Herodias* is a masterly reconstruction of the events leading up to the martyrdom of St John the Baptist.